INDIA AND CENTRAL ASIA
(CLASSICAL TO CONTEMPORARY PERIODS)

About the Editors

J.N. Roy, IPS (Retd.) is former Commissioner, Civil Aviation Security, former Consultant Ministry of Home Affairs and a Strategic Analyst. He is founding member of India-Central Asia Foundation (ICAF) and has abiding interest in developments in the India's neighbourhood and Central Asia.

B.B. Kumar, (*b.*1941), M.Sc. (Chemistry), M.Sc. (Anthropology), M.A. (Hindi), Ph.D. (Anthropology), former Principal, Science College, Kohima, was member, Executive Council, Academic Council, University Court, College Development Council, Examination Committee, School Board of Physical Sciences and other numerous committees of the North-Eastern Hill University, Shillong (India). He was Chairman, Hindi Board of Studies, and member, Board of Studies, of 'Science for Rural Development', Gandhigram Rural University, Tamil Nadu. He remained associated with a large number of NGOs as President, Vice-President, Secretary and member. He was founder secretary of Nagaland Bhasha Parishad and Thinkers Forum, Nagaland and Governing Body member of the Nagaland Peace Centre, a voluntary organization founded by Jai Prakash Narayan. Presently, he is Secretary, Astha Bharati, New Delhi and founding member of the Governing Body of India Central Asia Foundation, New Delhi. Indian Council for Cultural Relations sponsored his lectures on cultural and linguistic links between India and Central Asia in the universities/institutes of Tashkent and Samarkand.

Dr. Kumar has written/edited/co-authored 136 books and more than 100 papers. Presently he is editing Quarterly journals, *Dialogue* (English) and *Chintan-Srijan* (Hindi), both published from Delhi.

INDIA AND CENTRAL ASIA
(CLASSICAL TO CONTEMPORARY PERIODS)

Editors

J.N. Roy

B.B. Kumar

Published for

ASTHA BHARATI, DELHI

by

CONCEPT PUBLISHING COMPANY, NEW DELHI-110059

Cataloging in Publication Data—DK
Courtesy: D.K. Agencies (P) Ltd. <docinfo@dkagencies.com>

International Seminar on India and Central Asia : Classical to Contemporary Period (2004 : New Delhi, India)

India and Central Asia : classical to contemporary periods / editors, J.N. Roy, B.B. Kumar.

p. cm.

Most of the papers presented at the International Seminar on India and Central Asia : Classical to Contemporary Period, held at New Delhi during 1-3 March 2004 and contributed articles; previously published in the quarterly Dialogue.

Includes bibliographical references.

Includes index.

ISBN 8180694577

1. India—Relations—Asia, Central—Congresses. 2. Asia, Central—Relations—India—Congresses. 3. Asia, Central—Politics and government—Congresses. I. Roy, J. N. II. Kumar, B. B. (Braj Bihari), 1941- III. Title.

DDC 303.482 540 58 22

ISBN : 81-8069-457-7

First Published 2007

Published and Printed by
Ashok Kumar Mittal
Concept Publishing Company
A/15-16, Commercial Block, Mohan Garden,
New Delhi-110059 (India)

Phones : 25351460, 25351794
Fax : +91-11-25357103
Email : publishing@conceptpub.com

PREFACE

The Central Asia forms part of our immediate neighbourhood in east Central Asia and extended neighbourhood in the West. India was geographically nearer to the Central Asian republics before partition of the country in 1947. Apart from common contiguous borders, climatic continuity, similar geographical features and geo-cultural affinities, India and Central Asia have long traditions of socio-cultural, political and economic contacts since remote past. Their relations have been multi-dimensional, deep, old and continuous. We have common concerns about international terrorism, religious extremism and drug-trafficking. India and Central Asian republics may develop mutually beneficial trade relations as the latter ones are very rich in energy resources. The two regions also have geo-strategic importance for each other. The book highlights all these aspects in the papers contributed by the scholars of India and Central Asian republics.

Astha Bharati, Delhi published two issues of its Quarterly English journal *Dialogue* with focus on Central Asia during April-June 2002 (Vol. 3, No. 4) and October-December 2004 (Vol. 6, No. 2). The scholarly papers on themes related to Central Asia by Indian and Central Asian scholars were published in other issues of the journal also. The papers written by Professor Lokesh Chandra, Professor Devendra Kaushik, Dr. S.P. Gupta and Dr. S. S. Toshkhani, included in this book were published in *Dialogue*, Vol. 3, No. 4. All other papers included in the book were presented in the International Seminar on "India and Central Asia: Classical to Contemporary Period".

The above-mentioned International Seminar was jointly organized by Indian Council for Cultural Relations and Astha Bharati, Delhi on March 1-3, 2004 in New Delhi. It was inaugurated by Dr. Najma Heptulla, the then President, ICCR and Vice-Chairperson of the Rajya Sabha. Her inaugural address is also included in this book.

Eminent scholars from India and Central Asia presented papers in six working sessions on various themes related to "Historical, Cultural Links and Interactions", "Indo-Central Asian Relations in

Medieval and Modern Periods", "Politics and Democracy", "Geopolitical and Strategic Perspective" and "Economic Development of Central Asia".

We would like to thank Dr. Najma Heptulla, the then Chairperson of ICCR and Vice-Chairman of Rajya Sabha and the then Director General of ICCR and all the officers of ICCR for their help organizing the seminar. We thank the scholars who contributed papers in the seminar and for the Special Numbers of the *Dialogue* on "Central Asia." We also thank Ashok Kumar Mittal and his staff of the Concept Publishing Company for publication of the book.

—Editors

Contents

Preface *v*
Notes on Contributors *ix*

Part - I
Historical, Cultural and Religious Links

1. India and Central Asia : Links and Interactions 3
—B.B. Kumar
2. Notes on Central Asian Buddhist Iconography 34
—Lokesh Chandra
3. Historical and Cultural Relations between Kazhakhstan, Central Asia and India from ancient times to the beginning of the 20th century 43
—M.Kh. Abuseitova
4. Hindu Gods in Western Central Asia 57
—S.P. Gupta
5. Religious, Cultural and Artistic Links between Ancient Kashmir, Afghanistan and Central Asia 63
—S.S. Toshkhani
6. India and Central Asia : Cultural Relations in Middle Ages 78
—Evgeni Kablukov
7. India and Central Asia 1947-1991 83
—Surender Gopal
8. Cultural relations between India and Tibet : An Overview of the Light from India 91
—Claude Arpi
9. Indo-Uzbek Literary and Linguistic Relations Throughout 11-18 Centuries 111
—Azad N. Shamatov

Part-II
Politics/Geo-politics and Democracy in Central Asia

10. Political System and Democratic Discourse in Central Asia : A View from outside 123
—R.R. Sharma

11. Central Asia : Changing Geo-Political Alignment in the Aftermath of 11th September 134
—Devendra Kaushik

12. Geopolitical Perspectives on Central Asia : An Indian View 143
—Nirmala Joshi

13. Politics of Oil and Natural Gas in Central Asia—Conflicts and Co-operation 156
—R.G. Gidadhubli

14. India and Post-Soviet Asia : An Appraisal of India's Central Asia Policy 172
—Sheel K. Asopa

15. Central Asia : Tulips have Different Hews 190
—P.L. Dash

Part-III
Islamist Radicalism in Central Asia

16. Central Asia after Collapse of USSR and Islamic Radicalism 211
—Muzaffar Alimov

17. Religious Extremism in Central Asia : A Case Study of Uzbekistan 226
—Ramakant Dwivedi

Part-IV
Economy and Energy Resources

18. Perspective of Economic Development in Uzbekistan and Relations between Uzbekistan and India 247
—Surat Mirkasymov

19. Economic Changes in Central Asia and Indian Response 251
—Gulshan Sachdeva

20. Basic Directions and Mechanisms in the Formation of a Joint Power Market of the Central Asian States 273
—Gulmira Kurganbayeva

21. Scientific and Cultural Cooperation Development between India and Tajikistan 295
—Sanavbar Vohidova

Annexture I : Inaugural Address—*Najma Heptulla* 301
Annexture II : Some Statistics on Central Asia and India 304
Index 308

Notes on Contributors

Professor Meruert Abuseitova, Director, Institute of Oriental Studies, Almaty, Kazakhstan

Dr. Muzaffar A. Alimov, Director of History and Research Centre, Dushanbe (Tajikistan)

Dr. Claude Arpi, Tibetologist, Auroville, Pondicherry.

Professor (Mrs.) Sheel K. Asopa, Professor (Retd.), International Politics, Rajasthan University, Jaipur.

Professor Lokesh Chandra, eminent scholar, former Member of the Parliament, Chairman, International Academy of Indian Culture, New Delhi.

Professor P.L. Dash, Director, Centre for Central Eurasian Studies, University Mumbai.

Dr. Ramakant Dwivedi, Associate Fellow, Institute for Defence Studies and Analysis (IDSA), New Delhi; founding member, India Central Asia Foundation.

Professor R.G. Gidadhubli, Professor (Retd.), Central Eurasian Studies, Mumbai University; founding member, India Central Asia Foundation.

Professor Surender Gopal, Professor (Retd.), Patna University.

Dr. S.P. Gupta, former Director, Allahabad Museam; Chairman, Indian Archeological Society, New Delhi.

Dr. Najma Heptulla, the then President, Indian Council of Cultural Relations and Vice-Chairperson of the Rajya Sabha.

Professor Nirmala Joshi, School of International Studies, Jawaharlal Nehru University; New Delhi; Director, India Central Asia Foundation, New Delhi.

Dr. Evgeni Kablukov, Chief of the Chair of Oriental History, Bishkek, Kyrgyzstan

Professor Devendra Kaushik, the then Chairman, Maulana Azad Institute of Asian Studies, Kolkata.

Dr. B.B. Kumar, Editor, *Quarterly Dialogue*, founding member, India Central Asia Foundation.

Dr.(Mrs.) G. Kurganbayeva*, Deputy Director, Kazakh Institute for Strategic Studies, Almaty.

Dr. Gulshan Sachdeva, Associate Professor, JNU; founding member India Central Asia Foundation.

Professor Azad N. Shamatov*, Chairman, South Asian Studies Centre, Tashkent, Uzbekistan.

Professor R.R. Sharma, Dean, School of International Studies, JNU and former Vice-Chancellor, Jammu University.

Dr. Surat Mirkasymov, Former and the first Ambassador of Uzbekistan in India; Professor, Institute of Oriental Studies, Tashkent, Uzbekistan.

Dr. S.S. Toshkhani, Chairman, NS Kashmir Research Institute, New Delhi.

Dr. (Ms.) S. Vahidova, Tajik Academy of Sciences, Dushanbe, Tajikistan

---

* Positions/posts held at the time of Seminar.

PART- I

HISTORICAL, CULTURAL AND RELIGIOUS LINKS

1

India and Central Asia

Links and Interactions

B.B. Kumar

India and Central Asia, with common and contiguous borders, climatic continuity, similar geographical features and geo-cultural affinity, have long traditions of socio-cultural, political and economic contacts since remote past. Their relations have been multi-dimensional, deep, old and continuous. There has been uninterrupted flow of men, material and the ideas between the two. The Indian and foreign literary sources attest to the fact. According to *Zend Avesta*, the ancestors of Iranian, Indian and Turanian people were the three sons of Tratoria, namely, Arya, Sairimia and Tura respectively.[1] Abu Qasim Farishta gives a very interesting account of the geneology of the Indians and the Central Asians.[2]

The excavations in Southern Uzbekistan in the Amu Darya valley, in Afrasiab in the north-eastern edge of Samarkand and elsewhere in Uzbekistan, in Turkmenistan, Kazakhstan and in the Tak-ınak region of Kyrghyzstan provide ample proof of Indo-Central Asian links from ancient days. Extensive excavations have been done with remarkable findings at Kara Tepa, Fayaz Tepa, Dalverzin Tepa, Yer Kurgan, Ak-Beshin, Kranayerezka and Isyk-Ata. Sakas, Kushanas, Hunas, Turks and Mughals came from Central Asia to India. India had very intimate historic, cultural links with Eastern Central Asian regions of Xinjiang and Tibet also. Findings of the excavations and the discovery of manuscripts in Xinjiang and Tibetan literary documents provide enough material to establish our links. India had rulers of Central Asian origin. Dynasties of Indian origin ruled Khotan and elsewhere in Central Asia.

Ancient Links

Ancient Indo-Central-Asia links were well established. The leading pre-historians of Russia have discovered large remains of Sohan Culture across the difficult moutainous terrain of the Hindukush and the Pamirs in the valley of Oxus and its tributaries in Tajikistan, Kazakhstan and other places. The discoveries by V. Ranov, Kh. A. Alphasbayev and others in Soviet journals provide enough light on this subject. The first stage of Old Stone Age or Palaeolithic culture of Central Asia was named Borykazghan culture after the type-size in southern Kazakhstan. Ranov named it Soan culture of Central Asia. Diffusion of culture continued in the Neolithic stage and in Bronze Age culture also. There is marked similarity in Kangra valley neolithic culture of India and Gissan (Hissar) culture of Central Asia. Altin Depe, Khapuz Depe, Namazga Depe Tahirbai Depe, Anau, etc. in south Turkmenistan bear unmistakable stamp of Indus civilization.[3] T. Shirinov, in a paper presented in a seminar on "India and Central Asia (Pre-Islamic period)" held in Tashkent in the year 2000 on the subject on the "Contact between Central Asia and the Indian subcontinent in the second millennium B.C. has pointed out that "Cultural and trading relations between Central Asia and the Indian subcontinent in the III-II millennium B.C. were closer than they are described by many contemporary researchers."

Central Asia was well known during the epic age. Indian epics (*Ramayana* and *Mahabharata*) and the *Puranas* have numerous references of the region, its topography, mountains, rivers and the people. Many communities of Central Asia participated in Mahabharata War. Shakas and Yavanas (Greeks) have been described as degraded Kshatriyas by the *Mahabharata* and *Manu Smriti* (Hindu code). There is mention of Shakas, Pahlavas (Persians), Kambojas (Galcha speaking people of Tazikistan), Rishik (Yueh-chi or Kushanas) at one place in the Mahabharata (5.4.15). At another place, China, Huna and Shaka is mentioned (*Mahabharat* 2.47.19). Kanka (Kangyu of Sogd) are mentioned with Shaka and Tushara (Tokharian). Enough material on Central Asia is available in Medieval Sanskrit literature, and in Buddhist and Jain literatures.

Part of India and Central Asia were ruled together during Achaemenian, Seleucid and Kushana periods. The use of Indian languages and scripts, Buddhism, Hinduism and Islam, rule of dynasties of Indian origin in many kingdoms of Central Asia and that of the dynasties of Central Asian origin further deepened their links. In Transoxiana, the ruins of the Buddhist monasteries of the period from 525 BC to 700 A.D. have been found in Transoxiana.[4]

Two names figure prominently in the spread of Buddhism in Central Asia. They are of Ashoka and Kanishka. Pentti Aalto has mentioned[5] about an inscription on the wall of the gate of Chu-yung-kuan, a town on the road from Peking to Kalgan in Sanskrit, Tibetan, Hsi-hsia, Uigur, Mongol and Chinese languages, which reads: "The great and illustrious Cakravarti King Ashoka, having assembled the relics of Lord Buddha of great virtue, adorned beautifully the vast world with stupas, and made the great *Dharma* shine greatly throughout the world". Kandahar inscriptions of 258 BC in Greek and Aramaic says: that as a result of Ashoka's activity, "everything prospers over the whole earth". Kanishka, patronized Buddhism. According to Chinese tradition, it is said that Lord Buddha understood Kanishka's Yueh-chi language.[6]

According to the ancient Khotanese tradition, the kingdom of Khotan was established by Kutsan, the son of Ashoka in 240 BC. There is yet one other tradition which says that Khotan was founded by exiled Gandharan subjects of Ashoka. Language of the documents discovered in various archaeological expeditions of Khotan in Chinese Turkistan was Prakrit. It is the Gandharan dialect of Middle Indo-Aryan. The documents known as Kharoshthi documents are written in Kharoshthi script of India. Apart from the manuscript of Dharmapada, the documents have enough secular materials written on wood, leather and silk found at Lou-lan (Kroraina). These facts give credence to the tradition of Gandhara expansion to Turkistan.[7] In this connection, it needs mention that several dynasties of Central Asian states claimed Indian origin. Apart from the Vijaya rulers of Khotan, in the south there were many others, such as Pushpa and Deva ending rulers at Kucha, and those with Arjuna suffix at Karasahr (Agnidesha) in the north with Sanskrit/Indian names. Names, such as Anand, Buddhamitra, Dharmapala, Punyadeva, and Vasudeva; real titles, such as maharaja (great king), rajatiraja, avijitasimha (unconquered lion); and sometimes, mixed names, such as Vasu Mogiya, Vasu Kekeya, etc. in the records were indicative of Indian links.

Indo-Central-Asian interaction was most intimate during the Kushana period. However, the same continued even after that. Frescoes reminiscent of Bharhut and Ajanta caves has come to light in the excavations of Penjikent (Tajikistan), Varaksha (Uzbekistan) and Azhina Tepe (Tajikistan). A fresco carrying the painting of a blue dancer wearing tiger skin with a trident in the background at Penjikent is identified with Shiva, the Nilakantha (blue necked). A painting on the palace-wall at Varaksha shows a king hunting a tiger riding on elephant back along with his retenue. At Adina Tepe, a figure of sleeping Buddha (about 12 metre size) in Nirvana posture is found. These finds clearly show the influence of Indian tradition. A painted figure, supposed to be of a worshipper or of Indra, seems distinctly Indian in structure, colouring, costumes and style similar to some Ajanta figures.[8] Excavations have brought to light the existence of numerous Buddhist temples and caves with icons, paintings in Central Asia with Indian influences. But Central Asia has also assimilated diverse elements from other sources also. Local elements and adaptations are also not lacking.

An outstanding Buddha figure in Balawaste shows some significant non-Buddhist symbols like sun, moon, flaming jewels, etc. These were originally used in Hindu iconography and developed Tantric symbolism later on. The *shrivasta* mark, originally meant for Vishnu, was seen in the centre of the Buddha's chest. In other case there was depiction of the *samudramanthana* legend. Most of the paintings from Dandan Uiliq, Balawaste and Farhad-Beg-Yailaki sites of Domoko region of Khotan oasis had Mahayana Buddhist themes, but some popular Hindu divine figures were also depicted on them.[9] Kucha, an important seat of Hinayana Buddhism, reflected best of the Indian traditions in painting. The first out of the styles of the paintings clearly shows the influence of the Gandhara and Gupta traditions. Kizil cave paintings remind us of the Ajanta traditions. Indian elements in the art of Kizil is more prominently shown. The figure of Gopala with cows from the Cave of the Statues, the figure of Dilip as described in Kalidasa's *Raghuvamsha*, the graceful dance depiction of queen Chandraprabha shows it amply. The Ajanta style is clearly seen in the last one.[10] The theme is a Hindu one. The Indian motifs like lotus, multi-limbed divinities, e.g., multiple eyes (*Sahasraksha*) on the body of Avalokiteshvara in certain silk paintings of Tun-huang, may be cited as examples. In the cave of Thousand Buddhas at Tun-Huang, the artists painted the walls and the ceilings of the caves depicting scenes from the life of the Buddha, stories of the Jatakas and Bodhisattvas, as well as various Hindu gods and goddesses, like Shiva and Ganesha.[11]

Buddhism was introduced in Khotan by the king Vijayasambhava under the spiritual guidance of Arya Vairochana. The first monastery was established there in 211 BC. The religion spread to other southern states from there. Marco Polo visited Sachiu in this region and found that people were "for the most part idolators". Fa-Hien, travelling in the region during 399-414 AD, found that all the inhabitants of the Khotan region "professed Buddhist law, and joined together in its religious musk for their enjoyment." Hiuen Chwang also confirmed the fact. Fa-Hien was lodged in a monastery in Khotan where three thousand monks stayed. It was known as Gomati monastery. There were four great monasteries and many smaller ones there according to Fa-Hien.[12]

Buddhism had deep roots in northern Xinjiang (Chinese Turkistan), specially in the states of Kucha, Karashahr (Agnidesha), Turfan (Kaochang) and Bharuka (Aksu). Kucha was an important Buddhist centre since first century AD. It played important role in the propagation of Buddhism. Famous Buddhist scholar, Kumarajiva was the son of a Kuchian mother and Indian father. Balkh was an important centre of Buddhist sites and was known as 'Little Rajagriha'. The places around it had numerous *sangharams,* and statues of Buddha. It had a hundred convents and five hundred monks. There was a convent called *Navasangharama* outside the city. A former ruler built it. There was figure of Buddha studded with gems. The hall was also well-decorated with the same. It was often raided and plundered by the covetous neighbouring rulers. It had also a statue of Pishamen (Vaisravana) and it was believed that he protects the precincts of the convent. Tirmiz and Aksu each had ten *sangharamas* and a thousand monks. Chaghaniyan, Kubadian, Sumana and Kulab had few *sangharamas* and monks each. Northern Xinjiang had the followers of Hinayana sect.[13]

Buddist link with Xinjiang are well-known. Buddhist and Hindu Buddhist icons have been found in Buddhist temples of Khotan, Kucha, Dandan Uiliq and other places. Buddhist and Hindu links in western

Central Asia, as stated earlier, has also come to light after excavations by Soviet archaeologists.[14] The central regions of the western Central Asia was specially rich in art and architecture. This region, known as Sogdiana had multi-layered links with India. R.H. Sulemanov, in a paper presented in a seminar held in Tashkent in 2000 AD on "India and Central Asia (Pre-Islamic period)" has brought out many Indian parallels in ancient cults of Sogdiana. He has specially mentioned about the funeral rites among the tribes and the same in Vedic tradition, the cult of fire worship and Mithraism (Sun worship; Mithra/Mitra is Vedic Sun god, Iranian word is Mihir), the legend of Gandharvas (water deities) and the Ganges. Place names such as Kanka or Ganga has also the Central Asian connections. *Mahabharata* mentions the name of Kanka (Kangyu tribe). The water deity was also worshipped in Central Asia as perfect women.[15]

Apart from the *Puranic* cults mentioned above, the worship of five Hindu gods in Sogdiana, namely, Brahma, Indra, Mahadeva (Shiva), Narayana and Vaishravana needs special mention. Brahma, Indra and Shiva had the Sogdian names of Zravan, Adbad and Veshparkar respectively. The four armed goddess riding the lion may be Durga.[16] Portable fire altars associated with Mahadeva-Veshparkar, Brahma-Zravan and Indra-Abdab found in a mural of 8th century at Penjikent also needs special mention. It may also be mentioned that the name of Iranian supreme god Ahur Mazda in this case,[17] and that of Iranian river goddess Anahita Harahwati Ardavisura in the case metioned above is not used in Central Asia. Russian scholars have related three or four armed deities in west Central Asian murals, Hindu and Buddhist God Vishwakarma (creator of everything; Sanskrit) and a case of an obvious transformation of Indian cults.[18]

A fragment of Kharoshtji inscription discovered by Russian scholar A.N. Burnshtan in Tajikistan, and translated by J. Harmatta, is attributed to the second-first century B.C. on paleographic grounds. It reads : 'Narayana, be victorious'. Paintings of Shiva from various sites of eastern and western Central Asia, and that of the Ganesh, Kumar/Kartikeya, Mahakala, Durga, Digpalas and of Vishwarupa Krishna at various places of Central Asia confirm Hindu linkages.[19]

God Shiva appears on certain coins of Gondophares, Maues and several other kings who ruled Central Asia and India. The coins of Kushana rulers also have Shiva with his consort Uma and the son Kartikeya-Kumara. Vima owed personal allegiance to Shiva.

Ancient Land Routes

India and Central Asia were linked through many land routes. The Indian traders, at the close of 1880s, started bringing goods to Central Asia through Persia. This new trade route was less dangerous and cheaper. They asked for and received permission from the Russian authorities to use even a more advantageous route to Central Asia after the construction of trans-Caspian railway. The route was from Bombay port to Black Sea port of Batumi and then across Caucasus to Central Asia.[20] Takshashila and Purushpura on either side of the Sindhu river were connected with Indian trade routes on Indian side and Central Asian trade routes on the other. Strategically located, Takshashila, the capital city of Gandhar, was the terminus of several major inland routes and the starting point of the great trade routes connecting India and Central Asia. A route towards the north passing through Kashmir valley to Gilgit, Yarkand and Kashgarh connected it do eastern and western Turkistan. The western route passed through Pushkalavati, Purushapura (Peshawar) and Kapisha (modern Begram) to Bactria. The route from Kapisha to Bactria ran through Bamyan and number of passes—Robat, Dandan, Shikan and Karakotal; followed Dana Yousouf river route to reach Mazar-i-Sarif and then Bactria. It was the oldest and most frequented route. Hiuen Tsang reached Bactria from Samarkand and then followed this route to reach Bamiyan, Kapisha and Purushpur through Khaibar pass. Bactria became very important as natural converging point of several routes. Babylon, Susa-Herat, Samarkand-Tashkent in the Oxus valley in the north, and a number of routes from Kashgarh in the west. The importance of Takshashila-Kapisha-Bactria route increased during Achaemenian period when Punjab was its satrap and during Seleucid period when it became royal highway to the west. Two routes connected Bactria to the Oxus valley. Strabo, Pliny and other geographers have mentioned about Caspian Highway going towards the Caspian Sea. Indians favoured this route for trade to the Black Sea ports taking advantage of the navigability of Oxus river. The route to Tashkent via Samarkand went farther to the north-east to Turfan. Tashkent-Turfan route passed through the northern parts of Tien Shan range and through Kulja and Uranchi cities. Khojend lies about 150 miles south-east of Tashkent.[21] Alexander suffered a military disaster while passing through Samarkand or Marchanda. He went up to Khojend, known as Alexandria Eschate (farthest) at that time.[22]

Kashgarh, on the western fringe of the Taklamakan desert in Tarim basin, in between the Tien Shan range on the north and Kun-lun mountain range in the south, was on farther west, which became prominent due to the development of the silk route and silk trade. Two routes emerging from Kashgarh passed though the important places located in the series of oases on the outer periphery of the oval shaped trough-like Tarim basin desert. Imortant places, like Yarkand, Karghalik, Keriya, Niya, Endere, Charchan, Charkhlik and Miran, and after skirting the salty Lop-nor marsh, Tun-huang and An-hsi were located on the southern route. It passed through the southern periphery of the desert on the northern foot-hills of Kun-lun. The northern route, on the northern periphery south of Tien Shan, passed through Uch-Turfan, Aksu, Kucha and Korla. There was bifurcation of the route at Korla towards south-east and north-east. The south-eastern route passed through Kuruk Darya, Lou-lan, etc. and terminated at Tung-huang. Kara shahr and Turfan were located on north-eastern route. The route made a great arch through Hami, and then ended at An-hsi. Tashkent-Kulja-Urunchi route met Akshu-Kucha-Karashahr route at Turfan. Hiuen Tsang followed Hami-Turfan-Tashkent-Samarkand road, descended from Oxus valley to Bactria, and then reached Purushapura in India through Bamiyan, Kapisha-Purushapur route. An alternative route links India to Kashgarh via Bactria through a route passing south of Pamir. Hiuen Tsang in 644 A.D. for his return journey to China and Marco Polo for his journey to Cathay in 1273A.D. used the same. Passing from Bactria to Badakhshan up the open valley of Wakhan, it goes to Sariqol south of the peak Muz Tagh Ata, and then to Tashkurghan and finally, descending the hills to the Kashgarh and Yarkand. A route from Kashmir valley through Gilgit, Darkot and Baroghil passes meets Badakhshan-Wakhan-Sariqol route at Sarhad.[23]

Central Asia in Ancient Indian Literature

The Indian epics and *Puranas* mention about the earth consisting of seven *dvipas* the number varies in some cases. *Dvipa*, ordinarily, means island. *Panini* derives it from *dvi + ap*, meaning 'land between two arms of water'.[24] However, the Puranic dvipas stand for continents or tribal or national territories.[25] It signified all types of natural or human regions—big or small.[26] The barriers may be water, sand, swamp, high mountains or thick forests.[27] Jambudvipa is at the centre of all. Mount Meru is at the centre of the Jambudvipa. It needs mention that India and Central Asia form part of the Jambudvipa. Mount Meru is the Pamir knot.

Details of the mountains, rivers, vegetation, climate, etc. of the dvipas have been given in most of the Puranas, and some scholars tried to identify specific geographical region basing on the same. Al-Beruni, as for example, located Pushkardvipa between Cina and Mangala (perhaps China and Mongolia).[28] Jambudvipa, also known as Sudarshandvipa, is said to be circular in shape[29] and surrounded by the sea on all the sides. It has six mountain ranges—Himalaya, Hemakuta, Nishadha, Nila, Sveta and Shringavat[30]—and nine zones (varshas)—Hari, Bhadrashva, Ketumal, Bharata, Uttar-Kuru, Sweta, Hiranyaka, Airavata and Ilavrita.[31] According to the *Markandeya Purana*, Jambudvipa is depressed on the south and north and elevated and broad in the middle.[32] The elevated region is known Ilavrita or Meruvarsha; mountain Meru is at the centre of the same. The nine divisions of Jambudvipa according to different Puranas, such as *Matsya Purana* are: Ilavrita, Ramyaka or Ramanaka, Hiranmaya or Hiranyaka, Uttara-Kuru or Shringashaka, Bhadrashva, Ketumal, Hari, Kimpurusha and Bharata.[33] The first division, as mentioned above, is centrally located, the next three and the last three in the north and south respectively, and the remaining two, Bhadrashva and Ketumala to the east and west respectively. The geographical detail of the region is given in the Mahabharata's Bhishma parva in detail and in other puranas also. *Markandeya*[34] and *Brahmand Purana*[35] divide Jambudvipa into four regions shaped like four petals of a lotus. From Dialogue four rivers flow from mount Meru; namely Sita, flowing to the east through mountains to the Bhadrashva region to the sea; Alakananda flowing to the south through India to the sea; Chakshu (or Vakshu or Oxus) flowing through the mountains towards west to the Ketumal region, and Bhadra flowing through northern mountains and Uttar Kuru region to the sea.[36]

Vayu Purana details the mountain ranges, valleys river systems, etc. of the geographical region of Jambudvipa making it possible to identify some of their geographical features. The description of the northern regions of Jambudvipa, according to S.M. Ali, 'covers a very vast area, from the Urals and the Caspian to the Yenisel and from the 'Turkestan, Tien Shan ranges to the Arctic. It describes topography of the whole land very accurately and in some cases picturesquely .....'[37] Bhadrashva, in the east, is identical with the basins of Tarim and Hwangho rivers, i.e., the whole of Singkiang and northern China'.[38] Ketumala to the west of Meru, through which river Chakshu (Oxus) flows, corresponds to western Turkestan.[39] It is believed to cover 'practically the whole of the ancient Bactria which included the whole of the present Afghan Turkistan (north of Hindukush), the lower Harirud valley, the basin of Murkhab Kashka system (all south of the old bed of Amu Darya) and the basins of the Surkhan, Kafirnigan, Vakhsh and Yaksu rivers...'[40] Hari[41] and Bharata represented western Tibet and India respectively. The area around Meru, the mountainous region, was Meruvarsha or Ilavrita. The area across the Himalayas and Hindukush from Pamir up to Arctic was known as Uttar Kuru. Arctic was known as Somagiri.[42] There is numerous mention of the region in the *Ramayana* and the *Mahabharata*, the two Indian epics.

Valmiki, in the *Ramayana*, gives graphic picture of Uttar Kuru and Somagiri.[43] Sugriva, while sending the monkeys to the north for searching Sita describes the route and the countries in that direction. Among others, he commands them to search Sita in the lands and towns of the Dardas, Kambojas, Yavanas and Shakas.[44] He describes Uttar Kuru and Somagiri (the arctic region). There is the sea and the Somagiri in the extreme north. The route is extremely difficult one. The region is without the sun and yet very much lighted. There are no national boundaries there.[45] Arjuna brought water from the northern sea for the coronation of Yudhisthira.[46]

Mahabharata describes Meru (Pamir), Meruvarsha around it, Ketumala to its east, and Uttar Kuru to its north.[47] Meru, according to the Indian classical literature, is located at the centre of the earth. The conference of the Devas (gods) was held at mount Meru to Java decide about the churning of the sea.[48]

Central Asian People in Indian Classical Literature

There is numerous mentions of the people of the Central Asia in Indian literature, especially in the *Ramayana*, as stated above, and the *Mahabharata* and the *Puranas*. Shaka, Darada, Pahlava, Kirata and Parada are said to be Kshatriyas of good birth.[49] It was suggested to invite Shaka, Pahlava, Rishik and Darada kings in the Mahabharata war from Pandava side.[50] Mahabharata mentions that Arjuna brought tribute from Uttara Kuru[51] and another Pandava hero, Nakula defeated Hunas, Pahalvas, Yavanas and Shakas.[52] Yudhisthira received tribute from Uttar Kuru.[53] Shakas, Hunas and Tusharas also paid tribute to him.[54] It needs mention that Tusharas are also known as Yueh-chi (in Chinese language) and Kanishka belonged to that community. Tusharas were present in the *Rajasuya Yajna* of Yudhisthira.[55] They participated in Mahabharata war from the Kaurava side.[56] They were ferocious warriors.[57] The name of Tushara-Giri (Tushara mountain) finds mention in *Mahabharata*, *Harshacharita* and *Kavyamimansa*.[58] Chakshu river (Oxus or Amu Darya) flows through Tushara, Lampak, Pahlava, Parada and Shaka countries, according to the *Vayu Purana* and *Matsya Purana*.[59] It shows that these countries belonged to the Central Asia.

India's contact with Central Asia is ancient one. The inhabitants of Uttar Kuru seem to be legendary fellows in the epics and latter literature, but as historic ones in the *Aitareya Brahmana* according to the author of Vedic Index. Uttar Kuru is the Divine land (region of Devas) for Vasistha Satya Havya, but Atyarati wants to conquer it.[60] Indians remember Jambudvipa during their daily worship which includes Central Asia.[61]

Immigration of the people from Central Asia to India is a well-known fact of history. Shakas, Yavanas, Hunas, Turks, Mongols and Pathans came to India. Most of the immigrants were absorbed in Indian society. Yavanas and the Maga Brahmanas came from the north-west. Patanjali's *Mahabhashya* and *Gargi Samhita* echo frequent incursion of the Greek chiefs from Bactria to India. Varahamihira, the famous astronomer, was a Maga Brahmin.[62] Here, it needs mention that Indian tradition, says about out-migration of Shakas, Yavanas, etc. from India.

Sagara was an ancient Indian king. His father was defeated and humiliated by some Kshatriyas. He was forced to live as an ascetic in the forest. Sagar regained his kingdom in due course and wanted to take revenge and kill his enemies. His priest Vasistha intervened to save their lives. He persuaded Sagara to spare them. They were forced to abandon their religiously ordained duty and declared dead while living (Jivanmrita, a man abandoning his ordained duties and considered dead while living). Brahmana priests abandoned them as they stopped performing their religious duties. They were degraded socially; became Vrishal/Vratya/Shudra/Kshatriya Shudra. Sagara killed Haihayas and Talajangha Kshatriyas. Shakas, Yavanas, Kambojas, Pardas and Pahlavas became Vrishala (Kshatriya Shudras).[63] According to Mahabharata, Shakas, Yavanas, Kambojas and Mahashakas were Kshatriyas. They became Vrishala due to not availing the benefits of the contact of the Brahmanas.[64] Lack of proper conduct is also said to be the reason for such degradation for Tushara and others.[65] Anushasan Parva of *Mahabharata*, further says that some, Kshatriya communities—Mekal, Dravida, Lat, Paundra, Kanvashira, Darad, Darva, Chaur, Shabar, Barber, Kirat, and Yavana—were degraded due to their envy for the Brahmanas.[66] *Manu Smriti* regards Shakas, Yavanas, as degraded Kshatriyas reduced to the status of Vrishalas.[67]

According to Sagara legend mentioned above, Shakas, Yavanas, Kambojas, Pardas and Pahalvas were the inhabitants of India. In historic time, they were mostly settled in the Central Asia and the countries west of India. This phenomenon pre-supposes their out-migration from India. Patanjali, in his *Mahabhashya*, considers Shakas, and Yavanas to be the migrants from India.[68]

As discussed above, considerable geographical information about India and its neighbourhood in Central Asia is available in the Puranas and the Indian epics. The same is the case with medieval Indian literature. *Kavyamimamsa* of Rajshekhara, Kalhan's *Rajatarangini*, some lexicons, Sanskrit and Buddhist prose narratives and fables, etc. provide valuable information in this direction. Gunadhya's *Brihatkatha*, Somdeva's *Katha-Saritsagar*, Kshemendra's *Brihat-Katha-Manjari* and its Jaina adaptation, *Vasudeva-Hindi* provide valuable information and insight for understanding the geography and other information about India and its neighbourhood. Kalidasa's epics and dramas provide graphic picture of the northern mountain region of India. This is especially so in the case of *Meghdoota*, and *Vikramorvashiam*. He brings refreshing reference of Uttar Kuru.

The fables and narratives in the books mentioned above provide valuable information based on the experiences of the travellers. It needs mention that Central Asia was frequently visited by Indian traders, monks and scholars. Ruling dynasties, such as that of Khotan claimed Indian origin. Shakas, Hunas, Kushanas of Central Asian origin ruled parts of India. Monarchs of Turk and Mongol origin ruled India and continued to have Central Asian links to some extent. The knowledge about the region was reflected in the classical and medieval literature of India. In this connection, it needs mention that perceptional haziness has developed due to change in the names of regions, places, mountains, rivers and the people. There have been shifting frontiers. One group of people have often replaced the others. However, many names, items of trade, the geographical features, etc. have not changed considerable, Kubha, Gomati, and Vakshu and Gandhar have become Kabul, Gomal, Oxus and Kandahar. The community names of Shaka, Huna, Kushana have not changed. The items presented to the Mahabharata hero/monarch Yudhisthira are still known to be produced in the region. This has led many scholars to identify the names of the Central Asia and co-relate them with those mentioned in the Indian literature.

Tashkent, the capital city of Uzbekistan, and Samarkand, the ancient capital of Sogdiana and that of Timur and Babar, are ancient cities. The old name of Tashkent is Chach. Pulleyblank wanted to connect it with Yenisseian word for 'stone': Ket. *Tyes*, Kot. *shish*, Pumpokolsk *cys*. He sees it as a relic of the Huna occupation of the Sogdiana in the fifth and sixth centuries. However, as the word finds place in the inscriptions of Shapur I (240-272 A.D.) and therefore, it had earlier currency. In the old Chinese records, Tashkent is transcribed with the hieroglyph '*shih*' that is stone. The name is linked with Turkic *tash*, 'stone' and may be considered a translation of the older names of the city. It is pointed out that the older names of the city before '*Chach*' also had the meaning 'stone'. The inhabitants of the area, according to Chinese sources were *Ch'iang chu* or *K'ang chu*, very likely of Tukharian origin. *K'ang* may mean some kind of stone in Tokharian. In Hindi, '*kankar* is pebble. According to *Sutralamkara*, a painter of Pushkalawati visited the country *Ashmaka* (meaning stone or stoney) and out of his piety decorated a Buddhist monastery. The place is identified with Tashkent. There was a tradition that *Sutralamkar* was written by Ashvaghosha. Others attribute its authorship to Kumarlat, the founder of *Sautrantika* school of Buddhism. Ashmak, was the name of a north-western country, according to the *Brihatsamhita* of Varahamihira. Kumarajiva knew the great cities of the North like Alasanda and Tashkent.[69] The Name of Tashkent). It needs mention that the word *Tashkent* first appears in *Ta'rikh al-Hind* of al-Beruni.[70]

The name *Kanka* appears in Mahabharata with the names of other tribes of Central Asia. It is the same as *Kang* mentioned earlier. At one place, it comes with Shakas and Tukharas (*Shakas tusharah kankascha;* Mahabharata.[71] At another place, it comes with Shakas, Tusharas and Pahlavas (*shakas tusharah kankashch.pahlavashcha).*[72] *Kankas* are mentioned twice in *Bhagawata Purana*, together with the Kiratas, Hunas, Andhras, Pulindas, Pukkasas, Abhiras, Yavanas and Khasas;[73] and then again with Kiratas, Hunas, Yavanas, Andhras, Khasas and Shakas.[74] A point which needs to be kept in mind here is that the names of the neighbouring communities are often clubbed together in the classical Indian literature. However, this is not done if the social factor, such as the mobility in the social frame, is discussed.

Panini in his *Ashtadhyayi* has mentioned the word *kantha.* The word in *Kashika Sutra* denotes 'town' or 'city'. The 'kand' or 'kent'of Tashkent, Samarkand, Yarkand, etc. is the same as the above-mentioned *kantha.* Tashkent and Yarkand, I am told, were also known as 'Dakshikantha' and 'Yahvarkantha' respectively. The Sanskrit word for 'Turk' is *Turushka.* The first syllable of the name is found in the name of 'Turvasu' in classical Indian literature. The second syllable 'shka' is a superlative suffix found in the name of Kanishka; the meaning of 'Kanishka' is the youngest son.[75]

The last syllable of the Central Asian nations is 'stan'. It is related to the Sanskrit 'sthan' and Persian 'stan', denoting land or place. Kasyapa was a seer and progenitor of the living world according to the Indian mythology. Phrigia is called Phrugia in Greek. Indian literature has Bhrigu, a seer. I am not sure whether 'Phoenic' of the word 'Phoenician' can be derived from Semitic roots. Sanskrita has the word 'Banik', the traders. I feel the deep study of the languages and cultures of Central Asia may help Indians in understanding themselves better. The reverse may be equally true.

Contacts during Medieval and Modern Periods

Indians pleasantly remember Mirza Abdul Rahim Khan-e-Khana and Mirza Ghalib. The former was an eminent Hindi poet. He was a

Turkmen. His father Bairam Khan was the tutor-guardian of the Mughal Emperor Akbar. Mirza Ghalib was an eminent Urdu poet. When we remember Central Asia, we lovingly remember both of them. Both had their roots in Central Asia. Babar, the founder of Mughal dynasty in India was the ruler of this area. Some Sultans were scions of the Turkmen, Khilji and Tughlak tribes. Babar, the founder of the Moghal dynasty in India was the king of Farghana in Central Asia. The number of *manasabdars* (high ranking noble) in Delhi Sultanate and Mughal courts was very large. During first hundred years of the Delhi Sultanate, the immigrant groups, such as the Turks, Khaljis, Ghurids and Tajiks maintained very strong grip on power. As much as fifty per cent of the appointments made on the accession of Muhammad-bin-Tughlaq was from among the amirs of Khurasan, which included Turks, natives of Mongolia and Persia. Several hundred people from Central Asia came to India with Babar. The nobility comprised mainly of Turanis (Central Asians) with a sprinkling of Persians (Iranis). The number of the Iranis increased in the nobility of Humayun, the son of Babar after his exile in the Safavid court. Fifty-seven nobles accompanied Humayun to India, of which 27 were Turanis, 21 were Iranis and nine remained unidentified.[76] Turani stranglehold weakened during Akbar's rule when the Turani nobles revolted against him.[77]

The people from the Central Asia migrated to India due to various reasons. Delhi Sultanate and Mughal court patronized Muslim scholars, artists, soldiers and Sufi saints from Central Asia, Iran and the Arab countries. A galaxy of scholars and men of fine arts had clustered at the Mughal Court. There was large exodus to India whenever the economic and political conditions deteriorated in Central Asia. Mention is made of 15 luminaries in Mughal Court, namely, Jalali Kitobar, Dasturi Nasafi, Khwaja Sami Sadat, Ghubar, Mulla Mustafidi Balkhi, Munim Bukhari, Mustaidi Bukhari, and others. There is mention of 274 poets from Bukhara, Samarkand, Nasaf, Badakhshan and other places migrating to India.[78] Turanis were preferred as guards or watchmen (*pasbani*) and warriors. Turani soldiers received twice the amount in comparison of the Indians. It was easier for the refugee infiltrators to get such jobs.[79] There used to be massive migration from Central Asia during natural calamities. It is reported that 12000 people fled to India during 1730s when there was severe famine in Transoxiana. The people also left for India due to political disturbances, anarchy or tyranny.[80] People fled/immigrated to other countries from Balkh during the tyranic rule of Muhammed Bi. Many left their homes for India during the invasion of Bulkh by Abdullah Khan.[81]

The visit of scholars and Sufi saints from Central Asia to India is a well-known phenomena. Al-Beruni and Abdurazzak Samarkandi came to India from Khwarezm. Central Asian scholars, Al-Khwarezmi and Ibn-e-Sina were aware of the works of Indian scholars, Aryabhatta on Mathematics and Astronomy, and that of Charak and Susrut through their Arabic translations. Many Muslim Sufi saints came from Central Asian cities of Bukhara and Samarkand. Poets from Bukhara and Merv stayed at the imperial court of Akbar. Khwaja Parsa, Makhfi, Mirza Srajuddin, Furqat, Hamza Hakim Zadeh and other poets came from Central Asia to India even in the 19th Century. Tajjali Hindi, Agha Munir went from India. Poets like Nasim, Nasafi, Maharam, Mushrib and Shaukat popularized Indian style of poetry in Central Asia. A group of learned men in Khwarezm were engaged in the translation of Indian historical and literary works in Uzbeg language. Some translations, like that of Aryabhatta's *Ardha Ratrika* is available even now.[82]

Al-Beruni and Al-Khwarezmi were two scholars from Transoxiana, Central Asia. They perfected Sanskrit and Indian Sciences. Al-Beruni's '*Tarikh-ul-Hind*' provides encyclopaedic information about India. Al-Khwarezmi was highly interested in Indian mathematics; he produced an excellent astronomical 'Zij' based on Hindu parameters and methods of calculations. His works on Indian astronomy and mathematics were translated from Arabic to Latin in 1126 AD. It was entitled Liber *Algorizmi de Numero Indoren*. The importance of this publication in the development of European sciences is well-recognized. Adelard translated al-Khwarezmi's another work under the title of *Liber Ysogogarum.* Thus Central Asia was instrumental in the introduction of the decimal system and the concept of zero of Indian origin to the Europe.

Abu Mashar al-Balkhi was highly influenced by Aryabhatta's *Ardha Ratrika* in his study of astronomy. Some Uighur texts found in Turfan deal with lunar calculations based on Indian astronomy. The famous Bower manuscripts found in Central Asia deal with Indian system of medicine. Abu Mansur Muwafaq appreciated and adopted

Indian system of medicine. Hamara Pal came to India, learnt *ilmi tibb,* returned to Transoxiana and practiced medicine as *tabib hakim* and *jarrah.* Abdurrazzaq Samarkandi had appreciation for Indian drugs and brought some of them for use in Central Asia.

Scholars have noticed similarities in the paintings in India and Central Asia. The unique blending of Indo-Turani style in miniature painting was noticed at the turn of the sixteenth century. The Mughal miniature painting, to a great extent, owes to Central Asian masters for its evolution. Some Central Asian miniaturists of seventeenth century followed Indian style of miniature painting, especially those of the Delhi masters. Many miniature painters and calligraphers came from Central Asia and served in Mughal courts. Farukh Begh, a Qalmaq, joined Akbar's service. Muhammad Nadir Samarkandi and Muhammad Murad also came from Central Asia.

There were various sources through which Indian handicrafts, artisans, mechanics, stone masons and builders found their way into Central Asia. Timur brought large number of them to Samarkand. Horticulturists from Iran and Turan helped in the cultivation of trees. Skilled hands from Turkistan and Persia, under the patronage of Akbar, sowed melon and planted vines.

Indo-Central Asian contact was not restricted to the medieval period only. The links exist from the ancient period. Again the flow of men, materials and the ideas was never uni-directional. It was a two way process. Shakas, Hunas and the Kushanas migrated to India in historic period. Shakadwipi or Maga Brahmins of Central Asian origin have prominent place in Indian society. Indian epics, *Puranas, Jatakas*, Jain texts, fables etc. have numerous mentions and descriptions of the places, persons, mountains, rivers, etc. of Central Asia. Shakas, according to Indian tradition, belonged to India and were of Kshatriya Varna. They might have migrated to the Central Asian region in remote past. The same is the case of the Yavanas or the Ionian Greeks.

The Urdu language owes its origin to the Indo-Central Asian contact during the medieval period. 'Urdu' itself is a Persianized Turkish word, which originally meant 'the camp of a Turkish army'. In India, it means 'court' or 'camp'. The language, in its initial stages, was known as 'Hindi' or 'language of Hind or India'. It was also known as 'Hindwi' or 'Hindostani'. This language travelled to different places of India with Sufis or Muslim mystics, freely accepted various regional or local influences, and were also known as Gujari, Dakhni or Dehlavi.[83] Hindi language was also influenced by Turkic language. The number of Turkic words in Hindi, according to Dr. Bhola Nath Tiwari, a noted scholar, is not less than 125. Some of the Turkic words in use in Hindi language are: Urdu, Bahadur, Uzbak, Turk, Chaku (knife), Kainchi (scissors), Qabu (in control), Chammach (spoon), Top (cannon), Topachi (gunner), Barud (gun-powder), Biwi (wife), Chechak (small-pox), Lash (dead body), Sarai (inn) and Bewarchi (cook). Suffix-chi of Turkic language is very much in use in Hindi.[84]

India's commercial and cultural contacts with Central Asia extend to pre-historic times. India's trade with China in one hand and Europe on the other and its cultural intercourse with them partly depended on the Silk Roads through the heart of Central Asia. Central Asia and the Indian community living there played vital role in the trade relations between India and Russia. N.B. Baikova in her monograph (*Rol' Srednei Azii V Russko-Indiiskikh Torgovykh Svyazakh :* Role of Central Asia in Russo-Indian Trade Relations; Tashkent, 1964) has shown that the Central Asia was the connecting link in the trade between the two countries between first half of the sixteenth century to the second half of the eighteenth century. Publication of another volume provides further information in this direction. It was published in 1965. The documents published in Moscow in 1958 throwing light on Russo-Indian relations and the ample work done by Russian and Central Asian scholars provide ample material for study in this field.[85]

A colony of Indian settlers existed in Astrakhan since 1630s. Bukhara also emerged as the chief point of concentration of the Indians. Spread over all Iran, Afghanistan, Uzbekistan, parts of Central Asia and India, they were a great help in transmission of money through letters of credit. Pyotr Pashino, a Russian orientalist traveller and journalist, who visited India twice, reported about the Indians in Central Asia during early 1870s. He collected the materials by personally talking to Indians residing in Tashkent. He also used the materials collected by others from Bukhara and others places of Turkistan. According to him, the natives of Delhi, Bombay and other cities of India lived in many places of Central Asia.[86]

Indians occupied several caravanserais in Tashkent, Bukhara and Samarkand; had homes close to one another in old Margelan, which were known as Indian rows. Nemangan city also had Indian quarters.[87]

It may be mentioned that the Central Asians living in India had also their separate quarters or Maḥallas, such as the Mahalla-i-Khwarazm. Shahi, Mahalla-i-Samarqandi, Mahalla-i-Khitai, Mahalla-i-Atabegi. A separate mahalla in Ahmedabad was named after Bukhara. Haji Sadr Shah of Bukhara settled two villages—Shadrpur and Shahpur, which continue to exist as Shahpur and Shakarpur.[88] Such colonies existed in Central Asia, atleast, since 17th century and in India since the time of Akbar and Jehangir. Many Indians were merchants trading in items traditionally exported from India. But there were skilful jewellers, bookbinders, weavers, bakers, and farmers also among them. The merchants acquired monopoly position in the tea trade in Bukhara; they opened tea-packing enterprises in Samarkand. They sold indigo, muslin, cotton fabric, rugs kimonos, dyes, iron, copper and steel pots, sugar, etc. They exported raw silk, Russian porcelain dishes and manufactured goods from Central Asia to Afghanistan, Kashgar and India.[89]

The relation of the Indians with locals was cordial. They maintained friendly relation with the people of the cities and the villages of the region. The merchants maintained good relation with their Central Asian counterparts. Indians were also the source of information about India and its culture for the people of Central Asia. Indian traders established contacts with Central Russian firms after the region became part of Russia.[90]

Babar was the founder of his own empire in India. He came from Farghana valley. He has written much about his native place, about the wars he fought in his native place, in his *Babarnama*. He compares and contrasts, gives massive information about the land, the climate, and the people, their way of living, housing, village settlement pattern, vegetation, fruits, etc. He detests India's heat and dust; nostalgically remembers Central Asian melons. Abul Fazal mentions about the cultivation of melons in India. Not only *Babarnama* and *Ain-e-Akbari*, but the memoirs of other Delhi Sutanate and Moghal kings also provides information about Central Asia, the Sufis and others coming from there.

Many travellers from India have written their accounts of the land and the people of Central India. M.N. Roy, Raja Mahendra Pratap, Rahul Sankrityayan and others visited the region and have written about the same. Raja Ranjit Singh of Punjab sent his envoys there.

Mohan Lal's wrote his travel accounts. Iqitidar Sidiqi was there. *Tarikhe Munajile Bukhara* by Fazil Khan is a well-written book. Unlike Britishers, who had the tendency to denigrade, the Indian travellers wrote about the region and the people with warmth and as they saw it.

In Hindi language, the history of Central Asia by Rahul Sankrityayan is published in two volumes *(Madhya Asia ka Itihas). Sarthavah* (in Hindi) by Dr. Motichandra provides valuable information about the trade routes between India and Central Asia. However, much more need to be done by Indian and Central Asian scholars to re-discover their links from the ancient days to the present. The works of some of the scholars in this case needs mention, which are: *The Geography of the Puranas* by S.M. Ali, *Cunningham's Ancient Geography of India*, edited by S. Majumdar Shastri, N.L. Dey's *The Geographical Dictionary of Ancient* and *Medieval India* and D.C. Sirkar's *Cosmography and Geography in Early Indian Literature.*

Problem of Proper Interpretation

Icons and paintings of many excavations are not properly interpreted due to various reasons. Eminent Indologist, Dr. Lokesh Chandra has pointed towards misinterpretations of certain icons of Central Asian origin. A head from Khocho with the third eye of Shiva and all the features of that divinity was interpreted as that of a devata. Fragment of a wall-painting, found in the rubble of temple 9 at Bezeklik was identified as the head of a Brahmana. In reality, it is that of the Nilakantha Avalokiteshvara appearing as the metamorphosis of Shiva, the great Yogin, in the Nilakantha-sutra. Faragment of a mural painting from the Second Domed Cave, Kumtura is that of Vasishtha and Arundhati, and not, as broadly identified, of a Brahmin. The silk painting of an 'Angry Arhat' found by the Third German Expedition at the lower end of the cave of Eightyfour Siddhas on the foothills near Turfan, is, in reality, that of Dingnaga. Professor Lokesh Chandra has properly explained Tukhara melody and Tiered Stupa with Niches in proper Historical perspective.[91]

Central Asian Role in Spread of Buddhism and Indian Culture

Central Asia played crucial role in the spread of Buddhism and the

Indian culture. A large number of earliest Buddhist missionaries in China (Loyang) belonged to western Central Asia. Among them, there were two Parthians (An Shih-kao and An Hsuan), three Tusharas or Yueh-Chih (Chi Lou-chia-chi'en or Lokakshema, Chih Vao and Chin Liang), two Soghdians (K'ang Meng-hsiang and K'ang Chu). K'ang Chu came from K'ang-chu, which is known as 'Kangyu' in Russian literature and 'Kank' in Indian classical literature. Among the translators of Buddhist literature in Chinese, before the end of western Chin dynasty, 6 or 7 were Chinese, six were Indians and sixteen belonged to Central Asian communities. Of the last category, there were six Yueh-chi, four Parthians, three Soghdians, two Kucheans and one Khotanese.[92]

An Shih-kao (his Chinese name) was a Parthian crown prince, who abdicated his throne in favour of his uncle; dedicated his life for religious work; went to the East; settled in Loyang in 148 A.D. and translated up to 170 texts. Many men whose ancestors migrated from western Turkistan engaged themselves for the spread of Buddhism.[93] Parthian scholar associated themselves with the school of translators of Buddhist texts in China, apart from Ngan-She-Kao or Lokottama, was Ngan-Hivan. Kasyapa Matanga and Dharmatrata founded the school, but Ngan-She-Kao made the first organized effort in this direction. Indo Scythian monk Lokakshema was also among the first group of translators. Senghui, a Sogdian was the first to introduce Buddhism in southern China. Scores of Central Asian scholars like Kumarajiva contributed immensely towards the dissemination of Buddhist religion and thought in Central Asia and China through expositions and translations of sacred texts. Some of the best specimens of the Central Asian Buddhist scholars were Buddabhadra, Sanghabhuti, Gautam Sanghdeva and Punyatrats.[94] Apart from the Parthians, Sogdians, Indo-Scythians, Kucheans and Khotanese, the other teachers of Buddhism in Central Asia were Uighurs, Tibetans and Mongols. Central Asia has produced many Buddhist savants. It had also the Buddhas and Boddhisattvas, Amitabha, Avalokita, Manjushri and Kshitigarbha had Central Asian and Chinese linkages.[95] Sylvain Levi suggests that Manjushri was of Tokharian origin. Indian tradition links him with China. According to I-tsing, he dwells in China. Lokashema was also of Tokhara origin. Ghoshak was an important Buddhist scholar who was born in Tokharistan. A point which needs mention in Central Asian context is that the scholarship there was not only confined to the Buddhist scriptures. Kumarjiva also studied four Vedas, five sciences, Brahmanical Shastras and astronomy at Kashgar,[96] during his return journey from Kashmir after his study of Buddhist scriptures. Like India, Central Asia had great centres of learning. Sarvastivadins popularized the study of Sanskrit. The people of different ethnicity speaking different languages lived harmoniously in Central Asia.

Place like Kucha in Central Asia was the centre of Indian influenced music from where it spread to China. Musical instruments were taken to China from Kucha. One of the teachers of lute in China was a Brahmin. Another lute-player, Sujiva was from the Royal house of Kucha.[97]

Buddhism was dominant; it was in flourishing state. Yarkand and Khotan were the centres of Mahayana Buddhism. Kashgar, Kucha, Turfan and Shan Shan near Lob-nor were Hinayanist centres. The contact of the states of Tarim valley mentioned above was intimate and regular with India and the Oxus valley.

A very positive aspect of the culture of Central Asia was the harmonious co-existence of different religious groups and sects. There were Hinayanists in Mahayanist centres and *vice versa*. Brahminism existed with Buddhism. Manichaeism, and Nestorian Christianity also were practiced by some.

Language and Literature: Links and Interactions

As discussed earlier, Urdu language owes its origin to the Indo-Central Asian contact Hindi has large number of Turkic, Persian and Arabic words. Other Indian languages also have the words from these languages. Persian was the official language during the Mughal rule in India. Russian scholars have discovered some Indic languages in Central Asia. Pariah of Hissar Valley speak an Indic language of the same name in their home. They communicate in Uzbek and Tajik languages with their neighbours.[98]

Central Asia is a polyglots society. Different languages were spoken in Tarim and Oxus valleys. Linguistic scene did not remain the same at all the time. The language scenario changes with the change in the Ethnic composition with passage of time. Two languages were spoken in the Carly centuries of the Christian era, in Xinjiang. The northern language was named Kuchean. It was also called Tokharian or the language of the Tokharas or Indo-Scythians. The language, with two great western and eastern groups, was supposed to be an Indo-European language. The language spoken in southern Tarim basin was called 'Saka' and 'Khotanese'. The three other languages, written in the script of Aramaic origin, were Iranian languages. Two of them have preserved Manichean texts. Sogdian, the language of the region around Samarkand contained Buddhism, Manichaean and Christian texts.[99]

Uighur, literary form of the various Turkish idioms spoken north and south of Tien Shan, derived its name from the Uighur script, derived from the Syriac. It was widely used for Buddhist, Manichaean and Christian literature. Its use for Buddhist literature increased when Uighurs replaced Tibetan power in Tarim valley in about 860 A.D. and founded their own kingdom. Tibetan manuscripts have also been found in Khotan, Miran and Tun-huang regions. Prakrit recension of Dharmapada, and other documents knows as Kharoshthi documents have been excavated from Xinjiang. The language (Gandhari Prakrit) and the script (Kharoshthi) of the same are Indian. Wide use of Sanskrit in Central Asia, especially by the Sarvastivadin Buddhists is a well known fact. Khotanese, Agnean, Kuchean, Sogdian, Uighur, Turkish, Mongol, Manchu and Chinese manuscripts or tracts or the fragments have been recovered from Central Asia.[100]

Presently, Turkic languages are spoken in Uzbekistan, Kazakhstan and Kirghijistan. Tajik spoken in Tajikistan is an Iranian language. Uighur is a Turkic language. Some religious minorities speak their own languages.

Apart from the Scripts mentioned above, Brahmi was widely used in Central Asia. Its introduction in Central Asia and association with Buddism is supposed to be of earlier date than that of Kharoshthi. Three verieties of this script are traced in Sanskrit texts found there. The script was also used for writing Agnean (language of Agnidesha), Kuchean and Saka-Khotanese.[101]

The discoveries of an inscription of the first century B.C. in Tazikistan and an inscription on gold slab found at Dalverzin in Uzbekistan and some other inscriptions at Wardak and Kunduz in Afghanistan take us back before the Christian era, so far the use of Prakrit is concerned. As mentioned earlier, Kharoshthi documents were discovered from various archaeological sites in the Tarim basin, in

Khotan, Niya, Endere, Miran, Lou-lan and Kurak Darya. Over two hundred documents written in black ink in Kharoshthi script on different materials—wood, leather, silk and paper—were discovered. Sir Aurel Stein wrote: "At the Niya site, I found hundred wooden documents comprising correspondence, mainly official, contracts, accounts, miscellaneous memoranda and the like, all written in that Sanskrit language and the Kharoshthi script which during the first centuries before and after Christ were used on the Indian north-west frontier and in the adjacent portions of Afghanistan.[102] The inscriptions received at Miran were fresh even after the lapse of two thousand years. A large number of coins struck in Khotan or nearby places were also in the same script. The coins dated first century B.C. to 1st century A.D.[103]

Sanskrit was methodically taught in Central Asia. It was called 'Arshi' (Arya) in Tokharian. Many Sanskrit manuscripts, like that of Ashvaghosha's *Buddha Charit* and *Saundaranand Kavys* (discovered from Shorchuq), were found out in Central Asia during various excavations. Almost all the important Buddhist texts were translated in all the major Central Asian languages. The scholars not only studied the texts and translated them, but also wrote commentary on the texts. Grammar, astronomy and all other subject were methodically taught and studied. Bower manuscripts discovered at Kucha are medical texts.[104]

The languages of India and Central Asia had profound impact on each other. Genesis and development of Urdu and Turkic lexemes in Hindi are the results of Indian and Central Asian contact. Sanskrit has also the profound impact on the languages of Central Asia. The language of the region also had impact on Sanskrit. The Shaka and Slav languages, which were spoken in Central Asia, were intimately linked with Sanskrit. The relation of Turkic languages with the Aryan languages is very ancient.[105] Caldwell has given voluminous data and massive analysis of the links of the Turk-Mongol languages with South Indian language in general, in his *A Comparative Grammar of the Dravidian of South Indian Family of Language*. The work, however, had many shortcomings. Caldwell links Dravidian languages with the Sythian languages of Central Asia. However, the Scythian is a very loose grouping, and therefore, his study lacks sharp focus.

Some valuable information is also available in the *History of Central Asia* written by Rahul Sankrityayan in Hindi language. The vocabulary of Russian language given by him shows massive lexical similarity with Sanskrit. Here, it needs mention that the difference between the languages of Rigveda and Avesta, and that between Sanskrit and old Persian is mostly phonetic, and not grammatical. The Iranian languages of Central Asia and Iran are intimately related to the Indo-Aryan languages.[106]

Dr. Ram Villash Sharma, a well-known Indian scholar has brought many lexical, phonetic, morphological and syntactical similarities of Turkic and Mongol language with Indian languages in his Hindi publication, *Bharat ke Prachin Bhasha Parivar Aur Hindi*. Dr. Sharma compares the languages of Turk-Mongol and Fino-Ugrian family with the languages of India. He compares phonetic, lexical, morphological traits of Turkic, Mongol (Khalkh, Buriat) and Fin languages with those of the Indian languages.

Turkic, like many Indo-Aryan and Dravidian languages shows the tendency of palatization. But unlike Dravidian and Indo-Aryan languages, it does not use cerebrals. Turkic adds semi-vowel 'y' before some vowels attached to 'k' and 'g'. Arabian words 'katib' (secretary), malum (known) and 'majkur' (said earlier) become kyatip, malyum and majkyur respectively. This trait is found in Kashmiri also. Here 'a' in 'majkur' is shortened. The 'b' of 'katib becomes 'p'. Arabic 'kitab' and Sanskrit 'rang' become 'kitap' and 'rank' in Turkic language. Thus 'b' and 'k' are devoiced in that language. When pronominal suffix 'i' (his or her) is added, then 'p' is again voiced and the word becomes 'kitabi'. This trait is visible in Sanskrit also, as we find in such words as 'Jagadish', 'sharadagam', etc. Like Dravidian languages, no word of Turkic has initial 'r' and 'l'. This tendency has become somewhat lax in Dravidian languages. Tamil 'irandu' (two) is sometimes spoken as 'randu'. 'Reddy' is the name of a caste in Andhra Pradesh. Turkic and Dravid languages usually do not use two consonants together in the beginning of a word. 'Slav' is pronounced 'Islav' (as 'school' is pronounced 'iskul' in eastern India) in Turkic. English word 'club' is pronounced 'kulup' or 'klup'. Like Prakrit, some mid-consonants become vowels or semi-vowels. Persian 'agar' (if) and 'digar' become 'ayar' and 'diyar'. Fricative 'f' in borrowed Perian words becomes 'p' in Turkic languages. Fricative 'kh' of Arabic and Persian words usually becomes 'h'. Arabic 'fun' (art), khala (mother's sister), 'khabar' (news) and Persian 'hafta' (week) become 'pan', 'hala', 'habar' and 'hapta' respectively. Like Dravidian languages, the use of aspirates is not the trait of the Turkic languages. Most of the Indian languages use dental and palatal sibilants – s and sh. Cerebral sibilant 'sh' is used in mostly in Sanskrit words. The Aryan and Dravidian languages, and to some extent Turkic, has the tendency to convert dental and palatal sibilant into palatal 'ch' and 'chh'. In Sanskrit, the roots 'gash' गश (gam, to go) and 'prash' प्रश (to ask; prashna, question) become 'gachchh' and 'prachchh' respectively. Sanskrita 'bhash' भाष becomes 'peshu' पेशु in Tamil; the Sanskrit root 'ish' इष (ish, to drink) is transformed into 'ich' (drink) into Turkic.

Dr. Ram Vilash Sharma has pointed towards many similarities and parallels at lexical level. Turkic lexemes for Sanskrit 'kar' (to do), 'kal' (time), 'kup'(well), 'kati' (how many), 'kim' (who) are 'kil' (old Turkic), 'kara', 'kuyu', 'kach' and 'kim'. Turkic 'kara' (black), Tamil 'karu' and Sanskrit 'kar' (of 'andhakar') are related. Hindi uses relative suffix 'ka, ki, ke'; in Turkic, it is 'ki'. 'Janma' (birth) of Sanskrit is derived from the root 'jan'. In Turkic, 'dagum' (birth) and 'ichim' are derived from 'dagh' (to be born) and 'ich' (to drink). Turkic, Tamil and Russian languages use relative suffix '–im' as in 'Ahamadin' (of Ahmad; Turkic), Maganin (of the son) and Stalin (of steel). Negative suffix –ma in Sanskrit and –ma in Turkic is identical.

The syntactic pattern of Indian languages, except Khasi and Kashmiri is 'Subject-object-verb'. Turkic language also follows the same. However, like in Sanskrit in '*gachchhami*' (I go; gachchh, to go); in Turkic '*galirim*' (I come); the pronominal suffix follows the verb. Neither Sanskrit 'ami' or 'mi', nor Turkic 'im' are freely used as first person singular pronoun, I, as is done in Bengali and Marathi. The word for 'I' in these languages is 'aham' and 'ban' respectively. Turkic language uses pronominal suffix after the noun as in 'babam' (my father; baba = father, -m = my). It needs mention that 'Baba' is used for father in many Indian Languages. The pattern of adding pronominal suffix as well the suffix for 'I' in this case is of Indian origin. Arabic and Persian also follow the same. Both Hindi and Turkic add the verb denoting 'to do' to the noun to make verb ('karana' in Hindi, 'kam karna, to do the work; 'kilmak' in Turkic, namaj kilmak, to do or perform namaj). In many cases, new meaning comes when two words are added and density of meaning is achieved by re-duplication of words. The pattern of the formation of higher numerals in Turkic, Dravidian and many Munda and Indo-Mongoloid languages is the same.[107]

New discoveries in Central Asia and India during colonial days have brought out huge material about the culture and languages of the two regions. However, the colonial studies has also the drawbacks. In many cases, the cultural and linguistic continuum, both in terms of time and geographical spread was ignored; differences, rather than the similarities were emphasized.

The facts are often explained with narrow focus and misinterpreted. It needs mention that Indo-Central Asian linkages operated on wider canvass. The areas from Central Asia through India to South-East Asia and from West to East Asia shared many cultural traits. The precepts of divine kingship, apotheosis/deification of kings, cult syncretism, composite cult emblems, law, bureaucratic government and expressions in arts, norms, values and the ethos conformed in a large area from Central Asia to South East Asia. Deification of Kushana Kings, the kings of Java and Combodia and that of India treated as Vishnu's incarnation are not isolated phenomena. The writings of the Nicolo Seals of Central Asia (Miarark, Yasnu, Oezo; meaning Mihir; Vedic God Mitra or Sun, Vishnu and Isa or Shiva) pointed towards the same phenomenon as we find in 'Surys-Sevana (worship of sun god; in reality the Sun and Shiva are identified and worshipped together) in Indonesia and Panchayatan Puja (worship of five gods together) in India. Kharosthi documents found in Central Asia show the similarity in the social and cultural fields with India. The similarities extended to South-East Asia also. India, Iran, Greece, Central Asia and South-East Asia, in reality, formed a vast culture zone during Classical period. There existed cultural continuum in the areas mentioned above and the study of the cultures and languages in 'continuum frame' may remove haziness of ideas and may bring clarity in our perceptions.[108]

Reconciliation and amalgamation of myths and local adaptations operated in Central Asia also. It is believed that Asanga, a well-known Buddhist scholar, effected the amalgamation. Rhys Davids has confirmed the same.[109]

The study of the history and culture of the people with colonial past, at a time, suffers due to Euro-centric bias of the scholars.

The Indian scholars mostly rely on the translations of its classical literature by the foreigners. Their outreach to the original Russian, Central Asian, Chinese and Tibetan sources is poor. The work by Indian and Central Asian scholars may bring new facts to light and remove perceptional haziness. It is necessary that Indian and Central Asian scholars undertake massive study of each other's languages, society and culture. The gap in our knowledge about each other is a real one and needs to be bridged.

NOTES

1. Mansura Haider, *India and Central Asia: Linkages and Interactions,* in Central Asia, The Great Game Replayed, An Indian Perspective, Edited by Professor Nirmala Joshi, Delhi, 2003, p. 257.
2. Ibid.
3. S. P. Gupta, *Pre-historic Indian Culture in Soviet Central Asia*, in India's Contribution to World Thought and Culture, pp. 239-40.
4. Mansura Haider, op. cit., p. 264.
5. Pentti Aalto, *On the role of Central Asia in the Spread of Indian Cultural Influence*, in 'India's Contribution…', p. 249.
6. Ibid.
7. Ibid.
8. B.N. Puri, *Buddhism in Central Asia*, Reprint, Delhi (2000), p. 332.
9. Ibid, p.271.
10. Chhaya Bhattacharya, *India — A Major Source of Central Asian Art*, in 'India's Contribution…', p. 292.
11. Ibid, pp. 294-95.
12. Ibid, p. 297.
13. Mansura Haider, op. cit. pp. 273-74.
14. Ibid, pp. 271-72.
15. S.P. Gupta, op. cit.
16. R.H. Sulamanov, *Indian Parrallels in Ancient Cults of Sogdiana*, The paper presented in a Seminar on "India and Central Asia (Pre-Islamic Period)", in Tashkent (2000), Mimeographed.
17. S.P. Gupta, "Hindu Gods in Western Central Asia: A Lesser know Chapter of Indian History;" *Dialogue*, Vol. 3, No. 2; April-June 2002, Delhi, pp. 142-43.
18. Ibid, p. 143.
19. Yuriy Burayakov, *The Issue of Relation between Sogd and Indian* in the ancient times *and the early middle ages*; paper presented in 'India and Central Asia (Pre-Islamic period)' seminar held in Teshkent in 2000.
20. P. Banerjee, *Hindu Deities in Central Asia*, in 'India's Contribution to the World Thought and Culture', pp. 281-87.
21. Ibid, p. 110.
22. *The Cultural Heritage of India*, Calcutta (1991), (heritage refered as 'Heritage…') vol. VI, pp. 221-23.
23. Ibid, p. 223.
24. Ibid, pp. 223-24.

25. Panini, *Ashtadhyayi*, V. 4. 74; VI. 3.97.
26. *Cultural Heritage of India*, Vol. VI. p. 8.
27. S.M. Ali, *The Geography of the Puranas,* New Delhi, 1996, p. 37.
28. Ibid.
29. *Cultural Heritage of India*, VI, p. 11.
30. Ibid. quoted from *Mahabharata*, VI. 5.12.
31. Ibid. *Mahabharata*, VI. 6. 4-5.
32. Ibid. Ibid, VI.6. 8, 13, 37-38.
33. Ibid *Markandeya Purana*, LIV. 12ff.
34. *Matsya Purana*, CXIII. 26.31.
35. *Markandeya Purana*, LV. 20ff.
36. *Brahmanda Purana*, XXXV. 50.
37. *Shri Vishnu Purana*, 2. 2. 34-38
38. Ali, S.M., *The Geography of the Puranas*, New Delhi, 1996; p. 87.
39. Ibid; H. Raychaudhari, *Studies in Indian Antiquities*, (Calcutta, 1932), pp. 75-76.
40. Raychaudhuri, op. cit., p. 75.
41. Ali, S.M. op. cit., p. 97.
42. N.L. Dev, "The Geography Dictionary of Ancient and Mediaeval India", London, 1927, p. 74.; quoted in *The Cultural Heritage*, p. 12.
43. Kumar, B.B.; Central Asia: The Indian Links; *Dialogue*, 3:4, April-June 2002, Delhi; p. 175.
44. Valmiki's *Ramayana; Kiskindha Kand*, 43.39-59.
45. Ibid, 43.12.
46. Ibid, 43. 55. 60.
47. *Mahabharata*, Sabha Parva, 53.17.
48. Ibid, Bhishma Parva, 6.1.31; 7.2.
49. Ibid, Adi Parva, 17.
50. Ibid, Sabha, 52. 13-17.
51. Ibid, Udyog Parva, 4.15.
52. Ibid, Sabha, 28. 11-15.
53. Ibid, 52. 13-17.
54. Ibid. 52.6.
55. Ibid, 51.23-24, 30.
56. Ibid, 78.60.
57. Ibid, Bhishma Parva, 75.21.
58. Ibid. Karna Parva, 77. 19.
59. Ibid, *Harsha Charit* 760; *Kavya Mimamsa*, Last part of Chapter III; Mahabharata XIII. 836.
60. *Vayu Puran* 4.7.44; *Matsya Purana*, 121.45-46.
61. Kumar, op. cit., p. 176.
62. B.B. Kumar, *Looking East*, Dialogue 5:1, July-September 2003, p. 7.
63. *Cultural Heritage of India*, Vol. II, pp. 614-16.
64. *Shrimad Bhagvata Purana*, 9.8.4-7; *Shri Vishnu Purana* 4.3.42-48.
65. Maha., Anu., 33.21-23.
66. Ibid, 33.21; *Kovel Jataka*, 6, p. 110.
67. *Maha, Anushasan Parva*, 35. 17-18.
68. *Manu Smiriti*, X. 43-44.

69 Agnihotri, Dr. Prabhu Dayal, *Patanjali-Kalin Bharat* (Hindi), pp. 92-93.
70. Penti Aalto, Helsinki, The Name of Tashkent.
71. Ibid.
72. Maha., 2.47.1850.
73. Maha., 12.65.2429.
74. *Shrimad Bhagawat Purana*, 2.4.18).
75. Ibid, 9.20.30)
76. Communicated by Professor Lokesh Chandra during personal communication.
77. Meenakshi Jain, "Secularism: The Indian Historical Experience;" *Dialogue*, vol.5, No.1; October-December 2003; New Delhi; p. 47.
78. Ibid.
79. Mansura Haider, "India and Central Asia: Linkages and Interactions;" in Nirmala Joshi's *Central Asia*, p. 261.
80. Ibid, p. 258.
81. Ibid, p. 259.
82. Ibid,
83. Mansura Haider, op. cit.
84. *The Cultural Heritage of India*, Vol. V, pp. 642-43.
85. Bhola Nath Tiwari, *Hindi Bhasha*, p. 183.
86. Dr. Surendra Gopal, *India and Central Asia, Cultural, Economic and Political Links*, Delhi (2001), pp. VII-VIII.
87. Ibid, pp.26-27.
88. A. Lubarasky, "Indian Settlers in Central Asia," Chennai, *Vivekanand Kendra Patrika*, vol. 2, No. 1, February 1973, p. 108.
89. Ibid
90. Mansura Haider, op. cit., pp. 267-68.
91. Lubarasky, op. cit.
92. Ibid, pp. 108-09.
93. Lokesh Chandra, "Notes on Central Asian Bhuddhist Iconography," *Dialogue*, vol. 3, No. 4, pp. 33-42.
94. B.A. Litvinsky, *India and Soviet Central Asia*, in 'India's Contribution…', p. 268.
95. B.N. Puri, *Buddhism in Central Asia*, p. 102.
96. Ibid, p. 322-23.
97. Ibid, p. 172.
98. Ibid, p. 141-43.
99. Ibid, p. 325.
100. B.N. Puri, op. cit., p. 242-43.
101. I.M. Oranskii, "An Essayy on the Ethnography of a group of Indic Language Speaking Pariah" (in the Hissar Valley), in '*India and Central Asia*' by Surendra Gopal; pp. 139-42.
102. Ibid, pp. 179-81.
103. Ibid, pp. 182-84.
104. Ibid, p. 186-87.

105. Aurel Stein, *Ancient Central Asian Tracts*, Macmillan & Co., London, 1955, p. 28.
106. Samarendra Nath Sen, "India and the Ancient World; Transmission of Scientifid Ideas," in *Cultural Heritage.*, Vol. VI, pp. 228-29,
107. Ram Vilash Sharma, *Bharat ke Prachin Bhasha Parivar Aur Hindi*, vol. 2, Delhi, (1983), p. 243.
108. B.B. Kumar, Looking East, *Dialogue*, Vol. 5, No. 1, p. 8.
109. P. Banerjee, op. cit., pp. 282-83.

2

Notes on Central Asian Buddhist Iconography

Lokesh Chandra

The exhibition of the treasures of Central Asian art from the West Berlin State Museums held at the Metropolitan Museum of Art, New York has awakened fresh interest in understanding this important phase of Buddhist art. Several items call for more precise identification.

Śiva

A head from Khocho, dated to the 7th century, evidences Indo-Iranian work. It is identified as 'the head of a *devatā*.' It has half-open eyes, with a 'dreamy look': this is a *yoga* posture of intense meditation in which the eyes are concentrated on the tip of the nose. The shallow incision between the eyebrows represents the third eye. The hairdo has the centre parting "while the rest of the hair is swept up in tresses that disappear under a lozenge-patterned chaplet" (AASR 1982:158 No. 96). This hairstyle is associated with Śiva: "the hair parted in the centre and then swept up on the sides into a topknot is found on other Śiva heads" of the eighth century from Afghanistan. A marble face from Afghanistan is illustrated in Deborah (1982:101 pl. 22). It is remarkably identical with the Khocho head, which in all probability represents Śiva.

Two painted clay heads from the Cave of the Statues, Kizil (AASR 1982:70-72 Nos. 11, 12) are dated to the sixth century and have the third eye painted on the forehead. They were made from moulds. A great number of stucco moulds have survived and bear Sanskrit names of craftsmen on the reverse. Both have been identified as "head of a bodhisattva". The crown is similar to the aforesaid Khocho head. The style of the crown and the third eye confirm it as a representation of Śiva.

Nilakantha Avalokiteśvara

A fragment of a wall-painting was found in the rubble of temple 9 at Bezeklik (lit. "place of paintings"). It has been identified as the head of a brahmin "with long strands of hair, apparently wind-blown, the thick beard... This fragment, unlike most of the other paintings found at the site, shows the influence of the Indian school" (AASR 1982: 147 No. 81). The identification follows Le Coq (1913: pl. 39d). The third eye between the eyebrows raises new possibilities. The Bezeklik monastic complexes were situated on high cliffs on the right bank of the Sengim River. Winding paths lead to the top of the cliff where several hundred temples have been preserved. These geographic features recall the description of Mount Potalaka of Avalokiteśvara in Hsüan-tsang (Beal 1884: 2.233): "To the east of the Malaya mountains is Mount Po-ta-lo-kia (Potalaka). The passes of this mountain are very dangerous; its sides are precipitous, and its valleys rugged. On the top of the mountain is a lake; its waters are clear as a mirror. From a hollow proceeds a great river, which encircles the mountain as it flows down twenty times and then enters the southern sea. By the side of the lake is a rock-palace of the Devas. Here, Avalokiteśvara, in coming and going, takes his abode. Those who strongly desire to see this Bodhisattva do not regard their lives, but, crossing the water (fording the streams), climb the mountain forgetful of its difficulties and dangers; of those who make the attempt there are very few who reach the summit. But even of those who dwell bellow the mountain, if they earnestly pray and beg to behold the god, sometimes he appears as Tsz'-tsai-t'ien (*Īśvara-deva*), sometimes under the form of a *yogi* (a Pāśupata); he addresses them with benevolent words and then they obtain their wishes according to their desires". The hair of the Bezeklik head are in typical ascetic style, he wears the thick ear-rings of a yogin, and has the third eye on the forehead like Maheśvara. The trifoliate ornament around the ear-rings symbolises the trifoliate leaf of *bilva* or wood-apple tree, Aegle marmelos. This tree is sacred to Siva: its leaves are dedicated to Śiva and its fruit is the *avyakta* form of Śiva (Liebert 1976:43). The mural seems to represent the Potala Avalokiteśvara.

Avalokiteśvara appears as the metamorphosis of Śiva the great yogin in the Nilakaṇṭha-sūtra. These are eight translations of this text into Chinese:

A.D.	*Translator*	*K*	*T*	*Nj*
624-649	Chih-t'ung	K 292	T 1057b	Nj 318
650-661	Bhagavaddharma	K 294	T 1060	Nj 320
709	Bodhiruci	K 293	T 1058	Nj 319
731-736	Vajrabodhi	K 1270	T 1061	–
–	"	–	T 1112	–
723	Amoghavajra	–	T 1111	–
723	"	–	T 1113b	–
14th Century	Dhyanabhadra	–	T 1113a	–

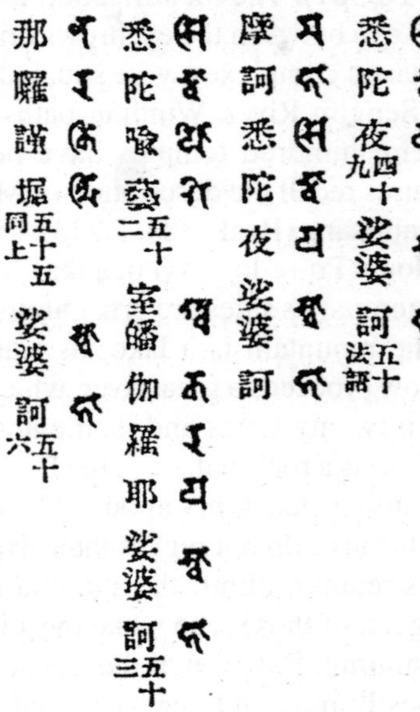

Bhagavaddharma translated the sūtra at Khotan, as we are infor-med by the colophon of its Chinese scroll from Tun-huang (Stein 3793 at the British Library). Thus the Nilakaṇṭha Avalokiteśvara was popular at Khotan in the first half of the seventh century. Twelve scrolls have been found at Tun-huang (Giles, 1957:105-106) which indicates his vogue at Tun-huang as well.

The version of Amoghavajra is most popular in China, Japan and Korea to this day. It is a Chinese transliteration of the lost Sanskrit text. It speaks of Nilakaṇṭha as the ascetic (siddha), the great ascetic (mahāsiddha), the lord of ascetic yogins (siddha-yogīśvara): siddhāya svāhā/mahā-siddhāya svāhā siddha-yogīśvaraya svāhā Nilakaṇṭhaya svāhā (Lokesh Chandra, 1979). The Bezeklik head is a remarkable portrayal of a great ascetic yogin.

The version of Chih-t'ung is the earliest and fuller than the vulgate version of Amoghavajra. Chih-t'ung's version invokes Nilakaṇṭha with additional epithets, like: *kṛṣṇā-jatamukuṭa e'oh* one with a diadem of black matted locks, and as unique in the fury of his laughter (*aṭṭahāsa*). The Bezeklik head "seems agitated as if taking part in a discussion. ... the slightly opened mouth in which a few teeth are visible all strengthen the impression of a heated argument". (AASR 1982:147). This posture represents the aṭṭahāsa, or furious laughter of Nīlakaṇṭha. The Bezeklik head in all likelihood is Nilalaṇṭha Avalokiteśvara as the great ascetic yogin, the mahā-siddha-yogiśvara.

Vasiṣṭha and Arundhati

Fragment of a mural painting from the Second Domed Cave, Kumtura has been identified broadly as a brahmin. The painting belongs to the early Indian-influenced phase, dated around A.D. 500. He has the typical dress of an ascetic and holds a flask (*kamaṇḍalu*) in his right hand. Behind him is a devatā, to which a rosary of beads appears to have been added later (AASR 1982:80 No. 18). This seems to be a representation of Vasiṣṭha followed by Arundhati. Vasiṣṭha is the owner of the wish-fulfilling cow Kāmadhenu and the leader of brahmarṣis: as such his attribute is the *kamaṇḍalu*, the gourd jar of ascetics with a narrow neck. Arundhati is renowned for her faithfulness to her husband Vasiṣṭha. She is the inseparable consort of the Sage. When a ṛṣi is accompanied by his spouse, they are most likely to be Vasiṣṭha and Arundhati. The question arises: does the couple occur in Buddhist art? Vasiṣṭha and Arundhati are in fact depicted in the Sino-Japanese *Garbhādhatu mañdala*. They are represented together (Esot. 206, 207) in the external quarter of vajras, wherein deities of the Hindu pantheon are shown. They head the deities on the east, followed by the sun (*Sūrya), Ketu, Mithuna*, Vṛṣa, Meṣa and so on. Arundhati is a personification of the morning star, which precedes sunrise, and thus she naturally comes before Sūrya in the maṇdala. Their Sino-Japanese names are Basu-sen (Vasiṣṭharṣi) and Basusen-kō (the consort ko of Vasiṣṭha ṛṣi). Vasiṣṭha has a bloomed lotus in the right hand while his soft turns a rosary. Arundhati holds a leaf and bud of a lotus in her right hand and a lotus flower in the left hand. The Sino-Japanese maṇdala can be dated to the eighth century. It is based on the Mahavairocana-sūtra, which was translated into Chinese by Subhakarasimha and I-hsing in A.D. 725.

Tukhara Melody

A divine musician was painted on the walls of the Prayer-Wheel Cave at Kizil, dated around A.D. 600-650 (AASR 1982:93 no. 29). Chinese records mention the introduction of melodies and musical instruments from Kucha since 138 B.C. to the eighth century A.D. (Liu Mau-tsai 1969: 99-108). Among the instruments from Kucha was the four-stringed lute. It can be seen in the hands of Sarasvati in the Sino-Japanese *Garbhadhātu maṇḍala* (Esot. 331). Sujiva, a member of the royal house of Kucha, came to China in A.D. 568 and introduced the seven keys of Kucha music: *sādhārita, kaiśika, ṣadja, ṣadja-grāma, ṣādava, pañcama, vṛṣabha*.

Chang Ch'ien brought back musical instruments and melodies from Kucha to the Chinese capital Ch'ang-an in 138 B.C. "Only the name of these melodies has come down to us: it is *Mo-ho-tou-le*. *Moho* is clearly the Chinese transcription of *maha* (great). As far as tou-le is concerned, the last word still remains to he spoken; it is perhaps a variant of Tou-k'u-le, or Tochara. The name of this melody suggests an Indian origin. Possibly this originally Indian melody was first known at Kucha, where, as we know. Tocharian was spoken in later days. It was the centre of Indian-influenced music in Central Asia, which later spread to China. At that early date Kucha must already have been under Indian cultural influence. In China, a son- in-law of Emperor Wu-ti (140-87 B.C.) wrote twenty-eight new tunes based on the Mo-ho-tou-le melody, which were played as military music" (translation of Liu Mau-tsai 1969:100 in AASR 1982:93). We do not find any Tukhara melody in Sanskrit texts, except Tururṣka-Gauda rāga in Sangita-ratnākara 3.383, or Turuṣka-Todi rāga in Rāga-vibodha of Somanātha 247. It is a strange coincidence of a historic leap that the Rāg Tukhāri should occur in the *Guru Granth* of the Sikhs (pages 1107-17). In the Tukhāri rāg (or *chant* = skt. *Chandas*), the first piece is the *Bārah māhā* 'twelve months' by Guru Nanakdev, the second by the fourth Guru Ramdas (p. 1113), and the third and last piece by the fifth Guru Arjundev. This affirms that the Chinese transcription of the melody Mo-ho-tou-le is indeed Mahā-Tukhāra.

Dinnāga

The silk painting of an 'Angry Arhat' was found by the Third German Expedition at the lower end of the Cave of Eighty-four Siddhas on the foothills near Turfan. It has been dated to the 8-9th century. The figure represented is not an 'Angry Arhat' but Dinnāga, the celebrated master of Buddhist logic. He is in a violent *mudrā* of disputation, vanquishing the heretics. A similar Tibetan painting can be seen in the Prof. Raghu Vira Collection at the International Academy of Indian Culture. Dinnāga is one of the Six Jewels (Tib. *rgyan drug*) of Mahāyāna in the Tibetan tradition. The eighty-four Siddhas as well as the Six Jewels are well established in Tibetan iconography. The fact that the painting was recovered from the Cave of eighty-four Siddhas lends support to its identification as that of Dinnāga. If so, it would be the earliest representation of Dinnāga in a militant mudrā: at Nalanda he had defeated Brahmaṇa Sudurjaya (lit. invincible) and other Tirtha dialecticians. Since he refuted the Tirthikas, he was called a 'Fighting Bull in Discussion'. "His whole life was passed in giving blows and receiving counterblows. Kalidasa, the prince of poets, warns *[in]* his poem to avoid the 'rugged hand' *(sthūla-hasta)* of Dinnāga. ...Mallinātha compares him with a 'rock' *(adri-kalpa)"* (Vidyabhusana 1920:273). The Buddhists were conscious of the awe-inspiring power of their knowledge. Their belligerent attitude against the heretics was expressed in violent terms, for example, in the Ratu Boko inscription of A.D. 792/3: "I pay homage to Him who is the fire of noble Dharma, who shines forth quashing the prevailing beliefs of outstanding heretics; struck by whose majesty the heretics *[*strong like*]* bulls panic away in fright, who in an instant reduces to ashes the numerous attachments to heresy and who burns out all bondages" (Lokesh Chandra 1980:7).

Tiered Stūpa with Niches

A free-standing tiered stūpa, designated Temple Y, was found at Khocho (AASR 1982: 55 fig. II:3). It rests on a Square base, with three stepped tiers, topped by a structure now lost. Each tier contains niches for statues on four sides. A staircase led to the top to conduct services, where the main image must have been installed. The main image should have been facing the east, and so also the staircase. The three tiers can represent the cosmology of *Triloka*, the three worlds of *kāmadhātu, rūpadhātu* and *arūpadhātu* (Matsunaga, 1969:43-56). These three realms are represented on the original lotus pedestal of the Great Buddha of the Tōdaiji Monastery (Paine & Soper, 1955: 23).

It is interesting that similar niched stūpa-like structures continued to be constructed by kings of Central Asian extraction centuries after they had been converted to Islam, when their meaning, function and symbolism had ceased to be relevant. In New Delhi, the Chor Minar has niches exactly like those of the Temple Y. It rests on a square platform, with one tier of niches topped by a tapering stele. There are three niches each in the south, west and north, on level to them there are two niches in the east, while the third niche of the east is on a higher storey, approached by a staircase. This upraised niche faces the rising sun. The morphology of the structure is strongly reminiscent of the Buddhist architecture of Central Asia. In its original function the twelve niches could have enshrined the Twelve Adityas, in which the upraised first of them in the east could have had the main image, consecrated daily by the first rays of the Rising Sun. The sun is the emblem of royalty and the cosmic symbol of its stability. The main niche could be rêached by stairs, which were essential for the daily services of the Image.

Cunningham (1883:149-150) says of the Chor Minar: "At 8 feet there is a belt of moulding all round, above which at regular intervals there are nine rows of round holes, about 9 or 10 inches in diameter. In each row there are twenty-five holes, so that there still remain 225 holes for the reception of as many human heads. Three more rows of holes would have raised the number to 300, and the height of the tower to 41 feet above the terrace. … That the tower was intended for the reception of human head, which was further confirmed by the discovery of something like human hair still sticking to the mortar in one of the holes. … When thieves were executed, their heads were cut off and stuck into these holes, where they could be seen by all the people. The women also pointed to the Kos-Minar close to the roadside, and said that all the travellers along the road could see the heads".

"I have read the numerous executions of dakaits and robbers whose heads were thus exposed, but, as well as I can remember, the numbers never exceeded 30 or 40 in a single gang. On the other hand, the recorded numbers of heads of prisoners taken in war usually ran up to many thousands. … Similar towers were erected by Firoz Tughlak in Bengal amounting to the incredible number of 180,000 heads". Babar won a decisive victory over the Rajput clans in 1527: "As a final disgrace a tower of the rajas' severed heads was built on the hill and Babar became Ghazi, Avenger in the name of God" (Godden, 1980:40, illus. on p. 41).

It seems that during its triumphant march across Buddhist Central Asia, Islam stuck the heads of Buddhist monks on the renowned and sacrosanct stūpas. Due to the height of the stūpas, these severed heads were visible from long distances and they struck terror in the hearts of the vanquished. They became the might of the new order, foreboding dread against transgression and preempting reversion. The historic Buddhist form survived with new political functions in the Islamic period which we witness, *inter alia,* in the Chor Minar.

REFERENCES

AASR (1982) *Along the Ancient Silk Routes*: Central Asian Art from the West Berlin State Museums, New York (The Metropolitan Museum of Art).

Albert von le Coq, (1913) *Chotscho: Facsimile-Wiedergaben der wichtingeren Funde der ersten koniglich preussischen Expedition nach Turfan in Ost-turikistan.* Berlin 1913, reprint Graz 1979.

Alicia Matsunaga, (1969) *The Buddhist Philosophy of Assimilation*, Tokyo (Charles E. Tuttle Company).

Bunyiu Nanjio, (1883) *A Catalogue of the Chinese Translation of the Buddhist Tripitaka*, Oxford (Clarendon Press).

Cunningham (1883) *Archaeological Survey of India Reports*, vol. XX, 1882-83.

Deborah E. Klimburg-Salter (ed.), (1982) *The Silk Route and Diamond Path*: Esoteric Buddhist Art on the Trans-Himalayan Trade Routes, Los Angeles (University of California).

Lokesh Chandra, (1971) *The Esoteric Iconography of Japanese Mandalas*, New Delhi (International Academy of Indian Culture), 1971.

Lionel Giles, (1957) *Descriptive Catalogue of Chinese Manuscripts from Tun-Huang in the British Museum*, London (The Trustees of the British Museum).

Rumer Godden, (1980) *Gulbadan: Portrait of a Rose Princess at the Mughal Court*, London (Macmillan London Ltd.).

Guru Granth (1969) *Sri Guru Granth Sahi,* Liu Mau-tsai; Liu-Mau-tsai, *Kutscha und seine Beziehungen zu China von 2 jh. V. bis zum 6 jh.*, Wiesbaden (Asiatische Forschungen vol.27).

Lokesh Chandra (1979) *Nilakantha Lokesvara as the Buddhist apotheosis of Hari-Hara*, New Delhi (International Academy of Indian Culture).

Lokesh Chandra (1980) Lokesh Chandra, *Cultural contacts of Indonesia and Sri Lanka in the eighth century and their bearing on the Barabudur*, New Delhi (International Academy.of Indian Culture).

Robert Treat Paine & Alexander Soper, (1955) *The Art and Architecture of Japan*, Harmondsworth (Penguin Books Ltd.).

Samuel Beal, (1884) *Si-yu-ki, Buddhist Records of the Western World*, transl. from the Chinese of Hiuen-Tsiang (A.D. 629), London (Trubner & Co.).

S. Subrahmanya Sastri, (1951) ed. *Ragavibodha of Somanatha*, Madras (Adyar Library), 1945.

S. Subrahmanya Sastri, (1951) ed. *Sangita-ratnakara of Œarngadeva)* Vol. III—adhyayas 5,6, madras (Adyar Library)1951.

T = Taishµo Tripitaka (1929) Taishµo edition of the Chinese Tripitaka, ed. Takakusu Junjiro and Watanabe Kaigyoku, Tokyo 1924-1929.

Satis Chandra Vidyabhusana, (1920) *A History of Indian Logic*, reprint Delhi (Motilal Banarasidass, 1971).

3

Historical and Cultural Relations between Kazhakhstan, Central Asia and India from Ancient Times to the Beginning of the 20th Century

M.Kh. Abuseitova

Ethnic-cultural and trade contacts between Kazakhstan and India has lasted for many centuries and go back to migration of Aryan tribes from steppes of Eurasia to plains of Indostan subcontinent. Vedic literature, for example *Rigveda*, *Atharvaveda*, *Samhitas* etc., contains information about the presence of Indoarian tribes on the territory of Kazakhstan and Central Asia, though it is fragmental. In the Neolithic epoch most of the territory of Central Asia, Kazakhstan and Northern India was a part of large area inhabited by agricultural cultures close to each other, which went through similar processes of social development. Comparable research of the Neolithic cultures of Kazakhstan, India and Central Asia allows us to review in details the sources of the agricultural cultures of the South of Kazakhstan, Central Asia and the Northern India, particularly to observe stages of development of pre-Harappa and Harappa settlements. Archeological excavations in the north-western regions of India, in the centres of the Harappa civilization display an existence of intertribal exchange of goods already in ancient time. From Central Asia towns of the Harappa civilization acquired gems. In its turn there were discovered Harappa handicrafts in Central Asia. These facts display that there were processes of different goods exchange in Central Asian and Indian regions, before the appearance of the Aryans in India.The recent researches of archeological relics display that there existed contacts between towns of Sindh river valley and Central Asian and Kazakhstan settlements. These discoveries belong to the period of golden age of the Harappan culture. Some items are similar with those of the Harappan culture (metal goods, beads made of faience, pottery, ivory). Handicrafts from India as well as the local items that had obvious signs of Indian influence were discovered in Central Asia.

Archeological materials from Central Asia and Kazakhstan revealed facts of similarity of material culture of the Vedic tribes and Central Asian culture. For example, items found in tombs turned out to be similar with items that the Vedic tribes used in burial rituals mentioned in *Rigveda*, and that is very important. An appearance of nomadic conquerors might explain discovery of iron plates of armour of Katafraktaries in Taksila, in the layer of the first half of the 1st century AC. Heavy armour and heavy armored soldiers' tactic were worked out during many centuries in steppes of Eurasia, including tribes of the northern areas of Central Asia and Kazakhstan (iron plated armour of IV-III c. BC in Chirik-Rabat in the lower run of Syr-Daryya). Specific double-edged short iron swords with straight and crescent knob on a handle that were recently discovered in the second layer of Sirpak in Taksila (the first half of the 1 c. AC) are connected with the culture of the tribes of Eurasia steppes. Their shape was formed among Skiff-Sarmats tribes of the Volga and western Kazakhstan steppes. In Central Asia they were found in Northern Baktra in tombs of Tulkhar (II-I c. BC).

Disk-shaped bronze mirrors with a relief roller on the edge, cone-shaped salience in the centre and a small flank ledge that is a pin for handle of the type, which is known also on the territory of Central Asia were discovered in Taksila (the second layer of Sirpak).

Discovery of proto-Indian seal with two pictograms in Altyn-dep allowed to make an assumption that some of the inhabitants of Altyn-dep were able to read this "text". There is an assumption that one part of the ancient population of Central Asia, probably, spoke Dravid language. Cornelian beads with white ornament were found in Central Asia and South Kazakhstan in tombs near Varuh valley (Isfarin area), Tura-Tash, Shaushukum, Ungur-Kura, Taigak and others, and also in Horezm and Farhadstroy. In Central Kazakhstan such beads were found in Sak complexes of the same period.There were no large deposits of good cornelian in Kazakhstan and Central Asia. Jewellers got it from Arabia, Iran and India. Professor Lemmlein G. G. thinks that the beads are Indian-made (Kambei, Gudzharat). Linguistic data of Beily H., who analyzed the origins of Avesta terms 'instrument', 'weapon' and adjective 'armed' in his work "Ariana", is very important. Later they entered Sogd language and Sanskrit. In Sanskrit and Prakrit this word forms complicated epithets and is met in the meaning of 'horse armour'. Sanskrit started to use Iranian terms with the meaning 'horseman' and 'saddle'. We might assume that corresponded words could penetrate to the Indian languages not earlier than VII-IV c. BC as a result of contacts with nomadic tribes of Central Asia, and namely with the Sak tribes. Contacts between India and Central Asia in the sphere of weaponry are witnessed by the fact that term for 'chest armour' came to Sanskrit from Iranian. Ethnic-cultural contacts between Central Asia, Kazakhstan and India became more intensified and regular in the period of emergence of the first large state formations on the territory of India (the Mauryas and Kushan empires), Buddhism and the campaign of Alexander the Great.

Buddhism played a great role in development and intensification of contacts between India and Kazakhstan. The penetration of this religion into Kazakhstan and Central Asia started a new era in the relationship between these two regions. The influence of Buddhism was so strong and diverse that a new culture was formed in Central Asia and Kazakhstan. This culture gathered the best that was made by Indians and population of Central Asia and Kazakhstan in the previous centuries. We shall review some typical facts of the mutual influence of India, Kazakhstan and Central Asia. Presence of many Buddhist temples and centres in Central Asia and Kazakhstan can be a nice example of mutual contacts and prove evidences of the Buddhist tradition about spreading of Buddhism over Central Asia and Kazakhstan under Kushans. Spreading of Buddhism in Central Asia under the Kushans was accompanied not by blind acceptation of the ideas of ancient Indian culture, but by their understanding and combination with local cultural traditions.The most interesting from archeological discoveries is written Buddhist Sanskrit manuscripts in Brahmi and Kharoshthi. Paleographically they are close to Gilgit manuscripts of "Pradzhnyapa-ramit" literature ("*Vinayapitaka*") and dated approximately by VII-VIII c. AC. Of a big scientific interest is Buddhist Sanskrit manuscript of Sarvastivad's school. Approximately it is dated V-VI c. AC.

Adherents of Buddhism in Central Asia and Kazakhstan did not just translate from Sanskrit and Prakrit, but interpreted it themselves. Local variants of Indian types were worked out. Great similarity of Kara-tepe inscriptions with some Indian epigraphic relics indicates the penetration of written traditions directly from India. Having researched temple complexes and Buddhist works scientists came to the conclusion that there were adherents of Buddhist schools of Sarvastivad and Mahasanghik under the Kushans in Central Asia and Kazakhstan. Sources inform that there were a lot of adherents of Vaishbhashik's school in Balh under the Kushans. His adherents were Central Asian theologian-monks Ghosaka and Dharmamitra known for their comments on Buddhist religious texts. Ghosaka was ascribed to make a huge commentary on "*Abhidharmapitaka*". Dharmamitra, Termez born, was a commentator of "*Vinayasutra*". The sources name five more Buddhist monks, natives of Central Asia and Kazakhstan who worked in China in II-IV c. AC on translation to the Chinese and interpretation of Buddhist texts. And finally, Indian Graffiti inscriptions discovered in Central Asia and Kazakhstan, display that Indians (or people who knew Indian languages and writing) continued to visit this region after the III c.

According to the inscriptions discovered in Central Asia, in the Kushan and Gupta periods, Indians settled there and built large temple complexes. There are also written evidences of the direct contact between Central Asia and India. These are Buddhist manuscripts on birch bark and palm leaves, which were found in Central Asia. Decline of Buddhism in Central Asia and Kazakhstan took place by the VII-VIII c. AC. According to a story of a traveller who visited Samarkand in 630 AC Buddhist temples did not function and population was hostile to Buddhists. Another traveller in VIII c. witnessed the same. Apparently, with the coming to power of Gupta dynasty in India (IV-V c.) that led to state disconnection between India and Central Asia, the direct contact with Indian culture was impeded. New Kazakhstan archeological materials and analysis of written sources allow us to assume that Eastern Turkistan and Chinese influence on spreading and development of Buddhism in Zhetisu was dominating. Information about the constructions of Buddhist temple in Suyab proves that the temple was build in 692 by the order of Van Chzhen Zyan, a military viceroy of Beshbalik, after he captured Suyab. We should share the opinion that an influence of India-China-Eastern Turkistan direction on development of Buddhism in Zhetisu was dominating. New researches displayed that Buddhism was spread over Zhetisu even after X-XI c. when Islam was dominating and the Buddhist temples were destroyed. That was mentioned by Kahsgari. But already in the middle of the XIII c. Rubruk G. the ambassador of Luis IX to the Mongol Khan Munke, informed about Buddhist temples in the northeastern Zhetisu. Spread of Buddhism over Zhetisu in this period was connected with Naiman invasion headed by Kuchluk. According to "*Tarikh-i Rashidi*" by Mirza Muhammed Dulati, there was a furious struggle between Kuchluk and Gurkhan of Karakitais were Kuchluk was a winner. Kuchluk seized Kashgar and Hotan, and his tribes settled alongside the Emil and Kiiyalik rivers. Then he forced local inhabitants to reject the religion of Muhammad and to choose another religion. According to Dulati, people began to wear Chinese clothes, i.e. Buddhist.

As it is known after the destruction of the Zhungar khanate by Zin empire in 1758, the Chinese conquered Eastern Turkistan and seized some part of the territory of Big and Middle Zhuzs, including Zhetisu. One part of the Kalmaks was used by the Zin empire in guarding its western borders. The Buddhist temples and monasteries belonged to those Kalmaks. In 1863 anti-Chinese rebellion of Dungans began under the religious slogan of fighting for Islam. Soon the rebellion involved Zhungariya. The Uigurs of Kuldja region actively participated in the same.

In 1864 the rebellion spread over the whole Eastern Turkistan. The Chinese garrisons were eliminated, their fortresses and settlements were destroyed and the Buddhist temples and monasteries were destroyed too.That year was the last Date of Buddhism's existence in Zhetisu and Eastern Turkistan. One of those destroyed monasteries was the monastery of Sumbe. It was mentioned by Valikhanov C.C. in 1854. Ruins of this monastery were discovered on the right side of the Sumbe river, near Shaartas mountain in Almaty oblast 320 kms away from Almaty. In its turn, apparently, in Central Asia and Kazakhstan was formed an image of Buddha with a belt of stylized flame (connection with Mazdeists' ideas) (Kara-tepe complex).We can mark two periods of penetration of Indian elements into Central Asian painting: Kushan period (I-VIII c.) when influence of Indian art was direct; early medieval (V-VII c.) when influence of Indian art was indirect. Archeological discoveries of the last decade revealed Buddhist memorials of the I-VIII c. on the territory of Central Asia: in Ayrtam, Kara-Tepe, Fayaz-Tepe (near Termez), Adzhini-Tepe and Kalayi-Kafirnigan (in south of Tadjikistan), Ak-Beshim (north of Kirgizstan).The first period is represented by small amount of Buddhist literature.

At the next stage (V-VII c.) Buddhism extended its borders and Buddhist art in Central Asia reached its pick. Simultaneously cultural contacts between Central Asia and India became more intensified. As an example we can consider Central Asian painting, represented by large number of relics, including wall-paintings of Buddhist temples in Adzhina-Tepe and Kalayi-Kafirnigan, paintings of palaces in Varakhsha, Pendzhikent, Afrasiab, Balalyk-Tepe, Shahristan, where Central Asian and Indian elements are joined together. Influence of Buddhist art is obvious. However, Central Asian artists did not obey all the canons blindly. Local sculptors and artists, builders and architects used traditions and skills that had already been developed in Central Asia and Kazakhstan, and they managed to combine them with cultural norms of neighbouring countries, especially of India and Afghanistan. Anthropo-morphologic and zoo-morphologic terracotta (monkeys, elephants, rhinoceros) from Dzhanbars-kala, Angka-kala, Torpak-kala, Gyaur-kala have many analogies with the famous Ajanta paintings. Indo-Central-Asian contacts are vividly seen in architecture of the "hall of black-skinned warriors" of Torpak-kala palace. Central Asian and Kazakhstan Buddhist painting has an image of Indian heavenly body that is sun (Surya). We find a parallel to this in images of sun chariot in the sculpture of Bodh-Gaya (I c. BC) and Hair-Khan (V c. AC) and in Bamian painting (V c. AC).There are parallels of winged lions in the Indian art (sculptural disk from Bharhut). Images of the Indian mythology penetrated into Central Asia together with the Buddhist ideas and iconography. There are some pictures in Central Asian painting that are connected with iconography of Shiva. Pick-topped "skiff" hat, which is unusual for India, is painted on several other sculptures from Mathura, and some terracotta14 from Taksila. Influence of the Indian artistic methods was reflected on different statues of dancers, which were found in the hall of the object III in Pandzhikent.After the Arab conquest of Central Asia, and later of India, the old cultural traditions were transformed and even abolished. The tradition of monumental painting weakened and was limited by decorating of palaces and other secular buildings. Book miniature, which illustrates only secular books, became the leading form of painting in the medieval period.

Many Chinese pilgrims of V-VIII c. crossed Kazakhstan and Central Asia on their way to or from the Indian holy places. Travel notes of those pilgrims display that the routes existed for a long period. It allows us to assume that the contacts between Kazakhstan, Central Asia and India were quite stable in the early medieval period.There are some evidences of spreading over Kazakhstan and Central Asia of fairytale plots from "*Panchatantra*" (III-IV c.), Indian story-collection of worldly stories, which were translated into Sogdian language.

Turkic element itself began to appear in India quite long ago. Tribes of the Northern India in V-VIII c. many times fell under the power of Ephtalite or Turkic conquerors, thus entering into political and ethnic contacts with Central Asian tribes. At the same time Epthalites and Turkic governors were affected by the developed and ancient Indian culture and very often promoted its spreading over their northern domains, i.e. Central Asia. For example, many sources give information that there were a lot of Buddhist memorials in Badiyan, the capital of the Ephtalites.

The Turks regularly invaded India under the leadership of Gazni governor Mahmud (998-1030) from 1001 till 1026. Under the successor of Mahmud the capital of Gaznevids was removed to Lahore. In the 70s of the XII c. governors of a small vassal princedom Gur got advantage from disturbance and seized Gazni in 1173, and in 1186 they seized the capital of their former master Lahore city. Brother of the governor Gur Muhammed Guri defeated Indian princes quarreling with each other and seized the whole valley of Yamuna and Ganga.

After a murder of Muhammed Guri one of his Turk slaves, a commander of his guard and viceroy of the northern India Kutb ud-din Aibek (1206-1210) declared himself an independent sultan of the Indian domain of the Gurids with the capital in Delhi. Thus the Delhi Sultanate emerged. Under the Iltutmysh the superiority of Turkic-Muslim commanders was formed. In commemoration of Illtutmysh there was erected Kutb-minar minaret in Delhi. Its construction began under Kutb ud-din and was finished under

Iltutmysh. Military aristocracy was formed from Central Asian Turks at that period. They created powerful organization "Forty", called so due to the number of its founders.

At that time the Mongols often conducted raids, and in 1241 they managed to seize Lahore. Giiyas ud-din Balban (1265-1287) got the power in 1265 after death of Nasir. After he became a sultan Balban managed to fight back the Mongols and build a number of fortresses on the northwestern borders. His ruling was full of fighting for strengthening his power. It were the Turks who due to their knowledge of Mongolian war methods managed to resist and even fight back the Mongols, and thus save the country from terrible pillage.The Delhi sultanate was the beginning of intensive penetration of Turkic culture into India.

At first the conquest of India by natives of Central Asia led to the growth of caravan trade between India and Muslim East. Coins of Delhi sultans are found not only in Persia and Central Asia, but even near the Volga. So far as the main force of the army of Delhi state was cavalry, and horses could not be bred due to the absence of pastures in India, horses were the major item of Indian import. However, soon the conquest of the Mongols and destruction of several towns in Iran and Central Asia led to decline of the Indian caravan trade.Under Aibek such Indian regions as Gwaliar, Ajmer, Benaras, Ratanpur, Patna, Kalanjhar and Bengal recognized the power of governors of Delhi sultanate. And that promoted the consolidation of India and spread of Islam over India.

The most influential part of gulyam's guard consisted of representatives of Kipchak tribe Ilbari, whose domain was situated in Western Kazakhstan and lower run of the Volga before Mongolian invasion. Under Eltutmysh who was a native Kipchak (Ilbari) gulyam emirs formed the most influential group in the ruling elite of the Delhi sultanate. Eltutmysh's policy was directed to consolidation of Turkic gulyams near him by appointing them to different posts both in the military and the state apparatus. According to Dzhuzdzhani, Eltutmysh had 25 commander-maliks from Ilbary tribe, Turki-karakitais, and other Kipchak tribes and natives of southeast Kazakhstan.

A consolidating effort of the Turkic governors of India made a positive effect and in the XIII c. Delhi was one the most important cultural centres of India. Basis of that Indian culture that later became known as Indo-Muslim were founded under the Delhi sultanate. This culture was a result of combining of cultures of different people, of their mutual influence. Scientists and poets from Otyrar, Samarkand, Bukhara, Gerat, Balh and other towns found "new Motherland in India and enriched its culture by their work and increased its glory".

An important feature of the cultural development of the Delhi sultanate in the XIII c. was formation of a style of Indian historic chronicles in Farsi. An outstanding representative of this style was a historian Dzhuzdzhani, native of Gurgan, who was under the protection of sultan Eltutmysh. His works saved for history an information about an important role of Desht-I Kipchak natives, ethnic ancestors of the Kazakhs and other modern Turkic people.

The empire of the Great Mogols emerged in the northern part of India in 1526. Emir of Fergana Zahir ad-din Muhammad Babur (1526-1530) started this dynasty. Establishment of a strong and organized state in India governed by Turkic-Muslim dynasty intensified penetration of new traditions, which were connected with culture and art of Central Asia and Kazakhstan, into this region. He was very educated and observant person, thus he understood art very well. His memoirs "*Babur-name*" were written in simple, clear manner.

According to "*Babur Nama*", Kazakh tribal aristocracy along with number of other fellow Turkic soldiers took active participation in the campaign of Babur. Turkic aristocracy made great influence over development of Mogul empire. Sources testify that Indians have preserved the genealogical tree and the tradition of shadzhara (shezhere). It is well known that founder of Kubt Shah (Kuli Kubt-al-Mulk) dynasty was from Turlestan and his encirclement was from this town. It is possible to discover other examples/dynastic chronicle, which testify wide phenomenon and significance of Turkic influence in life of Indian society. During this period, great traditions of cultural intercourse and contacts of Central Asia and Great Mogul Empire existed. Central Asia played special role in promotion of Indian culture. From the beginning of the 16th century Indian merchants from Northern India started trading in the north to Afghanistan, Iran, Central Asia and Kazakhstan. However, new aspect of Kazakhstan-Indian relations during 16th to 18th centuries is not well explored. Peculiarities of Kazakh-Indian trade was that it was conducted through the mediation of Central Asian, Indian and Afghani merchants.

Kazakhs mainly traded with cattle, which was driven through Central Asia to India. Among the goods, transported in caravan included horses. Considerable quantity of horses were driven to India from Bukhara; horses of Kazakh strains were especially preferred. There are documents giving data that Kazakh merchants drove about 40 thousand horses to India.Important information is available in written sources of Indian historiography such as "*Bukhar-Nama*", "*Tarih-I Rashidi*", "*Akbar-Nama*", "*Alamgir-Nama*" and others. In this connection it is necessary to pay attention to these manuscripts, archive materials, which are in custody of India and abroad, particularly in India Office in the Great Britain, which are yet to be studied properly.

According to sources there was regular diplomatic relationship between the Mogol empire and Bukhara. From the 2nd half of the XVI c. an intensive development of Indian-Central Asian trade took place in regard to seizure by Portugal of such big trade ports as Goa, Diu, Daman. As a result the Mogol empire lost its sea trade routes. Under these conditions the role of ancient caravan routes through Afghanistan to Central Asia, Kazakhstan and Russia increased. Positive effect was made on the development of Indian-Central Asian trade by the capture of Kazan (1552) and Astrakhan (1556) by Russia. From that time onwards the role of Central Asian merchants as mediators of Indo-Russian trade significantly increased.

Growing economic ties became a precondition for strengthening political relationship between Central Asia and India. Already in 1572 Akbar received the first ambassador of Bukhara, Hodzha Altamysh. According to Abdulfazl Allami, the author of "Akbar Shah's history", the ambassador had a letter from Abdullkhan to Akbar. The next mission from Abdullkhan came to India in 1575 with a proposal to divide Iran. Akbar send reciprocal mission to Bukhara with Mirza Fulad as ahead.

Bukhara ambassadors visited India in 1585-1586 once more. The head of the mission was Mir Kureish. The mission brought some pedigree horses and camels, furs and luxuries as presents. At the same time there was a reciprocal mission from India to Bukhara headed by Hakim Humam and Sadr Dzhahan, which went together with the Bukhara mission from Lahore on 28.08.1586.In the following years the Mogol empire and Central Asia and Kazakhstan exchanged missions for many times. The main purpose of those missions was solution of political and economic-trade problems in the region.

Aforementioned facts display that political ties between India and Bukhara in the second half of the XVI c. were very intensive and both sides aspired to peaceful relationship between each other, taking into consideration their own interests.

Conquests of Babur and his successors extended the borders of the Mogolian state. Numerous Indian and Muslim princedoms and states were replaced by centralized state, which stretched from the Himalayas to the Narbada river and from Arab sea to Bengal gulf. Consolidation of almost whole territory of India under one power promoted development of trade and crafts. Culture and art were also at the stage of raising. In architecture a nice example of the symbiosis of Central Asian and Indian art is Taj-Mahal. To build it emperor Shah Jahan gathered famous architects, craftsmen and masters from India, Central Asia and other countries. Thus Muhammad Hanif came from Kandahar and Muhammad Said from Multan. Masters of a cupola building such as Ismail-khan Rumi (local), Muhammad Sharif from Samarkand and Kazim Khan from Lahore were also invited. Besides that decorators and calligraphy masters from Bukhara, Delhi, Lahore, Kanauj and other towns took part in construction. From Bukhara came two "flower sculptors Ata Muhammad and Shukur Muhammad. That international group first created wooden model, and then started its construction that lasted for many years. Central Asian architectural tradition and Indian one, which originated from constructions of the VI and VII c., were vividly reflected on this building.

Babur in his "Memoirs" indicates that 200 stonemasons from Hindustan, Azerbaidzhan and other countries took part in construction of Timur Beg's mosque in Samarkand. When Babur came to India he brought many builders, including the Indians who earlier worked in Samarkand and Bukhara. An interesting sample of construction that probably originated from nomadic yurtas of the ancestors of the Great Mogols is an image of yurta in the picture showing the birth of Salim. It is known that Central Asian miniature masters Muhammad Murad and Muhammad Nadir Samarkandi worked in the court workshop of the Great Mogols. Several miniatures of Mogolian school had signatures of artists, which proved their ties with Central Asia. Muhammad Nadir Samarkandi was one of those artists. His nisba tells that his ancestors and he himself were from Samarkand. Works of this master that were made in siyahi kalam technique are quite famous. They are portraits of Jahangir, Shah Jahan and some courtiers.In its turn the Indian miniature school influenced Central Asian miniature painting. As a result of such cooperation some artistic methods appeared in the Bukhara painting. They are typical for the Mogolian school of miniatures.

Emergence and rapid development of a fine miniature school in the courts of the Great Mogols were prepared by the whole history of painting development in India itself, and also by specific historic conditions in India in XVI c.

Miniature painting of Central Asia developed as a secular art in the medieval period. By the time of emergence of the Mogolian school miniatures of Central Asia had been developed and improved for a long time, and thus its influence on the Indian painting was natural. However, several decades later it in its turn got an impulse for development from the Mogolian miniatures. There was fruitful process of mutual enrichment and renewal. Achievements of the Indian and Central Asian schools, each of them having its own old traditions, always were accepted creatively.

Exactly under the Mogol empire India was dramatically affected by the Turkic culture and the Turkic people. The Turks promoted the golden age of Muslim culture in India. Literature and lyrics in the Persian developed, elements specific for the Muslim architecture appeared, basis of the Indian miniature school were founded. From the time of the Turki appearance under the leadership of Babur, Indian culture develops in absolutely different way. Significant changes happened in the social life of Indian people. The basis of the caste system was undermined.

In the XIX c. Indian-Kazakh relationship bacame absolutely different due to the changes in the geopolitical situation in Asia. Epoch of great geographic discoveries that began little earlier and covered many parts of the world unknown to Europeans reached Central Asia, including Kazakhstan.

Indian-Kazakh relationship, in addition to the traditional trade-economic and social ties, became military and politic one. The main problems was of competition between England and Russia in Central Asia and Russian offense to Kazakhstan. Persistent struggle between British India and Russian defined military and political climate in the region, and character of relationship between India and Kazakhstan.

In the XIX c. relationship between India and Kazakhstan became more intensive and diverse than in the previous centuries. There were some reasons for that. The first, that relationship developed during changes in geopolitical situation in Central Asian region where the interests of 3 powers (Great Britain, Russia and China) collided. So-called "Great game" involved Kazakhstan also. Economic, cultural and political contacts between Kazakhstan and India proceeded against a background of intensification of interests of the powers that were fighting for the leadership in Central Asia. The second, Kazakhstan was not independent state any more and its contact with the world was under the control and was defined by Russia. That circumstance made a certain effect on the relationship between Kazakhstan and India. The third, English travellers actively began to make researches in Central Asia and Kazakhstan.

Movement of the English from the British India to Central Asia and Kazakhstan was accompanied by the same action of Russia on the north. It promoted activation of intercultural, trade and political contacts between two regions. The territory of Kazakhstan as well as the territories of other states of the region became an object of attention of research centers of the British India.

There were several English expeditions to the region that had scientific, political and economic purposes. Thus, Kazakhstan and Central Asia were visited by Ashton Dilke (1873), Delmar Morgan (1880), Landsdel (1882, 1892), count Danmore (1892), Littledeil (1890, 1893), Clive Bigham (1895), Kobbold (1897) whose reports were published in the British India, were discussed in the meetings of the Royal Geographic Society. That process was very useful for closing in between two countries. Thus Indian scientific and social circles got information about culture, history and ethnography of people of Central Asia and Kazakhstan. They made detailed description of geography, political and economic situation in Kazakhstan and neighbouring regions of Central Asia.

In the sphere of military contact we can mention visits of Indians to Central Asia and Kazakhstan who sought help in their fight against the English. Thus, two representatives of Kashmir maharadzha visited Tashkent in November of 1865. Turkistan was visited in 1867 by an envoy of raja Indor who sought friendship and proposed help in the case of a war between Russia and England. Baba Ram Singh who sought help for the Singh's struggle against the English visited Samarkand in 1879.

Specific feature of Indian-Kazakh trade relationship was that it was realized by merchants of India, Turkistan and Central Asia who delivered goods to both countries.

As a result of aforementioned processes by the end of the XIX c. India got a certain scientific image of Central Asia and Kazakhstan. Basis of future scientific and cultural contacts between India and Kazakhstan was founded.

The second aspect of the Indian travellers' activity in the XIX c. was the formation of Central Asian policy of the British India and later of Indian Republic. The main ideas and concepts of the modern Indian policy towards Central Asia were developed exactly in that period, and the reasons of many present geopolitical and political contradictions emerged in the XIX c.

4

Hindu Gods in Western Central Asia

S.P. Gupta

It is common knowledge that Hinduism pervaded several countries of South-east Asia which witnessed the rise and fall of several Hindu dynasties. The rulers of these dynasties got constructed many temples for Hindu gods and goddesses, Shiva and Vishnu including. Along with Shaiva and Vaishnava religions, Buddhism also penetrated the land between Myanmar and Indonesia and flourished side by side as twin brothers, sometimes in one and the same temple complex. The Chinese or Eastern Central Asia is also known for Buddhist and the so-called Hindu-Buddhist icons in Buddhist temples of Khotan, Dun-Huang, etc. However, what is commonly less known is the fact that the five Muslim populated Republics of the erstwhile Soviet or Western Central Asia, Tadjikistan, Uzbekistan, etc., did not witness the prevalence of Hindu gods and goddesses, even though Buddhism had some presence there. The purpose of writing this article is to show that this was not the fact.

In the Central part of this region, there flourished the region anciently called Sogdiana, covering largely the state of Uzbekistan. There were centres where great works of art and architectures flourished, viz. Varaksha, located near Bukhara, Afrasiab, the ancient site of the capital city of Sogdiana, in the outskirts of Samarkand, and Penjikent, an ancient small city, around 60 kms east of Samarkand. Their flourishing period is bracketed between 5th century A.D. and 9th century A.D. Belonging to 8th-9th centuries bracket are also the works of great art reflecting Indian influence in nearby sites, such as the Shahiristan. Buddhism, of course, flourished in a big way in Kirghizia, Tadjikistan and southern Uzbekistan where several monasteries have been excavated, dating back to 1st century B.C.-A.D. bracket. It may be noted that the Arab Muslims entered this area in the 8th century, often destroying non-Muslim art and architectural remains.

The most important site for our study is Penjikent, a commercial town with bazaars, covering an area of 13.5 hectares, in which around 130 houses and shops have been excavated. The structural remains of these two to three storied houses, some of them very large, including wooden posts and walls, have yielded many sculptural remains and remains of painting. It is in them that we get the representations of Hindu gods and goddesses as well as many decorative elements and narrative scenes. It may, however, be noted that the Hindu gods and goddesses depicted here were having some local overtones in the sense that the form and iconography as well as their names had local origins. In other words, as we see in south India, the north Indian Kartikeya became Murgan but the iconography remained the same, in Penjikent also the people who adopted the Hindu gods and goddesses have them local names. This cross-fertilization of cultures is the hallmark of Penjikent's Sogdiana civilization of the pre-Islamic period. It may be noted that Hinduism alone was not the external element which combined with the local pre-existing culture of Sogdiana, in which a very popular regional religion called 'Manichaism' was extant. In the north Iranian Culture, Zoroastrian in particular was much more dominant. Nestorian Christianity was also existing here. In fact Sogdiana was the melting pot of cultures coming from various directions through the long-distance trade mechanism.

Sogdiana witnessed Hinduism in the worship of five gods, viz. Brahma, Indra, Mahadeva (Shiva), Narayana and Vaishravana. It may be noted that out of these five, the first three Hindu gods were identified with their own three gods. Brahma was identified with their own god Zrvan, Indra with Adbad and Mahadeva with Veshparkar. The last two had no local counterparts to impose upon the Hindu gods. The Sogdian manuscripts have described them in iconographic terms, for example, Brahma-Zrvan has been described as a god with a beard, Indra-Adbag has been described as a god with a third eye, Mahadeva-Veshparkar has been shown with three faces. As a matter of fact, some of the pictures bore the names of these gods. V.A. Livshits deciphered such a label as 'Veshpur(kar)' under a three-headed god.

At Penjikent a four-armed goddess riding a lion, sometimes found near the image of Shiva is often depicted. It is possible that the goddess meant here was Parvati although some scholars would like to identify her with the Iranian goddess Nana depicted on some Kushana Coins.

The Sogdian god Veshparkar. Sketch of mural from Panjikent XXII : I. Eighth Century

Enthroned deities. Sketch of mural from Panjikent XXIV : 2. Eighth Century

Main hall of a Panjikent home. At bottom, a mural depicting a goddess and donors. Reconstruction by L.L. Gurevich

Sketch of mural from the northern wall of Panjikent VI : 41-42. Sixth Century

Four-armed goddess on a dragon. Sketch of mural from the northern chapel of Temple II, at Panjikent, Sixth century

A mural of 8th century at Penjikent has three portable sacrificial fire altars. Much of this picture is gone but what remains has at least the picture of Mahadeva-Veshparkar. Thus, the two remaining gods supporting two other altars could be Brahma-Zravan and Indra-Adbag. As a matter fact, the name of the Zoroastrian supreme god Ahar Mazda was totally avoided here, for whom Indra-Adbog was the substitute.

Camel and ram have been used as a mount of some gods with Indian features whose identity is very difficult to make. Dragon has also been used as a mount but the identity of this multi-handed Indian goddess from Temple II of Penjikent is not possible at this stage knowledge.

The Russian scholars working here have been doing excellent work and much of the archaeological remains of Penjikent can be seen in the Hermitage Museum, St. Petersburg.

REFERENCES

Albaum, L.I. *Zhivopos' Afrasiaba*, (Tashkent, 1975) Azarpay, Guity, *Sogdian Painting*, University of California Press (Berkeley, 1981).

Barthold, W., *Turkestan down to the Mongol Invasion*, 22nd ed. (London, 1958).

Belenitskii, A.M. and Marshak, B.I. *The Paintings of Sogdiana Ibid*, pp. 13-77.

Henning, W.B. "The date of Sogdian Ancient Letters", *BSOAS*, Vol. XII (1948), pp. 3-4.

Litvinshi, B.A. "Freski Kalan - Kafirnigana", *Voferug sveta*, (1976), pp. 44-46.

Negomatov, N., *Ushtrushana v drevmosti irannem srednevekov'e* (Dusharnbe 1975), pp. 137-151.

Shishkin, V.A., *Varaksha* (Moscow, 1963).

Smirnova, O.I., *Ocherki iz istorri sadda*, (Moskva 1970).

5

Religious, Cultural and Artistic Links between Ancient Kashmir, Afghanistan and Central Asia

S.S. Toshkhani

The Bamiyan Tragedy

The destruction of the two colossal Buddha images at Bamiyan, and of numerous other masterpieces of Buddhist art elsewhere in Afghanistan, in March 2001, left the whole civilized world shell-shocked and outraged. For centuries the two gentle giants stood serenely watching over the lush-green Bamiyan Valley spread between the Hindu Kush and Koh-i-Baba, guarding many a secret of Afghanistan's pre-Islamic past. But, perhaps, afraid of facing up to and accepting this past and all that it signifies, the Taliban fundamentalists sought to obliterate it by destroying its surviving relics, and in a fit of iconoclastic frenzy reduced to rubble what was regarded as an invaluable part of world heritage.

The paranoid perpetrators of this heinous crime may have derived sadistic pleasure out of what they did, but to Kashmiris like me it sent shivers down the spine as it was reminiscent of the barbaric acts of the bigoted Afghan governors who ruled over Kashmir from 1753 to 1819. What is more saddening is that the Bamiyan Buddhas were two glorious symbols of that pre-Islamic cultural past a greater part of which Kashmir shared with Afghanistan. Inspired by their artistic grandeur, great Kashmiri kings like Lalitaditya too had built colossal standing images of the Buddha, one of them in the very heart of Srinagar, but no trace of them can be found today. In fact, ancient Kashmir and Afghanistan had such close religious, cultural and artistic links till at least the 11th century when the last Hindu Shahi king ruled in Kabul, that it can well be said that the people of both the regions lived, believed and thought much in the same manner. Astride the famous Silk Route, Afghanistan in turn became a centre for diffusion of Buddhist ideology and culture to Central Asia and China in the north-east and Rome in the north-west. It will be my endeavour in this paper to touch upon some aspects of this intimate relationship.

While it must be admitted that geographical proximity played an important role in the affinities between ancient Kashmir, Afghanistan and Central Asia, it must also be noted that Afghanistan did not exist as a distinct political entity in those times. So blurred were the boundaries between what constitutes present-day Afghanistan that the eastern slopes of the Hindu Kush mountain, whose ancient name was Nishadh, were a part of the *Saptasindhu* of the *Rigvedic* Aryans. This is confirmed by ancient texts like the *Rigveda* which has an entire hymn, the *nadi sukta*, devoted to the rivers flowing in the region. In this hymn, the rivers Kubha, Suvastu (Swat), Krum (Kurram) and Gomati (Gomal) flowing in Afghanistan have been mentioned together with Sindhu (Indus), Vitasta (Jhelum) and Marudvriddha that flow in Kashmir, indicating that both the regions formed a part of the geographical habitat of the Vedic people. What is more, names of some of the tribes living along the banks of these rivers have also been given. These tribes, according to Dr. Bhagvat Sharan Upadhyay, a great scholar of ancient culture and history of Asia, took part in the *dasharagya yuddha* or the "War of the Ten Kings" described in the *Rigveda*. Panini, the great Sanskrit grammarian who himself hailed from Shalatur, a village located near the confluence of the Kabul and Indus rivers, has also mentioned the names of some of the northwestern tribes like the Madhumants (Mohmands) and Aprits (Afridis) in his *Ashtadhyayi* (5th century BC). He has also mentioned the Kashmirikas or the people of Kashmir with whom he seems to have been quite familiar.

Kashmir and Gandhara

In Buddhist texts, Kashmir and Gandhara have been shown as one and the same *janapada* in a list of sixteen *mahajanapadas* or "great republics" that together constituted ancient India. This indicates that both were looked upon as one political and geographical unit in those times. The earliest Chinese references to the whole region as Ki-pin or Chi-pin seem to confirm this. The term appears to have been used in a rather vague or general sense for a variety of territories in India's northwest, including Kapisha and Gandhara in addition to Kashmir. It occurs in a passage in the Chinese Han Hanshu while describing the annexation of Kaofu (Kabul) by the Scythian king Kujula Kadiphises. There has been considerable discussion among scholars about the exact geographical identification of the term Ki-pin or Chi-pin. S. Levi takes it to mean Kapisha (modern Begram), while Chavannes is of the opinion that the Chinese used it to indicate Kashmir alone. The most acceptable view, however, is that of Vincent Smith according to whom it denoted both Kashmir and Gandhara, and also covered most of the present day Afghanistan. The *mahavamsha*, a Ceylonese chronicle of Buddhism, clubs Kashmir and Gandhara together in one chapter as Kashmir-Gandhara but in another chapter refers to monks hailing from Kashmira Mandala while relating an anecdote of a later date. In Greek records, Kashmir has been referred to as Kaspapyros (the name having been derived from Kashyapapura), and has been linked with Gandhara. *Milindapanha* a Buddhist philosophical work that gives an account of the discussion between Milinda or the Greek king Menander and his preceptor Nagasena, refers to the two regions as Kashmira-Gandhara. It must be noted that the discussions took place at a spot 12 *yojanas* from Kashmir. Ptolemy, the famous Greek historian of the 2nd century, went as far as regarding Afghanistan and Baluchistan as parts of India, perhaps because of the religio-cultural affinities of these regions.

Kalhana makes a clear distinction between Kashmir and Gandhara, but attests to the closeness of the two. In Rajatarangini, we find him making frequent references to Gandharan Brahmans who had settled in Kashmir. Soldiers from Gandhara, he says, were recruited in the Kashmir army for their martial qualities. He also relates the story of King Meghavahana who took possession of the throne of his ancestors in Kashmir at the invitation of the Kashmirian ministers. A pious Buddhist, Meghavahana prohibited slaughter of animals throughout his territories and even marched up to Lanka to enforce this edict. His queens Amritaprabha and Khadana built *viharas* in Kashmir.

In historical times proper, Afghanistan was occupied by the

Achaemanids of Iran and remained under their occupation from the 6th to the 4th century BC. It passed into the hands of the Greeks when Alexander snatched it from the Iranian emperor Darius III in 320 BC and continued to be ruled by successive Bactro-Greek kings, some of whom also controlled parts of Kashmir, till Seleucus Nicator suffered a humiliating defeat at the hands of the Mauryan emperor Chandragupta in 305 BC. He was forced to cede four of his provinces—Arian, Gandhara, Archosia and Propamisadae to Chandragupta Maurya.

Surely, it must have been during this period that Kashmir came into a wider political as well as socio-cultural contact with the people of the Afghan territories and also the Bactro-Greeks. While definite details of this contact have to be still explored, it appears that both Kashmir and Afghanistan were at that time dominated by Hindu-Buddhist culture, the Bactro-Greek kings being worshippers of both Hindu and Greek deities due to the dominant Indian influence. When Antiochus III invaded Afghanistan, he found it to be in the hands of an Indian king Sophagsena or Subhagsena.

The Role of Buddhism

One must admit, however, that it was the Buddhist religion that acted as the binding force to bring the people of Afghanistan and Kashmir together in those early times. And though Kalhana provides definite evidence about the existence of Buddhism in Kashmir in the pre-Ashokan days, it was only when "Asoka Piyadassi" was converted to the faith towards the end of the 3rd century BC that Buddhism acquired the character of a powerful religious movement due to the indefatigable zeal of the great Mauryan empror in its propagation. As stated in the *Mahavamsha*, and also in the *Ashokavadana*, Ashoka sent missionaries to different countries to propagate the faith, deputing Majjhantika to the Kashmir-Gandhara region. Subduing the local Nagas by his miraculous powers, Majjhantika is said to have won them over to the Buddhist way of life. Ashoka's edicts indicate the northernmost boundaries of his vast empire that included the areas inhabited by the Yonas, Kambojas and Gandharas, in other words Afghanistan. No Ashokan edict has been found in Kashmir indicating, according to Nalinaksha Dutta, that it "must have been brought within his ken in the later part of his life". Kalhana and other literary sources provide ample evidence of the fact that Ashoka made Kashmir a part of his empire and built the capital city of Shrinagari. It is said that during Ashoka's time 500 *arhats* belonging to the *sarvastivada* sect took shelter in the hills and vales of Kashmir to escape the ordeal of being drowned in the Ganga on the dictates of Moggaliputta Tissa, his religious adviser who branded them as heretics to curb dissent. In his later days Ashoka is said to have repented and apologized to them, persuading them to return. The *arhat*s being in no mood to oblige him,the piouss king made amends by building 500 monasteries for them and giving the whole of Kashmir as gift to the Buddhist *sangha*. It was thus that Kashmir became the most important stronghold of the *sarvastivada* school which believed that *nama* and *rupa*, name and form, are real. From Kashmir, which produced the bulk of missionaries to spread Buddha's message, concepts of *sarvastivada* travelled to Afghanistan and from there to Central Asia and China.

After Ashoka, the most important name in the history of Buddhism is Kanishka, the Kushana emperor belonging to the Yueh-chi tribe, who lent the support of his imperial power to strengthen the religion he chose to adopt. One of the greatest rulers of Asia, Kanishka developed the vast empire he inherited from his predecessors Kujul Kadiphises and Vima Kadiphises to the farthest extent—from Aral Sea to Bactria and through most of Afghanistan, present day Pakistan and northern India to what comprises Bangladesh today. Along with political expansion, Kanishka is remembered for nurturing Buddhism and popularising it almost as a folk religion throughout his territories and beyond. His reign proved to be a great stabilizing factor in Kashmir, ushering in an era of peace and prosperity during which a very close liaison got established between Kashmir, Afghanistan and Central Asian countries. Ruling from his capital at Purushpura, near the present day Peshawar, he built there one of the most magnificent and largest ever *vihara*, known as the Mahavihara. But his most notable achievement was the Fourth Great Buddhist Council which he convened at Kundalvan or Kanzalvan in Kashmir under the direction of the great philospher Vasumitra, who he considered to be his teacher. Besides Vasumitra, Buddhist luminaries like Parshva, Ashvaghosha, Sugatmitra, Vasubandhu, Jinamitra and Dharmatrata took active part in the deliberations of the Council which was held to "revise, review and re-interpret" the *vinaya*, *sutra* and *abhidharma* texts so that the purity and clarity of the Buddhist canon could be preserved. According to Hieun Tsang the deliberations of the Council were recorded in three hundred thousand verses of *vibhasha*s or expository commentaries, and Kanishka got all the treatises engraved on copper plates and enclosed in stone receptacles and deposited in a *stupa*. These treatises were sent to the great Sanskrit poet Ashvaghosha for being given a proper literary shape.

With the reconciliation of the views of 18 different schools of Buddhism at the Council and the composition of the *vibhasha shāstra*s, Kanishka was able to get much of the confusion created by the conflicting interpretations of Buddha's words cleared. While the representatives of all the 18 sects accepted the conclusions of the Council, a permanent schism between the Buddhists of the South who stuck to the old canon known as Hinayana and Buddhists of the North who adopted the new canon which developed into Mahayana came into existence. It was soon among the pine groves of Harwan that the great Nagarjuna propounded the theory of *shunyavada*. Kashmir thus changed the entire complexion of Buddhist philosophical thought of which it remained a world-renowned centre for the next one thousand years or so.

The emergence of the altruistic doctrine of Mahayana as the dominant school in the North with its emphasis on idealism, disinterested love, relief of the sufferings of others and salvation for every living being ,as against the strict monastic discipline of Hinayana seeking for the individual, catered very much to the devotional and spiritual needs of the human mind. Mahayana deified Buddha, giving him a place in the highest heaven – Tushita – from where he is supposed to descend on the earth to end the suffering of mankind. It was in this manner that the concept of the divine boddhisattvas or pre-destined Buddha incarnates came into being along with an entirely new pantheon of gods and goddesses personifying many of the Buddha's qualities and attributes. This had a tremendous appeal for the common people who found the strict asceticism of the old school too demanding. Kashmir not only provided the inputs from its masterminds to sustain the new doctrine intellectually, it also launched missionaries and scholars from its soil to different lands including Afghanistan, Central Asia and China for propagating it and translating and interpreting its texts. Kanishka's reign proved of outstanding importance in establishing this new canon firmly as popular religion throughout the length and breadth of his vast empire.

The Gandhara School of Art

Kanishka's patronage of the Buddhist faith inspired a tremendous upsurge in creative activity, leading to the development of the Gandhara School of Art. It arose as a powerful art movement originating in northwestern domains of the Kushanas with a distinct style characterized by a strong influence of Graeco-Roman classical art that dominated in that region and found a significant expression in exquisitely carved stone images of Buddha and Boddhisattvas. Yet it cannot be said that it was totally unrelated to the indigenous art that flourished at Bharhut and Sanchi. The Gandhara School is generally credited with having introduced the first representation of the Buddha in human form, the Greek god Apollo being regarded the prototype for it. But the view has been strongly contested by Ananda Coomaraswamy and K.B. Jaiswal. One thing that needs to be emphasized is that the development of Gandharan art could not have taken place without the spirit of "devotional theism", and that is what Kashmir has contributed through the medium of Mahayana texts in Sanskrit. Unfortunately this aspect has not got its due share of attention.

The Gandhara school patronized by the Kushanas is generally believed to have exercised a considerably strong influence on Kashmiri sculptural art. But unfortunately no examples of early Kushana art have survived in Kashmir despite the fact that Kanishka and Huvishka had respectively founded the towns of Kanishkapur (modern Kanispur) and Huvishkapur (modern Ushkur) there. Of these Ushkur did yield a rich haul of splendid terracotta heads and figurines, but these are of a much later date and display a stronger influence of Gupta baroque art. Kushana power was dealt mortal blow in the fifth century with the invasion of the White Huns, and with that the productivity of the Gandhara art came to an end though its stylistic features lingered on for some time and continued to find expression in Kashmir as well as some isolated pockets in Afghanistan and Central Asia.

It has been said that the final chapters of Gandhara art have their settings in Kashmir which continued to be a centre of Buddhist thought long after the Kushanas had gone. But this seems to be quite an exaggeration. While it is true that Kashmiri art absorbed influences from Gandhara and post-Gandhara art of the northwestern region, it was also equally influenced by Pala and Gupta, and even Ajanta, Bharhut, Sassanian and Hellenistic art, as the breathtaking range of figures and decorative motifs of the beautiful Harwan tiles seem to suggest. The tiles discovered at Hoinar, Hutmara, Kralachak Ahan and Takiya Bala too indicate different origins not necessarily of Gandharan or Buddhist inspiration. The terracotta heads and figurines discovered from Ushkur representing Buddha, monks, lay devotees etc. have been recognized as the finest examples of Kashmiri plastic art. Terracotta figurines and seals have been discovered from Semthan, Bijbehara also. The female figurines, according to John Siudmak, show obvious Helenistic features in costume though "the face and hairstyle have been Indianized".

As for the stone sculptures of Kashmir, the number of surviving examples before the sixth century is rather small. As Siudmak has rightly said, this is so because "most of Kashmir's artistic heritage was systematically destroyed in the early fourteenth century by Sikander Butshikan, one of the early Muslim kings, and many of the ruins were pillaged for the construction of mosques". Yet, whatever we are left with speaks of splendid achievements in artistic creativity that touched unprecedented heights during the rule of the Karkota and Utpala dynasties. One of the finest works of sculpture in the pre-Karkota period is the stone image of six-armed Kartikeya from Bijbehara shown with his peacock, displaying features that some scholars have compared with the Gandhara Boddhisattvas particularly in terms of its massive frame and jewellery. A typically Kashmiri feature of the image is the *vanamala.* Other notable examples of the Bijbehara school are a four-armed Durga image and Vishnu, the costume of the goddess displaying Hellenistic features. From Baramula one of the most impressive sculptures is the Fatehgarh Maheshwara which displays a more conspicuous Gupta influence.

Gupta art, according to Hermann Goetz, had started infiltrating from the fourth century itself "when Kashmir had not yet heard the last from the Kushan". By the end of the sixth century, he observes, its "pervasive presence" spread to Pravarpura, the new capital founded by King Pravarsena II, while in Pandrethan, the old capital, a new and vigorous style had developed. Showing some continuity with the

Bijbehara school, it absorbed some features of Gupta art, as can be seen in the extremely beautiful but badly damaged figure of the dancing Mother-Goddess. Among other important Hindu sculptures from Pandrethan, we have the giant three-headed Maheshwara, the four-armed Ganesha seated on a throne showing lions rather than the mouse, the life-size figure of Chamunda and the images of Indrani, Varahi, and Vaishnavi representing the *matrikachakra*, all having features of Gupta art with hardly any Gandharan traits. From Pandrethan we also have several Buddhist sculptures, which display grace and beauty. It was from the standing Buddha Padmapani, seated Bodhisattvas, Lokeshwaras and other Buddha images that "the classical and typically Kashmiri Buddha evolved".

Lalitaditya, a superhero of Kashmir history, who ascended the throne in 724 AD, launched extensive military expeditions which extended Kashmir's control over Afghanistan among other territories, making it a strong power in the region. Earlier his predecessors Tarapida and Chandrapida had conquered not only parts of Punjab and Himalayas but made tributary the Turki Shahis of Afghanistan. Lalitaditya's great victories and his imperial grandeur had their artistic and cultural consequences also. It was during his reign that Kashmir, after absorbing influences from different sources, developed its own idiom and style in art characterized by vitality, ingenuity, beauty and grandeur and animated by typical Kashmiri sensibility. This new style, in the words of Hermann Goetz, was "no longer classic, or late Gupta, Gandharan, Chinese or Roman but represented the characteristic Medieval art of Kashmir". It was an art that "gave the impression of greatness and grandeur", finding expression in colossal buildings like the great Buddhist monuments at Parihaspur and the Sun temple at Martand. This art, writes Goetz, did not descend from late Gandhara as "Gandhara art was at that time already defunct, and such influence as it exercised on the new development under Lalitaditya was due to inspiration from the Ushkur Stupa and the giant statues of Bamiyan rather than a direct handing-on of a craft tradition".

The Brihadbuddhas of Kashmir

This brings us back to Bamiyan and its, now destroyed, colossal Buddhas. According to Kalhana, a "glorious statue" of Brihadbuddha

(Great Buddha) was made by Lalitaditya at Rajvihara with thousands of *prasthas* of copper, and it "reached up to the sky" (iv 203) . Another colossal image of Buddha stood in the city of Srinagar in the time of King Sussala (1111-12 AD). Kalhana also informs us that Jayendra, the maternal uncle of King Pravarsena II, got a statue of Brihadbuddha erected at Jayendra Vihara, a monastery which he had built (*Rajatarangini* iii 355). Interestingly it was in this monastery that the Chinese traveller Hieun Tsang (Hsuan Tsang) had stayed after he had arrived at the Kashmir capital in 631 AD. It was there that he received instructions in various *shastras* from the chief of the priests and stayed for most part of his sojourn in Kashmir. Thus was established a tradition of building colossal images of Buddha in Kashmir, inspired probably by Bamiyan, which continued well into the twelveth century.

Of considerable importance from artistic and religio-cultural point of view are the paintings inside the numerous grottos projecting from the cliffs at Bamiyan. These frescoes display stylistic features that appear to have been derived from different artistic traditions, with the Sassanian and Indian traits dominating apart from the local Gandharan ones. The niche above the smaller Buddha has been beautifully painted showing an imposing figure of Surya, the Sun god on his chariot with his consorts. The pictorial decorations covering the entire niche of the larger 175-foot Buddha bear a clear Indian influence showing stylistic similarities with Ajanta. On the vault are painted flying divinities, probably *gandharvas* and *apsaras*, scattering jewels and flowers. There are also rows of Buddhas seated in different poses and "a complete pantheon of Boddhisattvas all seemingly in Mahayana tradition". Being a famous Buddhist religious centre, Bamiyan could not but have attracted artists from different countries, representing different artistic traditions. It is quite likely that among the Indian artists, who painted the murals, some must have hailed from Kashmir. May be they were commissioned for the job, as they were for decorating the walls of monasteries in Tibet.

Sharda Script

There are many more evidences of a close liaison between Kashmir and its northwestern neighbour in the first millennium of the Christian era, including inscriptional and numismatic evidence. Both Kharoshthi and Brahmi are known to have been the common scripts widely used in the the two regions in the early part of the era. In their book "*Archaeology of Afghanistan*", F.R. Allchin and N. Hammond show that Sharada was also introduced in Afghanistan in the sixth or seventh century, providing evidence in the shape of two inscriptions that throw light on the development of Brahmi into an early version of Sharada. They write : "The inscription from Gardez, now in Kabul, is engraved in two lines on the base of a marble image of the Hindu god Ganesha... It refers to Maharajadhiraj Shahi Khingila and dates to his sixth year. ...The second is the inscription on the pedestal of the Uma-Maheshwara image discovered in the Japanese excavations at Tapa Sikandar. The inscription refers to the Hindu Triad, "Brahma, the creator, Shiva the destroyer and Vishnu the preserver". A clay tablet from a miniature *stupa* from Gudas-I-Ahangaran, Ghazni, has also been found with an inscription in Sharada.

That the Shahis looked increasingly to Kashmir is borne out by their coinage also. "Between AD 750 and 1000, the Shahis issued silver coinage to provide currency for eastern Afghanistan and Gandhara—at first the kings of Kabul and subsequently, the rulers of Ohind", write Allchin and Hammond quoting Macdowell. Most of the coins have an obverse legend in Sharada script—either Spalpati Deva or Shri Samanta Deva. Another major group of coins has the obverse legend "Shri Samanta Deva".

Hindu Shahis of Kabul

It was during the second half of the seventh century, when Arab armies had invaded western Afghan provinces of Seistan and Herat and sent governors to control them that "popular non-Islamic kingdom" of the Turki and Hindu Shahis was set-up. The kings of the Turki shahi dynasty were Buddhists, but they also worshipped Hindu gods like Shiva and Durga. According to Al-Biruni, the Brahman minister Kallar who overthrew the last Turki Shahi king founded the Hindu Shahi dynasty. When Yaqub captured Kabul in 870, the Shahis shifted their capital to Hund or Waihund, the Udbhandapur of Kalhana, even though they temporarily recovered the city. Sebuktigin annexed Kabul in 977 and repeatedly raided the territory of the Shahi king Jayapala. Kalhana tells us that the Kashmiri king Shankarvarman (883-902 AD) and

Queen Sugandha (902-906 AD) reconquered Punjab and Afghanistan, keeping the Hindu Shahi kings of Kabul as vassals. However, during the reign of Queen Didda (950-1003 AD), they regained independece and made themselves "a formidable military power". Didda herself was the granddaughter of King Bhima Shahi of Kabul. Her marriage with King Kshemagupta of Kashmir united the ruling dynasties of Kashmir and Kabul. The Shahis were in Kashmir even before this. According to Kalhana, Shahis held offices in the court of King Lalitaditya. During the early part of King Ananta's rule (1028-63 AD), Shahi princes Rudrapala and Diddapala had taken refuge in Kashmir after the Shahis were defeated by Ghaznavid kings.

Kashmir and Central Asia

Buddhist and Hindu settlements had come up in Central Asia—a region that stretched from Afghanistan up to East Sinkiang (Xinjiang)—in the time of Ashoka, the great patron of Buddhism who introduced the faith in the region. When Kanishka took on the mantle of the great Mauryan king, its propagation received a tremendous boost and it continued to flourish there up to the tenth century before it succumbed to the onslaught of Islam. It is indeed amazing, as Dr. Bhagvat Sharan Upadhyaya has observed, that at a time when Jesus, the saint of Nazareth, was facing the tyranny of the Roman empire and his disciples were being preyed upon by hungry lions in their Colosseum, calm and peaceful Indian missionaries, a great number of them from Kashmir, were preaching Buddha's message of love and brotherhood to bloodthirsty tribes of Central Asia. Kashmiri monks and missionaries, traders and travellers were active from very early times on the routes to the north and south of the Takla Makan desert, interacting with people, propagating Buddhist thought and carrying Indian cultural influences with them. Art historian Anil Khosa is therefore right when he says that Kashmir has functioned "as a gateway of Indian culture for Central Asia" and it has been so "from the beginning of the transmission of Buddhism and Buddhist culture" in the region. Among the leading Kashmiri monk-scholars who propagated Buddhist ideology, translated religious texts and expounded important theories in Central Asia and China were Sangabhuti, Kumarajiva, Vimalaksha, Dharmamitra, Dharmatrata, Gunavarman, Buddhayashas, Buddhajiva, Ratnachinta and Prajnabala. Hieun Tsang (Hsuan Tsang) has attested in his travel account that "Kashmir is one of the most important and famous land in the spread and development of Buddhism". Kumarajiva, who was regarded as "one of the four suns of Budhism" and one of the greatest masters of the Buddhist philosophy of Mahayana, was born in the famous Central Asian town of Kucha or Kuchi as it was originally called as the son of a Kuchean princess Jiva and Kumarayana, son of a minister of Kashmir. A great genius, he was taken to Kashmir by his mother from the same route from where his father had come to study Buddhist texts. His great reputation as a scholar made the king of China to virtually abduct him to his country where he translated more than a hundred Sanskrit texts into the Chinese language, a good number of which are still available.

Sanskrit Buddhism

Soon Kashmir gained tremendous reputation as an important centre of what is known as "Sanskrit Buddhism", and missionaries, scholars and monks who set out from there to different places not only translated Buddhist texts but also tried to popularize the Sanskrit language and the whole wealth of knowledge it contained. Two Indian scripts as we have pointed out earlier served as the medium of this dissemination—Kharoshthi and Brahmi. While a special dialect of Prakrit called Gandhari Prakrit was widely in use and developed its own literature, particularly at Niya, Lou-lan, Endere and probably Khotan, the most important work found in it being the *Dhammapada* written in the Kharoshthi, Sanskrit language also held a place of eminence in Central Asia as well as Afghanistan. The people of this region not only studied Sanskrit texts, but were also conversant with other branches of literature like *Sariputra Prakrana* and *Saundarananda* by Ashva-ghosha. Sanskrit manuscripts in Brahmi have been discovered in a number of areas including Tumshuq, the Kucha region (Qizil, Qumtura, Kirish, Achig-Ilak, etc.), Shorchuq, the Turfan Oasis (Xocho, Yarxoto, Murtuq, Sangim, Bazalik, Toyoq, etc.), Dun-huang, Kashgar and Khotan region, according to B.N. Mukherji (India in Early Central Asia), besides those included in the famous Bower, Godfrey, Macartney and Weber manuscripts which have been discovered from the Kucha region.

Sanskrit in fact became the most important vehicle of both Hinayana and Mahayana forms of Buddhism in Central Asia, having been introduced there by the Sarvastivada School of which Kashmir was considered to be the stronghold. A large number of Sanskrit manuscripts comprising the sacred literature of these sects, mostly in fragmentary form, were unearthed from various Central Asian sites, like Kucha, Turfan, Agnidesha or Karra Shahar, Kizil, Tumshuq etc. These include almost the entire *sutra* and *vinaya* texts of the *sarvastivadin*s. Discoveries of important texts of Mahayana Buddhism, which was introduced in Khotan, Shan-shan, Kashgarh, Kucha and also possibly Niya in the fourth century, according to Mukherji, have also been made. Among the Sanskrit sacred works discovered besides *sutra* literature and *dharinis* is the complete text of *Udanavarga*, which is as important in *sarvastivada* as the *Dhammapada* in *theravada.* Dharmatrata, a famous Buddhist philosopher from Kashmir, is said to be the author of the work.

Apart from the Buddhist canonical works, other forms of literature were also popular with the ancient Central Asians, as we have mentioned above while referring to manuscripts unearthed by scholars in the region, like Ashvaghosha's Sanskrit drama Sariputra-*prakarana* and his *Saundarananda-kavya. Buddhacharit* by the same author has also been found from Sorchuq. Several manuscripts of hymns attributed to Matricheta, like the *Shatpanchshatika* and the *Chatuhshatakam* have also been recovered in Tumshuq, Karrashahar, Kucha, Turfan and Dunhuang. The poet was a Kashmiri and a contemporary of Kanishka, and he appears to have enjoyed immense popularity with the Sanskrit-loving Central Asians. What is interesting is that many of these religious and literary works had been lost in India. Many documents in Sanskrit have also been found not related to religious or philosophical themes but dealing with administrative, commercial, legal and even personal matters. These, particularly personal letters have been written, according to Aurel Stein, in the style shown in the Kashmiri manual on writing, the *Lekhaprakasha*. "Kashmir was directly connected with such things in Central Asia", writes Dr. Bhagvat Sharan Upadhyaya in his book *Brihattar Bharat*. "In fact many *bhikshu*s, Brahmin-monks had gone there. It is hardly surprising that they might have introduced the Kashmiri documentation system in these areas!"

Cultural Activity

Excavations by explorers and archaeologists like Albert Von Lekok, Count Otani, Baron Oldenbourgh, Grundwedell and most of all Aurel Stein have yielded a great wealth of materials in the form of *stupas*, *viharas*, sculptures and murals from ancient cities buried under the sands on the routes north and south of the Takla Makan desert. Chinese travellers like Fa-Hien, Che Mong, Fa-Yong, Oukong, Hieun Tsang (Hsuan Tsang) and Itsing, who came to India via Central Asia, almost all of them visiting Kashmir, give a fascinating account of the state of Buddhism in places like Turfan, Kucha, Kashgar, Niya, Bharuka, Agnidesh or Karashahar, Yarkand, Khotan and Niya in their travelogues, testifying to the important role of Kashmir in fostering religious, cultural and trade relations between India and Central Asia. The cave complexes and temples of eastern Turkestan—Kyzyl, Bezeklik, Kucha, Khotan, Endere and other places have their prototypes in the Hindu-Buddhist cave art of India while the monumental sculptures appear to have been inspired by the Gandhara-Bamiyan Buddhas and Bodhisattvas bearing obvious Indian influence. With the advance of Islam to Central Asia in about the ninth century, the cultural and artistic interchange between Buddhist and Hindu Kashmir and these regions fell victim to iconoclastic fury and a long and glorious chapter ended for ever. Looking back in time, the ties that bound Kashmir, Afghanistan and Central Asia in a close bond can prove to be a fascinating subject for study. An extensive exploration of this relationship is sure to bring many interesting facts about it to the fore.

6

India and Central Asia

Cultural Relations in Middle Ages

Evgeni Kablukov

First of all I would like to mention that during last four-five years I am not a scientist, I work in the Kyrgyz diplomatic service. But my background allows me to say some words on the topic. Taking this into account I would like to focus mainly on the problems which, as I see it, face the contemporary researchers in the field.

Central Asia is a vast region. World researches include in this region Tibet and Xinjiang (also known as Chinese Turkistan) of East Central Asia (now autonomous regions of People's Republic of China), West Central Asia with five former Soviet, and now independent, states of Kazakhstan, Kyrgyzstan, Tazikistan, Uzbekistan and Turkmenistan, Buddhist regions of Russia (Buriatia and Tuva) and Mongolia. But in this presentation I shall focus on West Central Asia with five former Soviet, and now independent states and the term "Central Asia" will be attributed to this region.

Due to India's (especially Northern India's) geographical proximity with Central Asia from the ancient times till the British occupation of India there was cross-regional and social interaction which led to forging of highly significant linkages. For many centuries Central Asia was an immense reservoir of human energy and skills where many conquerors and many religions left their still unextinguished marks. Many great and world religions were present, and some still are present, in the region: Zoroastrism, Buddhism, Christianity, Islam and others.Vast treasure of art materials, temples and manuscripts were explored by expeditions and individuals. Valuable and a lot of materials have also come to light in the excavations at Penjikent, Varaksha and Adzhina Tepe of the Western Central Asia by the Russian and Central Asian archeologists. All this allowed to see that Indian dialects Parya, Kavol, Jugi, Chistoni and Sagutarosh-hisori were present in Central Asia. The writings of Russian and other scholars reveal influence of Indian culture in folklore, geographical names, moral-ethical code and other spheres of everyday life and ritual in Central Asia. There is vast material providing information on Central Asia and its links with India in Russian, Chinese and Tibetan documents. The Chinese pilgrims have also left vast treasure of literature.

Indian links with Central Asia and *vice versa* have not been completely continues, for some centuries they were interrupted, sometimes very intense, as in the case of Kushana period, sometimes feeble, and two-way. Zia ul-Din Nakhshabi, the author of "*Tuti-nama*" ("Book of Parrot") was born in Central Asia. Al-Beruni came here, learnt Sanskrit and wrote *Tarikh-I- Hind* (The History of India). Abdurazzak Samarkandi also came here. Ibn Sina and Al-Khorezmi were acquainted with Indian scientific works. Two-way movements for trade and culture continued during Mughal rule and after that also. Alexander Burnes, the British agent, wrote that turbans of Punjabi white cloth were used by "whole of the natives of Bokhara and Toorkistan" during 1830s. There were about eight thousand Indian settlers in 19th and early 20th century in Central Asia. Every market and village had Hindu moneylender in Turkestan in1860s according to an observer. Indians had monopoly of book trade there.

The Silk Route, which connected China, Europe and India, passed through Central Asia. A lot of cities were established along the Silk Route. In those cities Indians settled and lived their own life; they had their own social and political organizations, language, scripts, literature, art, architecture and religion. Remains of hundreds of Buddhist shrines, stupas and monasteries of designs inspired by India; numerous Buddhist texts in Sanskrit, Prakrit or local languages, largely in the Indian scripts, Brahmi and Kharosthi; Sanskrit dramas and texts on medicine, astronomy and astrology written in Brahmi, hundreds of documents of administrative, commercial, legal and miscellaneous kinds, draft in Sanskrit, Prakrit or Central Asian dialects written in Indian scripts and tablets of Complete Brahmi script have been discovered from Central Asian sites. 764 Kharosthi documents in Prakrit language on wooden tablets, leather pieces and silk fragments, throw much light on the social, religious and political conditions of the Central Asia during early centuries of the Christian era. Aurel

Stein's collection from Xingjiang also included Central Asian art objects including paintings from Thousand Buddha Temple in Tun-Huang.

India's relations with Central Asia in early Medieval times corresponds with the spread of Buddhist teaching and worship. This initiated the one of the greatest cultural movements in history—the passage of Buddhist thought and philosophical ideas from one civilization to another and also the movement of Buddhist missionaries. Researches of Central Asian scholars reveal that Central Asia knew different schools of Buddhists. For example, Kyrgyz researches say that Kyrgyzs knew Tibetan version of Buddhism—Lamaism. Lamaist terminology may be found in "Manas" epic. And nowadays a part of Kyrgyzs in China confess Lamaism. With introduction of Islam Buddhism as religion dissapeared from Central Asia. Now there is vast amount of literature in Russian and local Central Asian languages on Buddhist monuments in Central Asia. But there is still a great field for research on the theme—what legacy Buddhism left on Central Asian people thinking and local philosophical and moral thinking, how much of this legacy have been included into Islamic thought in Central Asia. From Soviet time researches we know that in Tibetan culture *Jatakas* occupied very important role. They were not preserved in mummified form but were used as basic material by local writers and poets for illustrations of Lamaist dogmatics understandable to local people. The same case was also in the whole Central Asia. With removal of Buddhism from the scene its ideas and thinking could not dissappear from the minds of the people. The I. Moldobaev's paper is only beginning in this field. May be Buddhist ideas and thoughts may be found in Central Asian epics, folklore and even fairy tales.

Another splash in relations between India and Central Asia was during Mahmood Gaznevi reign and Delhi Sultanate times. At that times Persian language and literature were introduced to India. And mostly it has been done through Central Asia. Central Asia was not conquered by Islam by military means but they were Islamic missionaries mostly from Persia who introduced Islam in Central Asia. It is at that time when many Sufi scholars, poets and saints came from Central Asia and settled in Delhi, Kashmir and elsewhere in India. In many cases this was return of many Buddhist thoughts and ideas back to India.

Another possible theme for research is connected with another world religion—Chiristianity, to be precise with early Christianity. A legend says that Jesus did not die and was not took up by His Farther to Heaven. Instead, he set forth to India accompanied by Maria Magdalena. Their way went through Central Asia. There is a grave in Chinese Xinjiang belived to be a grave of Maria Magdalena. And there is a Jesus's grave in Kashmir called "Takht-e Suleiman" by local people. In southern part of Kyrgyzsrtan in Osh city we have a place called "Takht-e-Suleiman". It is a hill regarded to be a sacred place for local Muslim population. In Kyrgyzstan we have remnants of many early Christian monasteries belonged to Nestorians.

We may mention two-way road of cultural exchange between India and Central Asia. It is connected with Temurlang and his successors. But there was difference between Temurlang and his successors. Temur brought to Delhi great disaster: many buildings were burnt and looted, thousands of people were killed, except craftsmen and masons. Temur came to India to conquer and get enormous wealth. He took with him back to Samarquand Indian masons where they should learn also Persian art of building. It is believed that they constructed world famous architectural treasure of Samarquand—Gur-Emir mausoleum and other monuments in Samarquand and Bukhara.

But his successors better known in history as the Great Moghuls have returned their enriched skills back to India and these masons combined these two traditions and invented the higher skill that now is widely world known as Indian-Islamic architecture. Temur came to India for some time, his successors came for ever and presented to the world the epoch of the greatest splendor. Their royal court was filled with scientists, writers, musicians and poets.

And still there are about 250 manuscripts on history and literature of Central Asia, mostly in Arabic and Persian in the museums and libraries of India. Khuda Bakhsh Library, Patna is very rich in this matter. *Baburnama* and a book got compiled by Akbar has a lot of material on India and Central Asia. This is a great source for researches on Central Asian-Indian relations in medieval period.

And, in the end I would like to make a proposal. We may think and establish some kind of scientific panel to study and make researches on the wide theme—"Relations between Central Asia and India: from ancient to contemporary times". May be you know that the year 2003 was for our republic "Year of the Kyrgyz Statehood". Our scientists visited China and Iran in search of manuscripts, which may add something to our historical knowledge. Now they work on this material. Our scientists have a list of manuscripts which are kept in Indian libraries and archives. We should not leave any stone unturned in search and research of our historical legacy.

Central Asian scientists still make discoveries that firmly confirm deep roots of ties between India and Central Asia. Quite recently in Turkmenistan a treasure of 1515 coins of Vasudeva, Kushan king (III-IV A.D.), have been found. These coins will be kept in Turkmenistan National Museum and add valuable information and food for thought to our historians. At Issyk-Kul lake in Kyrgyzstan every year archeolo-gists find images of Indian gods which also adds a lot for understanding interaction on the Great Silk Route.

At present time the problem of material and cultural exchange between India and Central Asia is a matter of interest for researchers and scientists of Central Asia. A large conference "Buddhism and Christianity in Cultural Legacy of Central Asia" was held on October 3-5, 2002 in Bishkek, Kyrgyzstan. I believe that this was, may be, the first but not the last conference of this type in contemporary Central Asia.

7

India and Central Asia 1947-1991

Surender Gopal

During the Second World War the Soviets were fighting to save their homeland from Nazi occupation. When the Nazis encircled Leningrad (now St. Petersberg) and knocked at the gates of their capital Moscow, the Soviet shifted some of the Indian Indologists, Balavushevich, K.A. Antonova, etc., and some Indians to Tashkent, the capital of Uzbekistan. The group had two major tasks to perform: first, to keep studying India and secondly, to overhear messages exchanged by the allied powers over wireless even though they were partners of the Soviet Union. The later task was confidential; none of the Indian specialists put on this job was allowed to divulge anything about his work.

Historians like Balabushevich and Dyakov brought out brochures and articles on the labour movement in India.,Tahkent was now, as in 1920s, the major centre for Indian studies in the war-torn Soviet Union. Once the war ended, the Soviet specialists on India were repatriated to Moscow. Tashkent, however, retained its the prime position for Indian studies in the Soviet Central Asia. Several factors were responsible for this. The international situation had substantially changed.

The aftermath of the war saw decolonization and the emergence of India as a sovereign state though it was partitioned. Indians leaders, Mahatma Gandhi and Jawaharlal Nehru ensured that the new country became the torch-bearer of the ideology of anti-colonialism, anti-racism and liberation struggle. The Soviet authorities, initially, refused to take note of the new reality. The Soviet Press did not publish the news of Indian independence in August 1947. In the eyes of the Soviet leadership, India was a lackey of western imperialism. Even diplomatic relations were established with great diffidence.

Things changed after Stalin's death in 1953. Within two years Khrushchev and Bulganin were occupying the seats of power and they reversed Soviet policies.

Khrushchev decided to enlist the support of anti-colonial countries against the capitalist camp led the U.S. India emerged at the top of the list of non-Communist countries to be roped in as allies. Nehru, the Indian Prime Minister, had a strong Socialist bias and was enamoured of Soviet experiment of development through planned economy. He had visited the Soviet Union in 1927 and was actively associated with the League Against Anti-Imperialism, floated by the Soviets and their sympathizers. during its early years

The era of Hindi-Rusi Bhai-Bhai dawned. The Soviets in order to impress Nehru that Socialism was a powerful antidote to poverty, illiteracy and underdevelopment, cited the example of Central Asia where illiteracy had been obliterated, cooperative farming had been introduced and the hold of religion on the minds of people had been broken. Central Asia was put forward as a shining example of transformation of an undeveloped and backward region into a developed and modern one.

When Pandit Nehru visited the Soviet Union, he was taken to Tashkent to see how socialism had changed the face of a backward region. Indo-Soviet friendship developed. It was nurtured by government to government understanding and solidarity and backed by Indo-Soviet Cultural Societies (ISCUS), promoted by Indian communists and their sympathizers.

In the Soviet Union also ostensibly, a similar non-governmental organization was established to coordinate with ISCUS in India. Indo-Central Asian relations developed as an offshoot of growing Indo-Soviet friendship at the governmental level.

Geography and history, both helped to bring the two countries together.

As a resultant of growing diplomatic, economic and cultural cooperation, the Soviets established several big factories in India which required regular visits by Soviet and Indian officials to India and the Soviet Union. Regular plane services were started between two capitals, Delhi and Moscow.

In the late fifties planes flying between Delhi and Moscow needed a halt at Tashkent for refuelling. Air-India, operating between Delhi and Moscow opened an office in Tashkent. Tashkent had recovered its connection with India.

The Soviets decided to broadcast to India and Radio Tashkent was chosen for the purpose. The broadcasts were in English, Urdu and Hindi. They needed experts in both written and spoken Urdu and Hindi.

Persons required for the job were recruited in two ways. First, search was made for Indians on the Soviet territory who knew Urdu. The Soviets succeeded in finding one Indian expatriate, Hardat who had been sent to Siberian prison during the Stalinist regime and had been set free after Stalin's death. He could not travel back to India, as he had no valid travel documents.

The Soviets were still scared of unrestricted entry of foreigners. To get over this problem, they decided to ask some members of the Indian Communist Party to come over to Tashkent and work for the Tashkent Radio. Mr. Habib, a very active member of the Communist Party of India was selected for the purpose. The authorities were also able to locate a local Mr. Haider who knew Urdu, both written and spoken. Some Russians were also called in.

At this juncture other factors also strengthened Tashkent's role as a centre for Indian Studies.

Babajan Gafurov became the Director of Institute of People of Asia and Africa (now Institute of Oriental Studies), Academy of Sciences (USSR). He belonged to Tajikistan and was keen to promote closeness and traditional friendship between India and Soviet Central Asia; he persuaded Soviet Central Asian Republics to accord a special place to Oriental Studies. His advice was heeded.

The Soviet government also approved promotion of Indian Studies. While promoting friendship between the two countries, it would provide input to Soviet foreign-policy makers. The need was felt to train indigenous cadres, experts in Indian languages, especially Urdu and Hindi. The Soviet government decided that Soviet workers in India must have a Soviet interpreter, knowing Hindi and Urdu.

The Tashkent University, therefore, launched a programme for teaching Hindi and Urdu. After Moscow and Leningrad, Tashkent became the third major centre for Indian studies (not only Indian languages). Gradually Indian History emerged as a subject of study and research in Tashkent, both in the University as well as in the institutions, run by the Academy of Sciences, Uzbekistan Soviet Socialist Republic.

In 1962 further first time two language teachers, Dr. Qamar Rais for Urdu and Dr. Bhola Nath Tiwari for Hindi were invited to teach in Tashkent. Their spell as teachers helped local students to update their knowledge of Hindi and Urdu. It was also decided to students to Indian Universities so that they could develop their speaking skills in Indian languages they had learnt in Tashkent. The realization was reinforced when the Soviets decided to further strengthen Indo-Soviet friendship.

One area in which the Soviet Union promoted active cooperation with India was education. The Soviets first agreed to enroll Indian students for research courses in scientific, technological and social-sciences and humanities. The medium of study remained Russian and it was necessary to impart basic knowledge of Russian language to Indian students. Indian students selected for higher studies were to study Russian language for six months prior to taking up higher studies. A Podgotovitelny Fakultet or Preparatory Faculty was opened for foreign students in Tashkent to impart newly arrived students skill in Russian language. Foreign students including Indians arriving in the Soviet Union were admitted to this faculty.

This scheme attracted a number of Indian students; gradually the Soviets felt that this scheme be extended to undergraduate studies. The institutions in Uzbekistan from now onwards admitted Indian students to undergraduate courses. This was in addition to Indian students admitted to undergraduate courses in Patrice Lamumba University, Moscow. With the passage of time, the influx of Indian students increased; they were admitted to undergraduate courses located in other republics of Central Asia, in Tajikstan, Azerbaijan, etc. In early1960s, Tashkent became embedded in Indian consciousness because of a tragic incident.

The Soviet-Chinese rift widened under Khruschev and Soviets drew nearer to India. When the 1965 Indo-Pakistan War concluded, the Soviets offered their mediation . Tashkent was chosen as the venue for a tripartite conference. Soviet, Prime Minister Kosygyn, the Pakistan President, General Ayub Khan and Indian Prime Minister, Lal Bahadur Sastri attended it in January 1966. The meeting was successful and India and Pakistan signed Tashkent Declaration. Indian Prime Minister Lal Bahadur Sastri suffered cardiac arrest and passed away in Tahkent.

Later on a statue of Gandhi was installed in Tashkent and Hindi was made a subject of study in Indian schools. Tashkent TV frequently showed Indian films and Raj Kapoor-Nargis pair was well known in Central Asia. Tashkent was a must on the itinerary of Indian visitors as it showed how backwardness, economic and social could be overcome within decades, given the will power. Indians visitors were undoubtedly impressed and Tashkent also showed its appreciation of India by assiduously promoting Indian studies.

Azimzanova concentrated on medieval Indian history and translated *Babur-nama*, the autobiography of the founder of the Mughal Empire into Russian. Nelya Ismailova studied Urdu and Uzbek scholars took up contemporary Indian authors as subject of their doctoral researches. One of the students of Hindi and Urdu became the first envoy of Uzbekistan in Delhi. They also threw up a cadre of interpreters from Russian into Urdu and Hindi and *vice versa*.

The initial effort of historians was primarily directed at describing Indo-Central Asian relations before the establishment of the Soviet regime in the area. Scholar wanted to discover the past roots of Indo-Central relationship. N.B. Baikova in 1964 published her monograph *Rol Srednei Azii v Russko-Indiiskyn Torgovykh Svyazyakh* where trade contacts between India and Central Asia between the 16th and 18th Centuries were described.

Rasulzade's *Iz Istorii Sredneaziatsko-indiiskikh Svayzei vtoroi poloviny XIX nachala XX veka* (Tashkent, 1968) carried forward story of economic cooperation to the early XIX Century. Rasulzade's work supplemented that of Baikova's narrative. Another work focusing on Indo-Central Asian relationship in 1960s was published by Ilyas Nizamutdinov who also discussed diplomatic and cultural exchanges in the Mughal period.

But must effective initiative came from Babajan Gafurov, who organized a series of conferences in India and the Soviet Union on Kushan history. The Kushan empire extended over both Central Asia and India and had played a decisive role in propagating Buddhism in Central Asia. This was to be a joint endeavour and an important conference of Indian and Soviet (including Central Asian) scholars was held in Dushanbe (Tajikstan). From now onwards Indian archaeologists were able to visit Buddhist sites excavated by Soviet archaeologist and enrich their knowledge of Kushan history and more correctly evaluate India impact on Central Asian art, architecture, culture, religion and society.

In 1960s scholars, both Indian and Central Asian, firmly established the historicity of ties between India and Central Asia. In 1970s these ties were both deepened and broadened.

The Indo-Central Asian ties received further stimulus after 1971 Indo-Pakistan War. In this war the Soviets had openly come in support The theme was Indo-Central Asian relations and the activities of Indians in Central Asia which was known in outlines only. The UGC with the approval of the Indian government under its Area of Studies Programme sought to promote Central Asian Studies in India to nurture millennia-old historic ties.

In the School of International Studies, Jawaharlal Nehru University, a department of Central Asian Studies was created. Dr. Ram Rahul, who had earlier gone to the Soviet Union and visited several parts of Uzbekistan was made in-charge of this sector. He published books on Central Asia. The Indo-Central Asia ties further developed. Each Central Asian Republic forged special relationship with one of the major Indian states. For example, Bihar and Kyrghyzstan became closely linked. There were exchanges of delegations between the two.

In 1980 the UGC opened under the aegis of Kashmir University, Srinagar, a centre of Central Asian Studies. The choice of Srinagar for this centre was apt. For centuries Kashmir was on the route to and from Central Asia. Even today Kashmir is India's nearest point to Central Asia. For this reason during sixties or seventies when Indo-Pak relations were at the lowest point Indian planes could not fly over Pakistan on way to Moscow. They then flew above Kashmir and took a left turn after reaching the Pamir Plateau on way to Moscow.

The Centre continues to function and should next year celebrate its Silver Jubilee. It brings out a Journal where research articles on Central Asia are published. It has research scholars who take up different facets of Central Asian history, economy and politics. They have published a number of monographs. In India Prof. Warikoo produced in 1986, *Central Asia and Kashmir* based on diligent researches in different archives in India. He clearly brought out the position of Kashmir as a crucial link between the two regions.

A very important piece of research was carried on by G.L. Dmtriyev in Tashkent who assiduously worked in local archives and wrote about the Indian merchant community in Central Asia and described how they were affected by the Russian conquest of Central Asia. Unfortunately, the dissertation remains unpublished.Only its extracts have been printed. An English translation of his essay entitled "From the History of Indian Colony in Central Asia" is published in *Central Asia and India,* by Shipra Publication, Delhi.

The same author diligently worked in Central Asian archives and wrote a work on Indian revolutionaries in Central Asia in 1920s, *Indian Revolutionaries in Central Asia.* Thanks to Maulana Abul Kalam Institute of Asian Studies, Kolkata the book is now available in English. In mid-eighties, Prof. Devendra Kaushik, who went to Tashkent as a Ph.D. Student in 1962 published his book *Indian and Central Asia in Modern Times* in 1985, based on data collected from different archives in Uzbekistan. The book gave to readers in English an idea how close economic relationship existed between the two regions before the Soviet period

R.G. Mukhminova's book (Tashkent, 1985) *Sotsialnaya Differentsiatsiya Naseleniya Gorodov Uzbekistana v XVIIw.* Was significant because she published documents of the 16th and 17th Centuries to show that Indian artisans lived in Central Asia and some of them were extremely prosperous.

Scholars now started taking a multidimensional view. In *Iz Istorii Kultunykh svyazei Narodov Srednei Azii I Indii* (Tashkent, 1986) scholars in their essays attempted to describe the cultural exchanges between the two areas since Buddhist times. In 1980s monographs convincingly showed that the two regions were linked by a common history. In 1980s a new dimension was added to the relationship between the two regions.

The Soviet Union facing economic difficulties was in short supply of consumer goods. The government also decided to open up Central Asia and to invite foreign collaboration to develop its economy. The tourist sector which if developed properly promised quick and beneficial results to local economy.

The Government invited Tatas to build hotel in Tashkent. Larsen and Toubro was invited to construct a hotel in Samarkand. The two organisations were in the process of finishing their work when the Soviet Union disintegrated and the nature of politics and economy all over Central Asia changed suddenly. During 1980s local entrepreneurship was not inactive. They discovered that India could satisfy their needs in (a) textiles and (b) pharmaceuticals and (c) leather goods. Computers were available in India and they could also be brought to Tashkent. A local shop *Ganga* came up in Tashkent. It sold mostly goods brought from India.

The locals from Uzbekistan, Kyrghyzstan and Kezakhstan made regular trips to India and brought back stitched cotton apparels which were eagerly purchased. They also brought medicines, then in short supply in Uzbekistan and fulfilled an important public need.

Local effort was supplemented by some Indian students, who found that by bringing textiles and medicine on their return trips, they could easily finance their visits to their homeland. Some of these students gathered sufficient expertise to devote there energies to the burgeoning business in Central Asia. The increased travel necessitated that passengers be issued visa quickly by the Indian embassy. For this purpose a small branch of the Indian Embassy in Moscow was opened in Tashkent in 1980s.

When the Sovereign Republic of Uzbekistan was proclaimed in 1991 after the Soviet collapse, this office took care of the relationship between India and Central Asian Republics till proper arrangements were made by opening embassies in the capital different Central Asian sovereign republics.

Conclusion

The four decades discussed here saw continuous improvement in Indo-Central ties even though they depended to Indo-Soviet Relations. In 1960s they were put on a firm pedestal after scholars through their researches showed that they were millennia-old. In 1970s and 1980s several monographs appeared and institutions were set up in India to promote Central Asian studies. In 1980s economic contacts developed. India's private sector arrived in Central Asia to help develop tourist in destroy. Local entrepreneurs began visiting India and brought textiles and medicines which were sold in local markets.

The deepening of contacts necessitated opening of a branch of Indian Embassy, Moscow in Tashkent to facilitate quick disposal of visa applications. The small office looked after Indian interests when Central Asian Sovereign Republics were born after the collapse of the Soviet-Union.

8

Cultural Relations between India and Tibet

An Overview of the Light from India

Claude Arpi

Where to start?

When I was asked to make a short presentation on the cultural relations between India and Tibet, I immediately asked myself the question : Where should I begin? Indeed, these relations have been as old as the Himalayas.

Can we consider that this saga started fifty millions years ago when the Indian island collided with the Asian plate. Without this 'natural' accident, life could have continued undisturbed for eternity on the Indian island, but it was perhaps neither the destiny of Tibet to remain a sea for ever, nor of India to be a perpetual island. The Indian subcontinent had to meet the Tethis Sea and create a new range of glorious mountains and the highest plateau in the world. It is probably what my Tibetan and Indian friends call '*karma*'. Who knows?

Though, it would have probably stretched history back too far, this 'lifting' had incalculable consequences for the history of Asia.

Historical Note

I would like to mention here something which has always amused me. In 1959, India had a secular government, however, the Ministry of External Affairs sent "An Historical Note" drafted by its Historical Division to the Chinese government in Beijing. This note entitled "*Historical Background of the Himalayan Frontier of India*" deals with the mythological past of the Himalayan range.

The objective of the Indian government was to define the border between India and Tibet, the note apparently did not impress Mao

Zedong who professed a more materialistic ideology. In fact, in his memoirs a former Foreign Secretary of Pakistan, Sultan M. Khan, then Pakistani Ambassador to China, recounted that he was once called by Zhou Enlai who told him that it was impossible to discuss anything seriously with the Indians, because they were constantly mixing history with mythology and religion. The Chinese Premier was probably referring to this Note.

Nonetheless, the point is that the great Himalayan range has always been a cultural continuum. It has been porous not only to trade but also for religious, political and cultural exchanges. India has always looked at these mountains as very special. To quote from the famous Note :

> The Himalayas have always dominated Indian life, just as they have dominated the Indian landscape...

The earliest reference to the Himalayas is in the *Rigveda* which was written about 1500 B.C. It states that the Himalayas symbolize all mountains (10th Mandala, 10th Adhyaya, Sukta 121.4).

The *Kena Upanishad*, written some time about 1000 B.C., speaks of Uma the daughter of the Himalayas – Umam haimavatim. The legend is that Uma, the daughter of the Himalayas, revealed the mystic idealism of the Upanishads to the gods. This is an imaginative expression of the historical fact that the thought the Upanishads was developed by the dwellers in the forests and fastnesses of the Himalayas. For centuries thereafter, the striving of the Indian spirit was directed towards these Himalayan fastnesses. Siva was the blue-necked, snow-crowned mountain god; Parvati was the spring-maiden daughter of the Himalayas; Ganga was her elder sister; and Meru, Vishnu's mountain, was the pivot the universe. The Himalayan shrines are still the goal of every Hindu Pilgrim.

The Note continues with the long spiritual saga of the Himalayas. For our purpose, we should only keep in mind that the Himalayan range is a geographical and cultural entity though on one side there is Bharat and on the other side, Tibet. Mount Kailash as well as the lakes of Manasarovar and Raksas, located in Western Tibet, culturally belong to both India and Tibet. They are as fervently revered by the Buddhists in the Land of Snows as by the hundreds of millions of Hindus for whom it is the abode of Lord Shiva.

In conclusion, whatever is happening on one side or the other of the Himalayas has always been and will always be interconnected.

Therefore, the cultural relations between Tibet and India are something which will continue to exist for ever, even if at times it has to survive at a lower ebb.

Kingdom Shangshung

The official history of Tibet usually starts with the enthronement of Nyatri Tsenpo, the first king of the Yarlung dynasty in 127 B.C. However, modern research in the pre-Buddhist civilisation of Tibet have revealed a highly developed culture linked with the indigenous Bon tradition. This culture flourished in the kingdom of Shangshung, which is said to be located in Western Tibet (around Mt. Tise, another name for Mt. Kailash).

Shangshung Script

Buddhist Tibetan historians have often stated that Tibet did not possess its own script until 640 A.D. when Songtsen Gompo sent his minister Thonmi Sambhota to India. Therefore, it was assumed that without a writing system, Tibet did not have a cultural tradition. For these historians, the only source of the Tibetan culture was the Buddha Dharma which was introduced in a civilisational desert; the existence and flourishing of the Tibetan culture were related only with the spread of the Buddha Dharma.

However, for several decades, research has been undertaken in the Bon tradition. It has been shown that the original faith of Tibet not only had a large corpus of literature of its own, but also a script, known as the Shangshung script. Prof. Namkhai Norbu, who came to the West as a young man to assist Prof. Giuseppe Tucci and teaches at the University of Napoli, has been one of the pioneers who spearheaded research in this direction. In this he has been emulated by many Western and Tibetan scholars. He wrote :

> According to Bon historical records, the original source of Tibetan writing system is the Maryig (Mar script) of Shangshung. There are many evidences to support this fact. In the libraries of very old monasteries in Tibet, there used to

> be many ancient manuscripts handwritten in a script referred to as Mar-tsungs which is just like Tibetan U-med (Headless Characters) writing in which letters are high and vowels short. When I was in my home town in Derge, I used to take lessons in the Tsugs writing of Tibetan U-chen (With Head Characters) and U-med from a reputed challigrapher who was over eighty years old. One day he taught me a Tibetan Tsugs known as :
>
> Lhabab-yig (heaven descended script)... when I read the very ancient manuscripts written in Mar-Tsugs, I was able to observe and conclude that Lha-bab yig is the real Mar-yig.

It can also be proved that the origin and source of the Mar-Tsugs and the U-med which we use today are one and the same.

Other scholars said that it derived from an old Brahmi script.

Medicine

The Bon system of knowledge is often divided in twelve parts or "Twelve Lores". Most of them deal with astrology, divination, exorcism or mastery over spirits. One of the lore is called the "Lore of Healing" which has several aspects similar to the Ayurvedic system. The 'speciality' of the Bons was probably the knowledge of the natural forces and the way to deal with them. Many features were later incorporated in the Tibetan Buddhist system of medicine.

Philosophy

After the seventh century, the Bon philosophy interacted with the Buddhist philosophy and it is not easy today to discern the indigenous components. In fact, both have influenced each other and large similarties are found. However, many powerful myths widely used in Bon literature have similarities with the ones known in ancient India (the cosmic egg for example). It shows that India and Tibet certainly had strong and regular relations at the time of Buddha and even before.

All these aspects of the Indo-Tibetan relations need further research.

The Buddha

More than 2,500 years ago, an event which was to change the face of Asia and the world, occurred in India. A young Prince named Siddartha was born in a small state in the Himalayan foothills. He was to become the Buddha. No other human life had ever had such a profound influence on the cultural, social and political life of India, Tibet, China and most of the other Asian nations. The Buddha and his teachings have been at the core of relations between Tibet and India for practically 1400 years.

Historical Relations between India and Tibet

Tibet indeed is proud of its Indian heritage

Tibetan history has always emphasized the importance of Buddhism and India in the development of the culture of Tibet. As we have seen it has often been to the detriment of the local pre-Buddhist faith and culture.

From early times, India has always been considered as the 'Land of the Gods' in the Tibetan popular mind. The following legend demonstrates the strong association between India and Tibet many centuries before the Buddha Dharma was brought to Tibet.

In 127 B.C., the inhabitants of Yarlung Valley elevated Nyatri Tsenpo as the first king of Tibet. The legend tells us that he was a sort of god-like being who descended from the sky using a kind of 'sky-rope.' Nyatri, continues the legend, was originally from India; he was the son of a royal family related to the Buddha's family. Before reaching Tibet, he had been wandering between India and Tibet and finally came down in Yarlung Valley where he met some herdsmen grazing their yaks. The Tibetans believed that he had come from Heaven. Twelve chieftains took him on their shoulders and made him the first king of Tibet. His enthronement marks the beginning of the Yarlung Dynasty of Tibet. The Tibetan royal calendar still dates from that year.

Buddhism was introduced in Tibet in the fifth century A.D. during the reign of Thori Nyatsen, the twenty-eighth King of the Yarlung Dynasty. Once again, the Dharma came from the sky in the form of a casket falling on Yubulakhang, the royal Palace; the casket contained the Mantra of Avalokiteshvara, the Patron and Protector of Tibet. The king was unable to read the scripts, but kept them as a Holy Relic for future generations.

It was during the reign of Songtsen Gompo, the Thirty-third King of the dynasty, that Buddhism became a state affair.

After marrying a Nepalese and a Chinese Princess, the king converted himself to Buddhism. The importance of these marriages needs to be emphasized as they played a vital role in the spread of Buddhism in Tibet. Though Songtsen Gampo had other wives (in particular the daughter of the king of Shangshung), it was Bikruti (Bhrikuti, the Nepalese) and Wengshen (the Chinese) who most influenced the politics and religion of Tibet.

During his reign Tibet became the strongest military power in Central Asia. Though the Chinese Emperor and the Nepalese king were none too keen to 'present' their daughters to the Tibetan king who was considered uneducated and a barbarian, they had no choice but to accept the 'friendly' offer of their powerful neighbour.

Historically, Songtsen Gampo was the king who built the Tibetan Empire which extended to the Chinese capital Chang'an (modern Xian) in the East, to the Pamirs and Samarkhand in the West and the Himalayas in the South. It was the greatest empire in Asia. It was the time during which the capital was moved from Yarlung to Lhasa and a fort was built where the Potala Palace stands today. The adoption of Buddhism as the religion of the court is an important watershed in the cultural relations between the two nations.

Tibetan Script

Perhaps one of the greatest merits of the king was to have sent his Minister Thomi Sambhota to India with sixteen students to study Buddhism and Sanskrit. On their return, they developed a new script which is still in use today. Accurate translations of Buddhist scriptures from Sanskrit into Tibetan began soon after.

Usually, it is believed that the Tibetan script has been copied from the script used in Kashmir in the 7th century. The Dalai Lama when he visited India in 1956, told an audience : "*Thonmi Sambhota invented the Tibetan script based on the Nagari and Sharda scripts of northern and central India respectively.*"

Other theories exist. Even today, Tibetans use two scripts U-Chen (with headline) and U-Mey (without headline). Another theory is that the Lantsa script, a decorative script used by the Buddhists in Nepal is the origin of the U-Chen and the Vartu script has become the U-Mey.

A more acceptable theory is that the U-Chen script derives from a late Gupta script in use when Thomi Sambhota visited India. The U-Mey would only be an adaptation of the U-Chen, like the lower case is derived from the upper case in the Roman script. The great scholar Gedun Choeppel has demonstrated the evolution from U-Chen to U-Mey with a chart.

Whatever the theory, we believe it is obvious that the present Tibetan script has its origin in India. It is certainly the greatest contribution that Bharat could offer to the Tibetan culture. Apart from the script, the Tibetan grammar imported by Thomi Sambhota is based on a Sanskrit grammar in use in the great Indian *Viharas* during the 7th century. One can understand that if Sambhota had received royal instructions to translate as many Buddhist scriptures as possible, the easiest and the most accurate way was to adapt the Sanskrit grammar and syntax to the Tibetan language. It facilitated the rendering of the exact meaning of the sacred sutras. *The Kanjur* (108 volumes), which is the collection of the Buddha's sayings, could thus be accurately translated into Tibetan. An interesting fact is that today it is relatively easy to retranslate texts from Tibetan into Sanskrit and to rediscover the correct meaning of original texts which have disappeared more than ten centuries ago.

Numerous texts were translated during the reign of Songtsen Gampo; the king himself took a great interest in the translation work and became a scholar. For the first time, some of the Buddhist precepts were incorporated into the laws of the land. The Tibetan minister's visit to India was followed by hundreds of Tibetan scholars descending the Himalayan slopes in search of the teaching of the Buddha in its purity and integrity. Their only objective was to carry back the Buddha Dharma to the Land of Snows.

During the following centuries, a large number of Indian pandits, tantrics and siddhas would be attracted by the nascent spirituality on the Roof of the World.

Pandits and Tantriks from India

The thirty-seventh king, Trisong Detsen (741-798) sent emissaries to India and invited the great Indian abbot Shantarakshita to come to Tibet to teach the Dharma and ordain the first monks.

Richardson in his history of Tibet makes an interesting remark :

> "The religious foundations of Songtsen Gampo and his immediate successors were quite modest chapels and Buddhist influence probably reached only a small number of the people."

But the fact that the king himself adopted the new faith had incalculable effects on the religious, cultural and political future of Tibet. Soon after his arrival in Tibet, Shantarakshita faced a lot of difficulties due to the strong antagonism with the indigenous Bonpo faith. He convinced the king that the only solution was to call the great Tantric Master from India, Guru Padmasambhava. Only he could subdue the forces adverse to the Buddhist faith and overcome the resistance of the Bon practitioners.

There are many accounts of the magical powers of Padmasambhava, but in a very Indian (and Tantric) way, he always tried to convert and use the forces opposing his work instead of destroying them. These forces were later to become the protectors of the new religion.

After performing many rites, 'local deities' in Samye in Central Tibet were subdued and finally, the first Buddhist monastery in Tibet was completed in 766 A.D. The local deities became the Protectors of the temple and Shantarakshita could finally ordain the first Tibetan monks.

Under Trisong Detsen, Buddhism was established as a state religion and the principle of compassion and *Ahimsa* was inculcated into the rather violent and shamanistic population. The zeal shown by his people in the pursuit of war was thereafter used for inner researches. As Buddhism penetrated all aspects of life, the once barbarian tribes learned to respect all life forms down to the least insect. Fishing and hunting were banned and recognized as sins.

Samye Debate

Before dying, Shantarakshita, the Indian Pandit (known as 'Boddhisattva' to the Tibetans) predicted that a dispute would arise between the two schools of Buddhism that were at that time spreading in Tibet.

The first one—the Chinese school, probably influenced by Taoism— was of the opinion that enlightenment was an instantaneous revelation or realization. It could be obtained only through complete mental and physical inactivity and renunciation. This system of thought had spread throughout China.

The second school—taught by the Indian Pandits and known as the 'gradual school'—asserted that enlightenment was a gradual process, not an 'instant' one, requiring long study, practice and analysis and the accumulation of virtues and good deeds. Shantarakshita had brought these teachings with him when he came to Tibet and, having prophesized the dispute, he indicated that one of his Indian disciples would come from India to defend the theory of the Indian school. Over a period of two years (792-794), the famous debate, known in history as the 'Samye Debate' took place in Samye.

Hoshang, a Chinese monk, represented the Chinese stand known as the 'instant school' and Kamalashila who had come from India as prophesied by his *guru*, defended the Indian view. At the end of the debate, Kamalashila was declared the winner and the king issued a proclamation naming the Indian Path the orthodox faith for Tibet. The document was written on blue paper with golden letters and distributed throughout the Kingdom.

From that time on, India became the only source of religious knowledge for Tibet. This example is one of the many, which illustrates the important role played by India in the cultural, spiritual and political life of Tibet in the early period of its history.

The Return of Buddhism to Tibet : the Second Propagation

An empire is truly great when the spirit which built it can survive that empire's destruction and reappear under a new and more refined form.

This is what would eventually happen to the Buddhist civilization in Tibet after the systematic eradication of Buddhism by King Lang Darma who usurped the throne from his brother King Ralpachen at the beginning of the 9th century.

When King Lang Darma was killed by a Tibetan monk in 842, he had managed to destroy most of the Buddhist institutions in Tibet. An even worse consequence of the persecution initiated by the king was that for the next seventy years, no monk could be ordained.

Lang Darma's assassination marked the end of the Yarlung Dynasty. The Tibetan state lost its political homogeneity and became fragmented into several principalities (such as Yarlung, Purang or Sakya).

However, local princes or chieftains continued to focus their attention on their southern neighbours, India and Nepal. Due to the efforts of some of the rulers of the provinces of the erstwhile Tibetan kingdom, a revival of Buddhism became possible on the Roof of the World.

Perhaps because they were the closest to North India and at the same time had been spared by the Muslim invaders, the spiritual and cultural renaissance originated from the Himalayan regions of Spiti and Ladakh in India and Ngari, Tholing and Purang in Tibet.

Buddhism in India

Before looking at this renaissance movement, known as the Second Propagation, we must have a quick glance at the evolution of Buddhism in India during the closing years of the first millennium.

Though perhaps the Buddha never wanted to create a new religion, Buddhism as a structured new faith had slowly emerged in India, especially during and after the reign of Asoka. Many great monastic universities such as Nalanda, Vikramashila or Otantapuri flourished in North India. They were patronized by kings and very rich lay patrons. They were the main centres of learning and the repositories of the knowledge of that time.

Nalanda was the most famous of these great monastic universities and the curriculum covered not only Buddhist scriptures but also linguistics, medicine, astrology, debate and other sciences. Tantrayana had been incorporated into the teachings of these monastic universities, especially in Vikramashila, the monastery of Atisha who would soon play an important role in Tibetan history. Not only had the Pandits, the scholars and the abbots studied the Tantras, but many of them had intensely practiced these teachings and written extensive commentaries.

The Revival in Tibet

A few individuals personify this renaissance. One should cite: the Indian monk, Atisha Dipamkara; the Tibetan monk Rinchen Zongpo; the King of Guge Yeshe Od and also a Tibetan layman called Marpa. All of them symbolize the continuous movement of men and ideas across the Himalayas and the manner in which the Buddha Dharma was preserved in its integrity.

Though different in character, upbringing and education, they have all in their own way contributed much to the revival of Buddhism in Tibet. They were responsible for countless translations of the original teachings of the Buddha which were thus saved for posterity. Less than two centuries later, under the Muslim onslaught and the revivalism of Hinduism, these scriptures disappeared from their land of origin. In the first years of the second millennium, the monastic discipline declined quickly in Tibet and many original teachings were lost.

The Role of Yeshe Od, King of Guge

Guge was one of the principalities in Western Tibet; one of its kings, Yeshe Od was to become the main instrument in the renaissance of the Buddha Dharma on the Roof of the World. He ordered many young Tibetans to go to India to meet saints, yogis, siddhas and scholars in the great Indian *Viharas* and bring back to Tibet Buddhist manuscripts and translate them into Tibetan. The most famous amongst these Tibetan masters who travelled to the hot plains of India, was Rinchen Zangpo.

In those days, the frontier between Tibet and the Himalayan region was not a fixed border as it has become in the second part of the twentieth century. It was rather an 'undefined' borderline, at least culturally. For example, the influence of Rinchen Zangpo spread as much in the Tibetan provinces of Ngari or Purang as in Spiti, Lahaul, Kinnaur and Zanskar districts of North India.

Although he managed to get many monks ordained, Lhalama Yeshe Od realised that the doctrine of the *Tantras* was no longer understood and properly practiced by most of the members of the Sangha. Many pretended to be tantric practitioners, they often refused to follow any of the Vinaya's precepts opening the door to many perversions.

The king, very disturbed by this critical situation, decided to send Gya Tsondru Senge as an emissary to India. His task was to find a way to translate as many original Sanskrit texts as he could. He was also asked to try and locate a Pandit who would be able to subdue the negative forces and bring back the purity of the Dharma to Tibet. He eventually discovered Atisha Dipankara, a Bengali Master who had all the requisite qualities to re-establish the monastic rule in Tibet.

The king of Guge collected gold and sent it to Atisha to try to convince him to come and teach in Tibet. In order to find more gold, the king thought to visit Turkestan. Unfortunately, he was captured on the way by the powerful king of Garlok. Yeshe Od's nephew Jangchub Od, hearing of the king's fate, decided to pay a ransom to the Garlok king. He first offered one hundred gold coins, but the Garlok king told him that it was not enough. He went back and forth several times, but the king of Garlok repeatedly refused to release Lhalama Yeshe. Finally, one day Jangchub Od managed to have a private conversation with his uncle who told him that whatever gold he could collect should be used to go to India and to bring back Atisha to Tibet. He told him that his life was not so important and he was happy to give it as an offering to the renaissance of the Doctrine in Tibet.

Back in Tibet, Jangchub Od obeyed the last wishes of his uncle and sent a delegation to Vikramashila to meet Atisha who was informed of the sacrifice of the old king. It was difficult for Atisha to refuse the invitation. The party proceeded to Tholing where the King Jangchub Od received Atisha. From that day on, Pandit Atisha was invited to many places in Tibet where he taught the precepts of the Buddha, he consecrated temples and ordained new monks.

When he had left his monastery in India, Atisha had promised the Abbot of Vikramashila that he would return to India within three years. After three years in Tibet, Atisha decided to go to Purang near the Indian border to fulfil his promise. Atisha remained for a year at Purang and gave many teachings but never went back to India. The *darshan* of his country from the border town was enough to fulfil his vow.

We have gone into some details in this episode because it demonstrates the fervour and aspiration of the people of Tibet to bring back the Buddha Dharma to the Land of Snows in its integrity.

Tibetan Medicine

The Tibetan system of Medicine, known as *Swa Rigpa* (the Art of

Healing) is an interesting example showing India's influence on the culture of Tibet and the constant interactions between the two nations. As for all Tibetan traditional sciences, the medical system is said to originate from the Buddha Sakyamuni himself. However, the Tibetan historical texts, particularly. *The Survey of Tibetan Medical History* written by the Regent Desi Sangye Gyatso during the 18th century differs very little from the Vedic texts expounding the history of the Ayurveda. The only difference is that Buddha takes the place of Vedic rishis as the originator of the medical system.

The history of the Tibetan system of medicine is usually classified into three categories.

1. The spread of Medicine in the God Realm
2. The spread of Medicine in the Human Realm (in India)
3. The spread of Medicine in Tibet

In the spread of medicine in the God realm, the customary in-fighting between gods, the churning of the ocean in which is hidden the ambrosia of immortality, the using of Mt. Meru as stirring rod, the encounter between the Buddha and Brahma and the final recovery of the ambrosia are recounted. In the Tibetan tradition, it is Brahma who receives the teachings from Buddha : the medical science is thus transmitted through a text known as *The 100,000 Verses of Healing.*

In the second part, eight ancient Rishis teach Sage Atreya. His knowledge is compiled in the *Charaka Samhita* which is said to be the commentary of the knowledge taught by Rishi Bharadwaja. Atreya's disciples in turn wrote commentaries which became the basic root-texts of the ayurvedic system. Later the sage Susruta composed the *Susruta Samhita* which was later revised by Nagarjuna, the founder of the Middle Path (*Madhyamika*) school of Buddhism.

According to Tantric scriptures, the Buddha Sakyamuni taught the Four Tantras to four different types of disciples. He took the form of the Medicine Buddha, Bhaishaguru, and taught at the celestial palace of medicine in Tanadug, a place said to be located in the province of Uddiyana (modern Swat in Pakistan).

The different disciples of the Buddha heard the teachings according to their aptitude and needs. The gods heard the teachings as the *100,000 Verses of Healing,* while the Rishis were taught the

Charaka Samhita. The non-Buddhists received the *Krishna Isvara Tantra* and the Buddhist disciples heard them as the *Teachings of the Three Protectors*.

The history of the origin of Tibetan medicine is closely mixed with events of the Buddha's life such as the sermon on the Four Noble Truths or some other teachings at the Venture Peak near Rajagriha.

The Tibetan texts also record the life and teachings of Jivaka, a famous doctor who lived at the same time as Buddha and became one of his disciples. Nagarjuna is said to be the author of several treatises on medicine. His knowledge was transmitted to Asvaghosa who himself wrote several books, the best known being the *Astanga-hrdaya-samhita* (The Eight Branches) which is still today a reference for the medical students.

During the reign of King Songtsen-Gompo, physicians and medical experts from India, China, Central Asia and Persia were requested to bring their own system of medicine (it is said that some even came from Greece).

A century later, the famous physician Yuthok Yonten Gompo the Elder thrice visited India and later compiled the Gyud Shi (or Four Tantras) which is still today the base of the Tibetan medical knowledge. Using Indian medical scriptures, it incorporated some features of the other systems, particularly the indigenous system of Tibet. A very original and well adapted *Art of Healing* was born.

After 6 visits, Yuthok Yonten Gompo the Younger, who lived in the 12th century completed in India, the work of Yuthok the Elder (he is said to be his reincarnation). The 156 Chapters of the Gyud Shi are still considered as the assence of Tibetan medical knowledge and are studied as such not only in Tibet, but also by the Tibetans in exile in India and the local Amchis (medical practitioners) in the Himalayan region.

It is worth noting that *Astanga-hrdaya-samhita* still exists not only in its Tibetan translation (dating from Rinchen Zangpo's time), but also in its original Sanskirt version. It is a unique occasion to study both versions and marvel at the quality of the translation. It also helps to establish terminological parallels between both languages and shows the proximity of both literatures.

Buddhism Disappears from India

However, in the country of the Enlightened One, the Dharma soon disappeared under the onslaught of Muslim hordes from Central Asia. A new culture based on power and brutality replaced the old compassionate wisdom.

To be fair, it should be mentioned that, in the history, whenever strict adherence to the monastic rules stopped, degeneration overtook the Sangha. When monks began to aspire to political power and wealth, instead of consecrating their lives to the Dharma, India's strength vanished and the doors were wide open to invaders. This is probably one of several reasons for which Buddhism disappeared from India.

The sacrifice of the old king of Ngari had not been in vain, India through one of her great sons had restored the Buddhist precepts to the Land of Snows.

Tantric practitioners could again understand the deep meaning of the tantric scriptures and above all, the teachings of love and compassion of the gurus of Atisha could be transmitted to all – lay people, kings or lamas.

India showed her kindness to Tibet when the abbots and monks of the great *viharas* in India allowed the most knowledgeable among them to leave for the Himalayas to propagate the Buddha faith. Perhaps, the wisest amongst them knew that Atisha would not return to the hot plains of India and that their own Dharma would soon be replaced by a blinder and less compassionate one.

During this period, the political life of Tibet was deeply intermingled with its religious life. The modern concept of 'secularism' did not exist in India and Tibet. Any strong religious or spiritual personality was bound to have an influence on the politics of his times. This is what would happen during the predominance of the Sakya Lamas (13th-15th century) and later with the Dalai Lamas.

An interesting aspect of the decline of Buddhism in India is the migration of not only Indian monks and saints to Tibet, but also artists. As an author pointed out in his study of Tucci's discoveries in Western Tibet :

> "It is not only the inspiration of Indian art that was responsible for the beautiful frescoes adorning the walls though now in ruin, of Western Tibetan monasteries, but Indian artists themselves migrated into that country and settled there."

Tucci himself said that :

> "The sources of information speak not only of pundits and doctors invited to the court of the kings of Guge or having taken refuge there, in a period which marks the decline of fortune for Buddhism in India, but also of artists, specially from Kashmir who introduced there the Indian traditions."

In another study of Tucci's work in Tibet, Moulik had written :

> The Mussalman torment which was in its full swing at this time, the hostility of the new sects, the rebirth of the orthodox schools, already gave signs of the decline of Buddhism on the plain of Hindusthan. The monks and saints, the painters and sculptors, from the convents and universities, sacked and menaced by the Mussalmans, were gradually drawn into the Himalayan valleys, and were rescued by the magnificent piety of the Kings of Guge. Here on the immense desolation (speaking of today) reigned an unusual fervour of life, cities and temples, monasteries and markets. The artistic genius of India left there its admirable traces which the course of time and carelessness of man are going to obliterate.

At the beginning of the twelfth century, Tibet could no longer draw support from its southern neighbour. It had to find a new solution to survive and prosper.

Tibet turns North and East

The history of Tibet took another turn with the rise of the Mongol Empire at the end of the 12th century. After the Mongol hordes of Genghis Khan overran half of Europe and most of Asia, including China, the Empire of Genghis Khan became one of the vastest the world has ever known of. The Tibetans had no choice, but to ally with their powerful neighbours.

An arrangement was found. The Lamas (first the Lamas of the Sakya School of Tibetan Buddhism) became the teachers of the Mongol Khans who in turn gave military protection to the Land of Snows. India was nowhere in the scheme which continued for a few centuries under the Ming and Qing (Manchu) dynasties.

However, for a Tibet more and more close in on itself, India continued to remain the 'sacred land'. In the words of the Fourteenth Dalai Lama :

> "For us, it has always been the Holy Land. It was the birthplace of the founder of the Buddhist culture and the source of wisdom brought to our mountains hundreds of years ago by Indian saints and seers. The religions and societies of Tibet and India have developed in different lines, but Tibet was still a child of Indian civilization."

In 1950, India was still the main place of pilgrimage for all Tibetan Buddhists.

Modern Times

In August 1947, India became independent. The Indo-Tibetan relations were not a priority for Nehru's government which soon got embroiled in the Kashmir tangle. However, in July 1947, Delhi informed the Lhasa government that India was keen to continue to relate as before.

Eventually when the new Indian Republic took shape, the *Dharma Chakra* was included in the Indian national flag and the *Asoka Pillar* became the national emblem. It reminded the people of Tibet of the times when North India and Tibet were a cultural unit.

With the signing of the Panchsheel Agreement in April 1954, India accepted the Chinese contention that Tibet was a "Region of China". However, most of the clauses of the Agreement were related to cultural exchanges (such as right of the pilgrims) between India and Tibet.

Two years later, in 1956, the 2500th anniversary of the Buddha Mahaparinirvana was celebrated on a grand scale by the Government of India. The young Dalai Lama and Panchen Lamas were invited to participate. In a speech in Delhi the Dalai Lama declared:

> This year, with a view to commemorating the kindness shown by the Compassionate One, India is celebrating the 2500th Anniversary of His on a scale worthy of her great tradition. India has invited many distinguished guests from Buddhist and non-Buddhist countries to these celebrations, and I consider myself extremely fortunate in being able to attend them. We are convinced that such great deeds of India will

> not only strengthen our faith in the Dharma in the East, but will also go a long way in the propagation of the eternal truths in the West.
>
> If the Dharma spreads all over the world, it will undoubtedly yield good fruits for our future life; but even in our present existence, hatred, exploitation of one by another, and the ways and deeds of violence will disappear, and the time will come when all will live in friendship and love in a prosperous and happy world. I am glad to have an opportunity of expressing my humble appreciation of the efforts which many peace-loving great countries are making day and night towards the freedom of small countries and the elimination of aggression and war. I feel that our lives would be entirely aimless if the Dharma which was brought to our land by great scholars at such immense cost were allowed to decay.

Unfortunately for the Dalai Lama, less than three years after his first visit to India, he had to flee his country and take refuge there.

Himalayan Buddhist Culture

It is hardly necessary to mention that large parts of Northern India have shared a religion and cultural tradition with Tibet since the time of the First Propagation. The culture of Ladakh, Lahaul, Spiti, Kinnaur, Arunachal Pradesh or Sikkim is closely blended with the Tibetan civilization. It is worth pointing out that a Dalai Lama, Tsangyang Gyaltso (the 6th Dalai Lama) was born in the Tawang district of Arunachal Pradesh; very late in his life he was recognized as the reincarnation of the 5th Dalai Lama and taken away to Lhasa. Still many traces of his youth can be seen in villages around Tawang.

The exchanges between Indian Tibet (so called by many scholars) and the Land of Snows continued to flourish till the end of the fifties. I personally remember having seen in many monasteries of Hmachal Pradesh and Ladakh the photo of a Lama, Norbu Rinpoche. As a *yogi* he was highly revered by the local population. When I asked more details, I was told that he had received his training in yogic sciences (particularly the *Six Yogas of Naropa*) near Derge, in Eastern Tibet, today located in Sichuan Province of China. It tends to prove that till the middle of the 20th century, cultural exchanges between the Indian Himalayas and all the regions of Tibet were still very much alive.

Cultural Relations Today

The Dalai Lama crossed to India on March 31, 1959. During the next years, he was followed by more than one lakh of his countrymen. After being given asylum by the Government of India, he first lived in Mussoorie for a couple of years and later established his headquarters in Dharamsala (Himachal Pradesh). From here he strove to preserve the culture of Tibet which in Tibet was endangered.

Amongst others, he re-established several institutions:

The School of Medicine in Dharamsala (Men-Tsee-Khang)
The Tibetan Institute of Performing Arts in Dharamsala
The library of Tibetan Works and Archives in Dharamsala which preserves old manuscripts and published books.
The three great *gelukpa* (yellow sect) *monasteries* (Ganden, Sera and Drepung) in Karnataka.
The Tibet House in Delhi, a cultural centre for the preservation of the Tibetan culture in the Indian capital.

With the help of the Indian Government, a Tibetan University was opened in Sarnath (Uttar Pradesh). Not only it is now famous Central Institute of Higher Tibetan Studies providing facilities to students up to the Ph.D. level, but it has also started a very bold programme of re-translation of lost manuscript from Tibetan into Sanskrit. Luminaries like Prof. G.C. Pande have headed this Institution.

Most of the monastic universities which existed in Tibet before 1959, have today been re-established in India. One could mention:

The Sakya Centre in Rajpur (Uttaranchal)
The Mindroling monastery in Clement Town (Uttaranchal)
The Karmapa headquarters in Rumtek (Sikkim)
Several other important monasteries in Karnataka and West Bengal

The Bon tradition is also represented in Dolanji (Himachal Pradesh).

It seems that the Buddhist Pandits have returned to India after a long period of seclusion on the Roof of the World.

Though the cultural relations between India and Tibet have gone through difficult times, they have survived many onslaughts over the centuries. The presence of the Dalai Lama in India and the interest of the Government of India are the best guarantee to their survival.

9

Indo-Uzbek Literary and Linguistic Relations Throughout 11-18 Centuries

Azad N. Shamatov

Bearing in mind that Independent Uzbek Republic came to existence only not earlier than in 1991 i.e. at the end of 20th century one should consider that during the period marked above it had been representing a certain part of the greater Central Asia, comprising its contemporary regions like Tashkent, Sir-Darya, Farghana Valley, Samarqand, Bukhara, Qashq-Darya, Surkhan-Darya, Khwarazm and Karakalpakistan as a whole.

Moreover, literary and Language developments during the proposed period, as it is well-known, proved to have been going on as integrated process within the framework of various Medieval and New Times state structures moulded after Sasanid Empire's administrative standard.

As for Medieval India it is commonly regarded as an integral part of the whole geopolitical area defined widely as South Asia proper. That's why one can treat the Indo-Uzbek relations as interactions between South and Central Asia in the most broad sense.

As it is well-known the both regions from the ancient times were object of various foreign invasions and this phenomena has left its great impact on their cultural background embodying in itself a substantial relics of numerous influences and synthetic elements, so that one can mention Achaemenids Empire, partly including North-Western India (5-3 centuries B.C.), Alexander, the Great's Conquests, bringing afterwards Greek-Hellenic Cultural Influence on Buddhist Art (3rd century B.C.) and at last Arabian Khalifate (7th—8th centuries A.D.) affecting the destinies of local peoples for a millennia.[1]

It's quite natural that these factors immensely contributed to the social, political, religious, ideological, commercial, economic, cultural and domestic conditions formations in both regions.

In this respect a special role belongs to Arabic and Persian and their Literary Traditions. Earlier local cultural values had been enriched by Antique and Hellenistic science achievements as well as by well-developed religious and philosopical sources, inspired by ancient subjects and images of Judaism, Christianity and Pre-Islamic Arabians. There also let of highly artistic Poetry, which preserved and cultivated masterpieces of Ancient Semitic, Zoroastrian and Manichean Lore and Belle Letters having borrowed and absorbed in a brand new system of Versification, i.e. Aruz, which was subsequently elaborated to perfection in literary activities of various ethnic groups inhabiting the region.

We should take into account the great influence of Buddhist Culture extending to the vast territories including Central, South-East Asia and even the Far East. It can be distinctly traced in Ancient Turkic, Sogdian, Chinese, Mongolian, Tibetan regions some particular trends of this syncretic culture by its origin and development might be found also in other spheres of civilized activities like Philosophical and Social Thought, Architecture, various fields of Music, Choreography and Applied Arts as well.

Although some traces of this global process indeed had been already found and recorded in scholarly investigations but a complete recreation of the historical phenomena related has remained a far-reaching task could be accomplished by joint systematized efforts of scholars.

The present essay mainly observed only principal features of the process, outlined on the basis of original sources. Side by side with highlighting differentiation of the various aspects of the problem, our approach is directed at intercommunication of Indo-Muslim rapprochement and intimacy as a general course of cultural and historical process, which has been stimulated by linguistic processes of "Muslim Lexicon" borrowing, adaptating and assimilating in New Indian and Central Asian languages.

In this connection the main attention is given to the problem of Historical role of Indian Muslims as a new social stratum, which appeared in India by the midle of the 14th century. The same process in Central Asia had started more earlier and rapidly than in India since a local population had already consequent experienced Paganism, Zorastranism, Manichean, Buddhism and even Nestorian Christianity.

Thus, a considerable part of this social stratum was reinforced by newly converted Muslims from local Indians and Central Asians, and this phenomenon created the favourable pre-conditions for social and linguistic assimilation of non-Indian and as well as of non-Central Asian speaking ethnic groups.

In India at the primary stage of the coexistence of two religious communities there were two main features. The first was a formation of a new culture, which has synthesized the Indian and Muslim traditions and embraced many spheres of social relations, being under formation during the period.

The second one was an expansion growth and consolidation of reciprocal rapprochement, which defined synthetic phenomena in linguistic evolution of Northern and Southern India and accelerated the linguistic interference and following integration between both communities.

In its own turn the period witnessed devastating endless wars and campaigns, feuds and regional tumults, for instance. The most notable of these were Mahmud Ghaznavi's invasions and plunderings across both regions (998-1030), Mongols, i.e. Genghiz Khan's raids and conquests over Central Asia, Middle East and Caucauses (13th century) as well as subjugation of Central, East and South India by Delhi Sultans (14-16 centuries) and finally, invasion of India by Babur establishing Moghul Empire (16th century). Nevertheless it was presented by the historians as a period respectively more or less fruitful in terms not only of literary activities, but also of literary and language contacts between various parts of the region.

It seems appropriate to sketch briefly some synthetic phenomena in ethnic and social life which served as a definite historical background for the trends being investigated on.

The India an overwhelming majority of the research scholars put a particular accent on nobility of the Delhi Sultanate which "exhibited very miscellaneous origins, not just Turks, but also Khurasanis and other Persians (Tajiks), Ghuris and Kohjas"[2]. We find a definite presence among the Delhi Sultanate's noble class a lot of representatives from Central Asia, including Turks (the ancestors of the present Uzbeks, Turkmens, Kazakhs, Karakalpaks and Kyghizs) as well as of the Tajiks and Khurasanis, part of the population of modern Central Asia and Afghanistan from Itranian origin[3].

We also come cross a very significant fact of sending "a strong military contingent" by the ruler of Central Asia to Sind "to be present in the royal army camp in Thatta in 1346."

If our former data in general concerns with Delhi proper and some parts of Northern India, there is also an abundance of the facts on situation in Southern India. Paying attention at first to the Bahmani Kingdom in Deccan one can imagine an extremely complicated picture arising from a survey of ethnic diversity there. Referring to the paper of Muhammad S. Siddiqu "Ethnic Change in the Bahmanid Society."[4] We know that "the majority of local Muslims professed the Sunni faith" and represented a variety of newcomers from the various parts of Muslim world. We can refer to another observation of him, stating that "Distinguished alien figures like Sayyid Hussain Badakshi, Mir Ali Farrukh Badakshi. Khursro Khan Uzbek... were attained to his (i.e. Bahmanid) court."

He adds "moreover we consider as the most interesting that Jalal Khan (grandson of Jalal Bukhari) and etc... were... married to Ala'ad Din Ahmad's (i.e. the ruler's) sisters and..." "Another daughter of the Sultan became the spouse of a Chingizi prince, Shah Quli Sultan". So that becomes obvious that in spite of extensive influx of newcomers from many non-central Asian Eastern countries the Badakhshis (i.e. from Badakhshan), Bukharis (i.e. from Bukhara) and Uzbeks (as one of medieval Central Asian tribes which afterwards became an integral part of modern Uzbed nationality) have been representing a sizable and powerful group of Deccani nobility and relatives of the Sultans.

The same picture is in general of neighbouring Gujarat as well as to West Punjab.

One of the most popular medieval Sufis Hazrat Qutab-i-Alam was "an illustrious descendant of Makhdum Jalal Jahaniyan, the ancestor of the Bukhari Sayyids of Gujarat. He came from Uch, which now forms a part of Bahawalpur...in the West Punjab. Uch, though a small place in itself, has been associated with the names of Bukhari Saints and Ismaili missionaries".[5]

Now if we try to define a reasons of such a great exodus of people from Central Asia and its influx to India, Dr. Surendra Gopal, points out, that "Internal political upheavals in Central Asia immediately drew into their vortex the people inhabiting the fringe of the subcontinent...... The Islamized Turks mounted their invasions on India from Central Asia and established their empire here in the 13th century. Immediately, they were confronted by the Mongols whose occupation of Central Asia unleashed mass exodus raids continued from almost a century. The new rulers needed the skilful Central Asian horsemen for their cavalry. They required the litterati to occupy positions in the administrative hierarchy... In some measures the Indian subcontinent became a part of the Central Asian cultural scene[6].

Other authors give us much more details, like that "in the second decade of the 13th Century, Delhi received a large influx of Muslim scholars and theologians, artisans, handicraftsmen, physicians and men of administrative experience from Khwarizm (Khiva), Iran and Khorasan."

Reinforcing observations approach on this matter which is given in a publication of U.S.A. offered a refuge of scholarly fugitives from the Mongols. In the 13th century India became a cultural colony of the Muslim world at a time when the centre of that world was in enemy hands.

One must underline that though there are complicated impressions of diversity in ethnic contents of the newcomers to medieval India during the Delhi Sultanate and early Moghuls, nevertheless we can anticipate a sustainable foundation which preceded a cultural synthesis as a next stage of the historical development.

Meanwhile Turkish literature in India as well as Indo-Uzbek literary relations indeed represent a confused deal for the two main reasons. At first it depends on multilingual nature of the Central Asian newcomers to India. And, secondly, it is due to lower social status of Turkic language in comparison with Arabic and Persian both of which had been considered as major literary languages throughout the Muslim world including Central Asia as well. So the literary activities in Turki in Central Asia proper has been second rate next to Persian and Arabic, though the period of the 14th and 15th Centuries has been regarded as a flourishing one in the history of the Turki's Chaghatai form.[7]

As far as first traces of that in India are concerned one could notice that "when the pressure of the Mongols in Central Asia and the Eastern fringe of Khorasan grew stronger a number of scholars and poets found shelter in Sindh. One of them was Muhammad Aufi" ...in 1220. He was a famous Persian poet and writer. It is interesting to note that his second book "*Jawami al-Hikayat* (Necklaces of Anecdotes)... has been translated into Turki several times and was written at the request of his Turkish ruler Qabacha"[8]. It is propapably the only link in the chain of obscurity we consider prevailing in the Delhi Sultanate period about Turki Literary works.

Meanwhile in accordance with M-me A.M. Schimmel's observations the Turki was in fact "a language which must have been widely spoken in the subcontinent, since most of the Muslim conquerors hailed from Central Asia, and the military aristocracy was Turkic to such an extent, that "Turk" and "Muslim" became equivalents in some Indian vernacudlars".[9]

It led to retaining of several Turkic titles and terms in Indian history. For instance "in August 1249 the Sultan Allauddin Khilji awarded the title Ulugh Khan "a great Khan" Hasan Qarlugh, on Khwarazmi prince who had ruled Multan and Uch for some years".

It is also well-known that the Dynasty of Asafjans in Hyderabad Deccan among many other titles bore such a title as Chin Qilich Khan, "which in Turki means the Khan of Honest sword". Or one more else "like the Shahs the rulers of Golconda also had a "majlis-i kingash", which was summoned by the Shah during period of extremy emergence or where the existence of the state itself was in jeopardy". It nations besides Arbic majlis "an assemblance" also a word kingash of Turkic origin in the sense of "council".

Dr. A.M. Schimmel is very right in her remark, that "Turkish remained a favourite language in the feudal classes, and discovered new data on a real scope of Turki's circulation. In particular she found some marks of that in medieval Sind where several compositions in Turki reign of the Turki during the ruling families like the Arghuns and the Tarkhans. These are "Raudat as-salatin wa jawahir al ajaib" by Fahri Harawi and "Mathnawi maxhar ul-atar" by Jihangir Hashimi, which were edited by H. Rashdi and published in respectively at Hyderabad (Sind) in 1968 and at Karachi in 1957. The seed works belong to the early sixteenth century and seem to be legacy of the primary Turki literary production in India. Fahri Harawi had made his name for his delightful translation of the classic poet of Chaghatai Turki Mir Ali Shir Nawai, "Majalis an-nafais" in Herat under the title "Latifnama" into Persian.[10]

S.A.A. Rizwi in his, *Survey of the History and Culture of the*

Indian Subcontinent from the coming of Muslim to the British Conquest (1200-1700) notes that the Naqshbandi order's distinctive features were formed by Khawaja Abdul Khaliq (d. 1220) of Ghijduwan... near Bukhara." While surveying another Sufi order's activities in Medieval India we know that there are two other famous orders which are supposed to be originated from Central Asia. The first one of these belongs to S.A.A. Rizwi (*A History of Sufism, in India from the 16 to Modern Century)*, Das Munshi, New Delhi, 1983, "The Shattariya Silsila introduced by Central Asian emigrant Shah Abdullah (d. 1485) in the 15th century... the second one relates to the Suhrawardi order which in accordance with an information delivered by Mumtax Ali Khan was founded by Sheikh Qadi Hamiduddin of Nagaur, who "along with his father... came to Delhi from Bukhara via Farshor (or Peshawar) during the early 13th Century".[11]

Now it would be appropriate to move on language aspects of medieval Central Asian and Indian links. It is well known that an initial signs of these are traced as early as in the 11th Century while our ancestor Al-Beruni apart from his foremost Sanskrit studies left behind many examples pertaining to several New Indo-Aryan Languages. We could refer to the paper of George Morgenstierne from Oslo, "Modern Indo-Aryan words in Al-Beruni's India" (*Islamic Culture*, Vol. 19, 1958, pp. 319-322). He notes that al-Beruni, "was in fact, the founder of comparative studies in human culture. Analysing a number of numerals like Barkhu, Biya, Triya, Caut, Panci, Satin and so on, Morgenstierne remarks that, "It is obvious that we have here to deal with modern Indo-Aryan Numerals" (p. 320) and in particular those of Sindhi as Barhu for "one" and the ordinals bio, trio, cotho, panjo and so on.

In conclusion the scholar is inclined "to admit the possibilities of al-Beruni's list being patched together, the latter part belonging to a dialect with distinct affinities to Pashai (of Dardic origin). The present Pashai dialects are spoken by illiterate hill tribes, but they go back to the Hindu-Buddhist language of civilization of Kapisa, Lampaka and Nagarahara. Very possibly a closely related dialect was spoken also in Kabul, "the suburb of which had still a Hindu population in the second half of the 10th Century", with which al-Beruni may have been in contact.... The occurrence of Sindhi numerals is natural, considering the early contact between Sindh and Islamic world." (p. 322)

After al-Beruni a real missionaries of language links between Central Asian and Indian Culture one should highly appreciate the painstaking activities of Sufi saints and their orders especially of those which had originated from Central Asia like Naqshbandiyya, Shuttariya and Suhravardiyya.

Many scholars stress the contribution of the Sufi saints in the sphere of languages that they discouraged linguistic chauvinism, and they developed a common medium for the communication of ideas, known as Hinduvi. They also helped in the development of Panjabi, Bengali, Dakhini, Gujarati and other regional languages of India.

In the early history of these languages is the Khangah or abode of Sufi's which stands out prominently as the main nursery where the language of elite (i.e. Persian and Arabic) and the language of common man (i.e. a colloquial Indian one) came together and paved the way for the emergence of new languages intelligible to both.

It should be noted that the Sufi saints belonging to the different orders were reportedly highly educated intellectuals capable of communicating in many Oriental Languages. The Naqshbandiya Sufi related Shaikh Abdul Wahhab Mutaqqi who had settled in Mecca, used to deliver his lectures in Arabic for Arab students, in Persian for those who hailed from Persia and Central Asia and in Hindi for the benefit of the Indian Students-Hadith and Tafsir.

In this connection it should be pointed out, "the language of all these Sufi's in India, who had settled in different parts of the country, has certain common linguistic features. The metres used by them were mostly Hindi and occasionally Persian. The rhyming of all works whether of Hindi, or Arabic, or Persian origin was based on their similarity of sounds as they are pronounced by the inhabitants and their foreign accent was lost. In their mystical utterances the Sufi poets have freely borrowed from the Indian spiritual and intellectual atmosphere and Indian literary motifs. There verses were both discursive and lyrical and sometimes in the form of a folk-tale or questions and answers."

Sufi's role in Indian Language links was helped by tolerable atmosphere towards Indian culture and languages created by the Central Asian rulers of India, both Delhi Sultans and Moghuls as well, who reigned over 600 years as whole in the Indian History.

Dr. Kalika Ranjan Qanungo notes that, the Muslims seem to have taken to the cultivation of Hindi poetry even before the conquest of Delhi and Ajmer by Shihabuddin Ghuri... The earliest poets in Hindi were Mas'ud (1112 A.D.), Qutb Ali (1143 A.D.) and Akram Faiz (1181 A.D.), the last being a contemporary of Chand Baradai. Sixty-three years after the death of Chand, was born the famous poet Amir Khusrau. Son of a Turkish Amir...he was the first Hindustan born Muslim, who breathed a true Indian patriotism, upholding the greatness of everything Indian—languages, rivers, and her gifts of nature... These Muslim poets departed from the convention of singing lofty themes—kings and wariors, chivalry and philosophy, and set the fashion of depicting joy and sorrows of the country side..." (pp. 49-53)[12]

A perfect amity and tolerance between Hindus and Muslims having been patronised by the Mughals since Akbar onwards tended to foster the "Rekhta" of Urdu which represented the principle of unity in diversity, so marked a feature of Indian life if its best.

We came across a paper of Dr. S.K. Chatterji devoted to a verse by Guru Nanak in the "Adigranth" quoted by Emperor Aurangzeb. According to this Aurangzeb cited thus :

> *Tupi lende bawri dende gehare nilaja Chuha khadan mawli tikali banhe chaja.*

And Dr. Trilochan made the following translation of this: "Mad are those who bestow praises and honour on the undeserving and very shameless are those people who accept (such praise of honour).... The rat cannot fit into hole, yet has tied a winnowing basket to its waist with the assurance of carrying it into the hole."

While concluding the paper I have borrowed from these sources a long list of Sanskritic writings having been composed under the Mughals. For instance, there are about ten works on Astronomy, Civil Law, Medicine, Theology, Philosophy, Ethics, Music, Dancing, to be especially dedicated for the pleasure of Akbar. The list contains also five works compiled on the order of Jahangir concerned with Algebra, Philosophy, and Grammar. Besides one can find eight compositions which have been carried out either on request or under immediate influence of Shahjahan, his Queen Mumtaz Mahal, Aurangzeb, Shuja Shah, Dara Shikoh and Shayasta Khan, Aurangzeb's maternal uncle and general. These are devoted to various topics including poetical works, a treatises on Astronomy in Sanskrit metres, and works on auspicious moments as well as works on sentiments, moods, figures of speech and even the literary works containing prose and poetry. Apart from these they have also collected a bulk of data connected with Sufi order activities in developing a number of new Indo-Aryan Languages like Hindi, Gujarati, Bengali, Marathi, Sindhi, Kashmiri as well as of some Dravidian ones like Tamil and Telugu.

Note : The paper presented in the International Seminar organised by Indian Council of Cultural Relations, New Delhi and Astha Bharati, Delhi on "India and Central Asia : Classical to Contemporary Period" in New Delhi on March 1-3, 2004.

NOTES

1. Elio, H.M., *The History of India as told by its own historians,* London, V. 3, 1867-77.
2. *Islamic Culture Quarterly,* Hyderabad (India) Vol. 62, 1988, No. 4, pp. 1, 8, 17, 22, 23.
3. In compliance with Aziz Ahmad's opinion "Turks and Tajiks... were quite common in the Mongol armies of Central Asia, relating to Delhi Sultanate period (see Conversions to Islam in the valley of Kashmir" in *Central Asiatic Journal*, Vol. 23. 1979, pp. 3-18.
4. *Islamic culture*, Vol. LX, No. 3, 1986, pp. 61-81.
5. M.I. Dar, "Gujarat's contribution to Gujari and Urdu" in *Islamic Culture*, Vol. 27, 1953, pp. 18.
6. *Indians in Central Asia* in India (Bombay), Vol. 28, 1991, issue 52-53, pp. 40.
7. Second Edition, Vol. I, From the Beginning to 1800 AD and reviewed by Arnsli J. Embree, Columbia University Press, New York, 198, Part IV, *Islam in Medieval India*, p. 385.
8. Annemarie Schimmel, Islamic Literature of India, in "*A History of Indian Literature*" ed. By 1 Gonda, Otto Harrassowitz. Wiesbaden, 1973, p. 12.
9 The same work at p. 23.,
10. He enlarged the original by adding to it a new chapter with the biographical sketches of 188 poets and literary men not treated by Nawai, among the latter Mas' a Timurid prince. He until recently the seventies has been completely unknown to the world.
11. K.R. Qanungo, *Islam and its impact on India*, Calcutta, 1968.
12. *Ibid.*

PART- II

POLITICS/GEO-POLITICS AND DEMOCRACY IN CENTRAL ASIA

10

Political System and Democratic Discourse in Central Asia

A View from Outside

R.R. Sharma

The present day Central Asian States, namely, Uzbekistan, Turkmenistan, Kyrghizstan, Tajikistan, and Kazakhstan, came into being after the October revolution in 1917. They owe their existence to the Soviet nationality policy. Looked at from this perspective, they have, indeed, a short history as independent, separate nations. However, they share a host of common specifics, which include a common Turkic ethnicity, a Common Muslim Cultural tradition and language, a similarity of history, predominance of rural population, low socio-economic mobility, low level of technical skills and qualifications. Tajiks like to project their somewhat different identity in terms of Persian language, which was, in fact, the language of local rulers and elite before the advent of Turks and their language in Central Asia.

The apparent homogeneity is, however, quite deceptive. There exists a large diversity, which is articulated in many significant ways. For example, Uzbeks, who constitute the largest national group of over 17 million people, take pride in projecting their ethnic/national identity not entirely in terms of religious (Sunni) or linguistic (Turkic) bonds, but primarily in terms of superior urban civilization which had developed by the side of Amu-Darya and Syr-Darya. Tajiks also consider themselves as sedentary. As against this, Turkmens and Kyrghiz are basically nomadic. Therefore, their geo-cultural identity is restricted. Along with this, there is strong tendency, which cuts across practically all the Central Asian States, to closely identify with a specific region, and the ethnic sub-divisions. The articulation of identities in a variety of particularistic terms has severe implications.

Significantly, they also have fairly large ethnic minorities, such as slaves. All this makes the political scenario basically friction oriented, and hence rather fragile.

The process by which national independence was achieved by the Central Asian States was basically similar. Their emergence as Sovereign States was the result of the collapse of the Soviet State. The large mass of the people of these states did not wage any struggle for a separate nationhood. The fact of the matter is that there was no such moment at all. It is no exaggeration to point out that they somewhat reluctantly became independent states. The infrequent violent outbursts of national feelings were largely directed against other indigenous Central Asian ethnic groups, and rarely against the sizeable Russian population in these republics.

To put the matter in perspective, it needs to be clarified that "Central Asia inherited from the Soviet period a generally literate population, comparatively well developed state institutions and personnel, clear and for the most part legitimate state borders and modernized economic infrastructure." The region looked much better than the Middle East at the time of decolonization. At the time of collapse of the Soviet Union, the economies of the republics were reasonably in good health. They had realized respectable levels of economic growth. They were forging ahead practically in all walks of social and economic life. And then it came to a grinding halt in the first years of independence. The republics which were used to receiving help, and direction, from Moscow were now on their own with a whole host of economic, political and ethnic problems. The political elite tried to generate a belief that the road to their salvation must run directly to the outside world and not to Moscow. They took a few years to learn that a closer economic union with Russia, as well as other Commonwealth of Independent States (CIS) was essential to control the growing crises. Soon it also became quite obvious that the new situation called for a major economic and political reform. Perhaps the foremost imperative to move forward was, and is, to overhaul the political system. The republics were overflowing with several political problems, which were further aggravated manifold because of the tough neighbourhood. In fact, political reform is critical to ensuring economic growth and the security of the region. Political problems in Central Asia make quite a few economic problems more difficult to solve.

It is well known that there is a great deal of "democracy deficit" in all the Central Asian republics. Their political regimes are devoid of legitimacy as well long term political and strategic vision. The fragile character of the political system in these countries is largely due to "façade democracies" which have been imposed from above. The façade democracies have been instituted in these countries in accordance with the minimal principles of democracy, namely the so-called elections. Obviously, it has limited the efficiency and efficacy of the political structures. The lack of elite-mass linkages and socio-political dialogue not only retards socio-economic development, but also encourages traditionalist-conservative formations. It certainly pushes back the formation of a healthy civil society. The façade democracy is "static and fragile", and it invariably brings wide ranging instability and insecurity for itself, and most of all for its neighbours. This is exactly the outcome of existing situation in Central Asia. Political scientists have identified two democratic values, which are recognized as "twin pillars" in the democratic value system: Competition and Participation. The well known political scientist, Robert Dhal regards them as "the two theoretical dimensions of democratization." By competition, he means, "competition of elites", and participation implies "the participation of the whole population in the political processes." Dhal argues that participation and competition as basic democratic values have been invariably incorporated in the constitution of all democratic countries. However, there is a "huge gap" between the declared democratic values of the Constitutions and the socio-political realities in façade democracies. If we apply Dhal's model of democratic values to the countries of Central Asia, we obtain the following result.

Tyrannical Democracies

These are the gross distortions of majortian type democracies. The tiny political elite have manipulated the parliamentary majority, and refer to it for its legitimation. The elites act as tyrants and refuse the necessary compromise in political and social life. They refuse to establish "consensual democracy for the purpose of fundamental charge". Consequently, the political system resembles an "infantile disorder". The Central and West Asian countries represent an outstanding model of tyrannical, façade democracies.

The process of nation-building in Central Asia has muddled on. This is an obvious outcome of the fact that these republics have witnessed the emergence of authoritarian regimes, poor governance, and extensive corruption. The incumbent political elites are largely interested in holding on to power. They violate basic human values and brutalize their own people. Thus, they have created a nourishing environment for the growth of extremism and instability, both within and around them.

Apparently, all the five states in Central Asia are stable. They have not faced any major social turmoil or political dislocation after attaining independence in 1991. Tajikistan is, of course, an exception. The top most leaders of Uzbekistan, Turkmenistan, Kazakhstan and Kyrgyzsthan are unchanged and still control the reigns of power. From all accounts, the overwhelming bulk of population is not opposed to the political regimes in power. It is only a minority which is hostile to their governments. It is only a minority which is hostile to their governments. It is argued that "most Central Asians seem to value political stability, material well-being and personal security above all else, and they fear the violence and dislocation that accompanied Islamicization in Afghanistan and Chechnya." Some research surveys have also unfolded the fact that though the large majority of the people, in these republics describe themselves as believers, they however, prefer that the secular law should govern their societies. This goes well with the ruling regimes, which are formally secular. Obviously, the leadership feels secure and unchallenged.

However, the apparent calm is highly deceptive. After the demise of the Soviet Union, the economies of the whole region are in bad shape. In fact, the collapse of the Soviet Union "was a disaster for the region" in economic terms. Most of the republics have "lopsided economies," and there are huge disparities both between urban and rural areas as well as among regions. The proportion of poor, according to UNDP study, has jumped manifold. According to the World Bank, average wage in Tajikistan and Kyrgyzstan covers only one-third of the minimum needed to survive. Therefore, widespread poverty, declining rates of economic growth, "deepening income and wealth disparities, unemployment, organized crime and above all pervasive corruption serve as fodder for the mobilization of political grievances today, and they will continue to do so well into the future."

The apparent stability thus rests on a quicksand. It can vanish in no time. Obviously, "reducing poverty is seen as vital to stability in the region and international finance institutions, from World Bank to the European Bank for Reconstruction and Development have been pushing for faster economic reforms." However, it is easier said than done, because the political problems come in the way, and make many of the economic issues more difficult to solve. Also political power has become "increasingly intertwined with business interests, if not outright corruption."

Obviously, the crucial question is why are countries in the region "stalling, some would say backtracking, on democratic political reform?" While the ruling elite does not pretend to any democratic ambition, it is nevertheless fully aware that its chances of survival are minimal if it relaxes its grip on political power. Stephen Sestanovich, who was special adviser to U.S. Secretary of State and ambassador-at-large for the former Soviet Union from 1997 to 2001, informs that there is widespread belief in Central Asia that democracy is just not right for the region: "I have heard that argument from virtually every President in Central Asia. I have also heard it from despairing human right activists and from journalists who visit these countries from time to time, only to discover that things seem unchanged or worse from their last visit .... Central Asian elites know that if they are simply seen as backwaters of same sort of contemporary 'oriental despotism', they are not going to command the attention of the outside world, much less its resources." Therefore, the defensive argument that the countries in Central Asia are not ready for democracy or "even real constitutionalism" is an eye-wash. The argument is advanced to conceal the fact that the ruling elite are not ready for democracy. It is hard to imagine that the ruling elite would ever win an open election.

The view from outside is that Central Asia is "a heaven for tyrants and ruthless dictators and a poster child of acute economic underdevelopment and all the pathologies that go with it." The profound lack of constitutionalism and the rule of law is a huge hindrance in the evolution of healthy preconditions for social and political stability over the long run. It also perpetuates acute economic under-development, because the investors from outside feel greatly reluctant to invest in the face of instability and lack of transparent rule of law. The outside investors "want to know if the laws on taxation of their profits are going to charge whenever it suits the son-in-law of the president to take over their company."

While the ruling political party has held the political system to ransom, the opposition parties also seldom rhyme with political and moral rectitude, and credible alternative. They are there because of their regional or tribal affiliations rather than for their political vision, ideas and programme. It is aptly argued that "most conventional opposition parties are flimsy structures with little grassroots support." In many cases, the elements from the ruling elite have broken away to set up their own opposition groups, and they are like a "debating club", enjoying very little support. Their departure from the power structure in most cases is connected with power struggles, or "business interests rather than with their democratic conscience or distaste for corruption." Moreover, the opposition is hopelessly splintered into small groups, and is politically ineffective. Consequently, the base of the opposition goes on dwindling, and the people are loosing faith in their efficacy. Some of them eventually turn to Islamic radicalism.

No one would feel unduly concerned if it were an obscure region, or part of the world. But Central Asia is after all Central Asia, which is one of the most important regions of the world. It has indeed gained greater importance in the aftermath of 11 September, 2001 and particularly after President G.W. Bush declared his so-called global "war on terrorism", which he also labelled the "first war of the century." Central Asia is strategically placed between Russia, China and Europe. Moreover, "it lives in a tough neighbourhood", of Afghanistan, which continues to be a significant destabilizing force for both Central and South Asia. Geography ensures the continuing importance of the region. Thus, it has emerged as a major factor in the security scenario, both regional as well as global. Obviously, the major global and regional power, Russia US, China, India, Iran have a vested interest in boosting the security system in the Central Asia. In the absence of a viable collective security system in the region, the US has stepped in to fill the vacuum, and assume the role of "a security manager." It is estimated that the US in the last two years have advanced $42 millions to Kyrgyzstan, $40 million to Tajikistan, $45.5 million to Uzbekistan in security and humanitarian assistance.

Hence, the pressure, particularly from the West, to improve human rights and promote the development of civil society and free press.

The Central Asian states are listed "among no freedom nations" by various human right organizations. The US money that came together with the troops has not worked. This has only reinforced the pseudo-democratic regimes. In a testimony to the Senate in 2002, Lynn Pascoe, Deputy Assistant Secretary of State, outlined the US goal to push the Central Asian States towards free markets and democratic policies to strengthen stability. The contradiction between the proclaimed US commitment to democracy and the real action is obvious here like in all previous cases of the US cooperation with worst kind of dictatorships. This rhetoric obviously serves the US interests.

The Central Asian regimes, apparently believe that the problem of political instability can be addressed through tight controls. "Such control comes in varying shades, from blunt repression in Uzbekistan and Turkmenistan to more subtle legal guerrilla warfare in Kazakhstan and Kyrgyzstan, but everywhere the mix includes rigged elections. Some of the methods may differ, but philosophy is the same." It may give us better insight if we look the state of politics in each Central Asian republic Uzbekistan.

Uzbekistan was the first to offer the greatest promise of change. The president of the republic agreed in principle to support democratic reform and designed a new security cooperation and framework with the United States. It declared: "Uzbekistan reaffirmed its commitment to further intensify the democratic transformation of its society politically and economically (and set) priority areas such as building an open civil society, establishing a genuine multiparty system and independence of the media and strengthening non-governmental structures and improving the judicial system . . . improve the legislative process, develop low based government system . . . and enhance the legal culture."

It was indeed a tall list of reforms to be undertaken. In a way, it implied that the existing structure of governance was seriously flawed. Nevertheless, it was announced that there shall be a free and fair election for the new bicameral legislature in 2004. It has remained only an empty promise. To date, no independent political formation/ group(s) party(s) is operating freely in the country. There is no respite for the press and other media. The censorship of press continues to operate in one form or the other. There are various reports of relentless assault on press freedom. "In all the Central Asian republics, independent journalists seriously attempting to democratize the once-closed societies are either already behind bars, or have been sacked or physically assaulted, sometimes to the extent of suffering permanent injury and even narrowly escaping death. Reportedly, the political situation in Turkmenistan has "gone from bad to unsupportable since 2002." While the leaders of other republics make some effort, however small, to improve their democratic image, President Niyazov has no such democratic ambitions, or pretensions. In 1999, he got himself elected President for life and there is Stalinist personality cult around him, naming himself Turkembshi, i.e., "Father of Turks". The whole country is littered with his golden statues and palaces. This is in spite of the fact that the country has a very high level of foreign debt. He has targeted every section of political and social life, leaving the Turkmen intelligentsia diminished in numbers and bereft of its ability to function. There is pernicious corruption all over. Apparently, he is loosing support of the leftover political elite.

Kazakhstan

The republic has comparatively a much better record of democratization. Reportedly, the political opposition is functional, human right activists are apparently more vocal and the media enjoys a little more freedom. The economy of the republic is growing, and is the most growth oriented in the whole region. However, there are reports that the republic is sliding considerably in such areas as governance and freedom of press, electoral processes, etc. It is confirmed by the fact that President Nazarbayev managed to get a bill passed in the parliament "that conferred political legal rights to him and his entire family granting blanket immunity against any charge that he had already been made or that would be made in the future." The opposition has alleged that the republic is a "super presidential republics, where the president decides everything." The opposition, however, is not unblemished. Most of the opposition leaders have had a taste of power, and they are "much more politically savvy." They also have money "which buys some media influence".

Kyrghizstan

The republic stands out, comparatively, as a model of democratization in Central Asia. The regime, headed by President Asker Akayeb, is apparently "for more tolerant than any other Central Asian government." The regime has allowed a space, through limited, for the opposition to organize. It has also allowed, under pressure, to allow civil society to grow, and NGOs to operate at grassroots level. The other Central Asian leaders often refer to him that "he lacks the toughness" to restore order. President Akayeb, who was originally an academician, has declared that he shall actually step down in 2005. It does so; he will set an example, unmatched by any other leader in the region, who has extended their terms in a series of fake referendums.

Tajikistan falls in a different category. It descended into a civil war for the most part in 1990s. Finally, the peace agreement was signed in 1997, which was brokered with Iran's help. The Islamic Revival Party (IRP) allied itself with the United Tajik Opposition (UTO) and chose a nationalist agenda. The UTO was a signatory to the peace agreement and it was given 30 per cent share in government. The IRP has by and large honoured its promise to follow democratic rules. It is the leading opposition party in the country, which functions largely unhindered. However, lately, the party is becoming increasingly critical of the growing concentration of power, as well as the muzzling of the opposition. It is also a part of the political scenario that a number of Islamic groups have emerged and grown and they are visually active. This forces the Central Asian governments to follow a tougher stance against them, and follow a regime of tough and tighter controls. In the process, obviously, the rule of law becomes a causality. The political reform in the given circumstances takes a back-seat. This particular angle can hardly be ignored or minimized. Slow progress towards political reform can be rationalized. There is no credible political alternative to present leadership, which is basically secular.

There are several critical questions about Central Asia. The Central Asia is fairly important because of its proximity to Afghanistan and South Asia. The Russian withdrawal from Central Asia after the break up of the Soviet Union gave rise to a variety of security problems. The region was left without a security manager. Intra-regional feuds and rivalries eroded the possibilities of region-wide cooperation and consolidation. The "commonwealth of Independent States" did not live up to its expectations for a number of reasons. The Central Asian republics had therefore to content with domestic insurgencies, cross-border terrorism, growth of militant Islam, drug and gun running etc. The republics witnessed the emergence of authoritarian regimes, poor governance and extensive corruption. Because of political and security vacuum, the region has gradually emerged as a hotbed of factional and big power rivalries.

In 1997, the Deputy Secretary of State, Strobe Talbot, gave a major address outlining the US approach to Central Asia. He argued that the US has no compelling interest in the region. The region was in no way of critical, strategic importance to the US: "It has been fashionable to proclaim, or at least predict, a replay of 'great game' in Caucasus and Central Asia. The implication of course is that the driving dynamics of the region, fuelled and lubricated by oil, will be the competition of the great powers. Our goal is to avoid and actively discourage…." However, if "internal and cross border conflicts simmer and flare, the region could become a breeding ground of terrorism, hotbed of religious and political extremism and battleground for outright war." Strobe Talbot was, however, telling only a half-truth.

The strategic importance of the region grew manifold after September 11. Central Asia which was for some American analysts "a strategic quicksand" or a "mission too far" became mission immediate and urgent. To begin with, the US decided to be "Central Asia's security manager". However, Eugene Rumer makes a bold observation, which is at the heart of the issue. He says: "In the aftermath of September 11, though it would be short-sighted to define US interests in Central Asia merely in terms of operational counter terrorism requirements and ongoing military operations in Afghanistan. The tragedy of the terrorist attacks has given a new and very different meaning to the notion first articulated by US policy makers in 1990s…. the absence of geopolitical competition…"

This was officially confirmed by Elizabeth Jones, Assistant Secretary of State for Eurasian Affairs in a testimony before the US Senate Sub-Committee in December 2001. Jones testified that US had no intention of abandoning Central Asia after the Afghan War. She outlined four US priorities in the region: Combating Terrorism, reform, the rule of law, and Caspian Sea energy resources. Collin Powel also confirmed that Kazakhstan's oil was of "critical importance" to the US. Military presence is essential for the US to control Caspian Sea and Caspian energy resources. Apparently, this is a "sub-text of the war" in Afghanistan.

The US cannot however maintain its footprint in Central Asia without the active cooperation of most important regional powers, namely, Russia, China and Iran. Each of these nations has a huge stake in the region. These nations have offered their cooperation so far in the interest of regional stability and security. However, their concern for stability and security does not "outweigh fears of US preponderance". Tensions are bound to rise, and resolving the growing tensions obviously would be a formidable task. Russian Defense Minister, Sergei Iranov, in fact, reminded the US that it had promised to close down military bases in Uzbekistan and Kyrgyzstan after the completion of its military operation in Afghanistan. "We did not object to the bases, but set a condition that they operate only as long as it takes to stabilize the situation in Afghanistan", Iranov informed a NATO Conference in Colorado Springs. He went on to assert that the "CIS is an extremely important security zone for Russia … we have boosted and will further boost our presence in the Commonwealth of Independent States." Russia is thus showing a new assertiveness towards the CIS as a part of a broader revision of its "defense doctrine post-9/11." There is thus a clear signal to the US to accept Russia's dominant role in Central Asia. The signals emanating from the US indicate that it is working towards its known agenda of regime change in Central Asia also. The Russian Foreign Minister, Igor Ivanov, was forced to publicly declare: "It is to be regretted that the methods of pressure and interference in internal affairs that were used in Georgia are also being used in other countries. We are informed that the leaders of Central Asian republics are "on the U.S. hit list". Apparently, President Nazarbayev of Kazakhstan is at the top of the list. Several Kazakh officials have been reportedly bribed on behalf of several U.S. companies. There is a move to bring about a change of elite in Kazakhstan in the Parliamentary elections scheduled to be held in 2005. "Detailed instructions on 'how to make velvet revolution in Tajikistan' were reportedly "circulated in the capital Dushanbe against the backdrop of stepped up activity of Soros Foundation and demonstrative contacts of U.S. diplomats with opposition leaders" in Tajikistan. Obviously, Russia and the United States are heading for new rivalry in Central Asia.

11

Central Asia

Changing Geo-Political Alignment in the Aftermath of 11th September

Devendra Kaushik

In the wake of the tragic happenings of September 11, the only Superpower in the world was forced to act against the very forces it had created and nurtured during the previous two decades. Although, the effect of Septmber 11 was deeply felt all over the world, Central and South Asia witnessed tremors of great intensity demolishing the existing geo-political structure. In the region, within twenty-four hours of the terrorist attacks in America, Washington was knocking at Islamabad's door seeking support as a frontline state. On September 14, after a marathon meeting with his generals, President Musharraf announced that Pakistan would give total support to a US-led multi-national force to launch military action against the Taliban in Afghanistan from its bases. India was also reported to have offered three air bases as well as port facilities on its Western coast for use against the Taliban regime in Afghanistan. Subsequently, under pressure from the US and India following the terrorist attack on the Indian Parliament on December 13, General Musharraf also announced an internal crackdown on some militant groups in Pakistan. He also pompously abrogated the theocratic politics of his predecessor General Zia-ul-Haq, promising modernization of Pakistan. This new posture of the Pakistani military dictator was aptly compared by former Pakistani Prime Minister Benazir Bhutto to "Mullah Omar appearing on television, following the allied bombardment, to repudiate theocracy in exchange for avoiding conflict and continuing in power."

In early October 2001 President Islam Karimov of Uzbekistan who had reluctantly signed a military cooperation agreement with Russia in the year 2000 under the shadow of Taliban-supported threat of Islamic militants' incursion into Fargana, readily embraced the US as a new ally. By an agreement it gave the United States "extended use of Khanabad in the Karshi province, the biggest air base in Central Asia, used as the staging post by the Soviet Union for flying its troops to Afghanistan. With the acquisition of a permanent military foothold in Central Asia through its air base in Uzbekistan, America became a new player in the new version of the 19th century "Great Game". For sometime different interpretations of the Uzbek-US agreement were given. While Karimov said the agreement covered the mutual responsibilities and guarantees, the Americans asserted that their commitment was confined to only consultation. However, on 12 October 2001 a US-Uzbek joint statement was issued stating that the United States had extended security guarantees to President Islam Karimov's regime. Subsequently, Uzbekistan which had previously insisted that the United States could only use Uzbek facilities for humanitarian and search and rescue missions now sanctioned the use of its military facilities by the US armed forces for offensive military operations against Afghanistan. Some two thousand U.S. soldiers belonging to the 10th Mountain Division arrived at the Khanabad Airbase in Uzbekistan. Uzbek President Islam Karimov announced on 28 December that he had not set any deadline for US troops to pull out of the base. Uzbekistan has been playing a significant role in transhipment of relief supplies from the UN agencies by reopening its bridge of friendship, from Termez located about 40 miles north of the Afghan city of Mazar-e-Sherif.

In December 2001 the Kyrgyz Parliament agreed to allow the United States to set up a military base at Manas International Airport, some 30 kilometres from the Kyrgyz capital Bishkek. This base is going to have a strength of 3,000 troops. *The New York Times* reported on 10 January 2002 that the US military planners were considering rotating troops in the region every six months, for the purpose of increasing technological support and conducting training exercises with the Central Asian Republics. US analysts have predicted a long term military presence in the region dictated by the need to prevent a possible comeback of the Taliban and to ensure that all remnants of *Al-Qaida* are rooted out. It is also argued that the US troops in Central Asia are needed to protect the International Security Assistance Force (ISAF) which has been deployed in Kabul to help the new interim government to maintain peace.

American militancy presence in Central Asia has also been justified in the name of boosting regional economic development and sustaining democratic reforms in the region. This argument was advanced by Elizabeth Jones, Assistant Secretary of State for European and Eurasian Affairs, in her testimony before the Foreign Affairs Committee in December 2001. During his visit to Tashkent in early December 2001 the US Secretary of State Collin Powel, while addressing the press conference, declared that "the US interests in the Central Asian region stretched beyond the current crisis in Afghanistan".

Later on 7 January 2002 speaking at Bagram airbase near Kabul, visiting US Senator Joseph Liberman also indicated a significant shift in Washington's policy. He was reported to have said, "We learned at a very high and painful price the cost of a lack of involvement in Central Asia on 11 September and we are not going to let it happen again." US Deputy Secretary James Wolfowitz was reported to have stated that "by upgrading its military presence in Central Asia, the United States wishes to send a clear message to regional countries—especially to Uzbekistan—that it will not forget about them and that it has a capacity to come back and will come back whenever needed." The Uzbek press has carried reports about an economic agreement negotiated in early December pledging $150 million in loans and grants for economic reforms in the Republic. The US press reported that the US administration was considering abrogation of an earlier law which placed conditions on a number of former Soviet Republics' trade relations with the US based on their human rights record.

Central Asian leaders have publicly acclaimed the positive effect of American presence in their region on improvement of their economy. The Kyrgyz Prime Minister Kurmanbek Bakiev is reported to have stated that the presence of thousands of American soldiers would be a goldmine for his poor country. Although nearly 3,000 American servicemen and up to 40 planes are expected to arrive and be stationed in Kyrgyzstan from mid-December 2001 to mid-January 2002, only five military transport planes and 155 American servicemen have so far arrived in Kyrgyzstan. These military transport planes were used for delivering humanitarian aid to the northern provinces of Afghanistan. Three trains with military equipment were arriving in Kyrgyzstan every week. According to the Kyrgyzstan Security

Council's press release the US has granted Kyrgyzstan $3.5 million financial assistance for the year 2001 to be spent for purchase of spare parts of military helicopters as well as uniforms, transport vehicles and communication equipment for law enforcement and secret services of Kyrgyzstan. Kyrgyzstan also allowed use of its territory for delivering humanitarian aid to Afghanistan. Five thousand tons of humanitarian aid was reported to have been sent along the overland Osh-Khorog-Faizabad route. Kyrgyzstan is also hosting the staff of the Collective Deployment Forces of the CIS Collective Security Treaty. It has also received small financial assistance from China for strengthening its armed forces.

Kazakhstan which has no direct border with Afghanistan and did not face any serious threat to its security from the Taliban supported religious extremism, gave support to the US-led struggle against international terrorism in Afghanistan in the form of overflight clearances. It also offered Washington use of its bases. In his talks with the visiting US Secretary of State Collin Powel in December 2001, President Nazarbayev stated that "from the very first day, Kazakhstan declared it would be in a coalition fighting terrorism and would help with all the forces it has at its disposal". Later during his visit to the United States, President Nazarbayev reiterated Kazakhstan's intention to cooperate in the war against terrorism to its conclusion within the framework of international coalition.

Tajikistan which along with Russia, Iran and India played a significant role in helping the fight of the Northern Alliance against the Taliban regime, responded positively when the US Defence Secretary Donald Rumsfeld visited Dushanbe by offering three of its airfields, namely, Kulyab, Khojand and Kurgan-Tyube. It also assisted in the shipment of humanitarian aid to the northern part of Afghanistan. It was through Tajikistan that the massive Russian military assistance to the Northern Alliance was transported to launch an attack on the Taliban capital Kabul. However, unlike Uzbekistan and Kyrgyzstan, Tajikistan has not allowed stationing of US troops on its territory. Further, the Tajiks are believed to have consulted Russia on offering bases to United States.

Moscow which had in the beginning warmly welcomed the US military action in Afghanistan for reason of getting a free hand in dealing with religious extremism and secessionism in Chechnya, soon came to grief when the United States began to exploit its fight against international terrorism in Afghanistan to promote its geo-political interests and traditional foreign policy objectives in Central Asia and the Caucasus region, the soft underbelly of Russia. The Russian indignation at American policy of setting up military bases in its Central Asian backyard found expression in Russian State Duma Speaker Genadii Seleznev's warning in Kazakhstan's capital Astana in January 2002. Seleznev said, "I think that presidents, governments and parliament members will very carefully analyse what the status of the foreign army units expected to be deployed in Kyrgyzstan or in Uzbekistan will be, how they will behave in Tajikistan, on which legal grounds they will be deployed, for which period of time, etc. These of course are all issues to which we cannot remain indifferent. CIS countries that are members of the Collective Security Treaty, including those that I just mentioned cannot take a single decision without consulting each other. We do not wish to see permanent US bases appear here in the Central Asia region."

That a geo-political rivalry between Moscow and Washington was in full swing, became increasingly clear as the Russian supported Northern Alliance troops marched upon Kabul following a request by the then Afghan President and Northern Alliance leader Burhanuddin Rabbani. Russian forces arrived to repair the Bagram airfield near Kabul. This led Secretary of State Collin Powell to request his Russian counterpart Igor Ivanov to refrain from further moves in Afghanistan that could cause tension in US-Russian relations.

American suspicion of Russian intentions further deepened when the Northern Alliance troops entered Kabul in defiance of Washington. The Russian State Duma Foreign Relations Committee Chairman, Dmitri Rogozin, said at a round table discussion organized by a Russian periodical *Ruskii Zhurnal*, "it would be unforgivable to let the United States resolve all the issues of the Afghan peace settlement".

How a militarily and economically weak Russia would respond to a long term US military deployment in Central Asia and the Caucasus is not yet certain. For the present however, the leaders of Central Asian republics and Georgia seem to have turned a deaf ear to the Russian concerns about the US military intrusion into their strategic space. To meet this American threat in the Central Asian region, Moscow is for the time being trying to consolidate its relations with

Kazakhstan, Turkmenistan and Tajikistan. Apparently, it has reconciled itself to a long term US military presence in Georgia, Uzbekistan and Kyrgyzstan. In fact, Lt. Gen. Valery Manilov, a member of the Russian Federation council and former First Deputy Chief of General Staff has favoured adoption of a relaxed view of the matter and respond by promoting economic and political influence in the region by working with all parties interested in foiling terrorist plans. In his view, Russia should not be alarmed about new U.S. military bases even if they are set up near its southern borders. Instead he suggests stepping up by Moscow of its political, diplomatic and economic efforts to restore its traditional influence in the region

Since the disintegration of the Soviet Union, Turkmenistan has launched itself on a foreign policy course of permanent neutrality. It is not a member of the CIS Collective Security Treaty and the Turkmen president Saparmurad Niyazov has attended only a few CIS summits since 1992. Turkmenistan however refused to open its airspace and airfields to US war planes during the anti-Taliban military campaign in Afghanistan. On 7 January 2002, Niyazov rejected a German request to allow military aircrafts providing support to the UN mandated International Security Assistance Force to use Turkmen airfields. Turkmen Foreign Minister Rashid Meredov told journalists in Ashgabat after meeting Russian Foreign Minister Igor Ivanov that Turkmenistan would participate in the international efforts in Afghanistan only in terms of humanitarian assistance.

The joint Turkmen-Russian communiqué issued on 21 January 2002 at the end of Turkmen President Niyazov's visit to Moscow reiterated the support of Russia and Turkmenistan for a central role of the United Nations and its Security Council in international efforts for settling the Afghan conflict. The two countries reaffirmed their "devotion to the aim of reviving a peaceful independent Afghanistan free from terrorism and drug and living in harmony with their neighbours and the international community as a whole". The two Presidents declared their belief that it was impossible to remove the threat to stability in the Central Asian region "without an all embracing settlement of the protracted inner conflict". They also confirmed their striving for determining a new legal status of the Caspian Sea at the earliest by taking into account the interests of all Caspian states.

An International Conference on the Caspian Sea legal status

problem was convened in Moscow towards the end of February. At this conference Russia declared its readiness for compromise to help find a solution without winners or losers. American military presence in Uzbekistan and Kyrgyzstan has prodded Russia not only to work for a new legal status of the Caspian Sea acceptable to all coastal states, but also to launch a fresh initiative for establishing a Eurasian Alliance of Gas Producers. Such an alliance between Russia, Turkmenistan, Kazakhstan, and Uzbekistan was proposed by President Vladimir Putin in his talks with President Niyazov of Turkmenistan on 21 January 2002.

China too has recently taken steps to counter the threat posed to its security by US military presence close to its border in the Central Asian region. The foreign ministers of the Shanghai Cooperation Organization (SCO) met in Beijing in January 2002 where they endorsed a call for a neutral Afghanistan and opposed arbitrary expansion of the global war on terrorism to Iraq, Iran and North Korea described by President Bush as "axis of evil". China is also apprehensive of a nuclear war between India and Pakistan on its border. It is also scared of a growing effort by the two South Asian states to move closer to Washington. According to David M. Lampton, Director of China Studies at John Hopkins School of International Studies, China is haunted by a spectre of encirclement from Japan and South Korea in East Asia to India and Pakistan in South Asia.

It also perceives Russia as moving closer to West. Everything that happened since 11 September has reinforced such a perception of international developments by China. The Chinese Press for the first time disclosed that one hundred sixty-six terrorists were arrested in Xinjiang during the last three months of the last year. During the past decade more than one thousand outbreaks of terrorist violence have been acknowledged for the first time in the Chinese press. While meeting with the Foreign Ministers from the six member-states of the SCO in Beijing on 8 January, Chinese President Jiang Zemin is reported to have said that the most urgent thing at present was to set up a regional anti-terrorism mechanism among the six member-states of the SCO as soon as possible. In the statement issued by the SCO Foreign Ministers it was agreed that the UN and its Security Council should play a leading role in the anti-terrorism campaign and all actions in this regard should conform to the purpose and principles of the UN

Charter and other principles of acknowledged international laws. The joint statement further demanded that the scope of the actions should not be expanded arbitrarily and the actions should not interfere in the internal affairs of any nation and should help safeguard the long-term interests of regional and world peace. The SCO Foreign Ministers decided to set up an anti-terrorist organisation in Bishkek. The SCO Foreign Ministers meet in its joint statement declared that the anti-terrorism campaign should be carried out at all levels—worldwide, regionally and nationally and should not be prejudiced or have double standards.

Both Moscow and Beijing seem to be keen to carry New Delhi along with them in their struggle to prevent the establishment of the US global hegemony under the cover of fighting international terrorism. The possibilities for ushering in a multi-polar international system through forging trilateral cooperation between India, China and Russia were discussed during the New Delhi visit of Russian Foreign Minister Igor Ivanov. Both countries agreed to initiate a trilateral discussion including China on the joint development of energy resources and combating international terrorism. The Chinese Prime Minister Zhu Rongji who visited India in January this year expressed shared concerns about eliminating terrorism in the region. Zhu Rongji also stressed the need to raise bilateral economic cooperation between India and China. President Nazarbayev of Kazakhstan during his visit to New Delhi in February this year pleaded for India's participation in the Shanghai Cooperation Organization. Nazarbayev expressed the belief that India's membership of the SCO would add to the strength of the organization.

Notwithstanding the murmuring of protest against the US conduct of changing the geo-political situation in the region in its favour in the name of fighting international terrorism, it will be no exaggeration to say as Russian publicist Vyacheslav Kostikov has written that a substantial re-division of the sphere of influence has taken place in the world. In the United States they have already started speaking about the Bush doctrine which it is claimed is going to determine the history of human freedom. As President Bush declared in his Annual State of The Nation message to the Congress, "America is strong as never before". According to Kostikov, America has made the following nine significant gains :

1. Under cover of anti-terrorist rhetoric the United States has succeeded in establishing its presence in the Central Asian region. The countries of this region were in the centre of the "Great Silk Route" representing the shortest strategic road for transporting goods and resources from South East Asia, India to Europe.
2. It has created a springboard in a region which contains one of the richest oil and gas deposits.
3. The United States has weaned away Pakistan from China. Having lost the support of Islamist fundamentalists, President Musharraf is now totally dependent upon the United States.
4. It has demonstrated the exactness of its latest weaponry which will promote their sales in the World's arms market.
5. Bypassing the NATO, Washington has shown to the Europeans that they are not capable of solving the global task without it.
6. The United States has flooded the World oil market with increased supplies as they needed cheaper oil and oil products for their Afghan operation.
7. America has confirmed its right to be called the only superpower in the world by creating in an unprecedented manner a broad coalition of states for solving its (America's) own problems.
8. It has strengthened its mastery over the oil producing regions in the Near-East and the Persian Gulf by destroying the Arab solidarity.
9. The United States has substantially devalued the role of the UN for which it had been working during the last 20 years.

Similarly, in his interview to the Russian newspaper *Komsomolskaya Pravda*, American political scientist S. Cohen frankly admitted that while the Romanticists can derive satisfaction from the victory over the Al-Qaida and Taliban terrorists, the United States has in fact more enduring goals to achieve—military hegemony, widening its sphere of influence at the expense of Russia and China, and access to the rich oil resources not controlled by the OPEC.

12

GEOPOLITICAL PERSPECTIVES ON CENTRAL ASIA

AN INDIAN VIEW

NIRMALA JOSHI

Often the twenty first century is being described as an Asian one. In the coming decades it is expected that Asian countries particularly India and China would shape the future developments in Asia. It was the break-up of the Soviet Union in 1991 that set in motion the process of change. New sovereign and independent entities had emerged on the world map changing the geopolitics in Eurasia in particular. In fact in Asia it is Eurasia that has become the focal point of world attention. Several factors help in explaining this change. Apart from the projected rise of India and China, the huge Eurasian landmass is richly endowed with natural resources including energy sources. Today ensuring energy security has become one of the top concerns of countries. The uncertainty in the Middle East and the Persian Gulf has accelerated the search for new sources of energy. In this context the focus is on the energy resources of Eurasia. Besides the security paradigm widened to include non-conventional threats. The phenomenal growth of extremism, terrorism and aggressive nationalism was demonstrated by the break-up of Yugoslavia, the events of 9/11 and the emergence of Afghanistan as the epicenter of terrorism and extremism. These dangerous forces came to occupy the centre stage of international security. In order to deal with such threats military security was no longer sufficient. Greater cooperative effort was required to deal with such transnational threats.

All these momentous changes were taking place in the vicinity of India. It was certain to have an impact on Indian concerns. In strategic thinking its vital interests lay in ensuring a secure and stable Central Asia. In view of the ongoing militancy in the Indian State of Jammu and Kashmir, stability in Central Asia was crucial for India. Any destabilization of the region could have adverse impact on India. Hence India began to consider Central Asia as part of its extended neighbourhood. The paper focuses on the geopolitical importance of Central Asia from the Indian perspective.

Geopolitics of Central Asia

One aspect that began to draw attention among others was the strategic location of Central Asia in the centre of Eurasia. The region is flanked in the north by Russia having the potential to emerge as a major player in international politics. The eastern periphery is flanked by China perceived as an upcoming power. Probably China could pose a challenge to the supremacy of the USA as the leading power. However, China's Western periphery adjoining Central Asia is vulnerable. The Xinjiang region is not only underdeveloped but is not integrated well with the mainland China. Xinjiang is home to an ethnic Turkic minority, the Uyghurs who are followers of Islam and have been seeking autonomy and at times even independence from China. In the changed environment of the post-Cold War China's strategy has been to develop close links with Central Asia particularly with Kazakhstan, Kyrgyzstan and Tajikistan which share a border with Xinjiang. The aim of Chinese strategy is to ensure that the separatist movement by the Uyghurs would gradually loose shine. To the west of Central Asia are located Turkey and Iran both aspiring to emerge as regional powers. South Asia and Afghanistan are located in the southern direction.

What has immensely enhanced the strategic location of Central Asia is sits abundant natural resources. This is a crucial factor ever since the question of ensuring energy security has become a central issue. Central Asia and the Caspian basin have substantial reserves of energy – oil, natural gas and hydrocarbons. Estimates about Central Asian energy reserves vary, but it is now being acknowledged that Central Asian and Caspian basin resources are significant. The possibility of unexplored reserves being high is indeed real especially in the Caspian region. What has added significance to the Central Asian reserves is that the West particularly the US is keen to diversify its sources of energy. The uncertainty in the Middle East and the Persian Gulf and the need to avoid the dictates of OPEC in terms of demand and supply and the American entanglement in Iraq have led to an intensification of search for new sources of energy, and that is what makes the Central Asian energy reserves to appear significant. Russia, Central Asia and Iran together hold the second largest reserves of natural gas in the world. It is against this perspective that the West has sought to control the energy sources of Central Asia. Prominent American thinkers such as Henry Kissinger has not hesitated to advocate the control of this strategic commodity by any means. Often the competition with Russia to control the energy sources of Central Asia, and to roll back Russian influence, if possible, is referred to as the new version pf the Nineteenth century "great game".

The geopolitical significance of Central Asia's increased tremendously when the global war against terrorism was launched in the wake of the 9/11 events. As mentioned Afghanistan under the Taliban had emerged as the epicenter of extremism and terrorism. Three Central Asian States Turkmenistan, Uzbekistan and Tajikistan share a border with Afghanistan. These forces could destabilize Central Asia was proved in 1999 when an attempt was made by the Islamic Movement of Uzbekistan (IMU) on the life of President Islam Karimov of Uzbekistan. It is well-known that under the Taliban IMU received full support from Afghanistan. Hence the Central Asian States welcomed the military presence of the International Security Assistance Force (ISAF) led by the US at that time. In their view perhaps only the West could guarantee their stability and security. Uzbekistan and Kyrgyzstan granted military base facilities at Karshi-Khanabad and Ganci near Manas airport respectively, while the other states extended military facilities. These facilities proved helpful in defeating the Taliban. Although the Taliban has been routed, the danger of religious extremism and terrorism has not been completely wiped out. Reports are appearing with greater frequency about the reemergence of militant groups in this region. Moreover, the military presence of ISAF now led by the North Atlantic Treaty Organization (NATO) has altered the geopolitical situation.

Apart from the strategic significance of Central Asia's location another aspect that is of equal importance is that the majority of the people of Central Asia are followers of Islam. They belong to the Hanafi School and are largely Sunni Muslims. The five Central Asian States are however secular, modern and opted for a liberal democratic polity patterned on the Western model. The transformation process is incomplete and often it is erratic and slow. The geopolitics of the Central Asian region could undergo a fundamental shift, if the forces of religious extremism, already present in the neighbourhood, could sweep the existing regimes out of power. For the present the prospect of forces of religious extremism gaining ascendancy appears dim. This is because Central Asia lacks the tradition of fundamentalism. Though the people of Central Asia are largely followers of Islam, they have never displayed fanatic tendencies. Several factors have moulded the outlook of the people. The famous silk route which passed through the region exposed the people to novel ideas and new cultures. Renowned centres of learning and culture Bukhara and Samarkand attracted scholars from all over. The strong and benevolent influence of Sufism, a strand within Islam spread the message of tolerance all over Central Asia. In this regard the Sufi brotherhood has tendered yeoman service to the people. The nomadic psyche still exercises a powerful influence on the people of Kazakhstan, Kyrgyzstan and Turkmenistan. The access to modern education, science and technology, health care facilities during the Soviet period have all played a role in shaping the outlook of the Central Asia. The people have imbibed a spirit of tolerance and benevolence. However, the present day dire economic situation and the poor quality of life especially in the Fergana valley, and the lack of openness and participatory politics is driving the underprivileged to extremism.

It should, however, be borne in mind that the Fergana valley had always been a stronghold of Islam. It was the settled way of life in the valley which gave the people enough leisure to imbibe deeply the teachings of Islam. Even in the Soviet period when religion was brutally suppressed, Islam continued to have the faithful flock to the creed. It was in the Fergana valley that the influence of the unofficial clergy was much stronger than the official one in Tashkent. The religiosity of the people in the Fergana was never in doubt. Forces of radical Islam began to gain strength in the wake of Soviet intervention in Afghanistan. The mujahideens, opposing the "godless communists" were motivated to fight the Soviets on the plea that "Islam was in danger". The Soviet withdrawal from Afghanistan and its break-up in 1991 provided these forces of religious extremism a powerful boost. Subsequently, the forces of religious extremism by now well entrenched in Afghanistan acquired a new and a dangerous dimension under the Taliban rule, namely international terrorism. Closely intertwined with the growth of religious extremism and terrorism is the drug trafficking that goes on from Afghanistan via Central Asia to markets in Europe. This pernicious activity sustains extremism and terrorism and has ill effects in terms of corruption, addiction and violence.

Developments in Afghanistan have had an impact on the Fergana valley. The peoples fervour for religion and the economic deprivation have led many to take to extremist activity. From across the border, external funding, safe sanctuaries and training is provided. It is in the Fergana valley that the threat of religious extremism is looming large. Even now the depleted ranks of religious extremism operate from the Fergana valley. The people, however, want a right balance between modernity and tradition. As one perceptive observer stated "One hand must hold the Koran and the other a computer".[1]

Indian Perspectives

Among the various dimensions of geopolitics of Central Asia the one that was of immediate concern to India was the destabilization of the region by forces of religious extremism. From this perspective the developments in the region and the role of Pakistan posed a challenge to Indian interests. After the overthrow of President Najibullah of Afghanistan in 1992 by forces of religious extremism supported by Pakistan, Indian concerns began to mount. It was felt that Afghan developments could cast their long shadow over Central Asia. A simultaneous development in the Central Asian States was the revival of religion. Perhaps a response to the brutal suppression of religion during Soviet times, Mosques and Madrassahs or theological schools sprang up. People began to observe religious practices with fervour. On the other hand, Pakistan's activities in Afghanistan and its interest in Central Asia increased manifold. The spread of the religious agenda in order to acquire strategic depth *vis-à-vis* India became the prime objective of Pakistan in the region. Its objective also included to integrate with the region by acting as a bridge between landlocked Afghanistan and Central Asia from the long term perspective. In short, to create a strategic integrated region with Pakistan perhaps playing a leading role.

India was already battling the forces of religious extremism and terrorism when fundamental changes were occurring at the regional and global levels. After the withdrawal of Soviet troops from Afghanistan in 1989, the US attention from the region decreased rapidly. But it left behind a massive problem. It had created war lordism, a massive refugee population, Islamic militancy and drug trafficking.[2] These forces received a powerful stimulus when the Taliban came to power in Afghanistan. The Kargil war of 1999 is an eloquent testimony of India's apprehensions. Indian concerns were well articulated in the Ministry of Defence Annual Report. It was stated "... since then terrorism has been India's primary and most immediate security threat. Its location at the centre of arc of extremist activism and terrorism, and next to its epicenter, that is, Pakistan has grave implications for India".[3]

Pakistani efforts to befriend the Central Asian States bore no fruit. Instead the Central Asian leaders lacking experience and expertise looked towards India for help and guidance in transforming their political and economic system as well as in managing the diversity of a multi ethnic and a pluralist society. Such an approach came naturally to the Central Asian leaders because of the past historical and cultural affinity, and it undoubtedly eased India's worry. All the leaders viewed religious extremism as a very dangerous tendency. A typical example is the following speech made by President Askar Akayev of Kyrgyzstan during his visit to India in March 1992. He said at the banquet speech "Kyrgyzstan is looking to India as an example, as it sets about restructuring its economy and socio-political system". Further he said, "We categorically reject extremism of any kind. Let it be neither extremism of communist type nor of religious fanatics".[4] Such an approach showed that the leaders of Central Asia viewed India as a friendly country with no hidden agenda to pursue and the secular, modern and democratic ethos of India attracted them.

With the rise of Taliban in Afghanistan practicing a mediaevalist variant of Islam and supported by Pakistan, Indian apprehensions for its security as mentioned increased phenomenally. The Taliban had vowed to spread its ideology in Central Asia by promoting extremism, while they provided support to the militants operating in the Indian State of Jammu and Kashmir. Indian concerns at the regional level were related to stability and security in Central Asia. It did not wish that the existing regimes be overthrown by religious groups. India realized that its security interests were also closely linked to stability and security of Afghanistan. In Indian thinking, "The September 1996 offensive of the Taliban which overthrew the Rabbani government and captured Kabul was believed to have been part of Pakistan's larger game plan to extend her influence in Central Asia".[5]

In Central Asia the Fergana Valley especially the Uzbek part was getting radicalized. With ethnic tensions, economic deprivation and external support it was easy to lure people into extremist and terrorist activities. By the end of the last decade the Taliban was in control of nearly 90 per cent of Afghanistan. It became easy for them to extend support to extremist groups operating in the Fergana Valley. The two main groups that achieved prominence were the *Hizb-ut-Tahrir* (Party of Islamic Liberation) and the IMU. The IMU is now a decimated organization. These two organizations were located in the Uzbek part of the Fergana Valley with branches in other States. The proclaimed goal of *Hizb-ut-Tahrir* (HuT), is the establishment of a Caliphate from Mongolia to the shores of the Caspian Sea. The organizational structure is highly conspirational one. It believes in *Jihad* and the rejection of existing regimes. The IMU aims at capturing Tashkent and overthrowing the government of President Islam Karimov. The fall of Tashkent could have a ripple effect and possibly affect the whole of Central Asia. The Taliban extended full support to IMU. In fact the IMU came into existence due to their support. It is not clear whether both these religious organizations had established links with those groups operating in India.

The commonality in approach to religious extremism and terrorism led India and the States of Central Asia to oppose these forces operating in Afghanistan and extend support to the Northern Alliance. After the devastating events of 9/11 Indian and Central Asian perception about religious extremism being the most dangerous and destabilizing tendency and that this was their primary challenge coincided even further. All supported as mentioned, the USA led international coalition forces against terrorism and the Taliban. The American led coalition forces have ensured stability and security in Afghanistan which has had a beneficial impact on Central Asia. With US military intervention in Iraq attention from this region has got deflected. Osama Bin Laden is still at large. India and the Central Asian States are concerned at the frequent reports suggesting a reemergence of the forces of extremism and terrorism. One view is that extremists have readjusted to the post 9/11 scenario faster than the States have. The Andijon Events of May 2005 when a large group of extremists stormed the prison killing in the process innocent lives indicates that the danger of extremism and terrorism has not been completely wiped out. Although the Taliban has been defeated extremist and terrorist infrastructure has not yet been dismantled. Presently the war against terrorism is a low key one. The terrorist acts in London, New Delhi and Varanasi in July, October 2005 and March 2006 respectively lends credence to the reports about their reemergence. Terrorist activity has escalated with the continuing conflict in Iraq. There is also the ever-present possibility of hostile radical elements gaining access to the weapons of mass destruction. In Indian perception Pakistan has a vested interest in a weak and unstable Afghanistan ... in pursuit of its quest for strategic depth *vis-à-vis* India and Central Asia.[6]

Closely associated with the rise of religious extremism and terrorism is the related growth of drug trafficking. In fact, drug trafficking and organized crime are linked to terrorism. The involvement of militants and criminal groups in the narcotic trade is a worrisome factor. Afghanistan has emerged as the largest producer of heroin. According to UN Report 65 per cent of drugs consumed in the West are from Afghanistan and pass through Central Asia via Namangan route. This has created problems in terms of corruption, addiction and violence. Border management in Central Asia is neither effective nor efficient. The task of management becomes difficult because of porous borders. Besides, the region has plenty of small arms which has the potential to destabilize. Most of the non-State actors have access to small weapons. Such illegal activities helps in sustaining extremism and terrorism. In this context both India and particularly some Central Asian States are being used as transport corridors.

The commonality of approach towards religious extremism has facilitated the creation of an institutional framework. India has set up Joint Working Groups (JWG) to deal with extremism and counter terrorism with Kazakhstan, Kyrgyzstan, Tajikistan and Uzbekistan. It provides for better coordination, sharing of experience and information, regular consultations and training facilities to build up para military forces. A regular exchange of visits of the Groups in this context takes place. While it is difficult to know what transpires at these meetings, the fact that they meet indicates the continuation of the commonality of interests.

The second dimension of geopolitics is that India's extended neighbourhood has drawn the attention of major as well as of regional powers. Central Asia has been witnessing intense competition among the major powers for control and influence. It implies that the Central Asian States could be drawn into the vortex of international politics leaving India with difficult options. Central Asia's strategic location at the juncture of major powers and its energy resources are the two crucial factors at the crux of the competition between the US and Russia in cooperation with China.

In the immediate aftermath of the break-up of the Soviet Union in 1991 it was expected that the Russian Federation would be accepted as a natural partner by the West. But all such hopes were dashed at the Budapest Summit of 1994. The Summit exposed the limits of this cooperation, which was aptly described by President Boris Yeltsin as "Cold Peace". Whether it was differing geopolitical perspectives or civilizational divide that could explain this development is difficult to say. Perhaps it could be both the factors. Since then various views such as "geopolitical pluralism and multi-culturalism" have been propounded in the West. It implied that the post Soviet space cannot be an exclusive sphere of Russian special interest. Even the West had vital interests at stake in this region. Russian response has been that a section of opinion has been advocating confederal tendencies, and if possible integration. Since the mid nineties however both cooperative and competitive tendencies are at play in the post Soviet space including Central Asia.

After the collapse of socialism and the breakup of the Soviet Union, it was assumed that NATO would also dissolve itself. But NATO reinvented itself. In the changed paradigm of the post Cold War NATO was able to identity an adversary against whom its members needed to be safeguarded. The adversary was instability. In the words of American thinker Henry Kissinger "NATO must keep pace with the developments in the international stage and cope with new risks, dangers and threats, which are smaller in scale, but make Western societies more vulnerable". The focus of instability lay in the post Soviet space or on the periphery of Russia. In fact Russia was considered as the biggest source of instability in Western perception. The Western prescription for instability on the periphery was the promotion of Western liberal democracy, human rights and peace. This would widen the area of stability. American approach was slept out by the then Deputy Secretary of State Strobe Talbott who said that the countries of Caucasus and Central Asia should be independent prosperous and secure. This would widen the area of stability in a strategically vital region that borders China, Turkey, Iran and Afghanistan.[7] In the ensuring competition American objectives were clear; to control the energy resources of Central Asia particularly its focus is on the Caspian Basin, to roll back Russian influence, if possible, and to fight the war on terror. Russian objectives were more comprehensive and substantial. Russia shares a long border with Kazakhstan. The border is man made; it is not clear where the Russian steppes end and Kazakh grasslands begin. Hence monitoring such a border is difficult. Besides, a large number of ethnic Russians reside in Central Asia, and ensuring their safety and security is an objective enshrined in the Russian Military Doctrine. Given its Chechen problem any spread of religious extremism would further complicate Russian security interests. From economic point it was to see that the Central Asian markets were open. In this connection it wants to develop the transport network and in the security sphere, perhaps to forge a confederation. The Chinese interest in the region has also grown tremendously. It focuses primarily on maintaining peace along its western periphery, and ensuring energy security. In the Istanbul Summit of NATO of 2004 Central Asia and Caucasus were accorded a special focus in their activity.

In this emerging competition the issue of laying a new export pipeline infrastructure assumed more political than economic dimension. It became a tool in the hands of West to isolate Russia. In due course the question of Baku-Tbilisi-Ceyhan Pipeline (BTC) was juxtaposed against the Caspian Pipeline Consortium (CPC) which transits through Russia up to Novorossyisk on the Black Sea. The pipeline issue became a symbol of the emerging subtle competition between the West on the one hand, and Russia on the other hand. A related dimension is the question of building a transport corridor that would reduce Central Asian States dependence on Russia. The TRACECA project supported by the European Union *versus* the North-South Corridor project initiated by Russia.

On the other hand the Central Asian States as mentioned are not mute spectators in the evolving rivalry. Their main objective is to assert their independence, as well as to overcome their landlocked status. The foreign policies especially that of Kazakhstan and Kyrgyzstan is to follow a multi vector foreign policy which aims at maintaining a balance. However, if pushed too strongly there could be an adverse reaction. This has happened in Kyrgyzstan and Uzbekistan. The US was asked to vacate the military base facilities granted by Uzbekistan. In November 2005 US military present was withdrawn.

In view of the expanding NATO, and its focus on the Russian periphery, Russia has forged strong cooperation with China. The positive Chinese response is because it perceives that the US wants to establish its presence near its Western part where the Uyghur problem makes the region highly vulnerable. In cooperation with China, Russia and the four Central Asian States have formed a regional arrangement the Shanghai Cooperation Organisation (SCO). Security concerns top the agenda of SCO. By asking the US to announce a time frame for the withdrawal of its military presence, the SCO demonstrated its confidence as well as its ability to deal with the dangers posed by religious extremism and terrorism. This was followed by the combined military exercise in the Asia-Pacific in August 2005. It was an impressive display. It also points to the fact that the competition is possibly being accelerated. A phase of reactivism by Russia in Central Asia seems to have started. It is not going to passively acquiesce with the West as it had done in the past. An equally significant development is the formation of the Collective Security Treaty Organization (CSTO) comprising of Russia, Belarus, Kazakhstan, Kyrgyzstan, Tajikistan and Uzbekistan. Through the CSTO Russia is attempting to build closer security and defence ties with its partners.

After the vacation of the Qarshi-Khanabad base in Uzbekistan, Russian military presence in the region is considerable. Besides the military bases in Kyrgyzstan and Tajikistan, Russia is likely to acquire a base in Southern Kyrgyzstan in Osh. There is, however, a view that Russia's strong military presence in Central Asia is a projection of its power and to bind the Central Asian countries close to it, than to tackle concerns relating to religious extremism, terrorism and drug trafficking. These issues require better border security and management as the targets are often dispersed.

At the broader level Russia and China have been advocates of a Multi Polar world as against the Western idea of a unipolar world. It is perhaps in this context that former Prime Minister Y. Primakov put forward the idea of Russia-China-India Strategic Triangle.

Hence we find that Central Asia holds immense geopolitical significance for India. But this extended neighbourhood is not as peaceful and stable as it should be. The main destabilizing issue is the danger of religious extremism and terrorism. The sources of this danger emanate from the same origin as it is for India. In this context it is essential that Indian efforts at reconstruction and development in Afghanistan succeed. A strong, stable and a prosperous Afghanistan will have a beneficial impact on both Central Asian States as well as India. With the growing significance of Eurasia in the coming decades, the geostrategic importance of Central Asia would increase manifold. The competition that exists between Russia and the US, at times overtly and at times covertly is not likely to escalate into a confrontational situation at least not over Central Asia in the near future. It appears that for the present the interests of the major powers are not hostile. This scenario could undergo a radical change, if China surges forward and poses a direct challenge to US leadership role in world affairs. The possibility of international coalition forces withdrawing from the region in the near future appears dim. As Frederick Starr in his Testimony before the US Senates Subcommittee on Central Asia and the Caucasus said in December 2001, "Bordered by nuclear states and formidable regional powers, all of which have close historic and cultural ties with the region, Central Asia cannot depend for its security on any one of them without imperiling the security of all countries. The US must therefore be prepared to keep its forces in the region until a comprehensive security structure is in place." Moreover, reports about re-grouping of extremists and terrorists makes it difficult for the Western presence to be withdrawn.

On the other hand heightened Russian activism in Central Asia and the trend of using its energy card shows that Russia does have the potential to emerge as a pivotal player in international politics. Today Russian military presence is substantial and it is continuing its efforts to bring about better coordination among its Commonwealth of Independent States members. China's presence in the region is increasing, but it is not yet an independent player. In the emerging scenario Indian presence in Central Asia needs to be enhanced. In order to be effective Indian policy should aim at a serious engagement of the region. Given the immense fund of goodwill for India in Central Asia, sit should not be a difficult task.

NOTES

1. *The Times of Central Asia* (Bishkek), 7 February 2002.
2. Svante Cornell and Regime Spector, "Central Asia More Than Islamic Extremists", *The Washington Quarterly,* Winter 2002.
3. *Ministry of Defence, Government of India, Annual Report* 2003-04.
4. *Indian Express* (New Delhi), 18 March 1992.
5. *Ministry of Defence, Government of India, Annual Report,* 2002-03.
6. *Ibid.*, 2002-03.
7. Strobe Talbott, Speech delivered at the Institute of Caucasus and Central Asia, School of Advanced International Studies, John Hopkins University, September 1997.

13

Politics of Oil and Natural Gas in Central Asia

Conflicts and Co-operation

R.G. Gidadhubli

During the last over a decade the Central Asian republics of the former Soviet Union have undertaken the task of economic transition from socialist system to market economies. Being sovereign and independent states, the task of transition has been challenging and quite formidable. The leaders of the Central Asian States have tried to mobilize oil and natural gas resources in which they are endowed, as one of major sources for the development of their economies. But oil and natural gas resources of the Central States have become objects of international politics, which has attracted major players including Russia and the USA. An effort has been made in this paper to examine various issues concerned and how they have affected the Central Asia States.

Central Asia's Oil Sector Before the Soviet Break-up

At the time of the Soviet disintegration, the Central Asian States (CAS) played a rather marginal role in the oil-energy sector of the former Soviet Union. This is evident from the fact that in 1991 out of the total production of 10.3 million barrels per day, the share of the CAS was less than 7 per cent. In the total estimated reserves of the USSR amounting to 57 billion barrels of oil, the CAS accounted for about 16 per cent. Resources located in Western Siberia, Eastern Siberia, Volga-Ural regions in Russia and Azerbaijan played a major role by virtue of their dominant position with significant reserve potentialities of oil and gas. Moreover, the oil sector of the Soviet Union in general including that of the CAS suffered from various problems such as the shortage of functioning production equipments, lack of modern technology etc. as a result of which over 16,000 oil wells were lying idle in the USSR as a whole. The position of natural gas was somewhat better although in 1991 output had slightly declined. The Soviet Union had already emerged as the foremost with regard to natural gas reserves in the world. The CAS had also been identified as the most promising areas of natural gas reserves in the former USSR. According to a report of the Congressional Research Service, in 1991 Turkmenistan and Uzbekistan in Central Asia (that is excluding Kazakhstan) had 2 giant oil fields and 14 giant natural gas fields among the large number of oil-gas fields in the former USSR.

Considering this situation, the oil industry of the Central Asian republics was politically less significant in the former Soviet Union although the natural gas sector started assuming some importance from the perspective of the Central planners. Notwithstanding this, even as the Soviet leaders started setting up joint ventures in the country in collaboration with some western oil firms under Gorbachev's policy of perestroika mainly to acquire western modern technology and equipments for oil extraction and processing. Some oil and gas wells were also set up under such joint ventures. For instance, the Tengiz oil field in Kazakhstan was being developed and expanded with the collaboration of the Chevron Oil Company with estimated investment requirement of about $ 20 billion to develop the oil fields over the next 40 years. This joint venture was to deal with the problem of toxic hydrogen sulphide gas in the Tengiz oil field. This joint venture was also to be a test case for success as it was an object of intense contention between reformers and hard line communists on the question of sharing of revenue and juridical authority between Moscow and Kazakhstan. However, after the Soviet break up, the Chevron firm was to deal only with Kazakhstan.

Oil and Gas Resources of CAS—Post Soviet Period

It is an important to note that oil and natural gas resources are not uniformly distributed over the five CAS. Among the CAS, Kazakhstan is well endowed with oil and natural gas resources. According to the Energy Information Administration of the USA, the total potential reserves of oil of Kazakhstan are estimated at about 92 billion barrels, out of which proved resources are about 18 billion barrels. In the case of Turkmenistan potential reserves of oil are 80 billion barrels of which proved resources are 2 billion barrels. These resources are located mainly in the Caspian Sea region. In comparison to these two states of Central Asia, Uzbekistan has only about 2 billion barrels of potential oil reserves. But Uzbekistan and Turkmenistan have abundant reserves of natural gas. Kyrgyz Republic and Tajikistan are relatively less endowed with oil-gas resources. During the last decade efforts have been made by all the Central Asian countries to explore hydrocarbon resources in their territories. Thus as per the Uzbek official sources, intensive efforts of exploration have indicated that out of 171 discovered fields, 73 fields possess hydrocarbon reserves and their total potential reserves of oil could be 5 billion tonnes. Exploratory work being carried out by Kazakhstan and Turkmenistan has indicated large reserves of oil and gas.

There seems to be some political angle with regard to the estimates of oil-gas resources of the CAS. This is evident from the fact that in the immediate aftermath of the Soviet break-up, some hype was created in the West about the huge hydrocarbon resources of the CAS. For instance, Turkmenistan was called the 'Kuwait of the 21st century' by some Western commentators. Similarly, there were speculations as to whether Central Asia could be an alternative to the Middle East for oil supplies to the world markets. In fact, this raises the question about the international significance, both politically and economically, of the hydrocarbon resources of the CAS. While there is no doubt about the vast hydrocarbon resource potentialities of the CAS, there has been some sober assessment about the hydrocarbon potentialities of the CAS from the global perspective. Considerable exploratory work has been carried out and is still going on which alone could determine the realistic position in the years to come. Notwithstanding this, according to some experts, oil and gas resources are certainly important sources for meeting the world energy needs in the years to come. More importantly, it is also opined that the oil and natural gas resources of the CAS may not be an alternative source to the Middle East, but certainly additional sources to those in other parts of the world.

Oil and natural gas have also played an important role in shaping intra-state political relations of the CAS. This is partly because in comparison to these three states, the other two Central Asian countries, namely the Kyrgyz Republic and Tajikistan lack hydrocarbon resources but have abundant water resources being upstream countries for the two large rivers, namely Syr Darya and Amu Darya. While the Kyrgyz Republic and Tajikistan are critically dependent upon Kazakhstan and Uzbekistan to meet their domestic needs for oil and gas, the latter being down steam countries are dependent upon Kyrgyzstan and Tajikistan for water flowing into the rivers. Hence, under ideal conditions there could be greater co-operation among these Central Asian countries for mutual benefit. But proper understanding is yet to emerge. In the past the domestic needs of Tajikistan and Kyrgyz Republic for oil and gas were met without any difficulty as they were part of the former Soviet Union. But during the last decade their dependency factor has been felt in the evolution of the interstate political relations of the CAS. Occasionally differences have arisen during the last few years when Uzbekistan stopped the supply of natural gas to the Kyrgyz republic. It appears that there could be several reasons such differences. For instance, the Uzbek officials allege that they were reacting to the actions of the Kyrgyz Republic, which did not release water into the rivers flowing downstream into the Uzbek republic. Similarly, there were other reasons such as the delays in the payment for the supply of energy on the part of the Kyrgyz republic due to which Uzbekistan and Kazakhstan occasionally decided to stop the supply of oil and gas. However, so far in such situations with the political intervention at the highest level of the presidents of the countries concerned, such issues were sorted out. But there is need for ensuring greater co-operation and durable understanding among the CAS on common issues such as energy and water resources for achieving the mutual benefit of the countries concerned.

How far have the oil-energy resources benefited the economic development of the CAS? What is their political significance for the CAS? These are some of the questions that arise in understanding the political and economic significance of this sector for the CAS. So far as Turkmenistan is concerned oil and natural gas are crucial items for the development of its economy. They constitute the major share in hard currency earnings for the country. Hence, the oil-energy sector occupies a predominant share in the GDP of Turkmenistan. In the case of Kazakhstan oil-energy sector does play an important part in the economy of this country. In 2005 oil exports constituted about a quarter of total export earnings of the country. According to some experts energy exports could be as high 60 per cent of total exports. But there are other mineral resources such as ferrous, non-ferrous and precious minerals, and chemicals, which contribute for the development of many industrial sectors of Kazakhstan. Hence Kazak economy is relatively more diversified even as oil and gas contribute significantly for the generation of financial resources for the country. In the case of Uzbekistan natural gas has potentiality to be an important item of hard currency earnings in the future. Even at present Uzbekistan does supply gas to the Kyrgyz Republic. Being well connected by pipelines with industrial centres such as Ural and West Siberia of Russia and parts of Kazakhstan, Uzbek gas was being supplied to these states. Hence, the proposal of the Russian President for the formation of an 'Alliance of Gas Exporting Countries', if materializes, will immensely benefit Uzbekistan both politically and economically in the long run. But Uzbekistan is also rich in precious minerals such as gold and non-ferrous minerals, which are also important for the economic development of the country. Notwithstanding these observations, oil and natural gas have great demand in the world energy market and hence they earn hard currency for the countries exporting them. Hence, the CAS have benefited particularly during the last 5-6 years when international prices for oil and natural gas have increased. This seems to be evident from the fact that between 2000 and 2005 the GDP growth rates of Turkmenistan have been quite high ranging between 10 to 20 per cent per annum. Similarly, in the case of Kazakhstan GDP growth rates have been fluctuating between 6 to 13 per cent per annum during the last three to four years. It appears that export of oil and natural gas seems to have contributed significantly for achieving this reasonably good economic performance.

Conflict of Interests Among the CAS

There have been few political conflicts concerning the oil and other energy resources of the CAS, particularly with regard to the issue of the legal status of the Caspian Sea. The issue has remained quite complex. During the last decade, the five countries concerned, namely Kazakhstan, Turkmenistan, Azerbaijan, Iran and Russia have not been able to come to any agreement to the solution of the problem of the division of the Caspian Sea. Hence, mainly at bilateral levels some agreements have been reached. For instance, in July 1998 the presidents of Kazakhstan and Russia signed an agreement on the division of the bottom of the Caspian Sea on the principle of 'modified middle line'. Subsequently, Russia and Azerbaijan reached a similar agreement. Turkmenistan and Azerbaijan signed a bilateral communiqué in March 1998 on the question of the division of the Caspian Sea on the 'middle line principle' and not on the 'modified middle line' principle. As a result of on-going efforts, in May 2003 Russia, Kazakhstan and Azerbaijan reached a trilateral agreement on some issues of the demarcation of the Caspian Sea. In July 2003 the Tenth Round of Talks was held in Moscow at the level of the deputy foreign ministers during which, the foreign minister of Russia hoped that the talks would focus on narrowing down disagreements over the legal status of the Caspian. On 8th September, 2003 at the Convention held in Asgabat, the five states agreed only on some technical issues such as the protection of biological reserves of the Caspian Sea. However, there were differences among these states on the substantive issue of the status of the Caspian Sea. Occasionally differences between Turkmenistan and Azerbaijan and Iran and Azerbaijan have led to serious conflicts. In this regard to discuss regional energy issues of the Caspian an international meeting will be held at the end of February 2004 in Turkey at Istambul in which major energy producers of the CAS, Russia, and other concerned countries such as the USA, UK, Turkey and several key international agencies including the World Bank, EBRD etc. will be participating. It appears that issues relating to the legal status of the Caspian, feasibility studies of transporting oil-gas from the Caspian including that through Afghanistan were to be discussed.

Mutual co-operation and collective effort seem to be lacking on the part of the CAS in developing their hydrocarbon energy resources. While it is understandable that each of the Central Asian countries tries to maximize economic gains from the resources located in its territory, there is competition among them to attract foreign investment and technology to explore and exploit oil and gas resources and also to export them to world markets. Lack of co-operation is evident from the fact that in July 2003 the Uzbekistan President Islam Karimov met the of Russia's Gazprom chief Aleksei Miller and sought Russian help for laying pipelines for transporting its natural gas bypassing Turkmenistan. An agreement has been signed between Uzbekistan and Gazprom of Russia to export 10 billion cubic metres of gas by 2005 from the level of 5 billion cubic metres exported in 2002-2003. As a further step in that direction joint efforts are being made to explore and develop gas deposits in the Ust-Yust are of western Karakalpakstan. It may be observed in this context that both Uzbekistan and Turkmenistan are major producers and exporters of natural gas and hence there is competition between the two countries. Hence, to maximize its own economic benefit Uzbekistan could have entered into this agreement with Gazprom of Russia.

Some efforts have been made during the last several years by the Central Asian leaders to bring about regional economic co-operation and even declarations are also made to that effect from time to time. But very often policies and declarations largely remain on paper. This could be partly because as opined by some analysts national policies of the CAS generally favour self-sufficiency and import substitution at the expense of promoting regional trade and rationalization of energy use.

Oil Politics Between the CAS and Russia

Oil and gas have become important elements in the political and economic relations between the Central Asian States (CAS) and Russia. During the last decade due to certain policies pursued and actions taken by the CAS and Russia, some situations have arisen which have caused differences and conflicts in their relations. There is one problem that has arisen because being landlocked countries, the CAS are geographically at a disadvantage in transporting oil and natural gas to world markets. During the Soviet era pipelines were laid linking the oil-gas fields of the CAS with other republics of the USSR and also with ports for exporting to world markets. The CAS were not directly involved in deciding whether oil and gas produced in their republics was to meet the domestic needs of the country or to be exported. After the Soviet break-up, the CAS are dependent upon the pipelines passing through Russia for exporting their energy products to world markets. The Russian policy makers in their own national interest would like to retain this situation so that the CAS would continue to be dependent upon Russia for export of oil and gas. But at the same time the policy makers of the CAS in their national interest have decided to create additional and or alternative routes for exporting oil and gas to western markets. As a result the concept of 'Multiple Pipeline Policy' has emerged which has received considerable support from the USA and many other western countries. But the Russian policy makers are not in favour of the Multiple Pipeline Policy of the CAS as it would reduce the importance of Russia for the CAS. For instance, on the Baku-Ceyhan Pipeline project there have been differences between Kazakhstan and Azerbaijan on the one hand and Russia on the other. The Baku-Ceyhan Pipeline from Baku in Azerbaijan passing through Georgia is to transport oil from the Caspian Sea to western markets from the Turkish port of Ceyhan. This Baku-Ceyhan Pipeline has become a reality in 2005 and has been assuming importance for Azerbaijan and also for the CAS.

There are proposals to lay pipelines from Kazakhstan through the bottom of the Caspian Sea linking the oil fields of Kazakhstan to Baku for export. This pipeline will bypass Russia completely. Presumably for this reason the Russian side has raised several objections. Firstly, some Russian scientists have observed that the pipelines passing through the Caspian Sea could be exposed to the potential threats from seismic tremors. Secondly, it is argued that the Baku-Ceyhan Pipeline is not economically viable considering the cost involved. The mountainous terrain of Georgia through which the proposed pipeline is to pass through, will certainly be adding to the cost of the project. According to a report published on the 9th January, 2004 in Moscow, Russia would not participate in the construction of the Baku-Ceyhan Project as this was not considered to be economically viable. In this context it was contended by some Russian officials that even in the case of the Caspian Pipeline Consortium (CPC) pipeline in which Russia has 24 per cent stake, there was hardly any profit for the country. While the details of Russia's calculations are not known, the basis of Russia's calculation might be different from that of the USA, Azerbaijan and Turkey, which have initiated the Baku-Ceyhan Project. Moreover, the investments in the infrastructure development yield returns over a long period. Apart from these finer calculations, more importantly there could be political interests on the part of the

Central Asian countries as also on the part of Russia in taking different positions on this issue. By March 2006 Baku-Ceyhan Pipeline has become operational and Central Asian countries have evinced interest in it.

Between Kazakhstan and Russia there were some hiccups in their relations in matters relating to oil. For instance, in 2001 there were differences between the two countries over the delay in the inauguration of the Caspian Pipeline Consortium (CPC) project, which is connecting Tengiz oil field with Novorussisk port passing through Russia. This project has been crucial for the export of oil from Kazakhstan and hence the Kazakh Prime Minister Q. Toqaev stated in May 2001 that Russia was taking 'negative attitude' which caused this delay. It appears that there were some disputes between the two countries regarding customs duty. Even when this dispute was resolved, the Russian contention was that an agreement was to arrived at by all concerned possibly including foreign oil companies such as Chevron etc. on the 'terms of the use of pipeline'. It appears that there were different views on issues such as the quantum of oil to be transported through the pipeline. There could be other reasons for such situations causing irritants in Kazakh-Russia relations. It appears that according to some Russian political groups the CPC would be a competitor for Russian oil exporters, while few even contended that Russian exporters should get preference over Kazakh counterparts in exporting oil through the CPC as the pipeline passes through the Russian territory. However, such arguments did not carry much weight with the policy makers in Russia and hence despite such views and arguments, the CPC was completed albeit with some delay and Kazakh oil has been exported to the Western markets. On the other hand, there has been closer co-operation between Kazakhstan and Russia in the development of oil-gas industry of Kazakhstan and their exports to world markets. This is evident from the fact that in April 2006 Putin has offered to the Kazakh President Nazarbaev to increase the quantity of export of oil through CPC from 28 million tones to 67 million tonnes per year. This was partly intended to ensure that Kazakhstan would remain close to Russia and not get more attracted in the Baku-Ceyhan Pipeline project.

Notwithstanding some differences, there has been growing co-operation between the CAS and Russia in the oil and energy sector, which has strengthened political relations between them. While Russia has strong geopolitical interest in Central Asia to keep these states under its sphere of influence, co-operation in oil and energy sector has been an added dimension in cementing such ties. It may be stated at the outset that Russia is not dependent upon the CAS for oil-energy resources for its domestic needs, since Russia possesses large reserves in its own territory. But by co-operating with the CAS in this sector, the Russian policy makers may be able to indirectly control oil-energy sector and in turn enhance its own influence in the world oil-energy market. This is evident from various policy measures and actions taken by Russia with the CAS during the last decade.

For instance, in March 2002 Russia's President Vladimir Putin proposed to the Presidents of Kazakhstan, Turkmenistan and Uzbekistan that together they could form an 'Alliance of Gas Producers'. As reported by Khabar TV on 1st March, 2002, the Commonwealth of Independent States (CIS) possessed 40 per cent of global resources of natural gas. Moreover, according to Russian experts Russia and the CAS have well developed transport system. Hence it is argued that these two factors taken together will give Russia and the CAS a clout to 'influence not just the European economy but the world economy as well'. While such a gas alliance has not been formed as yet, but as and when such a proposal materializes it would certainly benefit Russia politically and the CAS economically. Secondly, during the last decade Russian policy makers have been making efforts to bring about agreements among the Caspian Sea States on the issue of sharing of the energy resources of this sea. Viktor Kalyuzhny the special representative of the president of Russia has been an active negotiator in these discussions and often defusing the conflicts that have arisen among the Caspian Sea States as between Turkmenistan and Azerbaijan, between Azerbaijan and Iran and so on.

Thirdly, Russia seems to be following a two-pronged policy with regard to oil-energy resources of the CAS. As stated earlier, at the state-to-state level, the Russian government has been promoting its own national interest while extending cooperation with the CAS. During the last couple of years, Uzbekistan has come very close to Russia particularly after the Andijan incident when the USA has been critical of the Uzbek policy on the human rights issue. There is close cooperation between Russia and Uzbekistan in the energy sector.

Russia's state owned and private oil and gas firms such as the Gazprom, Rosneft, Lukoil have been taking active role both in terms of investment and extending technical help in exploring and exploiting energy resources of the Central Asian countries. For instance, in February 2003 the Turkmen President S. Niyazov invited Gazprom to develop deposits in the Turkmen sector of the Caspian Sea and he discussed with the Gazprom chief Aleksei Miller the scope for long term co-operation between Russia and Turkmenistan. Subsequently, on the 18th August 2003 the Turkmen deputy Prime Minister Yolly Gurbanmuradov signed an agreement with the Gazprom chief on the reconstruction and expansion of gas pipeline system connecting Turkmenistan oil-gas deposits with Russia. According to reports, Gazprom has entered into a 25 year contract for gas deliveries with Turkmenistan. Similarly, Russia's Gazeksport has agreed to deliver equipment and services as partial payment for Turkmen gas deliveries in 2004-2006. These facts indicate close co-operation developing between Turkmenistan and Russia in the energy sector both at the state level and private level. Russia has been following similar policy with other CAS. For instance, Russia's Lukoil chief Vagit Alekperov and Kazakhstan state owned KazMunGaz signed a MOU in Astana on 10th February, 2003 to create a joint venture to explore and develop an unspecified block in the Caspian Sea which is likely to contain recoverable reserves of up to 100 million tonnes of oil. Even as this project will be launched in 2004, during the last 8 years Lukoil has invested over $ 1.5 billion in the oil sector of Kazakhstan and total investment by this firm in future is expected to exceed $ 3 billion which has made this firm as the largest investor in Kazakhstan. On the 9th and 10th of January 2004 Russia's President Vladimir Putin visited Kazakhstan during which policy decisions were taken to further strengthen political and economic co-operation between the two countries in which energy sector figured prominently. Also during President Putin's stay in Astana on 9th January, 2004, he and President Nazarbaev issued a joint statement on bilateral cooperation in the energy sector, as reported by the *Interfax*. This joint statement also focused on the joint development of Kazakhstan's oil fields at the northern end of the Caspian Sea, the transport of Kazakh oil and gas to world markets, and cooperation in developing the electric-power industry.

Russia's political and economic interest in Central Asia is partly dictated by its 'Near Abroad' policy. While in the first half of the 1990s there was no active interest and involvement of Russia in the Central Asian countries for a variety of domestic and external factors, during the last several years and particularly under the leadership of Vladimir Putin, Russia has adopted a policy constructive engagement with the CAS. In this context oil and natural gas resources of the CAS have played an important role as already stated above.

Political and Economic Interests of the USA and Western Europe in the CAS

Western countries and particularly the USA have evinced keen interest in Central Asia after the Soviet disintegration. The availability of energy resources in the CAS has been an added element in the US policy towards Central Asia. This is evident from the US strong political and economic support and encouragement to the Multiple Pipeline Policy (MPP) being pursued by the CAS and Caucasian countries. In the US policy perspective, the MPP provides an additional opportunity to the CAS to reach out to the world energy market and earn hard currency for their economic development, which in turn, it was hoped, would help to enhance political stability and to support political independence of these newly independent countries. Moreover, according to some western analysts, the USA has specific political interest in the MPP and that is to restrict Russia's monopoly position over the export routes of oil-gas resources of the CAS. Moreover, MPP would ultimately enable the USA to achieve its geopolitical interest and that of containing Russia's sphere of influence over the Central Asian countries. Thus oil and energy resources of the CAS are an important component of the Great Game being played between Russia on the one hand and the USA on the other. The interest of the USA is evident from the policy statement issued in May 1998 by the USA and European Union on the 'Caspian Energy'. In this policy statement the importance of oil-gas resources of the Caspian including those in the CAS has been recognized as also its contribution to the economic prosperity, energy security and stability in the region.

The European countries have also been active in promoting MPP of the CAS, which is evident from the support to the Odessa-Brody pipeline project. In this project Ukraine and Poland are also major beneficiaries. Hence Poland and Ukraine have signed an accord on the16th January 2004 to set up a joint venture to construct a 556 km pipeline, which will extend the Odessa-Brody pipeline linking it to the port city of Polsk in Northern Poland. According to the deputy Prime Minister of Ukraine Andriy Klyuyev this extension project which was completed by 2005 "has enormous significance for the government of Ukraine and will positively influence cooperation with the European Union". He has stated that this project has the support of the European Commission. The European Commission Strategy paper 1999, which spelt out its programme for Central Asia 2002-2004, elaborated common problems and shared challenges of Central Asia. In this strategy paper it has been stated that one of the objectives of the European Commission is to support the CAS in making more sustainable use of natural resources of Central Asia, which naturally includes oil and natural gas resources. In fact, during the last decade the European Commission has given assistance of over $ 944 million to the five Central Asian countries for their economic development including development of oil-gas sector. Hence, the European Commission has supported this Odessa-Brody pipeline project, which has been built with the intention of pumping Caspian oil to Europe. Considering the future prospects of exporting oil and gas to Europe through this Odessa-Brody pipeline, the CAS have evinced considerable interest in this project. In fact, Kazakhstan has given top priority to Odessa-Brody pipeline project. At the same time for Ukraine this pipeline is important since it will give an opportunity to earn big money through tariffs on the oil being exported through its territory. But since this pipeline bypasses Russia, efforts have been made by the oil-gas lobby in Russia by proposing to Ukraine and Poland to make this pipeline run in the 'Reverse Mode' that is allowing oil to flow from Brody to Odessa so that it can benefit Russia. According to some reports TNK-BP oil firms of Russia have offered $ 60 to 90 million annually for accepting this proposal. But it appears that there is a strong pro-western lobby, which is in favour of oil being exported through the port of Polsk in Northern Poland. From this account it is evident as to how international politics is being played by vested interests in matters concerning energy resources.

Both Turkmenistan and Kazakhstan while keeping close political and economic ties with the USA have tried to exercise their option with regard to promoting close relations with Iran and for exporting oil through that country. During the last decade Kazakhstan has supplied oil to northern ports of Iran over the Caspian Sea and in turn Iran exported equal quantity of oil through its southern ports in the Persian Gulf. Similarly, Turkmenistan, which has territorial contiguity with Iran has been exporting oil and gas through Iran. With increasing scope for exports from their production, Turkmenistan seems to be interested in having a pipeline through Iran for increasing export capacity of its country, a proposal to that effect was made by the Turkmen President Sapramurad Niyazov to the Iranian Foreign Minister Kamal Kharrazi, who visited Ashgabat on the 15th January 2004 (Report of Turkmenistan.ru). In turn Iranian foreign minister stated that Iran would like to increase the amount of oil transited from Turkmenistan, and also would like to double its annual trade turnover with Turkmenistan to $1 billion. For Kazakhstan pipeline through Iran will be cheaper and hence will support this proposal although the USA is not in favour of this pipeline project as it passes through Iran.

China-CAS Relations in Oil Sector

China is emerging as one of the important players in the CAS oil-gas market. This is partly because China's energy needs are growing at an alarming rate of 10 million bbl/d over the next 10-15 years. Hence, to meet its domestic demand for oil and natural gas China has been vigorously exploring alternative sources of supply and the Central Asian countries offer a good source. During the last decade the leaders of China and the CAS have made several exchange of visits at various levels including at high levels, which has created cordial political relations among them. Moreover, the creation of the Shanghai Cooperation Organization (SCO) in which China and several Central Asian countries are members besides Russia has further brought these countries closer politically and economically. This favourable situation has brought the CAS and China closer in the energy sector. In the opinion of the Turkmen president the CAS have to work out new strategies and approaches for meeting the needs of the 21st century and in that 'orientation towards China will become the main direction of transportation of oil and natural gas pipeline projects of both Turkmenistan and Kazakhstan. In turn China has shown interest in undertaking the pipeline projects from the Central Asian countries towards east linking centres in China. One such project is a pipeline from Aktyubinsk in Kazakhstan to Xingiang in eastern parts of China. Economic feasibility could be an important factor for such a project to materialize since this Aktyubinsk-Xingiang pipeline will be 2,880 kilometres and estimated investment will be over 3.5 billion dollars. This will be perhaps the longest pipeline from Central Asia since CPC pipeline is about 1,900 kilometres, Kazakhstan-Turkmenistan-Iran pipeline about 1,490 kilometres. However, according to some experts, the ambitious Chinese plan to build the longest pipeline in the world, from Western Kazakhstan to China, at a cost of $10 billion seems to have run into financing difficulties. China has enhanced its political and economic interest in Central Asia particularly after the Shanghai Cooperation Organization has become an effective regional organization. To meet its own growing energy needs China has increased its investment in the energy sector in Kazakhstan and Turkmenistan.

There is a political angle also in this regard. Russia has been forging close political and economic ties with China during the last decade. In the energy sector also Russia has proposed pipelines from its eastern regions of Siberia and the Far East to China to export oil and gas to the Chinese market and these proposals find positive reaction from the Chinese leaders. The Russian leaders have also shown keen interest in linking oil and natural gas fields of the Central Asian countries with the Russian pipelines to export oil and gas to China. With this strategy apart from economic gains from the tariffs earned for transporting oil and gas through their pipelines, Russia will get political leverage over the CAS in such proposals.

In lieu of conclusion it may be stated that during the Soviet era even though oil and natural gas sector of the Central Asian republics played a rather marginal role, this sector has assumed considerable importance for the newly independent states of Central Asia during the last over a decade. The CAS have made considerable efforts to explore and exploit oil and gas resources in their countries considering the growing importance of energy resources in the world market. Moreover, oil and gas are major sources of hard currency earnings for the CAS. At the same time oil and gas of the CAS have become objects of international politics. Russia has been trying to retain and increase its hold on the energy sector of the CAS not so much as to make economic gain but more to enhance its political influence in the Central

Asian region. Hence, to achieve this objective notwithstanding some differences, there have been wider co-operation between Russia and the CAS in the oil-gas sector. At the same time the USA has been investing in the oil sector of the CAS and offering technical assistance for the development of energy resources in these countries. Moreover, the USA has been actively supporting the Multiple Pipeline Policies of the CAS. These measures are partly intended to meet its own energy needs but mainly to contain Russia's influence in the Central Asian region thus a New Great Game is being played. Moreover, China has been a relatively new entrant in the energy sector of the Central Asian region and it may assume more importance in the years to come considering its growing domestic demand for energy resources. In view of these complex political factors of great international significance, the Central Asian States can benefit economically from the availability of oil and natural gas resources in their countries if they can achieve their declared objective and sustain greater political co-operation among themselves.

REFERENCES

Central Asian Survey Vol. 1 August 2001.

Cohen, Ariel, *The New Great Game: Oil Politics in the Caucasus and Central Asia.* Backgrounder, The Heritage Foundation, Washington 25th January 1996.

Economic Intelligence Reports, Russia and Central Asia U.K. 1995-2003.

Gidadhubli, R.G. 'Politics of Energy Resources of Central Asia'. In "*Central Asia. The Great Game Replayed- An Indian Perspective*". Edited by Nirmala Joshi, New Century Publications, Delhi, 2003.

Gidadhubli, R.G. "Oil Politics in Central Asia," *Economic and Political Weekly*, Mumbai January 30, 1999.

Gizzatov, V.Kh. 'Legal Status of the Caspian Sea and Problems Connected with the Pipelines' *Cayst*, Monthly Journal from Kazakhstan, *Almaaty* (In Russian).

Menon, Rajan, 'Treacherous Terrain: The Politics and Security Dimension of Energy Development in the Caspian Sea Zone'. NBR Analysis, USA 1999.

RFERL Reports, New Line Prague, 'Russia and Central Asia Part I.' 1996-2003

Regional Analysis: Caucasus and Central Asia, September 2001.

US Energy Information Administration. Department of Commerce 'Caspian Sea Region', July 2001.

14

INDIA AND POST-SOVIET ASIA

AN APPRAISAL OF INDIA'S CENTRAL ASIA POLICY

SHEEL K. ASOPA

The collapse of the Soviet Union in 1991 came as a great shock to India. It took a long time in getting acclimatized to the changed scenario in its extended neighbourhood. The Central Asian republics attained independent sovereign status and looked to India for help and support. During the period 1991-1995, India was passing through a different phase of political instability and was not able to respond befittingly to the events like the Gulf War fought by US-led coalition against Iraq, collapse the Soviet Union, emergence of new states in the Central Asian-Trans-Caucasian region etc. The leadership and political makers cannot grasp the high stakes that India has in the Central Asia's stability, security, integrity and secular ethos.

The newly independent states of Central Asia had been viewed by the power-seekers in the region and outside as a "soft ground" for moving in to establish their sphere of interest. The theories of "power vacuum" and "great game"[1] were revived and regional and extra regional contenders for power and influence registered their claims on the oil and natural gas-rich regions of Central Asian-Trans-Caucasian countries.

The most difficult challenge to their survival as independent political entities came from Islamic fundamentalist forces active in Afghanistan. They intervened in the Tajik Civil War and made their presence felt in Uzbekistan's Ferghana valley and other regions. The role of Pakistan and Pak-US sponsored *mujahideen* in the Islamic campaign undertaken in Central Asia stirred New Delhi and it could grasp the danger posed to India's interests in the region and to the survival of Central Asian states. The belated, slow and half-hearted stand taken by India in 1991-92, placed it in the difficult situation *vis-à-vis* the Central Asians as now it has to catch up for the loss compensate for earlier empathy (inaction caused by confusion and sense of loss of the Soviet Union) by undertaking a vigorous campaign against Islamic fundamentalism and militancy in the capitals of the world, by supporting the Northern Alliance led by Burhanuddin Rabbani in Afghanistan, strengthening Tajikistan's secular forces in their war against the Islamic and redefining its ties with Central Asian republics.

India's Stakes in the Central Asia

India's stakes in the Central Asia have always been high on account of its vital cultural, economic and strategic interest in the region. The geo-political and geo-economical change and frequent bouts of fundamentalist uprising in the region have further intensified them.

India is opposed to the theory of "power vacuum" propounded by United States and its western allies. The newly independent states of Central Asia are "new states" but old civilizations, conversant with the intricacies of the international politics. They are capable of safeguarding their freedom, sovereignty and national interest.

They might be lacking in the experience of western style democracy but they are inhabited by highly educated and professionally equipped, disciplined people. They are conversant with the art of governance. The Soviet experience has turned them into highly developed society notwithstanding their weak political and economic structure. They do not need external power to shape their destinies.

India is not prepared to endorse the thesis of "great game" re-enacted by regional and extra regional power in Central Asia. At the time of the "great game" of the 19th century, the competition was between Britain and Russia for territories which had absolutely no positive role in the game. They were passive objects. Today, Central Asia is different and contenders are not two but many with diverse objectives and strategies. Central Asia itself is a major player and can counter-balance the contenders in this game.[2]

India's interest is in the peace and stabilities in the region. The region should remain integrated and no anti-Central Asian coalition and strategies be allowed to develop. India is careful not to take any position on ethno-cultural issues and localize issues between the republics but it has been extremely concerned when ethno-cultural conflicts were given religious colour and fundamentalist forces tried to exploit them. India has opposed to the foreign intervention in Chechnya and tried to restrain the nations from taking sides. India's stand was that it is an internal issue of the Russian Federation and is being fanned from outside to serve the vested interests of external forces. During the recent "War against Terrorism" the United States has itself has somewhat modified its stand on Chechnya issue.

India has high stakes in retaining the secular ethos of Central Asian region. Being Islamic and as adherent of Islam as a faith or religion is one thing and being fundamentalist and '*jehadi*' is just another. The later has interventionist strategy and proposes the military power, violence and subversive method of spreading Islam as waging *jehad*. The fundamentalist aims at Islamisation of all the Muslim countries by reverting them back from modernity to traditional fundamentalist way of living and thinking. *Jehad* aims attaining the same by force, violence and terror to compel the states to surrender the wish to fundamentalists. During the initial years of their independence, Tajikistan and Uzbekistan were subjected to fundamentalists' onslaughts. However, the timely and effective action taken by the CIS and Russia frustrated their designs. The events of 1991-92 shook India and literally awaked it to the challenge of fundamentalism. It promoted New Delhi to stand against the forces of fundamentalism in Central Asia for the sake of its own security particularly in the areas adjoining Afghanistan. India is seriously opposed to the revival of the scenario of 1991-92 in Central Asia.

The efforts made in the direction of "Turkification" and "Persianization"of Central Asia is resented by India. The Turkic and Persian ethos of Central Asian republics make them vulnerable to influence the Turkey and Iran. While keeping good relation with Turkey and Iran, India want to discourage the division of Central Asia into "Turkic" and "Persian" zones of influence. Integrity of Central Asia as a region is to be maintained. It is, in fact, in the interest of both Turkey and Iran as well as Central Asians and all others who are interested in the stability of region.

It is difficult to change the hardened perceptions of external contenders for power in Central Asia. In their drive to carve out a sphere of interest in the region, they are striving to eliminate the influence of Russia in the Central Asia. Russia is the key Eurasian power and all the projects and programmes that are initially proposed to keep Russia out are bound to fail. Russia's interests in the Central Asia are not just commercial and economic as of the West. Russia is tickly woven into the very fabric of Central Asian psyche and way of living and thinking. Owing to its size, recourses, manpower, technological know-how, superior military power and above all having perfect knowledge of the region and its people, Russia is well poise to exercise influence in the region and protect it against external encroachments. Geography is bestowed upon Russia the position of primacy in the Central Asia.

The so called "great game" besides being about oil and natural gas, is also about the political influence in the region. Russia is a participant in the game not only for the oil and gas, but because till date, it is sole country which is helping in the export of Caspian oil and gas to international market as all the pipelines traverse through its territory. They are built by Russia and are operated by Russia. Moscow wants to retain its position.

The United States, another major player in the "great game" is also not in the need of Caspian oil and gas. It needs to acquire control over its production and marketing purely for the commercial purposes. Its objective is to deprive Russia from its privileged position of being a sole exporter or owner of all pipelines. The United States want to break the Russian monopoly by constructing new pipelines on new route which do not involve Russia and Iran just to satisfy its own superpower interests.

China, another formidable player, is a new entrant in the "great game". China needs oil and want to be partner in its production and export. China is not averse to Russian control over the export of Caspian oil as it views Russian position as a counterbalance to American entity in the region. If the game goes on without Russia weak, Beijing is not perturbed because that way American remain engaged with Russia and feel compelled to keep a friendly stance towards China. China wants to buy time to develop its own transportation which could carry Central Asian oil to world market.

Turkey was the first country to envisage the possibility of revival of the "great game" as in views of its geographical proximity to the region and to Caspian Sea, Black sea and Mediterranean, and controlling the Turkish straits (Bosphorus and Dardanelles). Turkey has potential to emerge as a prospective exporter of oil through its territory. Ankara wants new pipelines to traverse through the Turkish territories. Joining hand with Iran, which has already developed effectively operative pipelines, Turkey can immediately enter into the international market. But to its utter dismay Ankara could not take advantage of Iranian pipelines as the United States is opposed to inclusion of Iran in the Caspian oil deals.

The anti-Iran stand of America literally pushed Iran towards Russia although it is not only the reason for the re-invigorated Russia-Iran ties. In the current international scenario, Russia is only supporter of Iranian interests. Russia is opposed to the Turkey's entity in the Caspian oil affair, so is Iran. Hence, it is left with not so much choice bit to support Moskow. However, Iran too, earnestly desire that United States lifts the sanctions that are imposed against Iran in 1979 in the wake of Iranian revolution led by Ayatollah Khomeini and the new pipelines passes through Iran as it will give great boost to Iranian oil industry.[3]

Afghanistan, India and Pakistan are lesser player in the "great game". Of the three, Pakistan has a great role because it was projected as a facilitator of America's interest in the Central Asia. It could mediate with the Taliban and Central Asian regimes on the question of construction of new pipelines. Simultaneously, it could also serve the purpose of *Jehad* and fundamentalism by propagating Islamic common wealth and Islamic oil market, etc. Afghanistan was the second partner in this strategy. The Afghan *mujahideen* and the later *Taliban*, both have been protégés of Pakistan. Hence, Afghanistan's role in the "great game" became unavoidable though it remained marginal. Independent Afghanistan is however, definitely going to play a much bigger and more constructive role in Central Asia.

India, did not like the growing role of Pakistan in Central Asia at the behest of America and Saudi Arabia although for different reasons. The increasing bouts of fundamentalist attack on Tajikistan and Uzbekistan and the Taliban's near-total control over Afghanistan compelled India to take a stand and come out against terrorism in Central Asia. India could not afford to be an onlooker in the face of changing geo-politics of region and the open contest between major powers for region's resources particularly oil and natural gas. India's stakes in Central Asia and Caspian energy resources are equally high.

Caspian Oil Scenario and India's Interests

Caspian Sea basin has substantial deposits of natural gas. India with its increasing need for energy is interested in getting access to the Central Asian-Caspian oil and natural gas. The oil scenario in the Caspian-Central Asian region is not encouraging due to the difficulties that obstruct the free flow of oil to international markets. The only pipelines that export Central Asian oil are under the control of Russia and they all pass through Russian territory.

The decade-long exercise of the United States and its allies to carry the Central Asian oil to the European markets without using Russian pipelines has proved futile. Construction of new pipelines on diversified tracts (bypassing Russia and also Iran) is also made impossible by the geo-politics of the region. The countries of Georgia, Armenia and Turkey through whose territories the pipelines are supposed to pass are involved in serious trans-frontier as well as internal ethno-cultural and territorial disputes. Bypassing Russia is difficult and Russia will also take every possible measure not to be denied its legitimate share in the transportation of Central Asian oil.

Russia cannot idly watch Central Asia's energy wealth slipping out of its hold. Knowing that Russian pipelines alone cannot carry the entire load of Caspian oil, it is trying to provide new routes by constructing additional pipelines particularly for the Azerbaijan and the Kazakh oil. But the overland routes linking Kazakhstan's and Azerbaijan oil resources on the Caspian Sea to the Black sea port pass through conflict-prone region of Chechnya. Turkey has offered an overland route that could bypass Russia. As an alternative to Baku-Ceyhan (Turkish route) Russia has sponsored the projects of building the Burgas-Alexndropolis Pipeline. Oil from Russian black Sea port of Novorosiysk would be transported by tankers to the Bulgarian Black sea port of Burgas and from there pumped to the Greek Sea terminal in Alexndropolis. This will circumvent the Bosphorous and the Dardanelles (Turkish straits) controlled by Turkey. This Burgas-Alexndropolis Pipeline will be 300 km. long and would cost 700 million dollars which is comparatively not a big amount. It is expected to be 10 times cheaper then the one suggested by Turkey i.e. the Baku-Ceyhan pipeline.

The negotiations on Baku-Ceyhan line have already been

finalized. Its length will be 1920 kms. And the estimate cost is 3 billion dollars. Besides the heavy cost the Pipeline runs through the eastern Turkey where Kurdish rebels are already fighting a prolonged battle against the government of Ankara. A similar problem plagues the Burgas-Alexndropolis pipeline as from Baku to Novorossiysk the route runs through Dagestan and Chechnya, the two conflict-prone regions of northern Caucasus—part of Russian federation. In this tussle, the major brunt is borne by the Caspian oil producing States of Azerbaijan and Kazakhstan and also Turkmenistan which are awaiting new pipelines to carry their oil and natural gas to international market.

President Nazarbayev of Kazakhstan and Suleyman Demiral of Turkey in June 1995 worked a plan to transport Kazakh oil via Turkey. It was also suggested that a consortium including Russian oil companies be set up and assigned the job of constructing the pipeline through Turkey. When the details were worked out, it was clear that the Baku-Ceyhan Pipeline would first evolve the use of existing pipeline—Atyiray-Astrakhan-Grozny-Baku that passes through Chechnya. The other alternative is to take the pipeline from Baku through Armenia or Georgia as Turkey has no common borders with Azerbaijan. Armenia and Azerbaijan are having a prolonged conflict over Nagorno-Karabakh. Hence, the route through Armenia and Georgia is almost impossible. The Baku-Ceyhan Pipeline has the blessings of United States and the European countries which perhaps has not assessed the nature of geo-politics in the region. A pipeline through the Caspian sea-bed between Mangyshlak in Kazakhstan and Apsheron in Azerbaijan and then to Baku through the Black sea port of Georgia to Turkey has been proposed.[4]

The option of constriction of a pipeline to the Indian Ocean ports of Karachi and Gwadur through Afghanistan was marred by the civil war between rival warlords in Afghanistan. The two other options are through Iran in the south from Turkmenistan to the Persian Gulf ports and the other, to the west from Kazakhstan through China to the pacific coast.

Despite India's immense desire to get into the oil business in Central Asia, it remains on the fringe only. It can have "swap" arrangements with Iran and yet another alternative available to New Delhi is to participate in the Uzen oil product with China.

In June 1997, China's National Petroleum Company (CNPC)

obtained major oil concessions in the Aktyubinsk area of Kazakhstan, competing with the US oil giants—Taxaco and Amoco. In this project, China had invested $9 billion and built a pipeline to Xinjiang. In August 1997, the Chinese oil company also won a tender for extracting 60 per cent of the oil in the Uzen field. The China has offered to India a portion of its oil concessions in Kazakhstan for joint production. The work has already been started on the construction of an oil and gas pipeline from Turkmenistan to Iran in spite of American opposition to any deal with Iran.

The commissioning of this pipeline along with the already functioning rail link between the Iranian port of Bander Abbas and Ashgabat, the capital of Turkmenistan, will go in a long way in ending Central Asia's economic isolation. China is vigorously working to ensure its future energy security by pursuing equity oil from regions as far apart as Latin America. But India does not appear much concern about increasing imports which are growing at the rate of 10 per cent each year and expected to reach a level higher then 270 million tonnes by A.D. 2020. As compared to China, India's progress on energy front is not satisfactory.[5]

Central Asia is becoming an important source of energy and powers of the world are struggling to secure a foothold in the region. India stands to benefit a great deal if it exercises its options wisely and acts upon them without delay and also sorts out its problems with Pakistan and China.

For the past 50 years and more, India's relation with Pakistan has remained uneasy for several reasons. The overland transit rout from Central Asia to Indian Ocean has to pass through Afghanistan and Pakistan. Peace and stability in Afghanistan and workable relation with Pakistan are a pre-condition to derive benefits from this route. The Central Asia is not much worried about the India-Pakistan factor. Turkmenistan has already signed up this project with the western, Saudi-Arabian and Russian oil corporations because it wants to export natural gas through Afghanistan to South Asian markets. India needs to take effective and well spelled out measures to arrive at an understanding with Pakistan about the safety of proposed pipeline.

New Delhi has yet another option and it is comparatively easy to work on. India needs to explore the possibility of reaching an agreement with Beijing for the use of its road to Kazakhstan through

Xinjiang province. India can use this road by just constructing a link road in Ladakh joining the Tibet-Xinjiang road passing through the disputed Aksaichin territory. Ladakh is already linked by road with the Indian state of Himachal Pradesh bypassing the Srinagar valley. The opening of overland route through China will help in reducing India's over dependence on Iran as the sole transit point.[6]

For India, the Xinjiang Project of China is most viable and shortest. China has achieved a major breakthrough in developing more than 200 wells in the region. China's efforts at developing comprehensive transportation infrastructure within Xinjiang and across Central Asia and Russia are likely to be highly benificial to India, if construction of pipeline is undertaken across Xinjiang-Ladakh sector, along the traditional trade route, the "Silk Rote Extension" (SRE) of the British era.

The SRE originating from Xinjiang could come through undisputed parts of Sino-Indian border along Kakakoram pass at Daulat Beg-Ulde into Nubra valley. In the past SRE has served the political and economic interest of the British in the region *vis-à-vis* Russia and China. India has a strong economic presence in Xinjiang until 1950s when the consulate from Kashgar was withdrawn under China's pressure.[7]

China's pipeline development fits very well as a viable energy supply route for India to get Central Asian oil. The newly discovered oil fields are located at a very short distance from Ladakh border, only a small land portion of south west Xinjiang separates link between Ladakh and the Central Asian republic of Tajikistan, Kyrgystan and Kazakhstan.

In view of the fast developing changes in the region, India should join China's project for enlarging the Trans-Eurasian development activities. Several reasons prompt an intermediate action on India's part. In the first place, the route will be the shortest and will pass through only one country, i.e. China, between Central Asia and India. The route does not have to cross any troubled areas of Pakistan or Afghanistan, nor has any thing to do with Iran, which is subjected to an undue American hostility. Secondly, it would promote trans-boarder trade between the Ladakhis and the Uighurs as well as enhance goodwill between India and China. The trans-frontier interaction between the people of both sides would help in reviving the pre-1950s relations between the two countries.

With the tie up between ONGC Videsh and China's CNPC, the possibilities for India's participation in the Xinjiang transportation project would enhance. The bilateral trade between India and China has registered a threefold increase, and the Chinese supply of enriched Uranium for Tarapur nuclear power plant in India and China's offer to share with India an oil field acquire by it Uzen (Kazakhstan) has already provided momentum to India-China relations. This venture would not only open new vistas of development for India, but also liberate it from the peculiar South Asian contradictions.

India has other option too, provided it shades its political misgivings and joins China, Russia and the Central Asian countries in a long term energy policy. India enjoys immense goodwill in these countries. With Iran too, India has good relations, India should venture for swap transaction under which Caspian oil for India can be swapped by Iran from Persian Gulf. The Chinese, Japanese and Western companies are investing billions of Dollars for infrastructure and pipeline projects from Caspian's off-shore to Iran's Northern refineries. India can take advantage of these developments.[8]

India should give a thought to the reasons which are responsible for keeping South Asia on the fringe despite its closer to the Central Asia region. The tumultuous situation in Afghanistan and chronic India-Pakistan dispute over Kashmir has so far stymied Central Asia's integration with South Asia. Pakistan's patronage of the Taliban further frightened the Central Asian's forcing them to move westwards to Turkey, Iran, Europe and eastward to China. India has a role in reviving peace and stability in Afghanistan. New Delhi should also think about half a century which has been wasted in dealing with a hostile Pakistan. How long it can afford to be in that state?

India's Central Asia Policy

Notwithstanding India's great concern for Central Asia and its increasing involvement in Central Asian affairs in the post-Soviet period, it is realized that India still lacks a well spelled out policy towards Central Asia.

India has excellent political, military and trade ties with former Soviet Union. About 70 per cent of India's armaments were of Soviet Union and several joint venture industries were working both in the

Soviet Union and India. There was a high turnover of India's exports of consumer goods to the former Soviet Union. India had set up consulate in Tashkent and India Airlines operated a bi-weekly flight to Tashkent. Thousands of Indian students were studying in Soviet Union. But all these relation has been dependent on India's relation with Soviet Union.

The collapse of Soviet Union hit India hardest. Overnight a good percentage of its air craft and tanks were rendered inoperative as the spare parts were not available any more. Its trade decline and political and diplomatic support New Delhi has been enjoying for half-a-century has been disappeared without a warning. New Delhi took a long time in overcoming the loss of the Soviet Union. That precisely was the reason for its slow response to the friendly overtures of the newly independent states of Central Asia.

The civil war in Afghanistan, rise of Islamic fundamentalist forces in Pakistan and its neighbourhood, civil war in Tajikistan, growing rivalry in major powers for acquiring the foothold in the oil and natural gas rich countries of Central Asia, Pakistan enhanced role in Central Asia with full backing of United States, the Gulf war and its after effects—all put together flabbergasted New Delhi to the extent of remaining confused and indecisive for quite some time.

However, the geopolitical compulsion, the security needs of the country and the fast changing political scenario in the neighbourhood made India realize what it was loosing by standing on the fringe and just letting the opportunities slip by.

The Indian Commerce Minister, Salman Khurshid visited Central Asia in the summer of 1992 and announced credits of $ 10 million each to Uzbekistan and Kazakhstan and $ 5 million each of other three Central Asian republics. India also supported Iran in building the railway link between Ashghabat and Meshed. India wanted to counter Pakistan's growing influence in Central Asia but its major concern was to receive old ties with Russian Federation. India's efforts culminated in President Yeltsin's visit to New Delhi in January 1993 when a new treaty of Peace and Friendship was signed along with a defence cooperation agreement whereby India agreed to pay for all military parts in hard currency.

India has to address multiple issues of Central Asia. Loss of Soviet power created serious security concern for India. Dianne L. Smith articulated India's concern as:

> New Delhi feared that South Asian instability would mirror the chaos of Caucasus. Boarder realignments, ethnic disputes, resurgent Islam and civil war would directly affect the territorial integrity if Afghanistan which in domino fashion influences Pakistan, Iran and Kashmir. In such an environment, drag trafficking, illegal arms and crime syndicates would flourish threatening not only Central Asia but all of its neighbours. Such a scenario would inevitably have consequences for India's national security.[9]

India was alarmed at Pakistan's call for Central Asia as a strategic hinterland and Islamic initiatives, such as the ECO, although India was aware of limitations of Pakistan in moving deeper into Central Asia as like India also lacks geographical contiguity with the Central Asian republics. Afghanistan and a small strip of China obstructed its way to Central Asia. The political instability and civil war in Afghanistan made construction of accessible route and transit prohibitive. An Indian analyst argued[10] that:

> The changed scenario of Central Asia made Pakistan to change its policy towards Afghanistan. Finding a solution of Afghanistan's problem became Pakistan's first priority when it realized that although 'Balkanization' of Afghanistan might lead annexations of South Eastern Pushtun region, it also could also affect Pakistan's own territorial integrity. A peaceful stable Afghanistan was necessary if Pakistan was to obtain a land route necessary for economic penetration.

However, Pakistan's growing presence in Central Asian affairs made India seek new security arrangements with the republic of Central Asia. But India did not make Pakistan an issue in its relation with newly independent states of Central Asia. India focused on bilateral economic programmes. India's special relationship with former Soviet Union provides New Delhi a conducive background "to begin afresh in Central Asia in commencing its trade and joint ventures". India has many things to offer to new republics particularly when they are shifting from "state controlled economy" to "market economy" and seeking integration with the globalize world economy. India has large, urban, educated elite fluent in English, a Anglo-Saxon judicial system, industry and management based on Western lines and on established share market.

Indian economic programmes concentrated more on two more stable, populous and comparative more developed republics of Central—Asia Kazakhstan and Uzbekistan. India offered credits worth $10 million to Tashkent in 1992 and 1993, and in 1992 signed a treaty on "the principles of inter-state relation and bilateral cooperation", promising cooperation in fighting terrorism, arms and drugs trafficking and extremist ideologies.[11] Special investments are made in construction of modern hotels in Tashkent, Samarkand and Bukhara. In 1992, India entered in the series of agreements with Kazakhstan also to develop its textile and hotel industry. India gave $10 million in aid to Almaty in 1992 and 1993.[12]

The Indo-Turkmen agreement of April 1992 and a ten year loan worth $ 5 million contributed to stronger ties between India and Turkmenistan. The agreement of 1992 promised cooperation in the field of gas extraction, chemicals and agriculture products, processing, hotel construction and banking.[13]

India is cooperating with the Central Asian republics in raising their bureaucracy and police force and imparting training to the security personals as well. India is cooperating ion the field of mining, oil and natural gas extraction and has direct flights to all the five Central Asian capitals.

Despite India's great desire to help Central Asian republics, it cannot make massive investments because of its financial constraints. Indian investors are also not coming in forth in view of privileged instability in the adjoining regions of Central Asia. Language difficulty and lack of proper knowledge about current situation is also a reason of less interaction between Central Asian republics and Indian business class. As discussed above, the apathy on the part of government in the initial years of the independence of Central Asian republics has done a great harm. By acting promptly at that time India, could have immediately resumed its earlier connections with the republics, and could provide great moral and material support to them.

New Delhi is taking serious measures for strengthening the existing ties and enlarging the areas of co-operation's with the Central Asian states, India, Russia and China together can workout a strategy for Central Asia and cooperate in its economic developments and promotions of oil and natural gas transportation. They can together help in retaining the secular ethos of the region and also serve as a deterrent to the evil designs of the Islamic fundamentalist and the drug mafia active in the region. The Russian proposal for the formation of a "strategic triangle" of Russia, China and India, seems a befitting answer to these treats.

Need for the Stretegic Cooperation

The American-sponsored coalition of Western and pro-Western countries supporting the "Unipolar world order" and "Globalized world Economy" seems set to dethrone Russia from its privileged position in Central Asia and acquire control over the natural recourses—oil and gas of the region. The Western countries are too eager to fill the "power vacuum" and take charge of the destinies and energy resources of the newly independent countries of Central Asia.

It is not an easy job to eliminate Russian influence and its role in Central Asia. Besides Russia, China has a common border with Tajikistan, Kyrgyzstan and Kazakhstan and the inhabitants of China's province of Xinjiang share an ethnic and religious affinity with the people of these three republics. In the post-Soviet period Beijing feels responsible for the security, stability and territorial integrity of the newly independent states of Central Asia. The threat of Islamic fundamentalism is as serious to China as it is to Central Asian republics and Russia.

After the collapse of Soviet Union, relationship between China and Russia has shown a marked improvement. The earlier misgivings about each other's policies and intensions, border conflicts, rivalries and subversive activities against each other have vanished. China today is the biggest buyer of Russian weapons and weapon technology and shares common interest in Central Asia.

In Central Asia, China considers Russia as a counter-balance to American designs and finds it a "stabilizing factor" in the region. China is not opposed to the Russia's privileged position as a sole exporter of the Caspian oil through its pipelines. Beijing only wants to acquire source of energy for its growing need of oil and natural gas. China wants to compete with the western oil companies in seeking concessions and winning exploration, extraction and transportation rights in the Caspian basin countries.

The Shanghai Agreement concluded between Russia, China and the three Central Asian republics (1996) which have a common border with China is a landmark in China-Central Asia relations as well as China-Russia relations. China is opposed to the geopolitical game plan of the West to oust Russia from Caspian oil affairs and establish their own supremacy in the region.

Both Russia and China want India to join them in forming a strategic partnership against the hegemonic designs of the supporters and promoters of the "unipolar world order". China prefers to see the world as a multi-polar system in which all regional groupings have an equal role and access to power sharing. The West is continuously trying to evolve a new system of pipelines and overland transportation system bypassing Russia (although it has not yet attained any success). It encouraged Azerbaijan to pump its oil to the Georgian port of Supsa on the Black Sea instead of the Russian port of Novorossisk.

The work on Baku-Ceyhan pipeline is also progressing. The main purpose is to deprive Russia of its "privileged status" in Central Asia. As already noted these pipelines will traverse difficult zones in Turkey (Kurdish areas) and Georgia (Abkhazia plagued with ethnic conflict) and it would be difficult to ensure safety and unobstructed flow of oil through these routes.

The environment for the formation of this strategic cooperation is conducive as Russia-India and India-China relations are showing increasing warmth and mutual understanding. India's relations with China have registered tremendous improvement since the visits of Indian Prime Ministers, Rajiv Gandhi and Narasimha Rao to China. The formal opposition expressed by China at the time of Pokharan II experiments did not make much difference to their relationship in other fields. The trade between the two countries has increased three-fold. China has refrained from making any comments on Agini II Intermediate range missile. China is supplying enriched uranium to the Tarapur nuclear power plant in India and has offered to share with India the Uzen oil field acquired by China in Kazakhstan.

Notwithstanding China's close collaboration with Pakistan in matters related to defence and its weapon supplies to Pakistan, China has made it clear that its relations with Pakistan are not detrimental to the interests of India and good relations with India is its priority in the new world order.

The relation between India and Russia had gone adrift for a while when the Soviet Union collapsed in 1991 and the Russian federation adopted the pro-West stance. It had shown total apathy towards the Third World and almost given up its cold cordiality and concern for its former clients. President Yeltsin in 1993-94 succeeded in rectifying the situation by receiving the old warmth in Moscow's relation with a number of Third World countries specially with India, which is its major trading partner in Third world.

India and Russia share equal concern for peace in region and are opposed to "international terrorism" and support of each other in endeavours to eradicate it. India and Russia have collaborated in defence related matters as well, and India is purchasing weapons, fighter aircrafts and other necessary armaments from Moscow. The understanding which has developed between the two nations during last 50 years is still unabated. Hence, it is not difficult for them to comprehend the new realities and their dictates.

Russia, China and India have several meeting points. All the three are close neighbours and share common historical and civilization ties that link them together despite some controversies and disputes over border and other issues. These three countries are nuclear powers and have material and scientific capabilities to promote the high-tech development of the region. They are equally concern about the threats from religious fundamentalism and militancy to their internal stability and territorial integrity. These three countries are subjected to foreign sponsored movements for secessionism in their territories.

Participation in proposed strategic triangle will pave the way to an understanding with China on construction of a link road joining India with Central Asia (Ladakh to Xinjiang) and facilitate India's participation in the Shanghai Agreement of April 1996, concluded by Russia, China and the four Central Asian republics—Tajikistan, Kyrgyzstan, Kazakhstan and Uzbekistan, with three of which China share 3000 kms. border. This agreement with China compensates for India's lack of geographical contiguity with Central Asia and facilitates strategic cooperation between India and China.

An appraisal of India's Central Asian police reveals that several lapses in the past were caused by its overestimation of the role of Islamic countries in the Central Asian republics. Devendra Kaushik suggested that:

> India need not to be deterred by the exaggerated prospects of

> Islamic states of Turkey, Iran and Pakistan acquiring exclusive influence over Central Asia, and evolve a pro-active policy in place of its current reactive posture, dominated by competition with Pakistan.[14]

The biggest before Indian foreign policy is to evolve measures that would safeguard the stability and integrity of Central Asian republics and save them from getting divided and standing opposed to each other. Unity of Central Asia-Trans-Caucasia as a region, despite the sovereign independent status is extremely important in the interest of region.

The increasing rivalry between the major contenders of power and influence in Central Asia is serious challenge to the stability in the region. India should try to defeat the "game plan" of these competitors striving to divide the region into various spheres of influence, and through a diplomatic persuasion try to forge a collective security arrangements and a collective project for the development of all the countries of the region regardless of their policy slants in favour of this or that big power. The US policy of excluding Iran and Russia, and bringing Central Asia under its exclusive control is a self-defeating exercise because the countries of the regions having cultural, ethnic, social, economic affinity as well as political interests to pursue through their relations with Russia are bound to remain closely related to Russia. Being a key Eurasian country, Russia cannot be excluded from Central Asia's political and economic life.

The Central Asian region needs to be insulated against the encroachments by Islamic fundamentalists, arms smugglers, drug mafia and international terrorists because the "silk road" can easily be turned into a "crime road" with such elements having a free hand. During their visit to Central Asia India's Prime Minster, Foreign Minister and other visiting dignitaries have emphasised upon the need of evolving a collective mechanism to fight religious extremists in the region. Recently, Former Prime Minister Atal Bihari Bajpai during his visit to Almaty to attend the CICA Summit again repeated India's resolve to cooperate with Central Asian republics in fighting against terrorism and fundamentalism.

India, with its good relation with the countries of West Asia, the Gulf and South-East Asia is well poised to play a constructive role in

Central Asia regardless of the fact that it lacks geographical contiguity, huge financial resources and easy access to the region.

NOTES

1. The term "great game" was coined by J.W. Kay in his book *History of the war in Afghanistan.* It was popularized by Rudyard Kipling in his novel Kim. where he used "great game" to describe the early 19th century rivalry between Great Britain and Russia over the Indian subcontinent – the land between Russia and India. Lt. Col. William R. Kunzweiler, USAF "The new Central Asian Great game", *strategic review* (summer, 1998), p. 25.
2. See, Stephen Blank, "Energy, Economics and Security in Central Asia : Russia and its Rivals", *Central Asian Survey* (1995), 14(3), pp. 391-93; and Dianne L. Smith, "Central Asia: A New Great Game?", *Asian Affairs* (Fall, 1996), pp. 147-175.
3. Dianne L. Smith, op. cit. pp. 151-152.
4. Amy Myers Jaffe and Robert A. Manning, " The Myth of the Caspian Great Game : The Real Geopolitics of Energy", *Survival,* vol. 40, winter, 1998-1999, pp. 112-129, also see Dorian, Ian Sheffield Rosi and S. Tony Indriyauto, "Current and Future Flows", *Post Soviet Geography,* 1994, Vol. 35, No. 7, pp. 412-430.
5. Devendra Kaushik, "India and Central Asia: Past and Present Relations and Future Hopes", *Contemporary Central Asia,* Vol. 1, No. 1 (1997), p. 237.
6. Ibid., p. 238.
7. P. Stobdan, " The Caspian/Central Asian Oil and India" unpublished paper, presented in the "Seminar on Geopolitics Energy Resources and National Development in Central Asia and Caspian Sea Region", New Delhi, 22-23 March, 1999.
8. Ibid.
9. Dianne L. Smith, op. cit. p. 156.
10. P. Stobdan, "International aspects of the conflict Situation in Central Asia: An Indian Perspective", *Strategic Analysis,* Vol. 16, No. 3 (June 1993), pp. 275-76.
11. Amita Singh," India's Relation with Russia and Central Asia", *International Affairs,* 71, No. 1, p. 79.
12. Ibid. p. 80.
13. Ibid.
14. Devendra Kaushik, "*India and Central Asia*", op. cit, p. 238.

15

Central Asia

Tulips have Different Hews

P.L. Dash

Introduction

Nearly fourteen years back, when the Velvet Revolution swept across the erstwhile Soviet Union, none had ever imagined that revolutions of various colours would once again sweep across the post-Soviet space. However, everyone had a fairly clear idea about the ensuing political chaos dismemberment of the Soviet Union had precipitated. All five Central Asian countries were bequeathal of the Soviet era–undemocratic, dictatorial, authoritarian and with a centralized economy. The political power stubbornly refused to reform all these years. All these countries, however, endeavoured to embrace what they themselves were not – western democracy, plural, multi-cultural civil society, freedom of press, independent judiciary and respect for human rights. Kirgyzstan was presumably the fore-post of all these modernizing elements in governance, the pioneer of democracy, the Switzerland of Central Asia. And its former president, Askar Akaev, who promised to build a paradise on earth was considered to be a liberator par excellence. Those who used these glorious eulogies to describe Akaev apparently forgot some fundamental truth.

First, all presidents were the product of a system that never espoused true democracy. All of them were schooled in the Brezhnevian style of democratic practice, implemented in their respective republics by ruthless leaders like the ilk of Rashidov, Kunaev and Gafurov. All of them were educated in the literature of socialist realism of Tengiz Aitmatov. It is in deed difficult for them to appreciate something that their cognitive process had never experienced. Secondly, once on the saddle of power, by virtue of being party secretaries and not by dint of their democratic merit, all these presidents endeared themselves more to their power centres than to the people. And this certainly alienated them from the masses. As a result, they have missed the moment to create the preconditions for democracy all through the post-Soviet ears. As a consequence, their countries lack the prerequisites of participatory democracy even after 14 years of their independence. The muzzling of the press, outlawing political opposition and efforts to create a pliant and friendly judiciary are all open evidences of undemocratic governance. The outcome was obvious: elections after election, the same president returned to power; some of them even went to the extent of declaring themselves president for life.

Thirdly, from the vantage point of their absolute power, the presidents failed to gauze the impact a tumultuous phase of transition that led to the abject poverty of their subjects. Instead of going to the people to solve their problems, they increasingly relied on the coterie of advisers who they had chosen as trustworthy aides. In an undemocratic environ, when the system was not geared to produce successors, they never looked beyond the coterie and the family and groomed their sons, daughters and other members of the family. As a result, they failed to create adequate political space for their citizenry to ventilate their political aspirations. The consequence was that filial democracy led to suppression of political parties and repression of political opponents. The outcome is : opposition is virtually absent in all countries. Wherever, it is present, it is nascent in form, compromising in content, and ineffective in practice. Perpetuation of one man as president and one party as the ruling party for over a decade betrays all norms of participatory democracy. Finally, when Central Asian countries emerged independent from the Soviet fold, the crimson hope that had appeared in the imagination of their populace, remained unachieved. On the political horizon across Central Asia, these imaginative dreams of democracy remains largely unachievable. On the debris of it, Kirgyzstan experienced Tulips revolution. Unexpectedly Askar Akaev had to flee the country and now apprehensions abound that Akaev's successor, Kurmanbek Bakiev, would be no better a ruler. The London Economist had aptly captioned an article on Akaev's exit: "One gone; four more to go". Delving deep into the pathology of Akaev's fall, one certainly wonders how more repressive regimes sustain in other neighbouring countries. The wonder provides the answer too: the more dictatorial the regime; the more its enduring capability to sustain in power, albeit peoples endurance rapidly thins out.

Bequeathal at Stake

Askar Akayev's track record of governance surprisingly ensured micro-economic stability to that country over the past decade. In 2004 real GDP grew by 7.1 per cent, exchange rate for the Sum was stable and the country's external debt was reduced from 130 per cent of the GDP in 2000 to 85 per cent in mid-July 2005. The country was planning to pay off its entire debt in the next five years.[1] Despite all favourable macro-economic indices, however, three things that impeded economic growth and social development were widespread poverty, rampant corruption and high level of unemployment. Should he fail to deliver good governance, these three social evils may pose a menace to Akaev's successor, Kurmanbek Bakiev. Desperate with the country's political fluidity, out of a total Kirgyz population of just over 5 million, 500,000 people or one in every ten person, had to seek work either in Russia or in neighbouring Kazakhstan.[2] The revolt that swept Kirgyzstan was a clear message of popular discontent with the Akaev regime. When radical alternatives of participatory democracy at the grassroots are unavailable, correlation of political power equation in any given country prefers opposition to the existing regime to come in power. This was what precisely happened in Kirgyzstan; and not a great political revolution.

Why is such alternative unavailable? Plenty of causes proffer a variety of arguments; some substantive, other frivolous. The world has witnessed innumerable typologies of regimes such as kingdoms, fiefdoms, Sheikhdoms, military dictatorship, constitutional monarchy, parliamentary democracies, presidential form of governments and so on. At the crossroads of her political history, Central Asia preferred a piquant combination of parliamentary democracy with strong, presidential form of governments. As a result, all countries have elected and nominated legislatures and all countries have strong presidents. The presidents were a legacy of the communist era. Therefore, the desire for ensuring a strong power centre has been transcendentally inherent in Central Asia, partly because of the traditions of patriarchal society and largely because of a legacy bequeathed from the Soviet yesteryears. If for a sizeable period of its seven decades plus history, the Soviet Union was ruled by just four leaders—Lenin, Stalin, Khrushchev and Brezhnev—and three of the four leaders save Khrushchev died in harness—why should Central Asian presidents bother to call it quit? Clan tribal loyalties further cement the bond with political power; and invariably all presidents have decided to stick to power unless forced to quit. Over the years, they have evinced their absolute power to control their countries that would have otherwise relapsed into civil wars. The saying that "power corrupts everyone; and absolute power corrupts absolutely" might be largely appropriate for post-Soviet Central Asian regimes.

One of the reasons why Central Asia as a region in general and individual countries in particular has not moved forward in political reforms is the pernicious legacy of yesteryears. Added to the legacy were individuals, who became presidents. Overnight many a communist ruler became self-proclaimed democrats, who talked of western parliamentary democracy as the model to emulate, Turkey or Iran as a model to follow and free market economy as their objective finale. They chose their like-minded cronies as advisers, who usurped power in the name of democracy and ensured continuity with little change. Change visited only when they were forced to change. Thus in all countries through the post-Soviet years a political tendency has taken roots that to change you have to force a president to go; voluntary abdication of power is ruled out and constitutional provisions are too rigid for the people and too flexible for the incumbent presidents to accommodate the desire. In the event of any exigency it can always be amended. Thus, the presidents of all countries have gathered a political elite as a solid legacy of the past era. They have formed a coteries where family and friends matter more than the people. It is people from this coterie, who get plum postings at home and abroad. It is these people who engage in profitable business and distribute favours to their chums. It is these people who form the power centre in Central Asian states. People are largely alienated from the power centres and a discernible schism exists between the rulers and ruled. In any given country, there are two types of lifestyle: one in the capital —gorgeous, pomp, and visible oomph laden with luxury; and the countryside—facing the morass of poverty and privation, suffering from the anemia of daily life.

Keeping aside the onerous task of erecting permanent political institutions, where these presidents have further embroiled themselves is the implicit efforts at propping up the image of their offspring to be inheritors of power. And Akaev was no exception. Askar Akaev has four children—two daughters and two sons. Eldest daughter, Bermet, has been working for years now as image maker of the President. Educated in Switzerland and working for long years in the UN office at Geneva, Bermet is married to Adil Toigonbaev, a Kazakh businessman, considered to be the richest man in Kirgyzstan, who is engaged in trading in aviation fuel supply from Turkmenistan to Kazakhstan. This is the couple seemingly most influential in the political life of the country. Akaev's second daughter, Saadat, is unmarried. She was educated in Switzerland and Boston. His eldest son, Aidar was an adviser to the Finance Minister, got married to Aliya, the youngest daughter of Kazakh President Nazarbaev—a marriage that did not last long. Akaev's younger son is studying abroad. This was the picture before Akaev left Kirgyzstan under duress of the opposition. His exit signaled chaos and bloodshed and implied that leaders sans vision elicit popular opposition, but the alternative arrangement available in the country may not be better than the previous regime. What an indelible mark in Kirgyz politics Akaev left! Like all other presidents he too groomed his children, rewarded plum diplomatic postings to people closest to him, business largesse was far too excessive for the near and dear ones than for the public. The outcome was polarization of Kirgyz society into rulers and the ruled. Under the shadow of this highly surcharged, polarized political scenario, the Switzerland of Central Asia turned into an arena of public protest the weight of which was too heavy for Akaev to bear with. It was Bermet, the eldest daughter, who was stoutly defending her father within and outside Kirgyzstan, after his ouster by a rowdy mob.

Kazakh President Nursultan Nazarbaev, also a solid legacy of the communist era, has three daughters—Dariga, Dinara and Alya in order of their birth. While Dinara is completely out of public gaze and engaged in charitable educational fund management, her husband, Timur Kulibaev, is the chief of a gas company called "Kuzmunaigas". Aliya is the Chief of a construction company "Elit Stroi". She also looks after production of mineral water in the country. First married to the son of Kirgyz President Akaev, Alya's marriage ended in divorce after the couple complained of irreconcilable differences on where to stay in Kirgyzstan as the husband wished or in Kazakhstan as Alya desired.

However, Nazarbaev's solid political support as heiress to the presidency is thrown behind eldest daughter, Dariga. In an interview to Eurasia Today, Dariga had admitted in 2003 that her father has encouraged her to enter politics, but her fate had so far taken a different turn. She has often been in the news as a press manager with considerable clout as daughter of the president and runs Khabar and El Arna television channels as well as radio station "Hit FM-Khabar". She has entered into direct politics by forming a pro-president youth forum "Asar". Registered in April 2003, as a youth organization, it soon began having branches across Kazakhstan with a view to supporting policies of Nazarbaev. The Asar made headlines in Kazakh print and electronic media for making direct foray into politics. With apparent support of President Nazarbaev, Dariga is heading a number of organizations such as Eurasian Media Forum, Eurasian Centre for Strategic Research, a member of the Board of Director of International Academy of Television Art and Science (New York), member of the National Commission on UNESCO, Honorary President of Gymnastic Federation of Kazakhstan, President of the Kazakh Fund for Image Building and so on. The list is too long to capture all her titles. She has become the most visible Kazakh personality in the media next to her father. Much as Nazarbaev wished to groom her, opinion across the board is divided as to whether she would succeed the President.

In an opinion poll conducted in the country, respondents were unequivocally equal in their opinion, when 32 per cent decreed that Dariga could not become president because she is a lady, 34 per cent endorsed the Russian syndrome that she would first become Prime Minister and then president as Vladimir Putin and 33 per cent considered her to be president should she win a presidential election.[3] Dariga Nazarbaeva's assertive political role as an elite Kazakh socialite and her outspokenness about future form of governance obviate an incredibly complicated political spectrum. On the one hand of this spectrum, there is the president, his daughter's political party, Asar, the coterie and the elite and the opposition party, supporting Nazarbaev. And on the other a vast majority of Kazakh people whose voice quickly evaporates into nothingness as worthless criticism.

Dariga has not only carried forward to villages the message of continuity of Nazarbaevism in Kazakhstan up to 2013, but also spoke in favour of one party rule in one of the Asar meetings that sent an unambiguous tiding to the people that "no single political party in Astana will have a chance to thrive, because this is the city of the president; he in fact, controls it".[4] In the absence of clear message from Nazarbaev himself, Dariga's claim covertly endorsed by her father implies that Dariga'a Asar is the potent force of continuity, particularly when she is first tipped to be a Senator, and then, to be nominated as Chairperson of the upper house. The Kazakh constitution provides for the Chairman of the upper house to take over in the event of an exigency such as death in harness or abdication of the president or demission of office by the president for whatever other reason. While this is the visible plan after 2013, up to that period Nazarbaevism is likely to sway in Kazakhstan.

Opposition Nomenclature

The leadership in all Central Asia countries is considered extremely capable, albeit authoritarian. Authoritarian because they have ruled their countries with iron hand, capable because they have avoided all major social and political upheaval that was sweeping Central Asia in the preceding years of Perestroika. Authoritarian because they mauled a nascent free press by snatching away the rights of journalists, capable because they have managed no regime change to prevail. Authoritarian because they have eliminated political opposition in their respective countries, exiled or arrested political opponents and capable because they have forged new policy frameworks—foreign and domestic policies alike in the national interest of their countries. Authoritarian because they have violated human rights off and on and capable because they have erected national armies and done all that have given these countries semblance of sovereignty. Logically, it was expected that after the collapse of communism, a new brand of non-communist leaders, especially those who were opposing Moscow, would run the state affairs after independence and hold the fort. However, in Central Asian countries, the reverse happened. Communists quickly changed their cloak and wore a new garb of nationalists/neo-capitalists/ democrats. They forced the opposition movement fizzle out. Any resistance to the new rule was treated mercilessly.

Although the political character of the regimes varied considerably country-wise, the leadership character remained unchanged, largely dictatorial and very often laden with ineffectual democratic attempts such as adoption of constitutions and conduct of elections. As a result, we have seen many elections and many constitutions. However, even fourteen years after independence, in none of these countries save Tajikistan, leadership has ever changed. On the contrary, efforts are afoot to perpetuate the present leadership by way of their glorification. The Opposition is effectively crushed and tangibly low. Three factors are responsible for this.

First, throughout the seven decades of Soviet rule, opposition was non-extant and dissidents were systematically hounded. They were either exiled or compromised. Thus by the time independence dawned, there was no root of opposition in Central Asia. Secondly, Central Asia's opposition to Moscow's rule was sporadic and uneven during Perestroika. The opposition was against Moscow, against Russian non-natives, ruling in Central Asia and against anomalous centre-periphery relations. The riots in Alma-Ata in December1986 and in Ferghana valley in June 1989 were bitter reflections of native feelings against the non-natives. They were not potent political opposition as in the Baltic states. In the new situation, however, the opposition is bewildered to fight against native rulers themselves, who were ex-communists and who thoroughly know the art of communist dictatorship. As a result, we witness a political phenomenon that says: the more a leader is thoroughly bred in the communist hierarchy, the more authoritarian is his rule in the country. Democracy is just a façade. Thirdly, the new opposition in Central Asia lacks a solid popular base. The leadership has appropriated power to garnish its rule too well to be tumbled too soon. A country-wise analysis of opposition therefore fits well into our scheme of things and two case studies are taken here for brevity of space.

Case Study: Uzbekistan

In the process of swift political developments following the coup in August 1991, the metamorphosis in Uzbek politics transformed the Communist party of Uzbekistan to Peoples' Democratic Party of Uzbekistan. Karimov became its Chairman and continued in that post until July 1996, when he wanted to abdicate the party. He proposed to a party plenum to quit in order to remain a non-party president. He did so on the face of mounting criticism about his authoritarian methods of governance. However, in reality, the Peoples' Democratic Party of Uzbekistan and Karimov have been ruling the country without any virtual opposition. The president's control is near absolute and those loyal to him bask in power and pelf.

Among the potential opposition parties, which were repressed, forced to toe the government line or forced to go underground were:

1. Birlik, founded in 1989 and banned in 1992 and subsequently registered as a social movement.
2. Adolat, founded in 1995, a pro-Islamic Social Democratic Party.
3. Fatherland Progress Party, a pro-government business party.
4. Islamic Renaissance Party, banned in 1991 because it advocated introduction of an Islamic system based in Shari'at. Soon it went underground and in Ferhgana valley and in Tashkent, its secret cells are still functioning. The Namahgani phenomenon of terror was its handiwork.
5. Erk, founded in 1990, is the only registered opposition party, ineffective enough though to counter the government. In 1994 it also passed through a series of repression, when its leaders, Erk General Secretary, Samad Murad and functionary, Otanazar Oripov were arrested.
6. National Revival Democratic Party, founded in 1995, a centrist party of Uzbek intelligentsia.
7. People's Unity Party founded in 1995. Not much is heard about its activities.

Two potential political opposition, Birlik and IRP, were initially ruthlessly suppressed and subsequently proscribed. In a semi-communist and demi-capitalist socio-political milieu that has come up during the past one decade, Karimov is the absolute hero. His words are laws, his quotations are extensively cited and streets and schools are renamed after him. The opposition, however, has been venting its feeling through expression of discontent in various ways. Throughout 1992-94, particularly in the Spring of 1994, the government was busy in arresting the opposition leaders.

The Spring repression in 1994 kindled no fresh hope for western style democracy. Karimov claimed that his country has her own path to future and the repression continued. In the evening of 18 July, 1994 an attempt to kill Karimov was made in the most unlikely of places—on the road to government building. Unknown assassins fired at his motorcade from high caliber guns. But nothing was reported to the press, except that the president was safe. In the specially conducted referendum in March 1995, Karimov extended his tenure of presidency up to 21st century, and when the century dawned to six more years.

The press as a pillar of opposition is virtually absent. Erk and its leaders were targeted because they published their party newspaper under the same name. There were reports about deportation from Tashkent of Russian journalists of major Russian newspapers. Izvestia was thus banned in the republic. The press that glorifies the performance of the government is tolerated well; critics have no place. It is a press controlled by the state, managed by the state and run by it where Karimov is as extensively quoted and as his deeds glorified. A contribution of Gorbachev's dual policy of Perestroika and Glasnost was freedom of expression and in all non-Russian republics including Uzbekistan, where writers, poets and intellectuals were at the forefront of liberation movement. However, in Uzbekistan it was the very intellectuals, who fell victims of an unsavory rule as prime target of the regime that replaced Soviet power.

On the personal front, Islam Karimov has two daughters—Gulnara and Lola. Both daughters are divorcees of their first husbands. Lola is not much in the news. After graduating from the Tashkent University, she has taken into business, and apparently does not nurture any political ambition. Quite contrary to Lola, the elder sibling Gulnara resembles her father in every respect—an economist by profession and a dictator in personal life. An amateur fashion designer by hobby, Gulnara is a product of the Tashkent University and by profession an economist with an added specialization on international security. She is now an adviser in the Uzbek embassy in Moscow, and in spare time, pursues her hobby of fashion design. Apprehensions are doing round about Gulnara as the best successor to Islam Karimov should he ever step down. In her personal life Gulnara had a stormy marriage with Mansur Naksudi, a Uzbek of Afghan descent settled in the USA, who was once upon a time the Chairman of the Coca Cola company in Uzbekistan. She is the most popular woman in the country, whom the political elite looks at with hope of continuing Karimovism in Uzbekistan after her father's exit from the scene.

Case Study: Turkmenistan

Turkmenistan remains by far the most dictatorial state in the region. It has an elected president, a constitution given to its people that provides for a presidential form of governance, a political party known as the Democratic Party of Turkmenistan. Yet democracy eludes Turkmenistan, opposition is not tolerated and the country is ruled by an absolute ruler, Turkmenbashi Saparmurad Niyazov, who symbolizes hopes and future of the Turkmens. His birthday, the 19th February, is declared a national holiday. In such a situation, one could only see that totalitarian rule of the Soviet yesteryears has been effectively replaced by authoritarian rule of the present president, and hence, to expect a viable democratic opposition to Niyazov's power is premature. Throughout the Soviet years, when the communists ruled, the country did not have an opposition. It was a one party rule, and one man rule by the party secretary. The government took decisions and the people said yes to endorse them. The embryo of opposition in Turkmenistan that took shape belatedly in the form of Popular Front Ogzybrilik in 1989, could not withstand the onslaught of power and disappeared in independent Turkmenistan. Its leaders fled the country and are waging a struggle from outside, mostly from Moscow.

Once, while being questioned about political opposition in Turkmenistan, Niyazov sharply reacted and said: "The Europeans, somehow consider presence of opposition as an indicator of democracy in the society. The more the opposition, the more are democratic rights and freedom. Maybe, this is an inevitable imperative for the Europeans. For oriental states and societies, the characteristic features are absolute power plus functional laws."[5] Thus Niyazov is an oriental ruler with absolute power in a energy rich country in a volatile region.

The political parties of Soviet and post-Soviet years have blended together in Turkmenistan on the face of a mighty state ruled by Niyazov, a communist dictator turned self-styled democrat. In the near total absence of opposition, one could list just three parties in Turkmenistan, that are visible in the political scene. All of them toe the government line and none of them pose any threat to the existing regime.

1. The ruling party, the Democratic Party of Turkmenistan was founded on 16 December, 1991. It was a reincarnation of the Communist Party of Turkmenistan. The party reformed itself just with change of the name with same functionaries of the fallen regime and with same institutions in place to run the state affairs. The party members were even assured of their seniority. This is the only registered political party.
2. Ogzybirlik, founded in 1989, is a popular front organization of the perestroika era. It was virtually dispersed, when the country promulgated an ordinance to the effect that any social organization to be politically active in the country must have two third support of the parliament. Despite the high-handed attitude of the president, pressure groups continue to operate in the country and a diaspora opposition is active in neighboring countries as well as in Moscow. They act under the banner of Turkmen Fund for Peace and Cooperation.
3. Peasants' Party, founded in 1993, consists of the deputies of the agrarian faction in the parliament. Since 70 per cent of the 4 million population live in rural areas, creation of a faction in parliament to represent this sizeable segment was tactfully engineered by the government as much to appease popular uprisings in far flung areas as to negate the voice of dissidents.

There are, however, three visible sections of viable opposition that might pose a threat to the regime. All of them operate from outside Turkmenistan because in Turkmenistan itself, their functional existence is impossible. The government has been trying to hold them at bay by different tactics. These opposition groups are political emigrants living outside Turkmenistan, Russian and Russian-speaking population in Turkmenistan, whose relatives have fled harassment; and Religious opponents, operating from neighbouring countries. It was fairly easier for Niyazov to handle political opposition in Turkmenistan because the opposition in Turkmenistan was often opposing itself, thereby contradicting their pronounced objectives with practical actions.[6] The leaders of most of these opposition groups were former bureaucrats who Niyazov knew well and these leaders have been envious of and fighting among themselves. Whether it is Abdi Kuliev or Boris Shikhmuradov or Murat Esenov—all of them were once loyal to Niyazov because they were his advisers in various posts.

Their personal political ambitions laden with envy and enmity, but shorn of any agenda for the future have been effectively juxtaposed by Niyazov, who doled out such favour to the people as supply of free gas and electricity on the domestic front, and stubborn refusal of any IMF help to ensure Turkmenistan's neutrality in international affairs. These steps facilitated Niyazov's mauling of the opposition and muzzling of the press. Niyazov has further endeared himself to the people by not endorsing family legacy as source of governance. He has a son named Murad, who is engaged in gas export business. Analysts say Murad himself is not interested in politics, but presumably he is the only hope and source of continuity of Niyazovism in Turkmenistan. Niyazov's daughter is not talked about at all. The press sometimes writes about the son; but not at all about the daughter. At least, till today. Niyazov has not groomed his children to be after political power, nor he is prepared to exit from the presidency by abdicating power in favour of someone.

Tajikistan: Democracy of a Different Taste

Tajikistan is the only Central Asian country, where officially, the Islamic Renaissance Part has been sharing power with socialists turned democrats in the government.[7] As evident through the years that followed the Soviet break-up, tangible support of the people from below and less of Central control by a debilitated government plunged Tajikistan into five years of civil war between 1992 and 1997. In 1997 a compromising accord, brokered by Iran, entailed a coalition of strange political bed fellows. Hewn out of fractious regional opposition groups, in the course of that civil war, Tajikistan is thus a different saga of democracy. Of all the post-Soviet Central Asian states, Tajikistan has a somehow a functioning democracy, where grassroots participations are evident in the pattern of existing power sharing by regional leaders of the country on an ethno-religious basis. The bloody years of the civil war has taught the country sanguinary lessons of history and leaders dare not venture into the arena of alternative power sharing, lest that would be more disastrous than the existing one. As a result, while negotiating a transition from socialism through a civil war to democracy, Tàjikistan has ensured a cooperative platform of participatory democracy, that in turn, has ensured so far viability of the regime as a functional democracy in the country.

However, more than half-a-dozen specific points that separates Tajikistan from other post-Soviet countries in that region are intrinsically imbedded in the obvious nature of its transition. First, no other country in Central Asia experienced a bloody civil war as did Tajikistan after the Soviet disintegration. Second, no other country was a frontline, vulnerable state to Afghan political volatility as did Tajikistan in pre and post-Soviet years. Third, in no other Central Asian country a whole contingent of nearly 20,000 Russian troops were stationed as did the 201st division of the Russian army in Tajikistan through the post Soviet years right up until February 2005. Fourth, no other country in Central Asia was as religiously and fundamentally ripened as was Tajikistan with her Islamic fervor rising high. Fifth, there is no other post-Soviet country in Central Asia where an Islamic party legitimately shared power with old communists and new democrats. Sixth, no other country in the region is as much central to narcotic trafficking to Europe from Afghanistan as is Tajikistan. Seventh, Tajikistan taught Central Asia the essence of coalition politics as did no other country and proved in practice that a combined efforts could sustain in power a seemingly diverse looking oppositions. Lastly, no other country save Kazakhstan is as ethnically clearly defined as Tajikistan in terms of the Uzbek Tajik conflict as well as North-South and East-West divides within the country. While Tajikistan negotiated a transition to its future, all these features told upon heavily on the layout of its governance, where unlike in other countries, such words as 'authoritarian' and 'dictatorial' would not hold out.

However, the process of transformations was not that smooth. It involved the same elements—old communists and their opponents. The political dough, however, was made here of different ingredients—the consequences of a civil war—that provided a different taste of democracy. 150,000 dead, 1 million displaced and the economy completely shattered—these were the outcomes of Tajik civil war the present generation cannot easily forget.[8] This was why a coalition with cohesive objectives for the upkeep of national interests held out clearly in Tajikistan. It was the primordial importance of this national interest that influenced politics in the country. However, when the telling impact of narcotic business as much as Islamic revivalism swayed events rapidly, the country got polarized. More than half of the country's able bodied citizens did not have jobs. They migrated to

Russia to earn their living. Only in 2004 some 280 million dollars—a sum exceeding the annual budget of Tajikistan—were sent from Russia to Tajikistan by these workers through banking channels. Friction arose in the coalition on the eve of 2004 elections on the basis that there are two Tajikistan—one, the city face of it with pomp and luxury; and the other the village majority, who struggled in penury to keep alive the memorabilia of Soviet yesteryears.

The pre-election opposition alliance in Tajikistan in 2004 was an effort to get together six political parties, two of which did not pass the rigors of registration. The remaining four were to join hands against the ruling Party headed by Imomali Rakhmanov of the Peoples Democratic Party of Tajikistan although all of them discerned that singularly they stood no chance against the ruling party. As a result, the Islamic Renaissance party entered into a pre-election alliance with the Socialist party and Socialist Democratic party in an effort to ensure free and transparent elections. It was a conscious effort laden with contradictory concerns. The contradiction lay in the fact that the IRP was the only opposition party in the Tajik parliament. On the one hand, the IRP did not wish to sever its relations with the ruling party; yet contest elections as a representative forum of all other existing opposition parties in Tajikistan. On the other, that was a difficult moment, a turning point in the annals of Tajik democracy that clearly implied that true democratic opposition is yet to emerge. The elections showed that the Islamic Renaissance Party, working in alliance with the ruling Peoples Democratic Party, could not serve the opposition objectives; nor it could serve as a tangible opposition front against that self same party in alliance with which it has ruled the country in post-civil war years. It also showed that all other opposition parties were in embryonic stage—only symbolic of the opposition with no practical presence in governance through the parliament. As elsewhere in Central Asia and devoid of the mores of participatory democracy, they were at their inceptive stage that would take years to grow.

Future Prospects

The Central Asian scenario throws little awesome prospects for any radical departure from the present. This ensures largely the continuity of present political fluidity rather than any abrupt change. This is simply because countries of the region are as much unprepared for radical change as the ruling regimes to embrace swift change. As a result, we have a scenario, where people are prepared for change, but they are unorganized. And leaders face unorganized or mal-organized opposition with abominable attitude; and unwilling to embrace change. They take recourse to repression as the only solution to ensure their style of democracy. However, such a situation begets a discourse on democracy, regime viability and governance with regard to each country and specific to each of the region's presidents.

Thus there has been more debate about children of the presidents succeeding them than debates of representative grassroots democracy. When the real problem is fundamental about nurturing ethos of democracy among the grassroots population, the solution proffered is superficial in choosing a successor little acquainted with the grassroots. The schism is too vast to bridge too quickly. Central Asian analysts have been looking to the periphery for alternatives which are unavailable. Whatever is available could be summarized as follows:

First, Central Asian leaders are reluctant to eschew power. They search for alternatives within their family and friends surrounding them, while the country requires them to demonstrate vision of democracy for the future. Contrary to the efforts of the leaders, local NGOs, supported by Western countries and under the aegis of the United Nations are busy in setting up democratic political institutions, erecting the edifices of judiciary and endeavouring to ensure the functioning of a free press—all three aspects are presumably three pillars of democracy that Central Asian leaders are known to have been unsupportive of. The outcome is semi-structured institutions trying to carve out a niche for themselves without patronage from the state, while the state supports centralization of power. In fact, the region is riddled with a fundamental question: peoples democracy or presidential dictatorship and centralized economy or free market?[9]

For immediate reference comes to mind how former Russian President, Boris Yeltsin handled the successor issue by nominating Vladimir Putin first as Prime Minister, who subsequently became the president after contesting an election. The shortcomings in this nomination was glaring if one harks back to those hoary Russian days when Yeltsin was unpopular. And this unpopular president picked up an apolitical non-entity to be his successor, struck a convenient, immunity deal with him for him and his family members not to be prosecuted for his many follies during his reign; and the Russians experienced a mood swing and said: Hurrah! This was Yeltsin style of democracy Russia had inculcated in the Central Asians. Much as you wish to emulate this style, you recall the pernicious tenets of this phenomenon. After all, it is people who must elect their president democratically; and not the president who should nominate someone of his choice to be endorsed by the people

The second choice is the Caucasian syndrome: Aliev after Aliev in Azerbaijan and Saakshashvli after Shevardnadze in Georgia. While Aliev's was a transfer of power within the family, Georgia's case was gory and gruesome. One recalls how gloriously Eduard Shevardnadze returned from Moscow to Georgia on 7 March,1992 to the applause of a cheering crowd to pilot a battered Georgia.[10] And how unceremoniously he was shown the path of exit in 2004. From the vantage point of Georgia's rose or Ukraine's pink revolutions, Azerbaijan's smooth transfer of power within the family holds emulative allurement for Central Asian presidents, much as they may not wish to face a Tulip revolution of the Kirgyz magnitude.

The third choice is Russia's emulative Putin phenomenon. Russia has been haunting Central Asia like none other. Putin had successfully contested a presidential re-election in 2004; and 2008 upcoming elections in Russia remains in the domain of question marks because Article 81(3) of the Russian Constitution states that "one and the same person cannot hold the office of president of the Russian Federation for more than two terms running".[11] While this constitutional provision is a wee bit disturbing to Central Asian presidents, some of whom have declared themselves president for life, they would prefer to wait and watch the Putin phenomenon unfold in 2008 to decide upon their future course of action. The February 2005 regime change in Kirgyzstan has turned paramount political apprehensions about successors into profound political fears for all leaders.[12] If 15 years of Akaev's rule in the "island of democracy" comes to an abrupt end by 5000 determined demonstrators, who stormed the Bishkek White House, can authoritarian regimes such as of Niyazov and Karimov be far behind? The Putin phenomenon of 2008 would certainly prove to be a belated escape route to the future.

The final and the best option is to go the disappointed people, beg their forgiveness for the follies of the past, appeal to them to forget the trauma of transition, convince them about the emerging political polyphony in a civil society, explain to them the vast difference between politics and economics of the socialist era and now and seek fresh ballot of legitimacy, of course with a change. After all it is they who are supreme in a democracy; and the presidents are their servants to serve them; and not lord over them. However, this is the only way out for Central Asian presidents for their safe and immune exit from politics to retirement. Meanwhile, they can take steps to groom political successors, corresponding to various stages of governance with clear-cut, short, medium and long-term objectives in such a fashion as: immediate successors to take over, middle aged political cadres to work for the prosperity of their countries at varied levels on various jobs; and grassroots level workers to create sound political base for a future civil society. This job is too difficult to undertake, but it is never too late to make a beginning.

NOTES

1. Kirgyzstan: Just like the Old days, *The Economist,* July 16, 2005, p. 31.
2. Ibid.
3. Alya Basimbaeva, Children of Power, *Russia and the Muslim World*, No.2, 2004, p.115.
4. Kairam Smagulov, *Assandi Times*, Alma Ata, 5 March,2004.
5. A.M. Vasiliyev, (Edited) *Post-Soviet Central Asia: The Loss and Gains*, Msocow, 1998, p. 171. (in Russian)
6. Sergei Simonyan, Opposition in Turkmenistan: Fight of the Chameleons, *Russia and the Muslim World*, No. 2, 2003, pp.108-111.
7. Z. Mamytova, Religious Ethnic and Clan Aspects of Conflict in Central Asia, *Russia and the Muslim World*, No.2,2004, p.101.
8. *Nezabesemaya Gazeta*, 17 May, 2004.
9. P.L. Dash, Political Landscape Across Central Asia, *Dialogue Quarterly*, A Journal of Astha Bharati, October-December, 2004, p. 134.
10. *The Independent*, 4 August, 1992.
11. Constitution of the Russian Federation, Moscow, Yurizicheskaya Literatura, 1994, p.121.
12. After the Tulips, *The Economist*, 2-8 July, 2005, p. 28.

PART- III

ISLAMIST RADICALISM IN CENTRAL ASIA

16

Central Asia after Collapse of USSR and Islamic Radicalism

Muzaffar Alimov

As a result of the collapse of the USSR in the early 90s, five independent states emerged on the map of Central Asia. From the very first year of their existence some of them, on one stage or the other, faced socio-political problems and threats to their security and internal stability.

The economic and social crisis that seized the Central Asian States after the downfall of the USSR was gradual and profound as compared with other CIS countries. As a result of the disintegration process of the countries of this region there is a significant decline in the socio-economic situation and in the material prosperity of the citizens. A sharp downfall in the living standards of the people is visible. There is degradation in the health and education systems and in the social-system as a whole, the number of the poorest people is increasing rapidly, there is increasing unemployment—mainly amongst the youth, and an increasing social stratification. With the weakening and corrupting of the law protection system, organized crime and corruption are also on the rise.

The GDP of the states of the region in the period 1992 to 1999 on an average decreased by 30-45 per cent.[1] There was a considerable downfall in the industrial production. During this period, three out of the five Central Asian States—Tajikistan, Uzbekistan and Kyrghyzstan slid to the category of the poorest states of the world.

During this period new threats emerged to confront these independent States. Foremost are the problems of inter-ethnic relations as well as of mutual territorial claims that arose from the very moment of independence. These have not only become serious irritants in the mutual relationship among the states of the region but also pose a hidden threat to the inter-political stability of the region. The Soviet period brought considerable changes in the territorial and ethnic structure of Central Asia in an attempt to solve the national and religious contradictions. However, Soviet policies destroyed the complex balance of ethnic, religious and mutual political relationship. The territories of Bukhara Emirate, Kakand and Khevo Khanate became parts of Uzbekistan, Tajikistan, Turkmenistan and Kyrghyzstan. A number of people were transferred to these republics forcibly, while many others reached here as a result of migration of labour force.[2]

With the creation of new borders by the Soviet powers, many people found no place in the formation of their governments. The Ferghana Valley populated primarily by Uzbeks was divided into parts that went to Uzbekistan, Tajikistan and Kyrghyzstan. The traditional centres of Tajik culture—Samarkand and Bukhara, became part of Uzbekistan. The southern part of Kazakhstan has a significant number of Uzbeks while the number of Kazakhs in Uzbekistan is no less either. However, with the open borders within the region during the Soviet era, such a division was practically not felt. But after the collapse of the USSR the nationalities that constituted the minority in these Central Asian States felt themselves under tremendous pressures from the majority after whom the states were titled.

The Soviet attempt to construct Central Asian nations along the European model of the eighteenth and nineteenth centuries could not be accomplished and left behind considerable 'construction material' in the form of primitive ethnic elements (tribal and ethno-territorial). It is this archived material that now manifests in social life after the collapse of the USSR.

In all fairness one must note that the process of nation building on the basis of titular nations, on a territory so poly-ethnical in structure as the previous Central Asian Khanate, in principle, was not the best of actions taken during the Soviet era and probably under any circumstance after acquiring independence, would have become the reason for serious controversies.

In this connection, particularly soon after the collapse of USSR, the question of interethnic coexistence became an important issue in the Central Asian states. As observed by A. Jacshenkulov: that the politics of central power on the cultivation of ethnical tolerance—

"friendship among the Soviet people"—had its positive fruits, but yet it could not overcome ethnic and religious controversies. The many problems of relationship among the people were so very difficult in their own way and had old roots that they could not be resolved even during the 50 years of Soviet power (ibid, p. 82). Consequently, as has been mentioned above, in the end of 80s and beginning of 90s, during the period of weakening of central power in the region, a series of conflicts occurred on ethnic grounds.

Obviously then, with the dawn of independence and subsequent intensification of interethnic conflicts within these states, the conflicts also got reflected—to an extent—in the official power politics of the states. A defined nationalism in that period, served as an ideological base for the construction of the new state, feeding on self-determination of the titular ethnic group, language, series of norms, traditions etc. and its imposition on the entire territory of the country.[3]

But such politics subsequently entered into controversy with quite a large number of national minorities living outside the boundary of their respective national states.

As in Uzbekistan, in the second half of 1990s, it was noticed that a powerful pressure was exerted on the Tajiks living in that country to move out. In Samarkand and Bukhara, books in Tajik language were removed from the libraries and the number of Tajiki schools in the country also decreased significantly. On the other hand, Uzbeks living in Kyrghyzstan were subjected to opposition from the official powers. It was only later in the 1990s, the nationalistic fervour of titular nationalities somewhat decreased and the government policies towards the minority nationalities became more considerable and tolerable.

In this background, the Russian speaking population of the region, which during the Soviet period were considered an important integrating factor for maintaining a balance of its own kind and served as a political stabilizer in the difficult interethnic relationships in a number of republics, now found itself in a peculiar situation. Later, when the socio-political status of the Russian speaking population, perhaps with the exception of Kazakhstan, changed substantially, and its number due to migration decreased significantly, the Russian ethnic group ceased to be considered the stabilising factor in interethnic relations (as it was earlier called).[4] After getting independence—particularly in separate regions of Kyrghyztan as well as in Tajikistan, calls for anti-Russian campaigns were heard. In the beginning of 1990s, one of the opposition leaders of Tajikistan—Shodmon Yusuf who was then the leader of Tajikistan's Democratic Party, declared Russians living in the country as hostages.

As is being done so today, actually it is needless to excessively dramatize the situation, suffice to say that interethnic relationships invariably give rise to clashes at the national level and become the reason for bringing about serious destabilization in the region. It is important to emphasise, that the issue of mutual relationship between different ethnic groups has become exceedingly delicate and sensitive and needs to be constantly handled and controlled by the governments. Today, one can say that due to skilful manipulation by the masses and the political short sightedness of the government, there is a possibility of the intensification of the inter-ethnic problems within different states.

At the time of independence substantial territorial grudges existed, practically between all the countries of the region. On Uzbek-Kyrgyz border alone, between 60 to 130 disputes were estimated.[5] A particular tense situation arose in Ferghana Valley. Very often different kinds of conflicts occurred between the citizens of Tajikistan, Kyrghyzstan and Uzbekistan. In the year 2000, Uzbekistan, in the absence of a fixed border, in a unilateral decision mined its borders with Kyrghyzstan and Tajikistan, attributing its action to the averting of attacks by the fighters of Islamic Movement of Uzbekistan (IMU) on its own territory. As a result of these mines many people perished.

Periodic border problems have become the reason of rising tensions between the bordering states of the region. In 2003, the work of border delimitation was almost completed between Turkmenistan and Uzbekistan and Tajikistan. However, more or less, the problems still remains unsolved.

Another major problem confronting the countries of this region is the issue of the division of water resources, which are vital for the production of hydroelectric energy and for agriculture. The main part of water resources of the region is concentrated on the territories of Kyrghyzstan and Tajikistan. Uzbekistan has found itself in a difficult situation, as it is dependant on these countries for water. Due to the absence of any agreement on the usage of water resources of the region even by 2003, the non-resolution of this issue is only worsening the already tense relationship between these states.

One of the significant peculiarities of the Central Asia Region concerns its topography. This region is characterised by a high population density particularly in the areas suitable for agriculture. A serious land deficit is sharply felt in Ferghana Valley where the population density and growth rate are very high and thus unemployment rate also high. Many people connect this factor with the complex socio-political situation in this region. It was here in Ferghana Valley that premeditated, organized massacres of Turok-Meskhenins were carried out and protests by Muslim extremists also held.[6] In Kyrghyzstan, some of its most fertile regions are traditionally inhabited by the Uzbeks, who have been called the "bearers of the culture of oasis" by A. Jacshenkulov, while the representatives of the titular nation occupy territories in prime hill areas and have been called "bearers of nomadic-culture and cattle breeders". In the opinion of the same author the above factor was quite instrumental in causing the tragic incident of 1990 (*ibid*). He also holds that one of the covert reasons for the origin of intra-Tajik conflict is also the lack of suitable land conditions as 93 per cent territory of Tajikistan is mountainous. These reasons were pointed out even in the beginning of 1990, after the infamous incident of 12-14 February in the city of Dushambe.

A complex problem aggravating the present situation is related to the demography of the region. Practically, in all the countries of the region after independence there has been a growth in population. Between 1991 to 2001 population increased by 44.6 per cent in Turkmenistan, by 20.3 per cent in Uzbekistan, by 15.7 per cent in Tajikistan and by 11.6 per cent in Kyrghyzstan. Only in Kazakhstan, the population decreased by 11.3 per cent, primarily due to emigration of Russian-speaking citizens. The demographic profile of the states of the Central Asian Region shows a growth in the population of the young.[7]

Here one may mention that during the Soviet era the above-mentioned controversies were resolved relatively successfully because of the then existing system of administrative planning and distribution. The powerful state machinery had the necessary resources for substantially diluting the existing problems. As a result of the disintegration of the systems of administrative power and control that existed and functioned in the framework of the USSR, and due to the destruction of regulatory mechanisms, the socio-economic and internal political situation intensified, and consequently affected the inter-relations of Central Asian states.

Another serious problem confronting the governments of the region was the illegal trafficking and use of narcotics. The tremendous growth of opium production in Afghanistan in the 90s made Central Asia one of the important links in the trafficking of drugs to the CIS and Europe and at the same time resulted in their direct sale in this region. The transit of narcotics through the states of Central Asia, along with other factors, created an atmosphere of crime, considerably increased corruption and caused damage to the authority of law organs. This primarily is in reference to Tajikistan, Uzbekistan, Kyrghyzstan and Kazakhstan, where the powerful narcotics organisations, to some extent, could even influence political decisions.

In spite of the opinion held by various researchers that Central Asian territory is not the main conduit in trafficking of narcotics from Afghanistan and Pakistan and that a large amount of narcotics (up to 70%) goes through the territory of Pakistan and Iran, nevertheless, the quantity which transits through Central Asian countries is also significant.

Deterioration in the milieu due to the illicit trafficking of narcotics also had a negative impact on the relationship between neighbouring states. In fact, due to the illicit trafficking of narcotics, at one time the image of Tajikistan suffered badly in the international arena and more so amongst other Central Asian countries and the CIS.

As the situation worsened due to above-mentioned problems, there was a general feeling of mistrust amongst the Central Asian states, which at times even led to personal hostility among their leaders. A struggle for regional leadership, unwillingness to compromise, and formulation of tough policies towards neighbours became the main characteristics of the interstate relationship in the 90s. A majority of researchers attribute the reason for the tension among the neighbouring Central Asian states to the unjustifiable tough stand taken by Uzbekistan.

According to them, Uzbekistan, in every possible way, by adopting methods unacceptable in contemporary international relations, has strived to become a regional leader. It is presumed that having conceptualized the reconstruction of "Great Turkistan", Tashkent is striving towards an unconditional domination in the region and thus playing a "fast destabilizing role in the regional system of international relations".[8]

In this background, in Tajikistan, Uzbekistan, and in southern regions of Kazakhstan, the phenomenon of Islamic fundamentalism is accelerating and precisely due to this reason extremist methods are being used for attaining goals. Some researchers attribute the reason for this growth to the decline in social consciousness as a result of breaking down of the old ideology, declining spiritual values, formation of an ideological vacuum and the absence of powerful ideological alternatives. The situation is described by the researcher R. Jangojin as: The "new period brought an untimely and considerable loss to the spiritual and moral values, and to the cultural achievements preserved by the people in the entire course of their history. However, another reason of anxiety is the mass social depression, loss of creative energy by people and its intelligentsia, of social orientation directed towards constructive reform of life".[9] Attempts by Central Asian states to create a national ideology by drawing attention towards its history and national heroes: Abai in Kazakhstan, Manas in Kyrgyzstan, Timurlane in Uzbekistan, Esmail Soman in Tajikistan did not succeed much. An ideological vacuum that was created in a definite time started filling up fast by different Islamic doctrines through an Islamic propaganda stimulated mainly by external religious forces. This factor, it is assumed, tremendously influenced the development of an internal political situation in the region, when as a whole, with the noble mission of restoring spiritual values, attempts were made to radicalize Islam, to convert the religion into a powerful instrument to attain geopolitical goals. As observed by the Uzbek researcher, A. Abbasova, this propaganda of "real Islam" was supported by illegal Islamic organizations that were interested in consolidating the radical Islamic forces and undermining the stability of the Central Asian countries in order to avert the Western and Russian influences.[10]

Looking back at the beginning of 90s, one notices a clear activation of foreign religious organisations in the countries of the Central Asian region. This period saw a rise in the number of foreign emissaries from Iran, Afghanistan, Turkey, Pakistan, and the Gulf countries. They were engaged in propagating different Islamic tenets and Pan Islamic ideas, which were irrelevant for the people of the region. Citizens of Central Asia were sent to study in various religious Institutes in foreign countries. According to the figures provided by the Ministry of Education, Science and Culture of Kyrghyzstan, 15,000 people went to religious centres in Saudi Arabia in the period 1992-1996.[11]

The early 1990s also saw the appearance of new religious organisations in addition to the already existing ones. Some such new religious organisations were: 'Islam and Democracy', and 'National Ahmed Muslim Group', in Kazakhstan; the 'Centre of Islamic Activities', 'Noor' (Ray), and 'Tablikh' in Kyrghyzstan.

The spread of Islamic fundamentalism in the countries of this region occurred primarily in the rural areas especially in Ferghana Valley, in Tajik-Prepamir, in South Kyrghyztan, and Kazakhstan. The researcher, M. Khrustalev, rightly characterised the process of the spread of fundamental ideas in the Russian region as: "Islamic fundamentalists are fast gaining strength and starting to claim power in those states, where capitalistic as well as socialistic modernisation in conjunction with population explosion is leading towards the fast impoverishment of a large number of people and forming great lumpen masses which are a powerful destructive force. With its show of poverty and democratisation it will not be difficult for the Islamic fundamentalists to overthrow the existing regime.[12]

Once peaceful, the Central Asian Region is now gradually turning into one of the instable points of the planet. The bloody civil war that started in Tajikistan in 1992 continues even after signing of the peace-agreement in June 1997. As a result of which about 100,000 people have died, and more than a million have became refugees and forced to migrate.

Reasons for the rise of intra-Tajik conflicts are yet to be studied and demand a deep analysis. The author would like to point out that in this context, one of the decisive roles in the escalating conflict is played by external factors. It is assumed that due to its geographical location, while safeguarding its border with Afghanistan, Tajikistan faced a strong negative influence from the south. Moreover, the immense ideological and logistical support from the outside created a sufficiently strong force capable of carrying out active armed struggle. In the northern region of Afghanistan special study camps were set up to prepare the future Mujahidins. At the end of 1993 armed opposition forces numbering about ten thousand, were situated in Afghanistan.[13] In fact, right up to the cessation of hostilities, activities of the forces of the United Tajik Opposition (OTO) received help from forces of Northern Alliance in Afghanistan. The armed support to Tajik opposition from A.S. Masud's forces stopped only after the active diplomatic pressure from Russia and Iran.

It is believed that after 1995 contacts were established between OTO and the Taliban.[14] An example of such a liaison was the support to the formations of Jumma Namangani, which entered into OTO in an organised way right till 1999. However, such relationships did not continue for long perhaps, due to their differences on ethnic principles.

A number of countries of the Near and Middle East, as well as international Muslim organisations rendered help to the war wing of OTO, which referred to this conflict as continuation of Jihad against communists. Fighting in these opposition forces were not only citizens of Tajikistan who underwent training in Afghanistan, but also Afghan and Arab mercenaries, including the well-known Hatab. According to some data, the arriving professionals included Arabs, Sudanians, Afghan instructors and terrorists formed more than 30 per cent of the opposition forces. Soon after its independence Tajikistan was flooded by thousands of mercenaries. By September-October 1992 "Brothers" were in Tajikistan from UAE, Malaysia, India, Bangladesh, Qatar, Jordan, Sudan, Pakistan, Afghanistan, Iran, Palestine, Syria, and Algeria.[15]

The internal conflict in Tajikistan became, perhaps, the first serious signal of the fast growing new danger for the region. In particular, the intra-Tajik opposition was forced to think seriously about the growing threat of Islamic Fundamentalism in Central Asia.

Meanwhile, even in other countries of the region the situation was not favourable. About the years 1995-96 in Ferghana Valley of Uzbekistan, the movement of Islamic Revival of Uzbekistan was formed which later transformed into Islamic Movement of Uzbekistan (IMU) under the leadership of T. Yuldashev, and D. Khodzhaev, and the most famous being Jumma Namangani. Groups such as "Toba" "Adalat" and "Islam Lashkarlari" founded the base of IMU. As a result of the tough measures taken by the Government in Tashkent, the leaders of these movements were forced to leave Uzbekistan and settle down in Tajikistan's Pamir Mountains where they joined the so-called Namagani Battalion and participated in skirmishes on behalf of the OTO. Later, leaders of OTO supported a strong contact with the Taliban and with the leaders of Al-Qaida, having received from them the necessary financial and material help. Its fighters received war and ideological training in the camps of Afghanistan and Pakistan. The situation became more difficult in the early 90s with the religious indoctrination of thousands of insurgents on the territories of these countries who then went on to form the framework of the movement. In the mid-90s, through the Chechnyan diaspora of Central Asia, a close contact was established between Uzbek Islamists and Chechnyan separatists. The so-called "Uzbek Front" operated from Chechnya and about 300 Uzbek fighters received training in the camps of the "Islamic Institute of Caucasus" located in Chechnya.[17] The leaders of IMU have declared and not just once, that their ultimate aim is to overthrow the regime of I. Karimov and establish an "Islamic Caliphate" on the territory of Uzbekistan.

In 1997 in the Namagan region of Ferghana Valley, extremists made a series of attacks on the local clerks and police employees, and instigated the locals towards anti-government acts. Similar terrorist activities were seen in Kyrghyzstan in the years1997-98.

A stage came in the year 1999, when the extremist organizations targeting the region started undertaking serious steps to realise their plans of creating an Islamic government. In February 1999, the supporters of IMU organized terrorist acts against the President of Uzbekistan I. Karimov, as a result of which 50 people were killed. Leaders of IMU took the responsibility of carrying out the shoot-out and declared that: "Our movement is being watched by the people of Uzbekistan, who would rather prefer the Islamic view. The history of a dark century dominated by Russian invaders and the rule of Bolsheviks is over, but we have still not achieved the freedom and opportunity to revive our Islamic life" (ibid, p. 154).

In August 1999 a big insurgency operation of IMU was carried out in Batkin region of Kyrghyzstan. This was aimed at destabilising the atmosphere and overthrowing the secular regime of I. Karimov and changing the existing social system. From the territory of Tajikistan, detachments of IMU fighters numbering about 2000 penetrated into Batkin region of Kyrghyzstan for subsequent invasion on the Ferghana Valley. The leaders of IMU expected to garner considerable support, particularly from this poor and thickly populated region. Intense fighting with the government forces of Kyrghyzstan continued till November.

An interesting fact is that, in IMU there were not only ethnic Uzbeks, citizens of Uzbekistan, but also there were Tajik rebels waiting in the wings, Arabian mercenaries, Afghanis, Uigurs, native

Chechnyans, Bashkirs, Tatars and people from other Muslim regions of Russia who had received training in the base camps in Afghanistan and Tajikistan.

In the year 2000 a similar attempt was made again. There are different opinions about Batkin and the Surkhandarya incident of 2000. It is evident that the act of the year 2000 was smaller in scale, localized and of a shorter duration than the incident that took place in 1999. According to some data available, this time there were only a couple of hundred fighters noticed in the Batkin region. As far as Sukhandarya province of Uzbekistan is concerned, the fighters appeared to have spent a long time in the region having left their families and immovable property behind and were discovered by chance.

At the same time there is a lot of information available about how Uzbek authorities manipulated facts about the presence of IMU fighters in the upper regions of Tupalang to deport en masse Tajik population from there to the plains of Sukhandarya region. In this process of migration, many migrants, particularly old people and children, died within a year due to malaria and other illnesses, succumbing to the new and unfamiliar conditions of the Amudarya flood lands.

Islamic Movement of Uzbekistan (IMU) attacks, at least in 1999, were well planned and organized and also well financed. It cannot be ruled out as is assumed by researchers, that these actions as well as detachments of S. Basaeva in Dagestan can be viewed as rings of the some chain and are parts of the grandiose plan of Al-Qaida. It is believed that a similar act in the summer—autumn of 2001 in Batkin did not take place only because the fighters of IMU were participating in the fighting activities from the side of the Taliban against the forces of the Northern Alliance in Afghanistan.

Another well-known religious organisation pursuing the objective of creating an Islamic government on the territory of Central Asia is: "Hizb Ut Tahrir al Islamia" (party of Islamic freedom). The Hizb Ut Tahrir (HT) was founded in Palestine in 1952 by a member of the Kaziat (Supreme Court) of that country Taqiuddin Nabakhan and is one of the branches of the movement "Brothers of Muslims" which was founded in 1928. As a consequence of the radical views the party was banned in many Arabian countries of the world. The first foxholes of the party in Central Asia were noticed in the beginning of 90s and its activities intensified in 1998-2000.

The ideological base of the HT is Pan-Islamism, and its activity consists of putting into practice its underlined teachings. Party ideologists, rejecting the armed methods of struggle, pursue their objective of uniting all Muslims, in the framework of one unitary Islamic government functioning on the basis of Shariat law. Presuming that the believers, particularly, in Central Asia are not ready to understand the idea of *Jihad*, party ideologists put before themselves the task to organise illegal religious propaganda with the help of oral appeals and discussions, distribution of papers and related literature. In other words, the parties are creating a base for peaceful evolution from the secular government to the Caliphate where Muslims will realise the advantage of Islamic government and secular forces will be compelled to hand over the power to the selected Calipha.[18] The idea of nonviolence particularly people wishing to join the party.

The structure of the party is characterised by a peculiar organisation and rigid conspiracy. HT primarily draws towards itself mostly youth from the agricultural rural areas. There have been incidents where law authorities have detained clerks, lower and middle ranking government officials.

In spite of the underground character of the activities of HT and repressive policies of the authorities, the work of the party has a high populist character. If its activities were earlier limited mainly to Ferghana Valley than later, pamphlets of HT and publications were displayed in other regions of Uzbekistan, Tashkent, and Kyrghyzstan, and also in the southern provinces of Kazakhstan. The number of party members is estimated to be in tens of thousands.

Moreover, in spite of a declaration of adoption of exceptionally peaceful methods of struggle, as per some information available, firearms and explosives were recovered during the arrests of party activists. Keeping this in view, one can presume that the party is likely to review the declared methods of work and start an armed struggle. The possibility of such developments is also evident from the incident of separation from HT in 1999 of the group of "Hizb an Nusr" (party of freedom) because of the latter's declared policy of resorting to radical means in case of punitive action from the authorities.[19]

It is important to mention here that the HT has a good global network. There is proof that one of its headquarters is located in London. The party collaborates with such organisations as "Hamas",

"Brothers of Muslims", and "Worldwide front of Jihad." The global activity of the party indicates the serious external support it receives, without which the very existence of the party for obvious reasons would have been impossible. There are evidences about the connection of HT with the activities of Taliban and Al-Qaida. Its open sympathies towards these organisations is indirectly hinted in its sharp anti-American announcements made soon after the beginning of anti-terrorist operations in Afghanistan and blaming the coalition participant-states of war against Muslims and Islam.

With such a complex background and keeping in mind the growing religious fundamentalism in the Central Asian states, in Turkmenistan the situation seems to be somewhat better. There has been practically no report of the existence of different kinds of underground organisations of religious nature or about problems of drug trafficking. This phenomenon can be explained to be due to the presence of a very strict administrative system in the country, which uses highly effective methods to control society, in front of which the existence of even legal parties is quite impossible leave alone the illegal ones.

At the same time, it is necessary to point out the unique stand of the Government in Ashkhabad in relation to DT. From the very beginning its stand was quite different from the position taken by other governments of the region and similarly from Russia on the issue of tolerance. Judging from the innumerous contacts of Turkmenian representatives with the Taliban, Turkmenistan *de facto* acknowledged the Taliban as the only legal power in Afghanistan, which position was undoubtedly connected with their plans of constructing a trans Afghanistan gas pipeline. For a long time diplomats of Ashkhabad strained to reconcile the leaders of Central Asia and the Taliban. In this connection one can presume that there was a tacit agreement between the Taliban and Turkmenistan about not having clandestine undermining activities against each other.

On the whole it is difficult to comment about any real plans of creating an Islamic government in Central Asia. It is unlikely, that the secular population of the states of this region would be ready to accept the new Islamic order. The acceptance of Islam by Tajiks, who were the natives of this region, was under the influence of Arab conquerors. The researcher E. Mamitova is of the view that till today Islam has not played a consolidating role, and it is regional, clan, tribal ancestral interests, and not some common faith, that play a great role in all, without exception, the states of Central Asia.[20] Moreover, as shown by many observations and researches, the day-to-day life and customs of the people of the region, though Islamic, are interweaved with the Pre-Islamic, Zoroastrian and in some cases even with the Buddhist beliefs and traditions. An example of not accepting Islam in its primitive form was the increasing dissatisfaction amongst Afghans towards the policies of Taliban, when in 2001 it was prohibited to celebrate "Navruz" a festival Zoroastrian in character but traditional for the Muslims.

Nevertheless, the threat of activation of radical Islam in the region, and the continuation of activities of the parties of religious character is very real and it would be a grave mistake to underestimate it. In the difficult socio-economic scenario, existing social inequality, the prospect of an alternate government system on the principle of Caliphate, becomes attractive for a part of the population. It is possible that the quantitative and qualitative rise of the illegal extremist organisations, to some extent, justifies the strict policies of Central Asian authorities that are working towards eradication or partly weakening the different types of legal and underground opposition movements.

Thus, it can be concluded that towards the beginning of the 21st century, Central Asia represents one of the most complex regions, with a large number of intertwined and problems, the main ones being illicit drug trafficking, the present difficult socio-economic situation, and the growth of religious fundamentalism acquiring the extremist form of radical organisations.

NOTES

1. A. Kashanov and B. Hussaimov, Problems of integration of states of Central Asia, *J. Central Asia and Kaphkaz,* No. 1 (13), pp. 79-95.
2. A. Jacshenkulov, *New independent states of Central Asia in the world community,* M: 2000, p. 83.
3. C. Golunov, Post Soviet borders of Central Asia in context to/with security and cooperation. *J. Central Asia and Kaphkaz,* No 5(17) 2001, pp. 166-179.
4. A. Jacshenkulov, *New Independence states of Central Asia in the world co-operation association,* p.306, M.: 2000, p. 88.
5. S. Golunov, Post Soviet borders of Central Asia in context of security and cooperation. *J. Central Asia and Kaphkaz.* No.5 (17) 2001, pp. 166-179.

6. A. Jacshenkulov, *New Independent states of Central Asia in the world community,* M: 2000, p. 87.
7. A. Topilin, B. Shylga, CIS states: problems and opportunities of socio-demographic growth. *J. Central Asia and Kaphkaz,* No. 3 (15), 2001, pp. 189-203.
8. O. Boronin, On the question of priorities of Russian policies in the Central Asia. *J. Central Asia and Kaphkaz,* No. 3 (27) 2003, p.103.
9. R. Jangojin. Some observations made on the situation of the governments of Central Asian region. *J. Central Asia and Kaphkaz* No.2 (8), 2000 p.160.
10. A. Abbasova, Question about the religious factor in modern Uzbekistan. *J. Central Asia and Kaphkaz,* No. 1 (13) 2001, pp.142-148.
11. A. Khanyazev, *History of Afghan war 1990 and conversion of Afghanistan into a source of threat to Central Asia.* Bishkek, 2002, p.161.
12. M. Khrustalev, *Political situation in the countries of the Central Asian region the perspectives of its growth. Central Asia in the External policy of Russia,* Moscow: 1994, p. 19.
13. C. Olimova and M. Olimov, Islamic revivalist party in intra-Tajiki conflict and its regulation. *J. Central Asia and Kaphkaz,* No. (13). 2001, pp.131-142.
14. A. Khanyazev, *History of Afghan war 1990 and conversion of Afghanistan into a source of threat to Central Asia.* Bishkek, 2002, p.125.
15. M. Olimov, *Problems of struggle with terrorism. The net of ethnological monitoring and early warning of the conflicts,* August, M.: 1998 p. 65.
16. Ibid.
17. A. Khanyazev, *History of Afghan war 1990 and conversion of Afghanistan into a source of threat to Central Asia.* Bishkek, 2002, pp. 172-173.
18. B. Babazhano, *Religious – opposition groups in Uzbekistan // Religious extremism in Central Asia—Problems and perspectives. Materials of the Conference of Dushambe,* 25 April 2002 p. 43-63.
19. Ibid., p. 57.
20. A. Mamitova, Islamic fundamentalism and extremism in the countries of Central Asia. *J. Central Asia and Kaphkaz,* No. 5 (11) 2000, pp. 57-63.

17

Religious Extremism in Central Asia

A Case Study of Uzbekistan

Ramakant Dwivedi

Introduction

Central Asia today is the area of the geopolitical opposition of world powers. The countries of this region occupy one of the most important geopolitical and geo-economic position which connects the states of Asia and Europe. The region is also gradually becoming one of the world's centres of hydrocarbon raw material production. The dismantling of the erstwhile Soviet Union led to the emergence of five independent and sovereign republics of Kazakhstan, Kyrgyzstan, Tajikistan, Turkmenistan and Uzbekistan. However, this historical development in Eurasian space little more than 15 years ago has failed to bring to the people of Central Asia[1] the changes in social, economic and political arena they had hoped for. Instead, they have had to suffer more poverty. Their continued hardship has been utilized by the extremist groups and organisations to promote their agenda based on religious extremism. The extreme form of Islam[2] has become an important issue in Central Asia today. Ideologues of extremism are determined to promote and ultimately establish their faith in this region. However, this is in sharp contradiction with the historical realities of Maveranahr.[3] The clash between secular and extremist forces in Uzbekistan has been around since 1991 and many violent incidents have occurred. Some Central Asian analysts attribute the rise of extremism to political deprivation, deteriorating economic conditions, corruption, and a steep drop in living standards, unemployment and poor governance in Uzbekistan. One may agree partially with this generalisation. However, it is also true that the Hizb-ut-Tahrir and Islamic Movement of Turkistan have the goal of setting up a Caliphate, a revivalist goal that rejects the modern state. The developments in Andijon City in Ferghana Valley (May 12-14, 2005) of Uzbekistan, clearly were not driven merely by social and economic demands. There are strong religious and political motivations[4] and reveal a power struggle with secular forces that will continue for some time to come. Experts have, also, pointed to external financial support to these extremists[5]. The organisers of the Andijon protests appear to have been impressed by the "Colour Revolutions" which had taken place in several of the former Soviet republics in recent times. Michael Hall, Director of the Central Asia Project of the International Crisis Group, has suggested that these "Revolutions" have cast their shadow, now, over Uzbekistan.[6] This appears to be an extrapolative leap from an inadequate data base. However, the case for continuous watch and study of developments is valid because Uzbekistan is a key country in the region and traumatic changes would have major geopolitical implications for Central Asia and its neighbouring region.

Islam in Uzbekistan

After the collapse of the Soviet Union in 1991, there was a revival of Islam in Central Asia. Uzbekistan and Tajikistan were the two most effected republics in Central Asia of this revival. A number of Muslim missionaries also arrived in Central Asia, mostly from Pakistan and Saudi Arabia. Funds flowed in for building new mosques and spreading 'Islamic teachings'. Ferghana Valley in Uzbekistan which has a dense concentration of people in whole Central Asia, also has a dense concentration of mosques.[7] It is not surprising, then, that most of the religious extremist groups got their start or found their greatest support in the Ferghana Valley.

Ideologues of extremism are determined to promote and ultimately establish their faith in this region. However, this is in sharp contrast to the historical realities of the region. The new Islamic groups, parties and organisations in Uzbekistan have advocated a kind of Islam that does not seem to follow the moderate form of either the Hanafi School[8] or the Sufi traditions.[9] This has ignited a long drawn struggle between the supporters and opponents of this ideology. In other words, contestation over Islam has become a security issue in the Ferghana Valley today. It is simultaneously a tool in a wider geopolitical struggle, one of the forms of anti-modernization, as well as a result of the ineffective nature of political and economic systems that increase the level of political risk.[10]

During the Soviet era, restraints were emplaced on the practice of Islam since the social and personal significance of religion was devalued.[11] After the collapse of the Soviet Union, political Islam began to assume importance in Uzbekistan. Before turning to the history of the emergence of the religious extremists groups, organisations, movement and parties, a brief anaysis of the main causes of religious extremism may here be useful.

Main Causes of Extremism

Some Central Asian watchers believe that political deprivation, and corruption have led to frustration and discontent, which has in turn given birth to religious extremism. Economic approaches emphasise the importance of socio-economic conditions as the cause of extremism. Graham Fuller has been stressing the relationship between the economic condition and the rise of extremism in Ferghana Valley.[12] The assumtion is that unemployment, poverty, monetary inflation and underdevelopment are the causes behind the resurgence of extremism. But it fails to explain why extremism is on the rise in some countries but not others where economic conditions are equally dire.

It is known that some schools of thought (ideological approaches) and movements within Islam are orthodox, uncompromising and strict. They are critical of Muslims who violate "authentic norms" of Islam. Salafism and Wahhabism are the movements which refuse to accept the religious, cultural and traditional practices in Central Asia.[13] John Esposito argues that religious extremists ignore classical Islamic criteria for a just Jehad.[14] Many Islamic scholars have also criticised "global Mujahideen" in Kashmir, Tashkent, Chechnya, Andijon and elsewhere for violating basic Islamic principles. They argue that Islam does not justify suicide attacks and cite passages from the Hadith of the Prophet Mohammed, "Whoever kills himself in any way will be tormented in that way in hell" and "Whoever kills himself in any way in this world will be tormented with it on the day of the resurrection".[15] Psychological and behavioural motivations, some argue, are the key elements behind the suicide attacks. Psychological approaches stress that people behave emotionally rather than rationally. Emotions become a stronger factor in taking decisions than logic and reason. Meanwhile behavioural approaches view religious extremism as a particular type of behaviour based on intolerance and exclusion.

To analyse the emergence of the religious extremist groups, movements, parties and organisations we need to apply a synthesis, however difficult, of their religious, cultural, sociological, political and ideological underpinnings.

Groups/Parties Having 'Islamic' Moorings

Followings are the groups and parties in Uzbekistan which have Islamic moorings. They are:

- Islamic Renaissance (Revival) Party of Uzbekistan (IRPU);
- *Adolat* (Justice);
- Islam *Lashkarlori* (Warriors of Islam);
- *Tovba* (Repentance);
- *Imonchilar* (Believers) or *Akromiylar*, or *Khalifatchilar* (Caliphate Supporters);
- Islamic Movement of Uzbekistan (IMU);
- *Hizb-Ut-Tahrir* (Party of Liberation);
- Islamic Movement of Turkestan (IMT).

Religious extremists are opposed to the traditions of Sufism[16] which have characterized Islam in many parts of Central Asia and they seem to have found some resonance in Uzbekistan.

These groups have converged on a set of demands[17]:

- Return to the basic principles and commandments of Islam, purification of Islam of all later heresies and 'distractions';
- A political system based on *Hakimiya* and caliphate;
- A legal system based on Shari'a, with administration of Shari'a of justice taking the priority over legislative and executive power.

The roots of religious extremism in Uzbekistan can be traced back to the 1950s. Muhammad Hindustani Rustamov or Haji Domla (teacher) was a very influential and unofficial spiritual leader in Central Asia. Born in Kokand in Ferghana Valley in about 1892, he studied in

Bukhara, Afghanistan and Deoband[18] in India. He returned to Uzbekistan in 1929 and was arrested on the charges of propagating Salafism. He spent 15 years in Siberia.[19] He moved to Dushanbe in 1947 and worked at the Institute of Oriental Studies, Academy of Sciences of the Republic of Tajikistan, and finally died in Dushanbe in 1989. In the 1970s, some of his followers[20] joined Wahhabism.[21] Their recorded speeches are still in circulation among Wahhabis and are being used to recruit new members. Recently, women are being recruited into Wahhabi groups in an effort to widen the social base. The adherents of "Wahhabism" in Uzbekistan thrive on the support of contacts with counterparts and *gurus* abroad. To evade scrutiny, citizens of Central Asia are given the cover of tourism to be imparted indoctrination and training in Turkey, Saudi Arabia and Pakistan. Secondly, monetary doles are given as seed capital for trainees to engage in some gainful business of their own on return.[22]

The Islamic Revival Party (IRP) of the Union of Soviet Socialist Republic (USSR) was established on June 9, 1990, in Astrakhan in the Russian Federation. It became active in Uzbekistan. However, the Uzbek branch of the Islamic Revival Party (IRP) could not function for long as it was banned by the government. But party members and supporters continued their work clandestinely. The Imam at the Ata Wali Khan Tura mosque in Namangan and follower of Rahmatulla Qori, Abd al-Ahad, along with his supporters called for the rule of Sharia law. They argued this would solve all the social-economic problems and end despotism, inequality and criminality.

Supporters of the banned IRP created the Adolat (Justice) Party in 1991. Two underground groups *Islam Lashkarlori*[23] (Warriors of Islam), and *Tovba*[24] (Repentance) were also established in 1991 in the provinces of Namangan, Andijon and Ferghana with the goal of establishing an Islamic State.[25] Adolat staged demonstrations in Namangan for the establishment of an Islamic State. An important incident occurred in December 1991 in Namangan city, when the members and supporters of the Adolat Party took over the headquarters of the then Communist Party of Uzbekistan. The Namangan city mayor did not give them permission to build a new mosque at a place of their choice. This prompted the Adolat party cadre to capture the Communist Party headquarters. *Imonchilar* (Believers), *Akromiylar* and *Khalifatchilar* (Caliphate Supporters), in one or other way, were also helping the 'cause' of creating a Caliphate. Akrom Yuldashev is considered the founder of this group.[26] Activities of these groups and parties mark the beginning of religious extremism in Uzbekistan.

Tohir Yuldashev Abdulhalilovich[27] has emerged as a 'strong' leader in Ferghana Valley by 1995 and religious extremists believed they could start a war to overthrow Islam Abduganievich Karimov's government in Tashkent. Alarmed, the Uzbek government effectively implemented Article 31 and Article 61 of the Constitution. Article 31of the Constitution states: "Freedom of conscience is guaranteed to all. Everyone has the right to profess any religion or none. The compulsory imposition of religious views is not permissible. It is prohibited to establish secret societies and associations." Article 61 states that religious organisations and associations are separate from the State and are equal before the law. The State does not interfere in the activities of religious associations. This Constitution of Uzbekistan was adopted on the 8th December, 1992 in Tashkent at the eleventh session of the Supreme Council of the Republic of Uzbekistan.

It is important to remember that so far all the extremist groups have emerged in the Ferghana Valley which accounts for 4.5 per cent of the territory of Uzbekistan but nearly 25 per cent population of the country.[28] Historically, the roots of Islam have been strong here, as stated earlier, whereas the other areas such as Bukhara, Samarkand and Khiva which had been traditional learning centres of Islamic and Sufi orders were less influenced by Wahhabism. Difficult social situation, high density of population and high unemployment provided fertile ground for the missionaries from countries situated in the south and south-west of Uzbekistan. Already 5 to 10 per cent of the population in the Valley follows the Wahhabi school.[29]

Another aspect which requires attention here is the relationship between the transnational drug trafficking lobbies and the religious extremist parties. Members and supporters of these extremist groups were involved in transporting opium from Afghanistan to Central Asia and beyond. This nexus continues while the area of operation and volume of trade had increased. According to the United Nations estimate, Afghanistan is the world's largest source of opium. The Drug money accounted for $ 2.3 billion in 2003—half the nation's economy. The country's total production of opium exceeded 4,000 tonnes in 2004. Though, area of poppy cultivation has reduced in Afghanistan in 2005 as per the UN report, however better yield of poppy per hectare has continued the nexus between transnational drug trafficking lobbies and the religious extremist forces.

Islamic Movement of Uzbekistan (IMU)

The Islamic Movement of Uzbekistan (IMU) was created by Tohir Yuldashev in 1996 soon after realizing that the United Tajik Opposition (UTO) would sign a peace accord with Tajik government.[30] He and his field commander Jumaboy Ahmadjonovich Khojiyev also known as Juma Namangani and Tojiboy were instrumental in expanding and strengthening the base of the IMU. Juma Namangani, a native of Namangan province joined the Soviet military service in 1987. He served for a short time in Afghanistan when Soviet forces were present there. From 1989 on he took up the study of Islam and received spiritual education from the well known Abdulvali Mirzoyev. From 1991 he became an active supporter of Wahhabism. The stated aims of the IMU and its present form are to overthrow the Government of President Islam Karimov of Uzbekistan and establishment of an Islamic State. Since its beginning IMU has been involved in transporting drugs from Afghanistan to Tajikistan and Kyrgyzstan on way to destinations in Russia, Eastern Europe and the West. Thus the drug business has been playing an important role in the sustenance of the IMU.[31]

Juma Namangani, who underwent special military training under Arab and Pakistani instructors in Afghanistan, commanded an armed formation. He took active part along with the United Tajik Opposition[32] (UTO) forces against the Tajik government troops. He has been an instrumental figure in training Uzbek militias to carry out sabotage and terrorist activities. It has been reported that he was killed in Afghanistan while fighting for the Taliban. Since then, Tohir Yuldashev has been taking both ideological and military command of this movement. Islamic Movement of Uzbekistan (IMU) has been responsible for carrying out killings of senior police officials in Namangan in December 1997.[33] This has prompted the Uzbek government to pass "Laws about Religious Practices" in the Oily Majlis (parliament) in May 1998 which put certain restrictions on the illegal religious mosques and Madrasas (*Madaris*) which were used by the IMU in carrying out their attacks in Namangan. These laws are aimed at tightening the government grip on the illegal religious practices.

The IMU leadership was held responsible along with the leader of the Erk (Freedom) Party Muhammed Solih by the Uzbek government for a series of bomb blasts in Tashkent on February 16, 1999 which left sixteen people dead and more than a hundred wounded. Uzbek President Islam Karimov survived this attack. This further intensified the government's hunt for the religious extremists. However, Uzbek government has been criticized for using this incident to marginalise genuine democratic opponents. A British expert believes that although the IMU was blamed for the Tashkent bombings in 1999, "the evidence has never been conclusive. In fact, there are strong indications that the Tashkent bombings were perpetrated by one of Karimov's political opponents who had ties to powerful organisations."[34] (The author was present in Tashkent when the blasts took place; and following discussions with the Uzbek scholars concluded that the possibility of IMU's involvement along with some transnational terrorists was very high). An important outcome of the trial which followed these bombings was that the leader of the Erk party was also found guilty of organising the blasts and was convicted along with the IMU leaders. The conviction of Salih left no hope that the Uzbek president would ever reopen dialogue with the Erk party.

In August 1999, IMU attempted an incursion into Uzbekistan. The objective of this incursion was destabilization in Uzbekistan and creation of Islamic state in the Ferghana Valley.[35] Second incursion took place in August 2000. These IMU fighters were trained at Tavildara region in Tajikistan. This has caused tensions between Dushanbe, Tashkent and Bishkek. In July 2001, IMU fighters attacked government forces in southern Uzbekistan. This series of events from Tashkent bombing in February 1999 to incursions into Kyrgyzstan in the same year as well as into Uzbekistan and Kyrgyzstan in 2000, and in July 2001 have caused a significant change in the threat perceptions from the extremist forces. Experts hold extremists responsible for May 13, 2005 events in Andijon city in Ferghana Valley.[36] Andijon is next door to Kyrgyzstan's Osh and Jalalabad provinces where the successful March 2005 demonstrations against the Kyrgyz President, Asker Akayev, culminated in his flight to Moscow. The movement was christened the "Tulip Revolution". The arrest of 23 businessmen or as the Uzbek government says "Akromilars" (followers of Akram Yuldoshev), were arrested under Article 159 of the Uzbek Criminal Code which pertains to unconstitutional activity. Their arrest followed by trial seems to have provoked revolt in Andijon. Supporters of 23 arrested "businessmen" were able to seize the buildings of the regional assembly for a short while, which were taken back by Uzbek security forces after a swift operation against "*Akromilar*". Here clashes between the "Islamists" and Uzbek security forces took a bloody turn. In all 187 people died in the clashes, as the Andijon Regional Prosecutor, Bakhtiyar Dekhkanov, told a news conference in Andijon City on July 13, 2005. This includes 94 "terrorists", 20 police officers, 11 military personnel, 57 civilians and 5 bodies are yet to be identified. Earlier, the Uzbek authorities listed 176 people killed and 295 wounded[37]. However, media reports put the death toll at more than 400. The unrest has also spread to Korasuv town from nearby Andijon. This has highlighted the question of international development and maintaining stability and security in the Central Asian region.

The Islamic Movement of Turkestan (IMT) known as the Islamic Movement of Uzbekistan (IMU) until the middle of 2003, has declared objective of overthrowing the constitutional system and to create the Islamic state. It was placed by the United State Department of States on the list of the 34 most dangerous international terrorist organizations. Islamic Movement of Turkestan (IMT) draws sustenance from financial support of international movements and donations from Uzbek diaspora in Islamic countries. In addition, IMT also periodically receives funds from special services in Pakistan and some other foreign countries. IMT comprises of several separate groups drawn from Uzbekistan, Kyrgyzstan, Tajikistan, Kazakhstan, Turkmenistan, Chechnya and Xinjiang Uigur autonomous region of China. After the reported death of Juma Namangani during the military action against Taliban in Afghanistan led by the United States, the post of the leader of IMT was taken up by Tohir Yuldashev. The leaders of IMT collaborate with a number of international and regional Islamic terrorist organizations and movements, in the first place, with Al-Qaeda, Taliban, Hizb Ut-Tahrir and Ikhvan-al-Muslimin. Some analysts believe IMT was backing the acts of terror in Uzbekistan in March 2004.[38]

After the Civil-war broke out in Tajikistan, Tohir Yuldashev started travelling to Afghanistan, Saudi Arabia, Iran, Pakistan, the United Arab Emirates and Turkey where he established contact with the Islamic parties and government agencies. Pakistan's Inter Services Intelligence

(ISI) provided funds and shelter to him and his supporters during 1995-98 in Peshawar, "the center not only of Pakistani and Afghan Islamic activism but also of pan-Islamic *jihadi* groups."[39] Pakistan's Jamiat-i-Ulema Islami (JUI) extended full support to the Islamic Movement of Uzbekistan. Funds were raised by the JUI to cover the cost of Madrasa education for the young Uzbek students.[40] This clearly suggests that support to religious extremism has become an integral part of Pakistan's regional strategy. Meanwhile, Saudi Arabia's financial and ideological support to the religious extremists in Ferghana Valley continued through 1990s. After the traumatic September 11 incident the Saudi government took some measures to control this assistance. However, financial and ideological assistance is still continuing to IMT through the large Uzbek Diaspora settled in that country. There is little doubt that Pakistani and Saudi linkages have been the important factors in promoting religious extremism in the Ferghana Valley.[41]

Hizb-ut-Tahrir (HT)

This Party was formed in 1953 in Bayt-ul-Maqdis in Jerusalem by Sheikh Taqiyuddin Nabhani. It is said to have had its connections with the Central Asia region as well.[42] However, it reappeared in the 1990s in Central Asia as a transnational and potentially far more powerful Islamist organization. It soon became popular with a number of followers in West Asia, North Africa and South East Asia. But it was banned in a number of countries and its followers were imprisoned.[43] The head office of the Party was for a while based in London. After London bomb blasts in July this year, the HT has come under tremendous pressure from Western countries. Whether it will be asked to wrap up from London is yet to be seen. The financial sources of the Party are not known but it publishes books, small booklets and reams of pamphlets to spread its ideology. It has got its website also.

Hizb-ut-Tahrir (HT) works at two levels. First, with the Muslim community; it explains the duty to work for the Khilafah (Caliphate) State and in living by Islam without losing one's identity. Second, it propagates Islam as a political and intellectual system to a wider audience.[44] HT is banned in all Central Asian countries. It is estimated that around 7000 to 8000 members of this party are in prison in Central

Asia most of them in Uzbekistan.[45] This figure appears to be exaggerated. HT leaflets were found in Tashkent in 1992-93. But today, it has become very active all over Central Asia. The main purpose of the Hizb-ut-Tahrir is to restore the Islamic way of life and to propagate the call (da'vat) of Islam in the world.[46]

The influence of "Hizb ut-Tahrir" is widespread in Osh, Dzhalalabad, Batken regions of Kyrgyzstan; Turkestan and Almaty regions of Kazakhstan; in Sogd region of Tajikistan, in the Uzbek part of Ferghana Valley and Tashkent region of Uzbekistan. During 1990-1998, the Party's focus was on religious propaganda and recruitment of new members. Small cells (Halqa) of 4-5 people were formed to carry out the activities of the party in various parts of the Ferghana Valley.

The Tashkent bombing of February 16, 1999 marked a new phase of activism. Party members started disseminating extremist leaflets in crowded places openly. The new form of the information propaganda also included the distribution of the audiocassettes among the people, that was not common earlier. Books such as *Muslim Brotherhood, Islamic State, Caliphate*, are being used as the manuals by the party members and workers. The aftermath of September 11, 2001, saw a temporary weakening of contacts between extremist and the terrorist organisations. But soon Hizb ut-Tahrir aligned with Al-Qaida, Taliban, and the Islamic Movement of Uzbekistan (IMU). The common cause became creation of a 'Caliphate'.[47] This position testifies that the radical methods of achieving the final goal seems to be more accepted in the activity of party.[48]

Both the IMU and the HT have common goals to overthrow the present-day secular Uzbek government. In early 2004, HT got divided in Central Asia. A splinter group of the HT known as *Zamots* was reportedly behind the attacks in Tashkent in Uzbekistan during March 28—April 1, 2004 in which more than 46 people were killed and tens of others were wounded. The suicide bombers have carried out attacks in Tashkent followed up by bloody clashes between the Uzbek security forces and terrorists who are believed to be members of the *Zamots.*[49] The recent suicide bomb attacks in front of US and Israeli embassies in Tashkent on July 30, 2004 in which seven people were killed and several others were wounded is also believed to be the handy work of this organisation.[50] However, HT has denied its involvement in these attacks while Islamic Jihad[51] and IMU had claimed responsibility.[52]

The suicide attacks of March, April and July 2004 and May 12-13, 2005 in Uzbekistan is clear pointer to an escalation of security threats and continued activism of religious extremist organisations.

The common uniting objective of all the named religious extremist groups is the creation of theocratic State in Uzbekistan. Whether it is planned or not, this objective finds resonance in countries like Saudi Arabia where Islam is religion, government and society. Religion is not a private matter between man and his creater. Official Islam should govern a Muslim individually and his interactions with society at large.

It can be summarised from the above mentioned analysis that the goals of religious extremist groups in Ferghana are similar. These are as followings:

- To overthrow the existing constitutional system and establish an Islamic Caliphate;
- Politicisation of Islam;
- To establish stable communication channels with foreign Islamic centres and organisations with similar political purposes;
- To mobilise funds for the Islamic parties for political purposes;
- To ensure participation in the State bodies for undermining political stability and discredit the secular form of government.

There are, inevitably, internal factors which tend to support the activity of extremist religious groups and parties, either directly or indirectly. These are:

- Socio-economic problems especially in the rural areas of the Ferghana Valley;
- Lack of reliable information and transparency on ongoing social, religious and political programme of the government;
- Absence of informed interaction and coordination between the various Muslim Boards *(Muftiyat)* of the Central Asian Republics; and
- Inadequate coordination and cooperation between the law-enforcement agencies of the Central Asian countries at the regional level about an effective intelligence exchange and control over illegal/banned religious extremist organizations.

International and Regional Cooperation against Religious Extremism

The Central Asian states especially Kyrgyzstan and Tajikistan are dependent on Russia to fight this menace. Russian focus so far has been on military methods. We now turn to an examination of the regional initiatives against religious extremism in Central Asia.

Shanghai Cooperation Organisation (SCO)

Cooperation within the framework of the Shanghai Cooperation Organisation (SCO) among the member countries against religious extremism and international terrorism is important. In the SCO summit held in Tashkent on June 17, 2004, all the member countries, i.e. Russia, China, Kazakhstan, Kyrgyzstan, Tajikistan, and Uzbekistan have expressed their determination to eliminate religious extremism. In June 2001, SCO member states signed *"The Shanghai Convention on fighting Terrorism, Separatism and Religious Extremism."*[53] By opening an Anti-Terrorism Centre in Tashkent the process has been institutionalised. The summit meetings of the Shanghai Cooperation Organization (SCO) held in Astana on July 5-6, 2005 and in June in Shanghai reiterated its commitment to fight against religious extremism.

Collective Security Treaty Organisation (CSTO)

Uzbekistan is a member of the Collective Security Treaty Organisation (CSTO), cooperation between Russia and the other Central Asian countries within the framework of the Treaty is another step in containing religious extremist forces in the region. Tajikistan, Kazakhstan and Kyrgyzstan have been taking part in joint military exercises along with Russia every year. The last one was conducted in Tajikistan early this year. The Strategic Partnership Agreement between the Republic of Uzbekistan and the Russian Federation signed on July 17, 2004 is a major development and is expected to contain the activities of extremist forces in this region. It signifies that both Russia and Uzbekistan are determined to join hands against destabilising forces in the region.

Operation Enduring Freedom in Afghanistan

Kyrgyz and Uzbek governments have cooperated with the US in its fight against the Taliban and Al-Qaeda in Afghanistan. Karshi-Khanabad air base in Uzbekistan, or K2, and Manas air base in Kyrgyzstan support the United States' air force to conduct air raids against Taliban targets. IMU fighters fought along with the Taliban against the US forces in Afghanistan. Though US led military action against Taliban has dealt a serious blow to Islamic Movement of Turkistan's presence in Afghanistan, there are reports that the Islamic Movement of Turkmenistan fighters are regrouping in Central Asia.[54] Clashes between the Uzbek security forces and the religious extremist in Andijon City in Ferghana valley on May 12-13, 2005 is a pointer to this.

It has been claimed that United States presence in Central Asia has played a positive role in neutralising extremist forces. Clearly, the destruction of the international terrorist infrastructure in Afghanistan has considerably reduced the threats from the religious extremists to Central Asian States. But some analysts[55] have expressed reservations about the effects of a prolonged stay of the US forces in Central Asia. The nature of the 'colour revolutions' in the former Soviet Republics indicate that these reservations are not entirely unfounded. The Central Asian states have joined hands with Russia and China to counter the US moves in the region. The implications for Uzbekistan are becoming clear as Islamic figures and opposition leaders are receiving warm welcome in Washington.

Religious Extremism in Uzbekistan and Implications for India

Will religious extremism in Ferghana Valley become a threat to India's security? From the Indian perspective, Central Asia has immense strategic and economic significance. The presence of Islamic extremists in Ferghana Valley has serious implications for the security of India. The outcome of confrontation between secular and extremist forces in Ferghana Valley is bound to effect all countries which have embraced a democratic, plural and secular form of governance. Extremist elements from Central Asian Republics have reportedly been found fighting along the Pak Mujahideens in Jammu & Kashmir. The nexus between the Islamic Revival Parties, the Islamic Movement of Turkistan, Jamat-e-Islami of Pakistan, Taliban and Al-Qaeda has been clear for some time. Victory of extremist forces in Ferghana Valley will give a major boost to the extremist forces not only in Pakistan, Afghanistan but also in India's Jammu & Kashmir and elsewhere. Geographic proximity of the region makes India an important stakeholder.

Conclusion

Religious extremism in Uzbekistan is a serious threat to security and stability in Central Asia. Declining economic conditions, corruption, sense of injustice and non-accommodative polity will attract followers to IMT and HT. Therefore, imaginative and creative initiatives by the governments to arrest the deteriorating economic conditions in the region are essential to weaken the appeal of religious extremism. The local population in the Central Asian countries (except a sizeable number in Namangan, Andijon and Ferghana provinces) is not in favour of radical Islam. However, they wouldn't resist if Islamic prohibitions are imposed on them in conditions of discontent. The consequences of the unresolved conflict in Afghanistan and transnational character of drug trafficking complicate the issue. Drug trafficking and organised crime is thriving along with extremism in Central Asia. Therefore, speedy reconstruction of Afghanistan and restoration of peace would also help addressing the issue of extremism in Uzbekistan. The role of external powers will remain an important part of the unfolding dynamic. Pakistan for example has strategic interest in creating centrifugal forces in both Afghanistan and Central Asia.

Central Asia is part of the "immediate and strategic neighbourhood" of India. The activities of Islamic extremists in Central Asia have serious implications for the security of Central Asian countries, India and Russia. Islam *per se* is not a threat to security and stability in the Central Asian region. However, Islamisation of politics and politicization of Islam on the line of IMT and Hizb-ut-Tahrir is a serious threat to stability, development and modernisation. A comprehensive, cooperative and coordinated plan of action is required on the part of all Central Asian countries to counter the threat. Also, the funding sources of extremist groups need to be plugged. As far as the issue of democratisation is concerned, one should welcome the emergence of genuine secular political opposition in Uzbekistan. However, these must not be prescribed and promoted from abroad. Human Rights, civil society and democracy are perceived locally as new instruments for perpetuating outside interference. Imposed from outside, these concepts will not work. They have to be home grown taking account of the historical, social, economic and political processes.

NOTES

1. The definition of Central Asia is without any territorial prejudice and is in accordance with the decision of the Head of States meeting held in Tashkent in January 1993 that encompasses Kazakhstan, Kyrgyzstan, Tajikistan, Turkmenistan and Uzbekistan.
2. This form of Islam is being preached and promoted by the Islamic Movement of Uzbekistan (IMU) now an arm of the Islamic Movement of Central Asia (Turkestan) and Hizb-ut-Tahrir which have been trying to gain political power in Uzbekistan.
3. Region between the Amu Darya and Syr Darya, i.e. Uzbekistan, South Kyrgyzstan and North Tajikistan.
4. Shirin Akiner, "Violence in Andijon 13 May 2005: An Independent Analysis" at http://www.silkroadstudies.org/new/inside/publications/0507Akiner.pdf (Accessed on June 25, 2005)
5. Ibid.
6. Michael Hall, 'Amid Western apathy, Uzbekistan can expect more violence' at http://www.dailystar.com.lb/article.asp?edition_id=10&categ_id=5& article–id=16344, (Accessed on June, 30, 2005
7. The author visited Ferghana Valley recently and found out that every Mahalla has a mosque which is not the case in the whole of Central Asia.
8. Abu Hanifeh al-Numan ibn Thabit ibn Zubta (699-767A.D.), the founder of the School has emphasised more on ra'y (opinion), qyias (analogy) and jima (consensus) in the interpretation of Islamic laws and principles.
9. The Naqshbandiya and Yasawiya Sufi orders.
10. Shirin Akiner, "The Politicisation of Islam in Post-Soviet Central Asia", *Religion, State and Society*, 31(2), 2003, London, p. 119.
11. Alexandre Bennigsen and Marie Broxup, no. 1, pp. 44-45
12. Fuller, G., "Central Asia: The Quest for Identity," *Current History,* 93 (582), April 1994, p. 147.
13. Interview with M. Sharafuddin, former chairman of the religious committee of the Republic of Uzbekistan, Tashkent, Uzbekistan, January 10, 2001.
14. John L. Esposito, *Unholy War: Terror in the Name of Islam*, Oxford University Press, Oxford, 2002, p. 157.
15. Bernard Lewis, *Crisis of Islam: Holy War and Unholy Terror*, the Modern Library, New York, 2003, pp. 153-154.

16. Sufism or *Tasawwuf,* as it is called in Arabic, is generally understood by scholars and Sufis to be the inner, mystical, or psycho-spiritual dimension of Islam. However, *Wahhabi* school of thought doesn't agree with this definition.
17. Rashid Ahmed, *Jihad : The Rise of Militant Islam in Central Asia*, Orient Longman, pp. 247-249, as cited in Poonam Mann, "Islamic Movement of Uzbekistan: Will it Strike Back", *Strategic Analysis,* 24 (2), 2002. Interview with the former Deputy Foreign Minister of Uzbekistan, Prof Abdusamat Khaydarov, New Delhi, January 29, 2005.
18. *Deobandi* Movement developed as a reaction to British action against Muslims and the influence of Sir Sayed Ahmed Khan, who advocated the reform and modernization of Islam. Named after the town of Deoband, where it originates, the movement was built around Islamic School (Darul Uloom).
19. Oliver Roy, *The New Central Asia: The Creation of Nations*, IB Tauris Publishers, London, 2000, p. 154.
20. Rahmatullah Qari Allama (Fergana), Abdulvali Qari Mirzoyev (Fergana), Ishaq Qori, Ismail Domla, Ibrahimjan Khukandi, Hikmatullah Qori (in Dushanbe), Muhammad Ali Marginani, Ubaydullah Makhsum (in Namangan), Abd al-Latif Andijoni, Muhammad Sodiq Qori (Mufti of Muslim Board of Uzbekistan 1989-93). See Ashirbek Muminov, "Traditional and Modern Religious Theological School in Central Asia," in Lena Johnson and Murad Esenov (eds.), *Political Islam and Conflicts in Russia and Central Asia*, Swedish Institute of International Affairs, Sweden, Conference Paper 24, 1999, p. 109.
21. This movement was started by Muhammed ibn Abdul Wahhab in the eighteenth century in Saudi Arabia. This is a puritanical sect. The chief feature of this sect is the call for a return to the 'pure' faith and practice of the seventh century as was practiced by Prophet Muhammad and his followers in Medina.
22. Rashid Ahmed, "Taliban Exporting Extremism", *Foreign Affairs*, New York, November-December, 1999.
23. Islam Lashkarlori was active till 1992. Uzbek government's action against the members of this group forced the leader and members of this group and Adolat Party leader, Tohir Yuldashev Abduhalilovich to leave the country in 1992. Most of the members went to Tajikistan and joined the Civil-War on the side of the UTO. On December 9, 1991, there was an encounter between Tohir Yuldashev and the Uzbek President Islam Abduganievich Karimov in Namangan where Yuldashev has demanded Karimov's resignation and asked him to declare Uzbekistan an Islamic State. See www.uzreport.com
24. This party was formed by Tohir Yuldashev and Juma A. Khojiyev together with the declared goal of Islamisation of Uzbekistan.
25. During my visit to these provinces I was told about these groups. Also see Ahmed Rashid, *Jihad: The Rise of Militant Islam in Central Asia*, Yale University Press, London, 2002, p. 139.
26. Shirin Akiner, no. 10.
27. Born in 1967 in Namangan province of Fergana Valley in Uzbekistan. He was leader of Adolat Party. He is talented speaker and organiser. Uzbek

government has named him as one of the conspirators behind the attempted assassination of Uzbekistan's President Karimov in February 1999. In May 1999, he obtained the Taliban permission to establish a military training camp for the Islamic Movement of Uzbekistan which he was leading in northern Afghanistan. After Taliban defeat and reported death of his field commander Jumaboy Ahmadjonovich Khojiyev in Afghanistan during US operation against Taliban, he has moved into the border areas between Afghanistan and Pakistan. He was reported to have injured in the last year (2004) Pakistani military operation in Waziristan areas.

28. "Calming the Ferghana Valley: Development and Dialogue in the Heart of Central Asia", (Report of the Ferghana Valley Project of the Council on Foreign Relations, Century Foundation Press, New York, 1999, p. 5.
29. Ibid.
30. Sulton Khamadov, *Mezhdunarodniy Contekst-Afghanskii Faktar, in Religiozniy Extremizm v Tsentralnoi Azii: Problemy I Perspectivy,* Dushanbe, Tajikistan, 2002, pp. 130-150.
31. Rashid Ahmed, no. 22.
32. A coalition of Tajik Islamists and democratic forces who fought against the Tajik government forces in the Tajik Civil war during 1992-97. Tens of thousands people were killed in this war which ended in June 1997 under a peace accord between both the parties. Since then UTO is sharing power.
33. *Pravda Vostoka* (in Russian), Tashkent, May 25, 1998.
34. Tamara Makarenko, "The Changing Dynamics of Central Asia Terrorism," *Jane's Intelligence Review*, February 2002, 1-2.
35. *Interfax:* August 24, 1999, 1618 h (Kyrgyzstan/terrorism/militants).
36. Shirin Akiner, no.4.
37. 'Prosecutor's Office presents report on Andijon to Parliament commission' at http://www.uza.uz/eng/news/?id1=5054 (Accessed on September 7, 2005).
38. Ibid.
39. Rashid Ahmed, no. 22.
40. Ibid.
41. Ibid.
42. The founder was a prominent Palestinian, a graduate of Al-Azhar University in Cairo and a member of Muslim Brotherhood. The leadership of this party was passed to Abdul Qadir Zallum.
43. It was banned in the Russian Federation in 2003 and Germany on January 15, 2003.
44. As told to Mahan Abedin for the James Foundation by the HT Executive Committee member Jalaluddin, *www.jamestown.org*, (Accessed on August 12, 2004).
45. *Ibid.*
46. http//www.hizb-ut-tahrir.org (Accessed on August 12, 2004).
47. *www.uzreport.com* (Accessed on August 6, 2004).
48. Rashid Ahmed, no. 22.
49. *www.uzreport.com* (Accessed on August 6, 2004).
50. www.uzreport.com (Accessed on August 12, 2004).
51. This is a known militant Sunni terrorist "brand" in use in Egypt, which was

spawned by the Muslim Brotherhood movement. In 1990s this movement was, led by Ayman Al-Zawahiri, merged with Bin Laden's Al-Qaida.

52. Ariel Cohen, "Terror in Tashkent", *The Washington Times* (Accessed on August 5, 2004).
53. http://hrw.org/english/docs/2006/06/14/eca13545.htm (Accessed on July 25, 2005).
54. For detail see www.uzreport.com (Accessed on May 29, 2005).
55. Babajanov, Bakhtiyor, "Replay of Great game in Central Asia," Paper presented at the International Seminar on *Recent Developments in Central Asia*, New Delhi, August 10, 2005.

PART- IV

ECONOMY AND ENERGY RESOURCES

18

PERSPECTIVE OF ECONOMIC DEVELOPMENT IN UZBEKISTAN AND RELATIONS BETWEEN UZBEKISTAN AND INDIA

SURAT MIRKASYMOV

Before beginning my paper I would like to say that the topic of the seminar fully reflects the ancient and contemporary relations between Central Asia and India, Uzbekistan and India in particular.

We can see the clear contours of four periods: the first, being the period when Central Asia played the role of a bridge for the spreading of ancient Buddhism—a religion which was born in India into China. It was during the Kushan period that Buddhism came to Central Asia, and southern Uzbekistan. The second period covers the Middle Ages when King Babur's settled in India, engaged in uniting and developing the country's economy, military, culture, architecture, agriculture irrigation system, etc.

The third period includes the Soviet period, beginning from the 1920s up to 1991. In this period relations between our countries grew from official relations to people's friendship. It was colossal! There was no sphere which was left untapped by bilateral relations. As a part of the Soviet Union, Uzbekistan also developed cultural, educational, scientific, tourist and other relations with India. Hundreds of Indian youths studied in the universities of Tashkent. Many young scientists did their Ph.Ds here and were trained in various plants, farms, institutions. We are sure of the contribution of these people in the fast development of India from the nineties to the present.

The fourth period reflects our relations from 1991 onwards, when Uzbekistan became a sovereign Republic, having direct relations including diplomatic were established between the two countries. The first three periods laid down the foundation for our present day relations. But are these relations strong and effective? Last November during the inaugural address at third India Central Asia Regional Conference in Tashkent, the Minister of Foreign Affairs of the Republic of India H.E. Yashwant Sinha said: "For us Central Asia is our immediate and strategic neighbourhood."

Uzbekistan also has the same position. Dozens of diplomatic documents on cooperation in different fields have been signed with India which are an evident proof of this. We can say that political, diplomatic, cultural, scientific, educational relations are developing, but economic and trade relations need more attention from both parties. As Mr. Yashwant Sinha mentioned: "As far as India and Central Asia are concerned, greater economic engagement is needed." All Central Asian Republics are connected by air with Delhi and other cities of India. Uzbek Airways is also functioning effectively. For the land and sea connectivity both parties already have some programmes planned. As the Minister confirmed last year, India, Iran and Afghanistan decided to open a new sea and road route through the Iranian port of Chahbahar. The government of Uzbekistan has also signed an agreement with the governments of Afghanistan and Iran to jointly construct a road which will connect the Uzbed city of Termez with the Iranian border via the ancient Afghani city of Herat. Once this road is complete, it will reduce the current distance between Uzbekistan and India by 1500 kilometres. No doubt that this road will serve other Central Asian countries, including the Asian part of the Russian Federation.

The historical meeting of the leaders of Pakistan and India during the SAARC summit meeting in Islamabad in the beginning of January this year and the decision to put their mutual distrust behind them and have a composite dialogue on all bilateral issues, including Jammu and Kashmir was welcomed by all. As the *Hindustan Times* correctly wrote "India Pak Kill Chill." A majority of countries, according to information received from capitals of different countries, welcomed the decision. We in Uzbekistan were also happy to hear this news. If negotiations will conclude with the signing of an encouraging agreement then the political atmosphere in the SAARC area will undergo a positive change and will help solve long awaited problems. Firstly, the political, diplomatic, economic, trade, cultural, tourism, sport relations will grow between the two neighbouring countries. Secondly, it will open the scope for quick development of economic and trade relations between Central Asian countries including Russia and Afghanistan and the SAARC countries.

As specialists calculated, the trucks with cotton silk, fruits, metal, fertilizer and other export goods from Uzbekistan starting from Termez city will reach New Delhi via Kabul-Peshawar-Lahor-Amritsar within 34 days maximum. For landlocked countries like Uzbekistan it makes sense. Inside the country there is a well developed infrastructure : automobile roads, airways, airlines, but there are still not many alternative roads connecting Uzbekistan with sea shores.

What kind of factors make India so attractive for the Uzbek party? The main factor is its great achievements in the process of liberalization of its economy: if in the beginning of the reform process it had only one billion dollars in its reserve now after just 13 years it has became $100 billion. The GNP has grown annually and crossed 7 per cent and in the last quarter of 2003 it crossed 8 per cent and India turned from creditor to debtor, its exports crossing the $50 billion mark. So we can see big positive changes in all fields of life of the Indian people: education, science, information technology, agriculture etc.

Of course, Uzbekistan has also tried to do the same and some good results have been achieved. The economy attained its pre-independence GDP level in 2001, the country achieved self-sufficiency in energy by 1995 and in wheat by 1998. Wheat product increased from 1 million tonnes in pre-independence times to a record of 5.4 million tonnes by 2002. A number of new industries were promoted in consumer goods, for example cars, TVs VCRs etc.

The government's development policy is aimed at building a "socially-oriented market economy". The strategic objectives announced soon after independence were :

- Achieving economic independence by reducing imports.
- Diversifying the economy from its raw material orientation to a more modern and competitive industrialized structure.
- Increasing the country's export potential and foreign exchange reserves to have a strong, stable currency.
- Expanding employment opportunities and raising living standards.

Here it has to be emphasized that the country had to face and overcome two expected difficulties on the way of implementation of it programme. First, lack of business experience as a result of about 80 years of the Soviet policy of "no private business", and the second minimal foreign investment into the economy due to civil disturbances and instability in neighbouring Tajikistan and Afghanistan. Now normal life in these countries has been stabilized. The aggressive policy of the Taliban government and its support of religious extremist groups had meant that the Uzbek government had to give more attention and higher expenses for the security of the country.

Now, after the great victory of the coalition forces against world terrorism, step by step new spheres are opening up for the speedy implementation of the economic reforms programme. The annual session of the European Bank for Reconstruction and Development and many other international seminars being held in Tashkent along with the growing GDP rate of over 4 per cent annually, strong government policy towards implementing reform programme educated and professional human resources plus rich natural wealth of the country have raised the confidence that the goals of the country will be achieved.

19

Economic Changes in Central Asia and Indian Response

Gulshan Sachdeva

In this paper an attempt has been made to understand economic changes in the Central Asian region in the last one decade. These changes have coincided with the Indian liberalisation process. It is described that although the countries of Central Asia have integrated in the global economy, their economic relations with India have declined significantly. Despite having close political relations, India is also absent from many of the new regional economic initiatives in the region. The paper ends with the assessment of Central Asian economic reforms and suggestions for improving Indian economic presence in the region.

Economic Developments in Central Asia

Since the collapse of the Soviet system, the five Central Asian countries Kazakhstan, Kyrgyz Republic, Tajikistan, Turkmenistan and Uzbekistan are witnessing transformation of their economic systems. All these countries have moved along this transformation to varying degrees. Despite having a very complex legacy (of central planning, dissolution of the USSR, distorted economic structures, ethnic problems), the region has made some progress in market reforms. Due to certain specific features (natural resources, strategic location, political systems and background of political elite) the region has used both standard as well as non-conventional strategies of economic transformation. The Soviet era leaders in more or less non-competitive regimes have tried to pursue economic stability while securing their own dominance in the new political system. They have also tried to learn a few lessons from the Chinese model of development.

In the early years, the break-up of the Soviet Union hit the region very badly for many reasons. Trade and transit was interrupted with new borders, increased transportation costs, illegal check points and collapse of traditional markets. Industrial and agricultural production was hurt due to disruption in access to inputs and markets. There was loss of subsidies for budgets, enterprises and households which were paid earlier directly or indirectly through social payments, as well as through below market prices on transport and energy. There was also loss of administrative structures and skilled labour as traditional Soviet administration collapsed and many Russians left the region. The access to secure water and energy resources was also lost in the region which was key for the agriculture, industry and household requirements. Countries in the region were left with large environmental burdens (including the Aral Sea ecological disaster, as well as industrial, nuclear and biological waste). Above all, there were also ethnic tensions and civil war (especially in Tajikistan).[1] All these were added complications to the 'normal' transformational problems faced by any country moving from a centrally planned economy to a market economy.

Despite a common historical and cultural background, including more than seven decades of Soviet legacy, the five Central Asian republics have had different abilities to cope with the transformation challenges.[2] As a result they have adopted different strategies. Even a quick view at the vast transformation literature, one could find "early and late reformers" as well as "radical" and "gradualist" reformers in Central Asia. The transition strategies adopted by these countries have also been influenced greatly by the political environment in the region and in their particular countries. Uzbekistan adopted a gradual and cautious approach to market reforms, while Kazakhstan and Kyrgyz Republic followed a relatively more aggressive approach. Turkmenistan and Tajikistan have cautiously joined later. These different policies have led to different macro-economic outcomes as well as different policy environments.

The countries of Central Asia in the first decade of their transformation displayed some common trends and some significant variations. However, output decline in all the countries in the region was very deep and longer. Recovery in some of the countries was further derailed with the fiscal financial crisis in the Russian Federation in 1998. According to the World Bank, Central Asia had an average of

Table 19.1 : Growth in Real GDP in Central Asia, 1990-2002

	1990	*1991*	*1992*	*1993*	*1994*	*1995*	*1996*	*1997*	*1998*	*1999*	*2000*	*2001*	*2002*	*6 DP 1989=100*
KAZ.	-0.4	-11.0	-5.3	-9.3	-12.6	-8.2	0.5	1.7	-1.9	2.7	9.8	13.2	7.6	84
KYR.	3.0	-5.0	-19.0	-16.0	-20.1	-5.4	7.1	9.9	2.1	5.1	5.3	2.0	2.0	71
TAJ.	-1.6	-7.1	-29.0	-11.0	-18.9	-12.5	-4.4	1.7	5.3	3.7	8.3	10.3	7.0	56
TURK.	2.0	-4.7	-5.3	10.6	-17.3	-7.2	-6.7	-11.3	5.0	16.0	17.6	12.0	13.5	96
UZB.	1.6	-0.5	-11.1	-2.3	-4.2	-0.9	1.6	2.5	4.4	4.1	4.0	4.5	2.5	105

Source: European Bank for Reconstruction and Development (EBRD).

about seven years of declining output in the first ten years, resulting in loss of almost 41 per cent of the initial measured output. The highest loss of output was in Kyrgyzstan and lowest in Uzbekistan.[3] This "transformation recession" is now over, the region is on a path of recovery.

Overall, the success of market-oriented structural and institutional reforms has shown mixed progress in Central Asia. According to different methodologies and classifications developed by major multilateral organisations as well as other independent agencies to measure reform progress in transition economies, Kazakhstan and Kyrgyzstan have progressed much faster. Similarly, Uzbekistan and Turkmenistan have been classified as countries which have achieved less progress in establishing market institutions. According to widely used indicators developed by the European Bank for Reconstruction and Development (EBRD), level of reforms concerning prices, foreign exchange and external trade, privatisation, enterprise reforms and banking sector is high in Kazakhstan and Kyrgyz Republic. In some cases it is comparable to Russia and Poland. Tajikistan has also made significant progress in price reforms, external sector reforms and small privatisation. The level of reforms in Uzbekistan and Turkmenistan is low, particularly in the external sector and enterprise and banking sector reforms. Except Kazakhstan, other Central Asian countries are quite low in Euromoney risk ratings.[4] The reform process in agriculture has resulted in (1) corporate units created by reconfiguration of shares inside the former collective shell, (2) successor farm (stay as is) created by keeping the share in the former collective, and (3) individual farms established by withdrawal of shareholders. Despite all these changes, in reality very little has changed in the form of farm restructuring in Central Asia.[5]

External Economic Relations

Central Asian economies inherited state-controlled foreign trade, which was subordinated to the central planning.[6] Within the integrated economic structure of the Soviet Union, Central Asian region has strong dependency on imports of energy, food and consumer goods. The production structure of the region was heavily oriented towards agriculture and mineral extraction. Because of lack of diversification, and high import dependency these countries were vulnerable to adverse trade shocks.

Table 19.2 : Progress with Transition: EBRD 2002 Indicators (Average Transition Score from 1 to 4)

	Enterprises				*Markets and Trade*			*Financial Institutors and Infrastructure*		
Country	*Private Sector Share (% of GDP 2001)*	*Large Privatisation*	*Small Priv. and Restructuring*	*Governance Enterprise*	*Price Liberalisation*	*Trade & Foreign exchange*	*Competition Policy*	*Banking Reform and Interest Rate*	*Security market & Non-Bank Mid-Liberalisation*	*Infrastructure FIs*
Kazakhstan	65	3	4	2	3	+3	2	-3	+2	2
Kyrgyz Rep.	60	3	4	2	3	4	2	+2	2	+1
Tajikistan	50	+2	-4	-2	3	+3	-2	-2	1	+1
Turkmenistan	25	1	2	1	2	1	1	1	1	1
Uzbekistan	45	-3	3	-2	2	-2	2	-2	2	2

Source: Transition Report 2002, EBRD.

External economic reforms in the region have covered five areas: liberalisation of foreign trade prices, reform of the trade system, market diversification, phasing out of barter trade and currency reforms.[7] Progress on these reforms has varied across the region. Although the role of state in foreign trade has been reduced throughout the region, progress has been more pronounced in Kazakhastan and Kyrgyzstan. Uzbekistan and Turkmenistan are more gradual with foreign trade liberalisation, particularly in the foreign exchange market. In the last one decade, exports have grown and significant diversification of trade has taken place.

The Central Asian experience with external trade could be classified in distinct phases. The first phase between 1991 and 1994 was a period of adjustments to the shocks of sudden dissolution of the USSR and sharp fall in mutual trade. During this period, all regional economies (except Turkmenistan) incurred sizable and persistent external current account deficits. The main reasons for this were : (1) the inherited economic structures (agricultural, industrial and household sectors) were highly energy intensive; (2) the demand for investment goods to replace this structure was high; (3) imports demand for western consumer goods was very high. The second phase was between 1995 and August 1998. During this period attempts were made to keep reasonable trade relations with traditional partners and to enlarge trade ties with the rest of the world. In the third stage, which starts from August 18, 1998, the region faced many negative impacts of Russian and Asian economic crises. With the sharp devaluation of Russian rouble, competitiveness of Central Asian commodities in traditional markets was affected. However, many of the negative impacts are eased since 2000 with strong recoveries in Russia and Central Asia.

Share of trade within CIS countries has declined in the region. However, as a result of some regional trade initiatives (discussed below) mutual trade in the region was increased, particularly in the initial years of transition. Since 1994, the share of trade with the non-CIS countries has been growing fast in both exports and imports. In the last few years about 70 per cent of Uzbekistan's trade has been with non-CIS countries. Although Russia is still an important partner at the regional level, the geographical distribution of trade has shifted from CMEA to EU (Germany and UK), East Asia (China, South Korea,

Table 19.3 : Merchandise Exports of Central Asia, 1992-2001

(Billion dollars)

	1992	*1993*	*1994*	*1995*	*1996*	*1997*	*1998*	*1999*	*2000*	*2001*
Kazakhstan	–	–	3.231	5.250	5.911	6.497	5.436	5.592	9.126	8.647
Non-CIS	1.398	1.501	1.357	2.366	2.732	3.515	3.266	4.100	6.750	6.015
Kyrgyzstan	0.317	0.396	0.340	0.409	0.505	0.604	0.514	0.454	0.505	0.476
Non-CIS	0.077	0.112	0.117	0.140	0.112	0.285	0.283	0.271	0.297	0.308
Tajikistan	0.193	0.350	0.492	0.749	0.770	0.746	0.597	0.689	0.784	0.652
Non-CIS	0.109	0.227	0.399	0.497	0.439	0.473	0.394	0.374	0.411	0.440
Turkmenistan	–	–	2.145	1.881	1.682	0.751	0.594	1.190	2.500	2.700
Non-CIS	0.908	1.049	0.494	0.951	0.610	0.300	0.442	0.700	1.200	1.300
Uzbekistan	–	–	2.549	2.821	4.211	4.026	3.218	3.200	3.230	3.110
Non-CIS	0.869	0.721	0.966	1.712	3.321	2.689	2.425	2.250	2.090	2.050

Source: UNECE.

Table 19.4 : Merchandise Imports of Central Asia, 1992-2001

(Billion dollars)

	1992	*1993*	*1994*	*1995*	*1996*	*1997*	*1998*	*1999*	*2000*	*2001*
Kazakhstan	–	–	3.561	3.807	4.241	4.301	4.350	3.687	5.051	6.363
Non-CIS	0.469	0.494	1.384	1.154	1.295	1.969	2.290	2.089	2.295	3.057
Kyrgyzstan	0.421	0.448	0.317	0.522	0.838	0.709	0.842	0.600	0.554	0.467
Non-CIS	0.071	0.112	0.107	0.168	0.351	0.273	0.401	0.341	0.256	0.210
Tajikistan	0.254	0.630	0.547	0.810	0.668	0.750	0.711	0.663	0.675	0.688
Non-CIS	0.132	0.374	0.314	0.332	0.285	0.268	0.265	0.148	0.115	0.150
Turkmenistan	–	–	1.468	1.364	1.011	1.183	1.008	1.500	1.780	2.250
Non-CIS	0.030	0.501	0.782	0.619	0.450	0.531	0.530	1.000	1.100	1.400
Uzbekistan	–	–	2.603	2.748	4.712	4.186	3.125	3.000	2.850	3.020
Non-CIS	0.929	0.958	1.202	1.630	3.195	3.047	2.256	2.250	1.800	1.920

Source: UNECE.

Table 19.5 : Kyrgyzstan, Direction of Trade *(Million US Dollars)*

Exports	*2000*	*2001*	*2002*	*3 Year Average (%)*	*Imports*	*2000*	*2001*	*2002*	*3 year Average (%)*
Total	501.9	476.1	480.5	–	Total	554.3	464.4	592.7	—
1. Germany	144.6	94.5	2.4	16.4	1. Russia	132.5	85.1	106.5	20.1
2. Russia	65.1	64.6	69.5	13.6	2. Uzbekistan	75.2	66.8	70.0	13.2
3. Switzerland	34.0	124.2	144.1	15.3	3. Kazakhstan	57.5	81.9	119.6	16.1
4. Uzbekistan	89.4	47.9	28.6	11.3	4. USA	53.8	26.7	43.4	7.6
5. Kazakhstan	33.4	39.0	34.6	7.3	5. China	36.9	48.6	59.3	9.0
6. China	44.1	19.4	38.2	7.0	6. Germany	25.1	24.3	28.9	4.9
7. UK	18.7	14.1	0.9	2.3	7. Turkey	26.7	15.8	17.9	3.7
8. USA	2.9	7.1	30.5	2.8	8. S. Korea	6.9	7.8	7.1	1.4
9. Tajikistan	7.4	6.7	7.1	1.4	9. Canada	11.3	10.9	10.2	2.0
10. Turkey	7.2	13.8	18.6	2.7	10.Turkmen'an	18.8	9.0	3.6	1.9

Table 19.6 : Kazakhstan, Direction of Trade *(Million US Dollars)*

Exports	*2000*	*2001*	*2002*	*3 Year Average (%)*	*Imports*	*2000*	*2001*	*2002*	*3 year Average (%)*
Total	9138.0	8646.8	9930.4	—	Total	5051.7	6362.8	6809.1	—
1. Russia	1783.9	1748.4	1743.6	19.1	1. Russia	2459.8	2890.9	2686.9	44.5
2. Bermuda	1358.1	1221.2	1325.3	13.7	2. Germany	333.7	471.4	624.5	7.7
3. Italy	891.9	970.9	600.9	9.0	3. USA	276.9	341.6	665.2	6.9
4. China	670.3	655.5	832.8	8.0	4. UK	219.4	246.3	152.0	3.5
5. Germany	566.6	509.6	905.9	7.0	5. Turkey	142.6	131.3	142.5	2.3
6. Switzerland	497.6	407.3	422.0	4.7	6. Italy	155.0	266.1	206.0	3.4
7. UK	231.0	295.0	47.2	2.1	7. China	154.0	169.2	244.3	3.0
8. Ukraine	268.5	490.5	532.3	4.6	8. Ukraine	79.8	154.9	168.1	2.2
9. Netherlands	240.0	144.9	123.6	1.4	9. S. Korea	82.5	106.5	115.6	1.7
10. USA	211.0	159.1	316.6	2.4	10. Japan	105.5	140.2	103.1	1.9

Table 19.7 : Tajikistan, Direction of Trade

(Million US Dollars)

Exports	*2000*	*2001*	*2002*	*3 Year Average (%)*	*Imports*	*2000*	*2001*	*2002*	*3year Average (%)*
Total	784.3	651.6	536.6	—	Total	675.0	687.5	704.5	—
1. Netherlands	178.2	194.4	2.8	17.7	1. Uzbekistan	185.6	150.7	163.6	24.2
2. Uzbekistan	97.8	87.2	94.7	14.5	2. Russia	105.1	129.4	88.0	15.6
3. Russia	258.8	104.7	64.4	20.4	3. Switzerland	0.6	2.1	2.1	0.22
4. Switzerland	72.2	52.2	54.1	9.0	4. Kazakhstan	82.4	89.1	96.7	13.0
5. Turkey	58.4	75.1	81.5	11.4	5. UK	86.9	2.5	1.2	4.5
6. Latvia	0.0	11.7	12.7	1.4	6. Turkmenistan	29.3	62.3	67.6	7.7
7. Iran	12.5	29.9	24.8	3.6	7. Ukraine	0.0	63.6	69.0	6.3
8. Hungary	1.0	38.8	65.8	6.1	8. Azerbaijan	63.1	33.5	36.4	6.5
9. Italy	21.4	5.8	18.9	2.4	9. Romania	41.0	10.9	11.8	3.1
10. Belgium	5.1	6.0	5.0	0.8	10. Iran	7.6	10.0	10.6	1.3

Table 19.8 : Turkmenistan, Direction of Trade

(Million US Dollars)

Exports	*2000*	*2001*	*2002*	*3 Year Average (%)*	*Imports*	*2000*	*2001*	*2002*	*3 year Average (%)*
Total	2505.2	1132.4	1218.9	—	Total	1787.8	1557.5	1432.5	—
1. Russia	1029.3	35.5	23.4	15.4	1. Ukraine	214.3	235.7	255.8	15.0
2. Iran	242.0	241.0	199.9	15.8	2. Turkey	253.3	115.8	125.7	10.1
3. Ukraine	164.9	182.1	197.6	12.9	3. Russia	254.5	153.4	152.3	11.6
4. Germany	404.8	5.8	10.5	5.8	4. USA	62.8	273.4	51.9	8.2
5. Turkey	186.0	65.2	70.8	5.8	5. UAE	146.6	158.2	168.2	10.0
6. Azerbaijan	37.1	122.9	133.4	7.7	6. Germany	52.6	140.6	173.9	8.0
7. Switzerland	91.9	0.8	0.8	1.3	7. Iran	90.9	98.1	104.3	6.2
8. Afghanistan	38.0	42.0	45.5	3.0	8. France	75.7	50.5	67.6	4.0
9. Tajikistan	29.1	56.7	61.5	3.9	9. Japan	144.4	35.9	6.0	3.6
10. Kazakhstan	5.3	70.5	76.5	4.2	10. Uzbekistan	35.3	38.8	42.1	2.5

Table 19.9 : Uzbekistan, Direction of Trade

(Million US Dollars)

	Exports	*2000*	*2001*	*2002*	*3 Year Average (%)*		*Imports*	*2000*	*2001*	*2002*	*3 year Average (%)*
	Total	2135.3	2028.1	1900.0	—		Total	2078.1	2303.4	2370.1	—
1.	Russia	602.0	527.2	327.8	23.8	1.	Russia	301.9	400.2	486.9	17.5
2.	Tajikistan	168.7	137.0	148.7	7.5	2.	S. Korea	253.5	380.3	412.7	15.4
3.	Italy	172.8	155.2	157.7	8.0	3.	Germany	233.3	227.2	211.4	10.0
4.	Ukraine	161.8	178.0	193.2	8.8	4.	USA	182.7	162.5	151.9	7.4
5.	S. Korea	94.5	124.3	134.9	5.9	5.	Ukraine	125.4	138.4	150.3	6.1
6.	Germany	67.6	56.4	44.2	2.8	6.	Tajikistan	107.6	95.9	104.1	4.5
7.	Kyrgyzstan	68.4	60.7	63.6	3.2	7.	Turkey	90.9	98.7	107.1	4.4
8.	Kazakhstan	66.6	72.9	79.1	3.6	8.	Kazakhstan	153.1	163.7	177.6	7.3
9.	Poland	36.7	82.3	89.3	3.5	9.	France	73.4	118.8	42.8	3.5
10.	Turkey	78.0	32.8	35.6	2.4	10.	Kyrgyzstan	98.3	52.7	31.5	2.8

Source: Asian Development Bank.

and Japan), North America (USA), and middle East (Iran and Turkey). China has been able to make some significant trade partnership with Kazakhstan and Kyrgyzstan. The commodity structure of Central Asian exports is mainly consists of mineral resources and agricultural raw materials. The main exports has been oil and gas products, ferrous and non-ferrous metals and grain in Kazakhstan; cotton fibres, gold, natural gas and non-ferrous metals in Uzbekistan; gold, tobacco and wool in Kyrgyzstan; aluminum and cotton fibres in Tajikistan; and natural gas, cotton fibres and oil and oil products in Turkmenistan. Import composition in the region has been changing. In the initial years imports consisted mainly of food products and other consumer goods. This structure of imports has been changing in favour of machinery and equipment etc.

Regional Co-operation Initiatives

Due to landlocked location and remoteness from major world markets, small domestic markets, rational use of water and energy resources and to integrate themselves with the global economy, the Central Asian countries have taken many regional and international trade and other economic co-operation initiatives. It is realised that developing regional markets would save large transport costs, exploit scale economies, and yield gains from trade, including those based on resource complementarity.[8] In the past, however, developing regional cooperation involving all five countries in the region has been difficult at the political level. Two big countries Kazakhstan and Uzbekistan have competed for the position of regional leader. As a manifestation of its declared policy of neutrality, Turkmenistan has resisted in participation in many regional forums.

All Central Asian republics are important members of the Commonwealth of Independent States (CIS). On the economic affairs, the CIS has not implemented a Customs Union or a free trade area covering all member states. In 1995, Kazakhastan and Kyrgyzstan formed a Customs Union with Belarus and the Russia. Tajikistan later joined this union in 1999. In October 2000, the Customs Union was transformed into Eurasian Economic Community (EEC). Its objectives include broadening of the co-ordination of economic social, industrial and financial policy of member countries.

In 1994, Kazakhastan, Kyrgyzstan and Uzbekistan also formed the Central Asian Union (CAU). The aim was to create a single economic region with improvements in payments arrangements and reduction in tariffs among member countries. In 1995, principle of free trade among member states was approved. A Central Asian Bank for Co-operation and Development was also created. In 1998, Tajikistan also became member of this grouping. During the same year the organization was renamed as Central Asian Economic Community (CAEC). In 2001, the CAEC was transformed into Central Asian Cooperation Organisation (CACO). Russia, Ukraine, Georgia and Turkey have been given observer status in CACO. All five have joined Economic Cooperation Organization (ECO), which also includes Afghanistan, Azerbaijan, Iran, Pakistan and Turkey. The main objective of ECO is to develop and improve economic infrastructure and transportation system in the region. All five have also become members of Organization of Islamic Conference (OIC), an intergovernmental organization with 56 members, established in 1971 in Saudi Arabia. Its aim is to promote Islamic solidarity by improving cooperation in the political, economic, social and cultural and scientific fields. Uzbekistan also became member of the GUUAM Group in 1999, a sub-regional formation of Georgia, Ukraine, Azerbaijan, and Moldova and Uzbekistan. The Group was formally founded as a political, economic and strategic alliance designed to strengthen the independence and sovereignty of these former Soviet Union republics. Some scholars have analysed GUUAM as product of the clash in American-Russian interests in the region. It was also considered an organisation to counterbalance EEC and to reduce Russian economic and political control in this region.

Kyrghystan has become member of the WTO and all others have shown interest in becoming its member. The European Union (EU) has granted Central Asian countries access to Generalized System of Preferences (GSP). It allows tariff reductions on manufactured products and ceratin agricultural goods. To encourage regional cooperation in the region, in 1997 Asian Development Bank initiated a programme called Central Asia Regional Economic Cooperation (CAREC). The operational strategy of the CAREC is to finance infrastructure projects and improve the policy environment for promoting cross-border activities in the areas of trade energy and transportation. The United Nations also started a Special Programme for the Economies of Central Asia (SPECA) in 1997. The objective of the programme is to strengthen regional cooperation in order to both stimulate their economic development and facilitate their integration into Europe and Asia. Another international initiative to promote poverty reduction, growth and debt sustainability in seven low-income CIS countries is also in operation the seven CIS countries are: Armenia, Azerbaijan, Georgia, Kyrgyz Republic, Moldova, Uzbekistan and Tajikistan. Along with these 7 CIS countries, the initiative brings together, the four sponsoring organizations: ADB, EBRD, IMF and IDA (WB) and a group of bilateral creditors/donors. Currently 24 countries participate in the CIS seven Initiative and in

Table 19.10 : Regional Economic Initiates in Central Asia

CIS	*EEC*	*CACO*	*ECO*	*OIC*	*CAREC (ADB) Initiative*	*SCO*	*CIS-7*	*GUUAM*
Kazakhstan	X	X	X	X	X	X	X	—
Kyrgyzstan	X	X	X	X	X	X	X	X
Tajikistan	X	X	X	X	X	X	X	X
Turkmenistan	—	—	—	—	X	X	—	X
Uzbekistan	X	X	X	X	X	X	X	X

CIS : Commonwealth of Independent States (with Armenia, Azerbaijan, Belarus, Georgia, Maldova, Russia, Ukraine).

EEC : Eurasian Economic Community, ex Customs Union (with Russia and Belarus).

CACO: Central Asian Cooperation Organisation, ex Central Asian Economic Community.

ECO : Economic Cooperation Organisation (with Iran, Pakistan, Turkey and Afghanistan).

OIC : Organisation of Islamic Conference (total 56 members, established in 1971).

CAREC (ADB) : Central Asia Regional Economic Cooperation (with Azerbaijan, Mongolia and Xinjiang Autonomous Region of China; Turkmenistan is also expected to join soon).

SCO : Shanghai Cooperation Organisation (with Russia and China). SCO began as a forum for discussing border delineation issues. As a result of threat of terrorism in the region it has lately focused more on security issues. Economic cooperation is also envisaged among members.

CIS-7 : An International initiative to promote poverty reduction, growth and debt sustainability in seven low-income CIS countries: Armenia, Azerbaijan, Georgia, Kyrgyz Republic, Moldova, Uzbekistan, Tajikistan.

GUUAM : Georgia, Uzbekistan, Ukraine, Azerbaijan and Moldova Group.

addition six organizations/countries hold the observer title. These include Canada, China, EU, OECD, Islamic Development Bank, France, Germany, Italy, Japan, Russia, Turkey, UK and USA. At the technical level, some other regional initiatives include the Inter-governmental Commission on Central Asian Sustainable Development, the Inter-State Water Commission, the Central Asians Energy Advisory Group and regional Electricity Grid.Table 19.10 summarizes major regional economic cooperation initiatives in Central Asia.

As a result of these initiatives, the Central Asian countries have made some modest gains. In the beginning of transition, mutual trade among Central Asian countries played an important role. Although regional trade has clearly developed in Central Asia, its growth has been uneven at best. The potential for expanding intra-regional trade remains considerable. Despite the common interest towards increasing trade, all the countries in the region have trade-restricting policies and practices. There are the barriers of tariffs, public policies, procedures and regulations, and weak financial systems. Some other policy-related constraints to trade include import quotas, export licensing requirements and transport restrictions. Arbitrary and often corrupt bureaucracies throughout the region administer regulations that are archaic and frequently conflicting. There are slow, difficult border procedures, multiple cargo inspections within a single country and prohibitions that prevent vehicles from transporting goods between countries. Other barriers to trade include transit fees and the costs of dealing with corrupt border officials and local police. Trade is also restricted by such practices as requiring importers to register contracts and currency conversion restrictions. In no country is there a healthy financial system that provides modern services to facilitate trade. Most of the trade is in fact conducted through inefficient cash transfers or barter.[9]

India's major initiative in the region so far has been Indian-Iranian cooperation in building North-South trade corridor. The main transport projects undertaken under this programme will be development of a new port complex at Chah Bahar on the coast of Iran, from where a road goes north to the border with Afghanistan. India will build a link from Zaranj on the Iran-Afghan border to Delaram from where all major cities in Afghanistan and further north Central Asian republics are connected. Another transport project involves the linking of the Chah Bahar port to the Iranian rail network which is connected to Central Asia and Europe.[10] When materialise, this initiative means speeding the flow of goods, especially energy, from Central Asia to Iran to India. Still the shortest route from India to the Central Asian republics is through Pakistan and Afghanistan.

It is evident from the above analysis that most of the regional initiatives in Central Asia are are either grouping to recreate lost linkages among the former Soviet republics or initiatives by multilateral organisation to strengthen regional linkages in the areas of trade, energy, water resources, infrastructure and communications. These are largely affairs within the former Soviet space. Other countries like China, Iran, Turkey, Pakistan and Afghanistan have also been able to create some formal structures for closer interactions, which will become useful in the long run. India is totally absent from any meaning regional economic initiative. India should now seriously pursue extending SAARC to Afghanistan and the Central Asian region. Because of the past result of the SAARC, if Central Asians are not interested in this grouping, then India should seriously consider creating another independent organisation involving India and some of the countries in the region.

Foreign Investment

During the first half of 1990s, Central Asia was considered highly risky because of breakdown of the trade and payments mechanisms and economic decline. As a result, the region had to depend on official bilateral and multilateral sources of financing new projects. Later, there was marked increase in private capital flows in the form of commercial bank lending and FDI, particularly in the traditional export oriented, resource based industries. All countries in Central Asia have tried to encourage FDI flows through far reaching reforms in their foreign investment laws.[11] Table 19.11 shows that these flows have grown (with some disruptions during 1998 crisis in Russia). On the whole, however, aside from Kazakhastan's oil and gas sector, FDI flow has been low, in large measures because of foreign investment climate. Turkmenistan has received about US $ 1 billion since independence, primarily in the oil sector. Kyrgyszstan has received some modest FDI flows, connected largely to gold mines project. There has been some improvement in FDI flows to Uzbekistan in the last few years. The United States has been major investor in the region which has been followed by Europeans. Some modest investments have been made by Chinese (in oil sector) and South Korean companies.

Table 4.11 : Inflows of Foreign Direct Investment in Central Asia 1992-2002

(Million dollars)

	1992	1993	1994	1995	1996	1997	1998	1999	2000	2001	2002
Kazakhstan	100	228	635	964	1137	1321	1151	1468	1245	2835	2583
Kyrgyzstan	–	10	38	96	47	83	109	44	-2	5	5
Tajikistan	9	9	12	20	25	30	24	21	22	9	36
Turkmenistan*	11	79	103	233	108	108	64	80*	100*	100*	—
Uzbekistan*	9	48	73	-24	90	167	140	121	75	83	—

*Net of residents' investments abroad.
Source: UNECE.

India and Central Asian Economic Linkages

During the Soviet period, all contacts with the republics of the USSR were through Moscow only. The nature and character of the then Indo-Soviet trade and economic relations largely determined these relations. In the post-socialist period, like other CIS countries, economic relationship with the Central Asian region has also declined considerably. The official two-way annual trade between India and the region has been about US $ 100 million in the last few years. Apart from Kazakhstan and Uzbekistan, economic relations with other countries are minimal. This relationship is also restricted mainly to traditional items. The main commodities being exported from India are pharmaceuticals, tea, readymade garments, woollen goods, leather goods, jute manufacturers, cosmetics, cotton yarn, machinery, machine tools, rice, plastic products, machinery and instruments, electronic goods, chemicals etc. Imports from the CAR are restricted to raw cotton, iron and steel, zinc etc.

Table 4.12 : India-Central Asia Trade, 1996-97 to 2002-03

(US$ million)

	1996-97	*1997-98*	*1998-99*	*1999-00*	*2000-01*	*2001-02*	*2002-03*
Kazakhstan	16.96	51.16	50.43	40.65	64.12	53.09	59.61
Kyrgyzstan	0.98	10.8	8.81	15.61	22.02	11.52	15.13
Tajikistan	1.53	1.12	3.04	4.72	4.10	2.56	8.73
Turkmenistan	1.65	1.70	2.03	6.03	3.83	6.30	15.70
Uzbekistan	10.74	20.3	14.50	22.91	19.98	23.80	25.62
Central Asia	31.86	85.08	78.81	89.92	114.05	97.27	124.79
% of Total	—	—	0.104	0.103	0.119	0.102	0.109

Indian Trade

To give impetus to bilateral trade, economic and scientific co-operation, bilateral inter-governmental Joint Commissions have been set up with the countries in the region. A number of high level visits have also taken place.[12] India has also extended credit lines ranging from 5 million to $10 million to almost all countries in the region. It has signed many agreements with these countries for technical economic co-operation under International Technical and Economic Cooperation (ITEC). So far about 1000 candidates from these countries have come to India and under the programme in various disciplines, such as, diplomacy, banking, finance, trade, management, small industry promotion, etc. ONGC Videsh has also been active in Kazakhstan. Despite all these developments, economic linkages between India and the region have been much below its potential. The main reasons are lack of information and connectivity. Lack of economic and financial sector reforms in the region could also have discouraged many Indian companies.

Co-operation in the energy sector is an obvious potential area. Since this region has great tourism potential, co-operation in the tourism related services would also be useful Information technology is another area where Indian services could be in great demand particularly when this region is undergoing a major transformation in the financial and other sectors. There is great scope for co-operation as some of these countries are blessed with high quality human resources. Indian consultancy companies could also play a very major role in the ongoing modernisation process in the region. Another area of major interest to Indian businesses would be to take part in the continuing privatisation process in the region. Compared to Russia and other east European countries, the region is still in the middle of privatising their huge state sectors. This could provide a huge opportunity for India as is shown by an NRI company Ispat International which has bought the 6.5 million tonne capacity Karaganda steel plant, a linked power plant and 15 coal mines in Kazakhstan. This deal has become one of the major success stories in the region. Ispat could turn around this loss making plant into a profit making venture. It has a work-force of 67,000 local workers. Some other Indian companies like Punj Llyod has also participated in oil pipeline projects in Kazakhstan.

Conclusions

Despite having a very complex legacy, the region has made significant progress in market reforms. The region has used both standard as well as non-conventional strategies of economic transformation. It has been successful in some economic stability. However, success with structural and institutional reforms is mixed. The inflation has been reduced, GDP is rising and production and trade has been diversified. Yet reforms have not been consolidated and the region is still vulnerable to external shocks. FDI in the region has been mainly concentrated in the energy sector and only Kazakhstan has been able to attract significant FDI. Most of the regional economic arrangements in the region are either grouping to recreate lost linkages among the former Soviet republics or initiatives by multilateral organisation to strengthen regional linkages in the areas of trade, energy, water resources, infrastructure and communications.

India's economic relationship with the Central Asian region has declined considerably in the post-socialist period. The official two way annual trade between India and the region has been about US $ 100 million in the last few years. The main reasons have been lack of information, connectivity, economic decline of the region and lack of economic and financial sector reforms in some of the countries. As these economies have picked up in the last few years, this is the right time to give a big boost to economic relations. However, a strong network of information regarding Central Asian economies is a must.

India is also totally absent from any of the regional economic initiative. India should now seriously pursue extending SAARC to Afghanistan and the Central Asian region.

NOTES

1. See Johannes Linn, "Central Asia : Ten Years of Transition," Talking points for Central Asia Donors' Consultation Meeting, Berlin, Germany. March 1, 2002. www. worldbank, org.
2. For details see Gulshan Sachdeva, " Understanding Central Asian Economic Models" in Nirmala Joshi (ed), *Central Asia : The Great Game Replayed : An Indian Perspective*, New Delhi : New Century, 2003.
3. The World Bank, *Transition. The first Ten Years : Analysis and Lessons for Eastern Europe and Former Soviet Union,* (Washington DC : The World Bank, 2002).
4. See various issues of *Euronomey* for country risk ratings.
5. For details of these reforms see, Zvi Lerman, Csaba Csaki and Gershan Feder, *Land Policies and Evolving Farm Structures in Transition Economies* (Washington DC : The World Bank, 2002).
6. For a comprehensive analysis of external economic relations in a socialist economy see chapter 14 in Janaos Kornai, *The Socialist System : The Political Economy of Communism* (Oxford, Clarendon Press, 1992).
7. For details see Jimmy McHugh and Emine Gurgen "External Sector Policies" in Emine Gurgen *et al. Economic Reforms in Kazakhastan, Kyrgyz : Republic, Tajikistan, Turkmensitan and Uzbekistan,* IMF Occasional paper No. 183 (Washington : International Monetary Fund, 1999), pp. 35-47.
8. See Renata Dwan and Oleksandra Pavliuk, *Building Security in the New States of Eurasia : Subregional Co-operation in the Former Soviet Space,* (London : M.E. Sharp, 2000); R. Sampat Kumar, "Central Asian Economic Integration : Emerging Trends", *Economic and Political Weekely,* May 2, 1998, pp. 1013-1017; Heribert Ddeter, "Regional Intergration in Central Asia : Current Economic Position and Prospects" *Central Asian Survey.* Vol. 15, Nos. 3-4, 1996, pp. 369-386.
9. Asian Development Bank website, (www. adb.org).
10. For details see C. Raja Mohan, "India, Iran Unviel Road Diplomacy", *The Hindu*, 26 January 2003 : Sudha Ramanchandran, "India, Iran, Russia Map out Trade Route". *The Asia Time*, 29 June 2002 and Stephan Blank, The India-Iranian Connection and its Importance for Central Asia, *Eurasianet*, 3/12/03.
11. Details about FDI laws could be found in Jimmy McHugh, "Capital Flows and External Debt" in Emine Gurgen et., op. cit., p. 54.
12. For details of these visits see S.D. Muni, "India & Central Asia : Towards a Cooperative Future" in Nirmala Joshi (ed), *Central Asia : The Great Game Replayed : An India Perspective,* New Delhi : New Century, 2003.

20

Basic Directions and Mechanisms in the Formation of a Joint Power Market of the Central Asian States

Gulmira Kurganbayeva

Introduction

The governments of Central Asian Region, namely Kazakhstan, Kyrghyzstan, Tajikistan, Turkmenistan and Uzbekistan have created a joint power market with the strategic aim of establishing an integrated cooperation between the states.

Utmost priority to such cooperation comes out of the need for establishing and developing mutually profitable economic ties in the power sector targeting domestic market with cheap electric power resources, meeting requirements of their consumers and increasing export potential to the third world countries.

In the framework of the Central Asian Region (CAR), a defined legal base has already been created for expanding integrated cooperation in the power sector. However, even after several talks and agreements in this regard, the development of integrated cooperation has not gathered the desired tempo. The main reason being that the competent organs of CAR have not yet worked out a concrete strategy for the realization of the plans.

Thus, in the present context, the need to chalk out a legal mechanism for the installation and smooth functioning of a joint power market has become a matter of utmost importance. For realisation of this mechanism, concrete measures need to be taken to strengthen cooperation in the power sector and achieve a balance between supply and demand of power resources in the domestic market. This will enhance transit potential of the Central Asian states and will create more opportunities for energy export to the Third World countries.

Analysis of the Condition of Units Dealing in Fuel–Energy in the CAR States

Analysis of the Power Condition in CAR States

The break up of traditional economic ties in the beginning of the 90s had a negative impact on the power situation in the Central Asian Region (CAR) countries. With the disintegration of a united national economy, practically all links between energy systems of the former state got snapped. Economic crisis in CIS states due to recession in the industrial production became the main factor for the reduction in the consumption of power in the former United Republics, which, in turn, affected its production. Details of power production in CAR countries are given in Table 20.1.

Table 20.1 : Power production in CAR countries *(In billion kWh)*

CAR countries	*1992*	*1993*	*1994*	*1995*	*1996*	*1997*	*1998*	*1999*	*2000*	*2001*
Kaz-n*	81.8	79.2	74.5	64.0	66.5	58.9	52.2	49.1	51.6	55.4
Kyrg-n*	12.0	11.3	12.9	12.3	13.8	12.6	11.6	13.1	14.9	13.6
Taj-n*	16.8	17.7	17.0	14.8	15.0	14.0	14.4	15.8	14.3	14.3
Turk-n**	13.2	12.6	10.5	9.9	10.1	9.5	9.3	8.8	9.8	10.5
Uzbek-n*	50.9	49.1	47.8	47.4	45.4	46.0	45.9	45.3	46.8	48.1

* Information from International Statistics Committee (CIS).

** Accounts data from the report of the World Bank on Turkmenistan for the year 1998 and Executive Committee of CIS on Electric Power.

The deepening of economic crisis in the CIS states and Central Asia, and the escalation of the disintegration processes affected the parallel work going on in the power systems and acted as an obstacle in the development of power units of CAR states in the beginning of the 1990s. The exit of power systems from joint venture became the main reason for the reduced efficiency of their work, for irregularity in power supply, for decrease in the volume of interstate power flow and irrational use of transit potential in CAR countries.

The governments of Central Asian states took appropriate

measures to overcome the economic crisis in this area and developed integrated cooperation in the power sector.

The main achievements of the CAR in the power sector are as follows:

1. *Creating a defined normative-law base for the functioning of power and passing appropriate laws on electric power and its storage.*

Realization of the indicated normative-law base documents facilitated market reforms in the power sector of CAR, the essence of which lies in breaking the monopoly of power blocks (power line, power transport) from power generation and its sale.

Insertion -1

Amongst the CAR and all CIS states, Kazakhstan is recognized as the undisputed leader in the redeployment of the units where an optimal organizational structure was created consisting of:

(a) National power system formed on the basis of interstate and intersystem power networks 220-500-1150KW controlled by AO "KEGOC";

(b) Regional Electric network companies (REK) containing distribution network of 110 kW and less and responsible for power supply at regional level.

(c) Electric energy producers—independent or integrated by powerful industrial users of power stations in the form of joint-stock companies.

Presence of the given structure facilitated the formation of wholesale and retail markets of electrical energy and power controlled by ZAO 'KOREM' established in the year 2000.

The main purposes of the creation and development of wholesale electrical energy and power market in Kazakhstan are providing free choice of power suppliers to end users, promoting competition between power producing industries, and ensuring transparency in laying tariff on electric power.

This way, in the energy sector in Kazakhstan, a favourable competitive ambience has been created resulting in an increased tempo of the development of units, stabilization of power supply of consumers and decreased tariff rates. In particular, the medium tariff on power in Kazakhstan equals to 1 cent / kWh.

Source: Programme for development of electric power till the year 2030, confirmed by the resolution passed by the Government of the Republic of Kazakhstan on 9 April 1999. No. 384.

2. *Adopting Normative Laws at the Inter-governmental Level for Creation of a Common Economic Area*

On 30 April, 1994, an agreement was signed between Kazakhstan, Kyrghyzstan and Uzbekistan on the creation of a Common Economic Area. It laid the legal foundation for economic cooperation in the Central Asian states and ensured free mixing of goods, services, capital, workforce and for enforcing the mutually agreed upon policies on payment, budget, taxation, tariff, custom duties and exchange rates. In the agreement, special emphasis was given to intensification of integrated cooperation between the participant states for the creation of a Common Economic Area.

On 26th March, 1998 the Republic of Tajikistan also joined hands with other states in creating a Common Economic Area and became a full-fledged participant of the agreement. In the same year on 17th June the "four" decided to form Central Asian Economic Society (CAES).

With the aim of realizing the agreement mentioned above on an international level, a programme was chalked out for creating a common economic space and another one for economic integration CAES states by the year 2000. The programme defined measures to be taken for intensifying integrated cooperation between state participants in all economic spheres including the electric energy sector.

3. *Passing a Resolution on Parallel Work of Energy Systems between Kazakhstan and Kyrghyzstan Republics and Republics of Tajikistan and Uzbekistan.*

This agreement played an important role in stabilizing electric power units, enhancing stability in the working of power systems, increasing interstate power flow and transit, thereby, successfully meeting the demands of consumers.

4. *Creation of Legal Base for Implementing Mutually Acceptable Policy on Hydroelectric Power.*

On 17 March 1998, a long-term agreement was signed by the governments of Republics of Kazakhstan, Kyrghyzstan and Uzbekistan for exploiting hydroelectric resources of the basins of the river *Sirdarya*. A year later the Republic of Tajikistan also joined in. This agreement will serve to stabilize water situation and power supply in the Central Asian Region (CAR).

However, even after creation of a legal base in this regard, the development of integrated cooperation could not reach the desired height and the problems of power sector of the Central Asian countries could not be fully resolved.

The main problems of power sector of the Central Asian Region countries are:

1. Insufficient level of cooperation between the energy systems and the absence of normative legal base.
2. Presence of an ineffective system of customs control in interstate power flow.
3. Absence of united approach in formulating tariff plans on power transit.
4. Lack of coordination in the utilization of fuel-energy and water resources.

Insertion - 2

In particular, in 2002, OAO "KEGOC" had cut off interstate electricity flow of 500 and 220 kW uniting single energy system of Kazakhstan and united energy system (OEC) of Central Asia.

The main reason behind the conflict was the regular occurrence of emergency situations in Uzbekistan, which threatened the stability of transit 500 - 220 kW in north-south Kazakhstan and similarly non-payment of electric power transit services by Kyrghyzstan, according to "KEGOC".

Source: materials collected in the sessions held by the Council of CIS on Electric Energy.

It is evident that for the economic growth of CAR countries, it is necessary to give top priority to expansion of integrated cooperation in power sector and formation of a joint power market with the aim of supplying cheap electric power to the CAR states and creating favourable conditions for its export to the third world countries. Special emphasis needs to be given to rational utilization of hydro-power resources, expansion of opportunities for interstate flow of energy and effective usage of transit potential of the CAR countries.

The given principles for creating a power market are reflected in important international agreements: European Energy Charter of

17 December 1991 and the Agreement on Energy Charter (AEC) of 17 December 1994.

In the above-mentioned international documents, a special role is given to the creation of corresponding legal terms and conditions in the states, which facilitate:

- Stimulation and promotion of market reforms in power sector.
- Development of mutually-profitable trading of power resources.
- Attracting investments in the power sector.
- Expanding transit power resources in the territory of the states and increasing transit supplies in the power deficient regions.
- Enforcing approved tariff policy of the states in the transit of power resources, ensuring non-discriminating and fair transit conditions for all the participating countries supporting the present and constructing new transit infrastructure in the power sector.

Considering the above-mentioned principles for the formation of power market, the Central Asian Region (CAR) states must plan out a general strategy for the development of power market. Main emphasis has to be laid on creation of approved a legal base in these states in order to accelerate development of business links between CAR countries in the field of electric power and to create necessary conditions for free and uninterrupted transit of power resources and enforcement of approved tariff policy of the countries in this field.

1. Analysis of conditions of the oil and gas extraction units and oil and gas-processing plants in CAR countries

The oil and gas extraction as well as the oil and gas-processing units constitute an important fuel energy complex of the power plants of the CAR countries. Their development has an important political significance especially for Kazakhstan, Uzbekistan and Turkmenistan.

An examination of the dynamics of oil extraction shows an uneven pattern of production. During the period 1992-94 the production dropped by 12 per cent to rise later up to 52 per cent. On the whole, during the years 1992-2002 oil extraction in the region doubled up to reach an absolute volume of 63.32 million tonnes in the year 2002 (Table 20.2).

Table 20.2 : Oil and gas condensate extraction in CAR countries

(Million tons)

CAR countries	*1992*	*1993*	*1994*	*1995*	*1996*	*1997*	*1998*	*1999*	*2000*	*2001*	*2002*
Kaz-n*	25.8	23.0	20.3	20.5	23.0	25.8	25.9	30.0	35.3	40.6	47.2
Kyrg-n*	0.1	0.1	0.1	0.1	0.1	0.1	0.1	0.1	0.1	0.1	0.1
Taj-n*	0.06	0.04	0.03	0.03	0.03	0.03	0.02	0.02	0.02	0.02	0.02
Turk-n**	5.2	...	4.4	4.5	4.4	4.8	5.5	7.0	7.4	7.9	9.0
Uzbek-n*	3.3	...	5.5	7.6	7.6	7.9	8.1	8.1	7.6	7.3	7.0
CAR	34.6	...	30.33	32.73	35.11	38.63	39.62	45.22	50.42	55.92	63.32

* Information from International Statistics Committee of CIS on Kazakhstan, Kyrghyzstan, Tajikistan and Uzbekistan and from the sites *http://www.centran.ru/, http://www.gazetsng.ru;/*

** Data from the Account of World Bank on Turkmenistan for 1998 and from site *http://www.turkmenistan.ru/.*

Kazakhstan, Turkmenistan and Uzbekistan are the leading producers of oil in the region.

Oil extraction is carried out mainly in Chingiz, Uzen and Karachaganak regions of Kazakhstan; in the Garashzuluk and Burun regions of Turkmenistan; and in the Kokdumalak, North Urtabulak and Kruk regions of Uzbekistan.

It can be inferred from Table 20.2 above that starting from the mid-1990s there has been an increase in oil extraction. This increase can be attributed to favourable competitive world market of hydrocarbons and a growth in the volume of export. On the whole, in Kazakhstan, there has been a steady increase in oil extraction during recent years. Export of oil and gas condensate in the year 2002 made up to 38.7 million tonnes.

Between 1992-2002 oil production in Turkmenistan increased by 42 per cent. Although till the year 1996 (inclusive) a decrease in oil production was noticed but since 1997 there has been a steady growth in its production. Turkmenistan falls into the category of oil rich states. In the year 1999 volume of production in the republic exceeded its domestic oil requirements by 40 per cent.

In Uzbekistan between 1992-2002 oil extraction (with gas-condensate) increased 2.1 times and in 2002 it made up 7 million tonnes. This oil was utilized not only for meeting domestic demands for liquid fuel but was also exported.

Kyrghyzstan and Tajikistan do not play any significant role in the development of oil and gas sector of CAR states.

According to the available figures in Kyrghyzstan, in the year 2002, oil extraction was 77 thousand tonnes and 65 thousand tonnes had to be imported. In the same year 53.7 thousand tonnes diesel fuel was produced and 84.4 thousand tonnes was imported. In the case of motor petrol 72.5 thousand tonnes was produced and 46.4 thousand tonnes was imported and in the case of fuel oil 158.5 thousand tonnes was produced and 36.2 thousand tonnes imported. In the year 2002 national self-sufficiency in oil products was only 30 per cent.

Industrial oil reserves are concentrated mainly in the Jalalabad and Osh regions. Intense work in the year 2002 changed the production by just 9 per cent as compared to the previous year. The transport sector can be considered the leading consumer of oil products in 2002 as it consumed around 42.9 per cent of total volume produced.

In Tajikistan, oil extraction dropped to an insignificant volume while the home-demand for oil and oil products increased to 25 times the volume of their production in 2002 (compared with 19.5 times in 1992).

As far as the development of gas-extraction industry is concerned, for the period 1992 to 2002, gas output in Central Asian Republics increased by 11.2 per cent, and its absolute volume was 125.24 billion m^3 in 2002. A considerable decrease in absolute volume of gas output in CAR was found in Turkmenistan, where it was 37.3 billion m^3, which was, partly, because of a decrease in its supply from Ukraine in

Table 20.3 : Gas output in CAR countries

(billion m^3)

CAR countries	*1992*	*1993*	*1994*	*1995*	*1996*	*1997*	*1998*	*1999*	*2000*	*2001*	*2002*
Kaza-n*	8.1	6.7	4.5	5.9	6.5	8.1	8.2	10.8	11.5	12.0	13.1
Kyrg-n*	0.1	0.04	0.04	0.04	0.03	0.02	0.02	0.02	0.02	0.02	0.02
Taji-n*	0.1	0.05	0.03	0.04	0.05	0.04	0.03	0.04	0.02	0.02	0.02
Turk-n**	60.1	—	35.7	32.3	35.2	13.7	11.4	22.8	43.0	51.4	53.5
Uzb-n*	42.8	—	47.2	46.8	49.0	51.2	54.8	55.6	56.4	57.4	58.6
CAR	111.2	—	87.47	86.88	90.78	73.06	74.15	89.26	110.9	120.8	125.2

* Information from International Statistics Committee of CIS on Kazakhstan, Kyrghyzstan, Tajikistan and Uzbekistan and from the sites *http://www.centran.ru/, http://www.gazetsng.ru;/*

** Data from the Accounts of the World Bank on Turkmenistan for 1998 and from the site *http://www.turkmenistan.ru/.*

1997-98 due to its debts of about $1.5 billion. Moreover, there were specific disagreements between Turkmenian gas suppliers and RAO 'Gasprom' on pipe carrying gas to Ukraine, regarding payment for the transits. These disagreements were only settled by the end of 1998.

Table 20.3 depicts the details of gas production. An analysis of the dynamics of gas production shows that the basic major gas-producing states of CAR are Uzbekistan, Kazakhstan and Turkmenistan.

It was only in the second half of the period under consideration, more so from 1999 onwards that there was active gas production in Kazakhstan, while in Turkmenistan and Uzbekistan gas production has dynamically increased during the last 8 years.

For the period observed, consumption of natural gas decreased by 17.4 per cent and in 2002 reached 60.37 billion m^3. Till date, volume of home production of natural gas surpasses its consumption in Kazakhstan by more than 2 times, in Turkmenistan—by three times. Contrary to this, in 2002, the share of home production of gas compared with its consumption was 5 per cent in Kyrghyzstan, while it was only 0.6 per cent in Tajikistan.

As far as the whole region is concerned, it may be called gas-surplus without hesitation, as the natural gas production in CAR as a whole was approximately 1.46 times its consumption in 2002.

Therefore, the gas resource industry present in this region promises a considerable increase in the gas output, and there are additional markets for its sale to which they have access.

Major gas deposits of Kazakhstan are spread along the boundaries of Caspian oil and gas province, South Mangeshlak and Turgaisk oil and gas regions, with more than 40 per cent gas deposits concentrated in the Karachagan Region. In 1997, an international consortium, which included the companies "AGIP" (32.5% Italy), BG (32.5 per cent Great Britain), Texaco (20% USA) and Lukoil (15% Russia), got the right to exploit these deposits within a period of 40 years. (The percentage refers to the division of the produce).

In Turkmenistan, the largest gas deposits are concentrated in the Amu-Daria gas province, where there is a gigantic deposit called Daulatabad-Donmez, in which almost half of all the gas reserves are accumulated. Similarly, large gas reserves are located at Murgab (Yashral deposits).

In Uzbekistan, large gas reserves are spread over the south-eastern parts of the Republics (Shurtan and Kokdumalak).

Regarding Kyrghyzstan and Tajikistan, it is worth noting that the oil-gas sector plays an insignificant role in the growth of the economy of these countries.

From 1992-2002, in Kyrghyzstan natural gas output decreased significantly—by almost three times. Industrially extractable gas reserves are located in Jalalabad and Osh regions and are found at a depth of 700-2500 m. A look at the consumption pattern of natural gas in the republics shows that the public-domestic sector plays the main role, which, in 2002, had a share of 61.5 per cent out of the total volume consumed. Remaining 34.3 per cent of gas is used by industries, which includes 28.2 per cent used in the production of construction materials. Kyrghyzstan basic requirement of gas is met by its supply from Uzbekistan.

In Tajikistan, natural gas production is limited and home demand is met by importing gas from Uzbekistan and Turkmenistan.

Major achievements of the CAR states in oil-gas sector are as follows:

2. *Increase in extraction and refining of oil and gas resources from the middle of 90s*

The creation of a favourable investment climate and drawing significant investments into CAR countries, has contributed to an increase in oil and gas extraction.

In all, for the period 1992 to 2002, oil output in Kyrghyzstan increased by 45.3 per cent, while that in Turkmenistan increased by 42 per cent, and in Uzbekistan – by 2.1per cent.

The corresponding increase in gas output for the above mentioned period was 38.2 per cent in Kazakhstan, and 26.9 per cent in Uzbekistan. In Turkmenistan, active gas extraction started only from 1999 onwards.

The rising trends of oil and gas resource extraction have stimulated the development of oil and gas processing industries in CAR countries.

3. *Adopting measures for effective utilization of the transport potential, for development of oil-gas transport infrastructure and for expanding export opportunities for supplying oil gas resources to third countries.*

(a) Most significant results in the direction were achieved in Kazakhstan, where great attention was paid to widening integration and cooperation with CAR and CIS countries in the oil-gas area.

No less important is the role played by increase in transit of Kazakh oil through Russian territory, carried out through the Atirau-Samara oil-pipeline and further by the Transoil pipeline system towards Bylorussia.

In export to third countries by Kazakhstan, the Chinese market is of prospective importance. In June 1997, an agreement was signed between Kazakhstan and China on constructing an 1800-mile oil-pipeline joining oil deposits of one country with the oil processing centres of the other, with China playing the role of an investor. The realization of the given project will undoubtedly become an important factor for development of the export potential of the Kazakhstan Republic.

(b) In March 1998, the Turkmenistan government reached an agreement with 'Monument Oil' company on taking oil from Burun deposits in west Turkmenistan to the northern boundary of Iran and its replacement with oil from the Persian Gulf.

In December 1997, a 250 km long pipeline was constructed connecting gas deposits in Korpeje in West Turkmenistan to the town of Kurt-Kui in northern Iran. For Turkmenistan, the given project opens opportunity to start natural gas export to Turkey through the network of Iranian pipelines.

In February 1998, the company "Royal Dutch/Shell" signed a protocol with Turkmenistan in accordance with which the company will carry out a TEO project to construct a gas pipeline connecting Turkmenistan with Turkey through Iran. The carrying capacity of this gas pipeline is estimated to be around 30-billion m^3 gas per year. The construction of another pipeline having similar carrying capacity is also being planned, which would be running through the Caspian Sea bypassing Iran.

Similarly, there are also prospects of constructing a gas pipeline from Turkmenistan to Pakistan through Afghanistan.

In this way, one of the priorities for CAR governments is the issue of effective utilization of transit potential and increase in exports supplying oil-gas resources to the world markets.

However, its realization faces a series of problems, which are:

1. Presence of an ineffective system of tariff control of oil gas resource supplies in CAR countries.
2. Disagreement in formulating tariffs for transit of oil gas resources within CAR.
3. Unsteady development of oil-gas transport infrastructure in CAR countries

In relation to this, for Kazakhstan (and similarly for other CAR countries) what is required is widening of cooperation in an integrated manner with the CIS countries —above all with Russia, and with other countries (for example with China). This is of utmost importance in order to develop the existing transport infrastructure and constructing new routes for gas-oil export.

Thus, an important priority of the economic policies of the Central Asian countries should be to make effective utilization of their transit potential by creating new transport systems as well as reconstruction of that which is already working, in order to increase the export flows of oil and gas to the internal and world markets.

From the above analysis of the conditions of the oil-gas field complex and of the main problems of its functioning, the following conclusions can be drawn:

1. In the Central Asian Region, the main producers of oil-gas resources are Kazakhstan, Turkmenistan and Uzbekistan. The demands of Kyrghyzstan, Tajikistan are also met by exports from the above-mentioned states.
2. In this connection, strengthening of mutual cooperation of the CAR countries is required towards the formation of a common market of oil and gas. This is also important for their economic growth.
3. In order to create this common oil-gas market in the CAR states, it is necessary for them to develop and effectively utilize

their transit potentials as well as oil-gas transporting infrastructures.

4. The economic basis for creation of this common oil-gas market of Central Asian countries has to be based upon agreed principles, customs, taxation and the Central Asian Republics' state tariff policy in the area of energy (power) engineering.

Examples of industrially progressive countries, particularly the Western European countries, which in the current year are making serious efforts towards creating a competitive power-resource market within the framework of the European Union, are showing that regionalisation of the energy (power) markets is the most essential condition for the future successful development of energy (power). *Emphasis is placed on the fact that even if any one particular country possesses significant power resources, it cannot ensure power-security if it stays out of international integrated processes.*

In creating the common oil-gas market, it is assumed that a balance would be achieved between the supply and demand of oil-gas resources, that payment would be made by the consumer at a sufficiently acceptable rate, and a strategic security would be created for the oil and gas reserves in CAR states, as well as conditions that would be favourable for increasing exports to other countries.

The Analysis of Condition of Coal Industry in The Central Asian Region Countries

In 1990s the coal industry of Central Asian Region countries suffered a serious setback. During this decade, in all the Central Asian Republics there was a fall and then stabilisation in coal extraction. In Kazakhstan coal extraction in the year 2001 dropped by 42.4 per cent as compared to 1991, and the corresponding decrease in Kyrghyzstan was by 77.2 per cent; in Tajikistan it dropped by 15 times, and in Uzbekistan it dropped by 36 per cent. The dynamics of the volume of coal extraction in the CAR countries are shown in Table 20.4.

Maximum fall in coal extraction was seen in its leading producer–Kazakhstan. The main reason of reduction in coal output of the Central Asian Republics is the fall in industrial production in all CAR countries. All Central Asian Republics are promoting the reduction in consumption of coal in real sectors of the economy, there is non-payment by consumers receiving coal, and the government subsidies on coalfields have been discontinued. Also, there was failure to achieve manufacturing capacities and in carrying out the basic groundwork, poor maintenance of mining equipment, difficulty in transporting from the hills, as well as high railway tariffs for the transit and supply of coal.

Table 20.4 : Extraction of coal in the Central Asian Region countries

(Million Tonnes)

Countries of central Asia	*1992*	*1993*	*1994*	*1995*	*1996*	*1997*	*1998*	*1999*	*2000*	*2001*
Kazakhstan *	127	112	105	83.3	76.8	72.6	69.8	58.2	72.4	72.9
Kyrghyzstan*	2.2	1.7	0.8	0.5	0.4	0.5	0.4	0.8	0.4	0.5
Tajikistan*	0.2	0.2	0.1	0.03	0.02	0.02	0.01	0.02	0.02	0.02
Turkmenistan	0.0	0.0	0.0	0.0	0.0	0.0	.0.0	0.0	0.0	0.0
Uzbekistan*	4.7	3.9	3.8	3.1	2.8	2.9	3.0	3.0	3.0	3.0
CAR	134.0	117.8	109.0	86.0	80.0	76.0	73.2	61.8	75.82	76.42

* *According to Information of Interstate Statistical Committee of CIS on Kazakhstan, Kyrghyzstan, Tajikistan, and Uzbekistan.*

The beginning of 1990s saw the closure of all unprofitable coal extraction enterprises throughout the Central Asian Republics and consequent decrease in volume of coal produced. This also contributed to the escalation of social-tensions in these states. The lowered coal production also considerably affected the inter-state delivery of this fuel.

Specifically, the level of delivery of fuel from Kazakhstan to Russia decreased by 35 per cent and to Kyrghyzstan by 73 per cent. There was also reduction in the export of coal from the CAR countries to other states of CIS resulting in a drop in its demand amongst the consumers leading to the closure of the main coalmines. At the same time there was a sharp rise in railway tariffs on delivery and transit of coal. (The increase in transport charges resulted in the cost of exported coal going up by even higher than 50%).

The development in industrial coal extraction in each CAR state are analysed below:

An analysis of demand and extraction of coal in CAR

countries as a whole shows that while Uzbekistan is self-reliant in coal, Tajikistan and Kyrghyzstan have to meet their domestic needs through imports from Kazakhstan and other CIS countries. In this context the main fact that emerges is that for the economic stability of CAR countries it is essential for them to widen their cooperation and to develop a common market for coal so as to fulfil their own domestic demands through heightened production, which would also enable them to export coal.

Basic Directions in the Formation of a Common Power Market of the Countries of Central Asian Region

The main step in the formation of a common market of power resources of CAR states is the development and functioning of an organised legal mechanism, which should lead to movement towards integrated cooperation in the field of power based upon the following:

(a) The Development of Mechanism to Saturate the Internal Market of the CAR States by Energy Resources and Expansion of Possibilities of Export to Third Countries.
(b) This factor should form the basis of market reforms to achieve balance between demand and supply of energy resources in CAR states. This would not only fulfil internal consumer demand but will also lead to exports to third countries.

Its realization proposes:

(a) Joint venture between competitive organs of Central Asian countries for a common fuel-energy balance (FEB).
(b) The development of an optimum scheme for the transportation of energy resources within CAR, and the creation of new transport systems as well as the renovation of existing systems leading to growth of export of energy resources of CAR countries.

It is necessary to adopt these at an inter-government level:

1. Concrete measures for defining and development of transportation routes.
   In the sphere of the formation of an electric energy market *a programme for erecting a grid network* for transportation and distribution of electricity within CAR and for export to third countries.
   In the sphere of the formation of a common oil gas market *a programme for construction of a modern oil-gas transport infrastructure* and renovation of the existing infrastructure through joint ventures within CAR countries.
   In the sphere of the formation of a common coal market *A mutual programme for construction of railway tracks* to deliver and distribute coal within CAR countries and for exporting coal to other countries.
2. Agreement on energy related tariffs, taxes, and customs policies between CAR countries.
3. Adopting measures for unifying and harmonising national legislations in the field of power.

   For the realisation of the above-mentioned interstate agreements leading to the formation of a power market, the need is to take steps to unify and harmonise national legislations. It is important to change customs codes by partly simplifying customs controls on the delivery of energy resources. This also applies to change in tax codes by partly changing tax policies so as to make them flexible. There is also need for legislation of power-sector tariff policies by CAR States governments.

4. The creation of a Council for the Formation and Development of Power Market in the Central Asian Region countries.
5. The creation of a finance-industrial group and joint enterprises on the production and transit of energy resources, and production of related equipment.

In the context of CAR this would mean:

In the field of formation of common electric energy market:

(a) Functioning of International Hydropower Consortium.

This Consortium was created in 2002 with the objective of rationalizing the usage of hydropower resources.

(b) Joint construction of the Kambaratinskaya Hydroelectric Station-1, 2 in Kyrghyzstan, Rogunskaya, and Sangtudinskaya Hydroelectric Stations in Tajikistan.

In the sphere of formation of common oil and gas market :

(a) The creation of an international oil and gas consortium.
(b) The formation of joint enterprises for the production of oil and gas equipments.

In the sphere of formation of a common coal market :

(i) The formation of joint coal-extracting and coal-enriching enterprises.
(ii) A joint working of Kara-Keche (in Kirghizstan), Zidda, Nazar-Ailok, Mienadu, Haqima (in Tajikistan) is of vital importance.
(iii) Developing integrated cooperation with other CIS countries is also equally important. In this process, an effective form of induction of capital can be from the exploitation of unrefined (raw) resources of the states of the Central Asian Region, and use of equipment produced in the Bylorussian Republic and the Russian Federation etc.

6. System of power exchange within the framework of the Central Asian Region

   The functioning of this exchange system shall help in meeting the consumers' need for energy resources, the creation of a normal competitive environment in the market, the formulation of equal prices for energy resources, and the determination of price-indices, which are reviewed by the market itself.

7. Formation of a unified information site in the field of power for states of the Central Asian Region

It is vital to create an appropriate website on the Internet about the activities of the various divisions of power sectors of the states of CAR.

8. Improvement of technological base for formation of a common power market.

In the sphere of formation of a common electric power market:

(a) Ensuring functioning of electric power systems of the countries of Central Asian Region in a parallel working regime.
(b) The creation of new power capacities with the purpose of ensuring power security to the countries of the Central Asian Region and that of meeting the needs of states of the CAR for cheap electric energy.
(c) Reconstruction and technical re-equipment of electric power enterprises.

In the sphere of formulation of a common oil and gas market:

(a) Increase in the depth of oil wells.
(b) Further development of underground gas reservoirs is required for increasing the reliability and availability of gas supply to the consumer.
(c) Reconstruction and technical re-equipment of oil and gas extracting enterprises and of the main pipelines is required along with the creation of new capacities and introduction of modern technologies.
(d) Apart from this, the development of the transit potential of CAR states indicates the need for creation of a capable oil and gas transportation infrastructure.

The above stated factors are a pre-condition for the vitality of the movement towards a common market, the realisation of which also necessitates the implementation of flexible taxation policies by states of the CAR, which in turn would facilitate the attraction of investments in the oil and gas sector of the Central Asian countries.

In the sphere of forming a common coal market:

(a) Improving the quality of coal production. Enhancing the quality of coal.
(b) For the reconstruction and technical re-equipment of coal extracting enterprises the following need to be undertaken:

- Reconstruction and technical re-equipment of coal extracting enterprises.
- Introduction of modern equipments and technologies in these enterprises.
- Increasing the cooperation between coal extracting and machine building enterprises of the CAR and CIS states. and restoration of mutually beneficial economic links among these countries.
- Creation of a favourable investment climate in CAR states through the implementation of flexible tax policies by these countries, which would enable an active attraction of investments into the coal extracting and machine building sector.

9. Creation of joint scientific and technical programmes on development of power in the CAR countries.
10. Providing trained and experienced personnel for the formation of a common energy market.
11. Safeguarding investments for formation of a common power market.
12. Implementation of an accepted ecological policy.

Today, the pollution of the air, water resources, and the accumulation of harmful and toxic substances pose a serious ecological problem. The further increase in Electro-Fuel cooperation of the CAR states will bring with it the load of pollutants released from its enterprises into the surrounding atmosphere.

The solutions of main ecological problems are possible by:

- Creating laws for environmental protection, including the ecological orientation of taxation of the Electro-Fuel cooperation enterprises, and harmonizing the national ecological and energy saving legislations.

- Introducing renewable sources of energy into fuel-power balance in order to lessen the negative impact of power-related activities on the environment and to conserve the potential of non-renewable energy resources for future generations.
- Improving the environmental-monitoring systems in the power enterprises.
- Modernizing the power objects.
- Lowering the emission of harmful substances as well as hot gases into the surroundings.
- Introducing ecological insurance.

Conclusion

One of the most important directions of development of world economy in present times is the tendency towards its globalization and regionalisation, particularly, through the creation of regional power markets and unions for the purpose of fuel power. It is already clear today that not a single country in the world, not even the ones that are abundantly provided with fuel energy resources, by not participating in the integrating international processes in the sphere of power, is in a condition to provide the needed security level for its power.

This development is particularly vital for the countries with a transitional economy, where the following are needed for their stable development:

- Wide influx of foreign investments.
- Presence of external market demands of the manufactured goods.
- Provision for secure and fair transport and transit of the energy holders via the territory of third countries.
- Working and realization of an agreeable and political line at the international markets for energy holders, etc.

An analysis of the socio-economical situation in the Central Asian Region (CAR) states led to the following inferences:

1. Central Asia Region (CAR) is such a region, for which integrated processes in economy, especially in *its power sector, was and will continue to be a vital necessity.*

Such a system was in existence for many years even during the existence of former USSR when there was a unified domestic complex. At that time there was a system of high and complimentary interdependence in the power sector between the republics of the USSR including those of the Central Asian Region. In our opinion, even now things are the same as far as the complex inter-industrial contacts are concerned, which were broken as a result of the disintegration of the USSR and were neither resumed in the perestroika period nor in the recently started process of reformation of markets.

2. The main aim of deepening of integrated interaction of the CAR states must be *the creation of a unified economic area, a main element of which is the common power market for the countries of Central Asia.*

   Its formation would result in the preservation and development of inter beneficiary industrial contacts between the CAR states in the field of power, saturation of internal market by cheap fuel energy resources, and the widening of opportunities for export of energy resources to third countries.

3. In this regard, creation of mechanism of formation and development of power market for the CAR states is of vital importance.
4. An important step in the process of creation of the above mechanism for the formation of a common market for energy resources within the framework of CAR, is the conceptualization and preparation of following documents at the inter-governmental level:

- Conception of formation of a common electric-power market for the CAR states.
- Conception of formation of a common oil and gas market for the CAR states.
- Conception of formation of a common coal market for the CAR states.

In the above mentioned documents the main tasks for creation of a common power market and the durations for its realization must be defined. In order to achieve the goal of a common power market, in our opinion, the following priorities need to be addressed:

- Joint creation by competent organs of the CAR states of a common fuel energy balance.
- Formulation of acceptable principles of trade, tax and tariff policies of the CAR states in the field of electric power and that of oil and gas complex and coal industries.
- Functioning of energy systems of Central Asia in a parallel regime.
- Rational use of transit potential of the CAR countries.
- Widening of construction of electrical grid-networks and creation of an effective oil and gas transportation infrastructure.
- Rational use of hydro-power resources of the CAR states.
- Creation of joint electric-energy, oil and gas as well as coal enterprises.

The realization of above mentioned directions will facilitate the deepening of integrated interaction of Central Asian Republic states in the field of power and formation of a common power market, which shall later become the base for a stable economic growth of these countries as well as for the creation of a unified economic area within the framework of the CAR.

The solution of the stated issues calls for a joint effort by competent organs, by international organizations and by institutes through the creation and realization of practical means for the formation of a common inter-complementary fuel and power complex within the framework of the Central Asian Region.

21

Scientific and Cultural Cooperation Development between India and Tajikistan

SANAVBAR VOHIDOVA

If to look at the mirror of a history, the communications and relations between India and Central Asia's states, in particular with Tajikistan, begin since antiquity. They include centuries, if not millenniums. India was a cradle of ancient civilizations and cultures with intensive interactions, intrinsic to its intensive interactions and dialogue.

It is necessary to note that after Iran and Central Asia, were seized by Arabs in VIII century AC. Zoroastrianism was superseded by Islam.

The followers of this ancient Iranian religion which have not wished to accept Islam, have exposed to most severe prosecutions and were compelled to escape to Eastern Turkestan, especially to India, where their descendants—Parsees profess Zoroastrianism till now[1].

After authenticity of AVESTA was proved by Anketil De Perrone, French scientific in 1826, and also due to the Christian Rask, Danish scientist which has brought from India the manuscript of the original, were set up by a fundamentals of the Iranian philology as a science[2].

German researches scientists like Hinz, Humbach, V. Lentz, English scientist like Mary Boys have proved that these monuments are oddments of a rich literary heritage of the peoples, dwelt in Central Asia before formation of the Mongolian power and having the state, culture and language[3].

On the one hand, all of them experienced influence of great adjacent cultures of India, Persia and China. On the other hand, the communications and relationships of these peoples were exhibited in the field of trade, policy and religion.

At Kushans period a huge civilization which was stretched from Khvarazm (Khorezm) till Pushkalavati (today's Peshavar) has left a noticeable track in political culture of this branch of Arian race. Sogdiana Area, and especially Zerafshan Velley kept in a history of its culture the story about redemption Dudkha from material and spiritual bounds of *Nirvana*.[4]

The conventional Indian thought, ascending to such monuments as Vedas, Upanishads, Brahmanas, Puranas, compiled laws of behaviour, great epics *Mahabharata* and *Ramayana* worthy delights.

Great German indologist Fridrikh Shlegel wrote L. Tik in 1803: "Here, purely, source of all languages, all thoughts and verses of human spirit : all without exception takes place from India".[5]

Important point is that in XVII century the Indian fashion reaches a full heyday. It puts forward (extends) a number of outstanding names, among which the first place is taken the king of the poets Saib, then follows Fayzi, Shavkat, Bedil and Amir Khosrou Dehlavi. It is "Golden Age" of a figure of Irsal-a Masal (usage of comparative or figurative expression).

Composite prospers multistage Muraat-a Nazir (symmetry of images), more often occurs Husn-a Tahlil (fancy substantiation)[6].

In Indian style there was something surprising and exciting, it is possible to judge it that in the given fashion the poets write both in Iran and India, Turkistan and Turkey. Osmani kasida falls under influence of gazels of Fayzi, Saib and Shavkat. Their fashion prevails in Osman transfer period[7].

The poetry of style "Sabki Hindi" preferred such forms (shapes) of, verbal art as: Gazel, Masnavi and represented itself lyrical and philosophical poetry. "Sabki Hindi" in opinion of A. Aziz is a style of Suffism going around by the radicals in Islam, in many respects bowed by the Buddhism, Hinduism and also Christianism, i.e. it is a syncretism phenomenon in a history of culture of the Earth.[8] It is necessary to note that in design of the manuscripts of Central Asia in XVI-XIX centuries as figurative and formation means gold was often used. The gold was general means at the solution of ideological space (spatial), temporary, rhythmic and colour of problems.

In the opinion of the known Russian orientalist E. Bertels the style "Sabki Hindi" became a phenomenon not geographic, not national, and to a certain extent social, for represented advance of poetry on social stairs[9]. It is necessary especially to note poetry XVIII-XIX of centuries, especially poetess Zebunniso which the outstanding German orientalist Herman Ette considers outstanding person. She was the daughter of Temurid Avrangzeb which lived in a seclusion, studied Arabian and Tajik poetry. Under an *alias* Makhfi, the princess has created a divan, saturated by progressive ideas condemning poverty and famine which is being experienced by people. She acted against depressing and violence women calling a modern language, acted on problems of gender policy still in XVIII century. Zubunniso wrote in the Tajik and Arabian languages lyrical verses, which were issued twice in 1940 and 1958 by S. Djavharizoda and A. Sidki. Her divan contains about 7000 verses[10].

It is necessary to note words of the professor Pandit Kashimat which has said: "for the Tajiks the music, which has stiffened in white mottled strings of Taj Mahal also is sonorous and clear as music sounding in deep poems of Bedil which was born, sang and has died in India far from people". Thus, India indeed is a storehouse of rich and miscellaneous cultural heritage[11].

It is necessary to note joint scientific cooperation of Tajikistan and India. A vivid example of this are the joint researches of scientific miscellaneous countries of the topographers, physicists, seismologists, botanists about discovery of Pamir. As one of the pioneers of Pamir is possibly to be called the Hungarian orientalist Aurel Shtein and Indian topographer Raya Bahadura Lal Singkh. Since 1879, Aurel Shtein was engaged in indology in Vienna, Leipzig and Tyubingen. In Germany became the doctor of sciences. In 1886 he was invited to work in Lahor and after that was forever connected with India. Aurel Shtein and Indian topographer Raya Bahadura Lal Singkh during the expedition have visited Vakhan, Garm, Shugnan, Daravaz. The topographic shootings of the first expedition of Sinkh and Shtein have filled up imagination about a relief of Pamir and considerably have updated a geographical map of high-mountainous Pamir.[12]

The development of cooperation of Tajikistan and India was more brightly expressed during the Soviet period. Orientalist, historian, statesman, academician—Babajan Gafurov has played the relevant role in revival and development of culture of the Indian and Tajik peoples. Studying a history, culture, science of the peoples of East, especially Hindus, lie could connect in world culture, culture and science of the Tajik people. Since 1956 to 1977, B. Gafurov worked as director of Institute of Oriental Studies of an Academy of Sciences, USSR. He was the president of International Association on Analysis of Cultures of Central Asia in UNESCO, vice-president of International Union on Eastern and Asian Researches, vice-chairman of the Soviet Committee of Solidarity of Countries of Asia and Africa, repeatedly has visited India on workshops through UNESCO[13].

One relevant occurrence was a meeting of Gafurov with the Prime Minister of India madam Indira Gandhi in Delhi in 1974. An example of cooperation of Tajikistan and India became in 1982 translation by the known Indian scientist Shashi Bushan of the book of Gafurov into Hindi. It is necessary to note that the great poet M. Tursunzade reflected in his poems the peoples India, Pakistan and African continent. Specially interesting are cycle of his verses "An Indian Ballad", "I from the Free East", "A Voice of Asia". In them the poet could reflect love to motherland, humanism of the East and Asia sons. M. Tursunzade was the chairman of the Soviet committee of solidarity of World-wide Council of a Peace and acted as the "ambassador of a peace" among nations[14].

Cultural and Scientific Cooperation Development between India and Tajikistan received a new impulse. The horizon of cooperation has been wided especially when Tajikistan became independent in 1990. After in Tajikistan India established its embassy headed by Mr. Mudkhu Kumar the cooperation became more brightly. In November 2003 after Prime Minister of India visited Tajikistan Mr. Atal Behari Bajpai there were signed a number of agreements and declarations between our states on orders and rules of obstacleless visits for persons having diplomatic passport.

Large opportunities for cooperation are in the fields like: hydro energy, development of agrarian products, construction materials, production, furniture, costumes, clinics, leather-shoes production, chemical, pharmaceutical and other branchs of industry.

The organization of joint ventures for production of high-technological production on the basis of the goods produced in India as well as cooperation development in the field of technology and services can be perceptively.

As for mutual beneficial cooperation in the field of science then India can has cooperation with Tajik Technical Institute in the field of modern technology, with Tajik Medical University also in the field of ancient medicine, with Institute of Chemists as well as with Institute of Oriental Studies and Written Heritages where one can find about 6000 old ancient manuscripts in Farsi, Arabic, Hindi and Urdu also 5000 exemplars of lithographs and 3000 exemplars of modern literature.

It is necessary to note that Tajikistan and India are closely tied by cooperation and partnership bounds which aims are mutual beneficial cooperation and assistance to peace building and stability in our region.[15]

Prime Minister of India Mr. Atal Behari Bajpai noticed: "The history of relations between our countries come out from the history of the common historic heritage[15].

For example the opening of the Indian Cultural centre in Dushanbe in January 2003 assisting to cultural relations and cooperation development between two countries.

It is necessary to note the date 18 February 2003—the beginning of direct air flight connections between Dushanbe and Delhi also the establishment of Tajikistan representation in India.

In the frame of visit of Bajpai to Dushanbe there was establish an exhibition "India Experience" where were exhibited agro machines, customer electronic goods, medical equipment, cars produced by new technology.

The matter of India acceptance to Shaghai Cooperation Organization, having taken geographic connection of India with Central Asia became an important factor in strengthening of friendship bounds and cooperation between countries.

In conclusion I would like to notice that India considered and indeed is the richest country of the World. "Not a land of milky rivers and kissel banks" but the place of great and famous culture and knowledge which serve as a envious thing for the rest world.[16]

Thus, it will be fully logic to believe that the India discovery opened new paths to cultural and educational treasures which till now are being under research in universities all over the world.

In India of those times there were developed science and technology that scientist up to the moment study ancient Indian manuscripts and texts to find new discoveries and keys to knowledge.

The India has been discovered till now, especially it is important the notices in notebook of famous german writer, Herman Hesse, a grandson of Basel missioners who had lived more the 20 years "I reached India and China not by train and ship, there must be searched magic bridges".[17] Is thought that India and Tajikistan have found "magic bridges" of cooperation having integrated roots, in the name of unification of two cultures in one civilized space, in the name of achievement of peace of safety of continent, and also in the name of development and discovery of science as a whole.

NOTES

1. Darmesterer, *The Zend Avesta*, Paris, 1892-1893.
2. Lukonin, V.G., *Drevnii i rannesrednevekovy Iran*, Moscow, 1987.
3. Marek, Ya., *Persian Literature in India*, Prague, 1967, pp. 27-35. Ibid. ....
4. Pandita, K.N., Tajikistan na perekryostke mirovykh tsvilizatsii// Tajikistan: Geopolitics, and International Problems, Conference Proceedings, Dushanbe, 1995, p. 64.
5. Ludwig Tieck and die Bruder Schlegel Grankfurt am Main, 1930, pp. 5-10.
6. Jan Rypka, *History of Persian and Tajik Literature*, Moscow, 1970, p. 336.
7. Ibid., p. 280.
8. Dodkhudoeva L.N., Khudozhestvennaya kultura knigi Srdenei Azzii b Indii, XVI-XIX veka, synopsis of DLitt dissertation, Dushnbe, 1998, p. 15. Bertels R.E., Ocherk istorii persidskoi literatury, Leningrad, 1928, p. 64.
10. Ethe, H. Neupersischen Literatur Strassburg, 1896-1904, S-212-220.
11. Pandita, K.N., no. 4, p. 65.
12. Vahidova, S. Novie mosty sotrudnichestva Tajikistana i Germanii// Tajikistan: geopolitika i problema mezhdunarodnykh svyazei. Materialy konferentsii. Dushanbe, 1995, p. 98-99.
13. Gafforov, U. Allomai Zamon// Khojent, 1998, p. 373.
14. Mirzo Tursun-Zoda, Kulliyot, Dushanbe, 1979, pp. 80-83.
15. Narodnaya Gazeta. Sovmestnaya deklaratsiya o druzhbe i sotrudnichestve, 19 Niovember 2003, Nos. 91-92.
16. *Perspective*, New Delhi, November-December, 2002, p. 16,
17. Palomnichestvo Hermann Hesse v stranu Vostoka// Vostok-Zapad, Leningrad, 1982, p. 206.

ANNEXURES

Annexure-I

INAUGURAL ADDRESS

NAJMA HEPTULLA

I am happy that an international seminar is being held today on the vital theme like India and the Central Asia. Scholars have joined us on this occasion.

India has had age-old linkages and interactions with the Central Asian countries. Over the, centuries close interaction of ideas, cultural diffusion and continuous exchange of literature, and technology, frequent commerce and human migrations. Disruptions in our neighbourhood brought new impulses of culture and creativity to India.

The legendry Silk Route not only facilitated rich trade between the two regions but also established cultural and academic linkages. The political exchanges between the two regions began rather early in our histories. There was a political interaction even before the Kushanas which continued till Mughals.

Significant contributions were made by these scholars, painters and artists along with their counterparts in India and other countries towards the enrichment of civilization. Active relations and exchange of ideas between the various countries have led to the opening of many new vistas and trends in the sphere of literature and paintings, often producing creative synergies. The Persian, Central Asian and European impact on Mughal paintings is a good example in this context.

The conquests facilitated interactions between artisans, architects and artists who visited India at regular intervals and settled in the country. Maulana Azad used to take pride in this historic destiny of India where many a caravans settled.

* Inaugural Address of the Seminar or 'India and Central Asia' by Dr. Najma Heptulla, Deputy Chairman, Rajya Sabha.

India was a hospitable land offering protection to refugees, poets artists and even embracing the invaders. The country attracted great attention due to its magnificent philosophy that respected and assimilated religious beliefs. Mahmud Ibni who travelled to India in 17th century, "wished to see the wonders and marvels of the world. Since India is full of rare diversities, fine monuments and secret openings."

There is definite proof of a link between the ancient cultures of Iran Sistan and the Indus valley. Vedic-Avestan rituals, the "fire cult", the sun worship are found as part of ancient civilizations of this region. There has been mythological linkage as is evident in the symbols, epics and scriptures of these ages. Haider Dughlat in the 16th century emphasized the complete freedom enjoyed by Indians in matters of religion, speech and action.

These traditional links between India and Central Asia were rudely interrupted by the British colonisers. The British administration perceived the depth and strength of our traditional links as a major threat to their own efforts to consolidate political control over India. The great leaders of our freedom struggle, Maulana Azad, Netaji Subhas Chandra Bose. Pandit Nehru, revived our linkages with Central Asia.

We have always valued our traditional linkages with Central Asian region. They are part of our heritage and culture. India cherishes relations with our neighbours. As Hon'ble Prime Minister has often said that one can change one's friends but not the neighbours. History bears the testimony that we have never forcefully occupied even an inch of land. For ages India has won only the hearts and minds of neighbours.

In the post-USSR period India established full diplomatic relations and opened Embassies in each of the Central Asian states. Happily, that was reciprocated so that we have the privilege of welcoming Ambassadors from many Central Asian states here today. Cordial political relations have enabled the governments and peoples of our nations to explore new areas of economic, commercial, scientific, technological and cultural cooperation, develop new systems of augmenting our mutual prosperity and improving steadily the quality of life of our citizens.

During my several previous visits to this region, I have always found familiarities and goodwill among people. There are distinct resemblances in the art forms, paintings and architecture. Indian cinema is extremely popular in Central Asia.

I shall suggest that our institutions of historical research, libraries and museum should collaborate more closely. We should be able to share the research works and manuscripts. Collaboration in research will give us the full dimension of linkages over the ages.

Further we can experiment with fusion in the art forms, music, cinema. We have been training young artists in classical Indian music and dances. And ICCR is proud that they have excelled in their pursuits.

There is a scope of translating the famous classical works of literature. This will enable us to appreciate the cultural and literary trends more closely.

ICCR has established Cultural Centres in Tashkent, Dushanbe and Almaty respectively. These Centres have been the nodal points in encouraging cultural and academic exchanges. We have been maintaining Chairs in Indian Studies in Tashkent and Osh. The Council has been pursuing the academic and cultural exchange programmes. We have been receiving artists and troupes from this region and they have been appreciated in India. The Council is pleased to host young students and scholars from Central Asia in the Indian universities and institutions. These young students are our cultural ambassadors in your countries. We would like to intensify these linkages even further.

I compliment Astha Bharti for envisaging this Seminar and am happy that the Indian Council for Cultural Relations has associated its efforts.

With these few words I welcome all the distinguished scholars and declare this Seminar open.

Annexture-II

SOME STATISTICS ON CENTRAL ASIA AND INDIA

CENTRAL ASIA INTERACTIONS

Extended Neighbours

Country	*Capital*	*Population (mn) 2003*	*Surface Area (000 sq.km)*	*Gross National Income ($ billion) 2003*	*Per Capita Income (in US $) 2003*	*Per Capita Income at Purchasing Power Parity (in US $) 2003*
Kazakhstan	Astana	15	2,725	27	1,780	6,170
Kyrgyzstan	Bishkek	5	200	2	330	1,660
Tajikistan	Dushanbe	6	143	1	190	1,040
Turkmenistan	Ashabat	5	488	5	1,120	5,840
Uzbekistan	Tashkent	26	447	11	420	1,720
INDIA	Delhi	1,064	3,287	568	530	2,880

Main Ethnic Groups, Religions and Languages in the Central Asian Republics

Country	*Main Ethnic Groups*	*Religions*	*Languages*
Kazakhstan	Kazakh 53.4%, Russian 30%, Ukrainian 3.7%, Uzbek 2.5%, German 2.4%, Uygur 1.4%, other 6.6% (1999 census)	Muslims 47%, Russian Orthodox 44%, Protestant 2 %, Others 7%	Kazakh (state language) 64.4%, Russian (official language) 95% (2001 est.)
Kyrgyzstan	Kyrgyz 64.9%, Uzbek 13.8%, Russian 12.5%, others 8.8% (1999 census)	Muslims 75% Russian Orthodox 20%, Others 5%	Kyrgyz (official) Russian (made official language in 2001)
Tajikistan	Tajiks 64.9%, Uzbek 25%, Russian 3.5%, Others 6.6%	Sunni Muslim 85%, Shi'a Muslim 5%, other 10% (2003 est.)	Tajik (official), Russian widely used in government and business
Turkmenistan	Turkmen 85%, Uzbek 5%, Russian 4%, other 6% (2003)	Muslim 89%, Eastern Orthodox 9%	Turkmen 72%, Russian 12%, Uzbek 9%, others 7%
Uzbekistan	Uzbek 80%, Russian 5.5%, Tajik 5%, Kazakh 3%, Karakalpak 2.5%, Tatar 1.5%, others 2.5% (1996 est.)	Muslims 88% (mostly Sunnis), Eastern Orthodox 9%, Others 3%	Uzbek 74.3%, Russian 14.2%, Tajik 4.4%, others 7.1%

Land Boundaries and Coastlines of Central Asian Republics

Country	*Land boundaries*	*Coastline*
Kazakhstan	Total: 12,012 km *border countries:* China 1,533 km, Kyrgyzstan 1,051 km, Russia 6,846 km, Turkmenistan 379 km, Uzbekistan 2,203 km	0 km (landlocked); [borders the Aral Sea, now split into two bodies of water (1,070 km), and the Caspian Sea (1,894 km)
Kyrgyzstan	Total: 3,878 km *border countries:* China 858 km, Kazakhstan 1,051 km, Tajikistan 870 km, Uzbekistan 1,099 km	0 km (Landlocked)
Tajikistan	Total: 3,651 km *border countries:* Afghanistan 1,206 km, China 414 km, Kyrgyzstan 8 70 km, Uzbekistan 1,161 km	0 km (landlocked)

(Contd....)

(Contd....)

Turkmenistan	Total: 3,736 km *border countries:* Afghanistan 744 km, Iran 992 km, Kazakhstan 379 km, Uzbekistan 1,621 km	0 km; (landlocked) [borders the Caspian Sea (1,768 km)
Uzbekistan	Total: 6,221 km *border countries:* Afghanistan 137 km, Kazakhstan 2.203 km, Kyrgyzstan 1,099 km, Tajikistan 1,161 km, Turkmenistan 1,621 km	0 km (landlocked) (*includes* the southern portion of the Aral Sea with a 420 km shoreline)

Economic Conditions in the Central Asian Republics
Growth Rate of GDP (% per year)

	2000	*2001*	*2002*	*2003*	*2004*
Kazakhstan	9.8	13.5	9.8	9.2	9.4
Kyrgzstan	5.4	5.3	0.0	7.0	7.1
Tajikistan	8.3	10.2	9.5	10.2	10.6
Turkmenistan	18.6	20.4	19.8	23.0	21.0
Uzbekistan	3.9	4.1	4.0	4.1	7.7

Inflation (% per year)

	2000	*2001*	*2002*	*2003*	*2004*
Kazakhstan	13.2	8.4	5.9	6.6	6.9
Kyrgyzstan	18.7	6.9	2.0	3.0	4.0
Tajikistan	32.9	38.6	10.2	17.1	6.8
Turkmenistan	8.0	11.6	8.8	6.5	5.0
Uzbekistan	28.2	26.5	21.6	3.8	3.7

Unemployment Rates (%)

	2000	*2001*	*2002*	*2003*	*2004*
Kazakhstan	12.8	10.4	9.4	8.8	8.4
Kyrgyzstan	7.6	7.8	8.6	9.0	–
Tajikistan	2.7	2.3	2.5	2.5	2.0
Turkmenistan	2.4	2.6	2.5	–	–
Uzbekistan	0.3	0.3	0.3	0.2	0.2

National Currencies: Exchange Rate to the US Dollar (Annual Average)

	Currency	*Symbol*	*2000*	*2001*	*2002*	*2003*	*2004*
Kazakhstan	Tenge	T	142.3	146.9	153.5	149.5	136.7
Kyrgyzstan	Som	Som	47.7	48.4	46.9	43.7	42.7
Tajikistan	Somoni	TJS	1.8	2.4	2.8	3.1	2.9
Turkmenistan	Manat	TMM	5200	5200	5200	5200	5200
Uzbekistan	Sum	SUM	237.3	423.3	772.0	971.0	1020.0

India-Central Asia Trade, 1996-97 to 2004-05 (US $ Million)

	1996-97	*1997-98*	*1998-99*	*1999-00*	*2000-01*	*2001-02*	*2002-03*	*2003-04*	*2004-05 (Apr-Dec)*
Kazakhstan	16.96	51.16	50.43	40.65	64.12	53.09	59.61	84.07	74.98
Kyrgyzstan	0.98	10.8	8.81	15.61	22.02	11.52	15.13	38.74	40.09
Tajikistan	1.53	1.12	3.04	4.72	4.10	2.56	8.73	8.42	8.13
Turkmenistan	1.65	1.70	2.03	6.03	3.83	6.30	15.70	28.55	18.74
Uzbekistan	10.74	20.3	14.50	22.91	19.98	23.80	25.62	42.84	36.93
Central Asia	31.86	85.08	78.81	89.92	114.05	97.27	124.79	202.62	178.87

Indian Exports to Central Asia, 1996-97 to 2004-05 (US $ Million)

	1996-97	*1997-98*	*1998-99*	*1999-00*	*2000-01*	*2001-02*	*2002-03*	*2003-04*	*2004-05 (Apr-Dec)*
Kazakhstan	4.39	15.13	38.0	27.19	50.08	45.70	46.88	74.81	61.70
Kyrgyzstan	0.98	10.79	8.70	13.80	17.59	10.95	14.67	38.20	39.74
Tajikistan	0.73	1.12	0.51	2.38	3.55	1.22	8.65	4.47	4.85
Turkmenistan	1.38	1.68	1.93	5.64	2.71	4.35	10.29	19.21	10.68
Uzbekistan	8.14	17.59	12.83	9.94	9.39	6.53	5.08	15.14	13.65
Central Asia	15.62	46.31	61.97	58.95	83.33	68.78	85.57	151.83	130.21

Indian Imports from Central Asia, 1996-97 to 2004-05 (US $ Million)

	1996-97	*1997-98*	*1998-99*	*1999-00*	*2000-01*	*2001-02*	*2002-03*	*2003-04*	*2004-05 (Apr-Dec)*
Kazakhstan	12.57	36.03	12.43	13.45	14.04	7.39	12.73	9.26	13.28
Kyrgyzstan	–	0.01	0.10	1.82	4.43	0.56	0.47	0.54	0.35
Tajikistan	0.80	–	2.53	2.33	0.54	1.34	0.08	3.95	3.28
Turkmenistan	0.27	0.02	0.11	0.38	1.12	1.95	5.40	9.34	8.06
Uzbekistan	2.60	2.71	1.67	12.97	10.58	17.27	20.54	27.70	23.28
Central Asia	16.24	38.77	16.83	30.96	30.72	28.50	39.22	50.79	48.25

INDEX

Abbasova, A., 217
Abdullah Khan, 18
Abhidharma, 67
Abhidharma Pitaka, 46
Abu Masher al-Balkhi, 18
Abuseitova, M.Kh., 43
Afghanistan, 20, 25-26, 34-36, 63-65, 74-75, 88-90, 96-98, 125-28, 130-32, 143-48, 150-64, 174-76, 178-80, 182-84, 217-20, 222-24, 231-32, 234-35, 248-50, 268, 283-85
  anti-Taliban military campaign, 139
  anti-terrorist operation in, 223
  fight against international terrorism, 138
  military operation in, 132, 135
  operation enduring freedom in, 239-40
  opium production in, 216, 231-32
  Soviet intervention in, 146
  US-led struggle against international terrorists, 177-78
Agreement on Energy Charter (AEC), 278
Agriculture irrigation system, 247
Ahimsa, 98
Ain-e-Akbari, 3, 21
Aitareya Brahmana, 13
Ajanta, 70
Ajantā figures, 6
  paintings, 48
Akbar, 17, 19, 21, 119
Aktyubinsk-Xingiang pipeline, 170
Al-Beruni,11, 16, 18, 73, 79-80, 117
Alexander Eschate, 910
  compaign of, 45
Ali, S.M., 22
Alimov, Muzaffar, 211
Al-Khwarazni, 18
Alma-Ata, 197
Al-Qaeda, 135, 142, 219, 234-36, 240
  activities of, 223-24
  grandiose plan, 221
Allauddin Khilji, 116
Allchin, F.R., 73
Alliance of Gas Exporting countries, 160, 165
Alto, Penthi, 5
Amir Khusrau, 119
Amu Darya valley, 3, 123-25
Ancient Indian literature, 19-12
Ancient land routes, 9-10
Anglo-Saxon judicial system, 183
Angry Arhat, 22, 38
Anti-modernization, 228
Anti-Russia campaign, 213
Anti-Taliban military campaign, 139
Antonova, K.A., 83
Arabian Khalifate,111
Archeological discoveries, 48
Arpi, Claude, 91
Arundhati, 37-38
Arupadhatu, 39
Arya Vairochana, 7
Aryabhatta's *Aradhna Ratrika,* 18
Asker Akaev (President of Kyrgyzestan),131,148, 190-195
Ashmeka, 15
Ashoka, 5
Ashtadhyayi, 16, 64
Ashvaghosha, 15, 26
Ashokavadana, 66

Islamic radicalism, 211-220
Islamic Renaissance Party, 204
Islamic Revival Party, 137, 230
Islamic teachings, 227
I-Tsing, 23

Jacshenkulov, A., 212, 215
Jaiswal, K.B., 69
Jamiat-i-Ulema Islami (JUI) 235, 240
Jalal Khan, 114
Jambudvipa, 11
James Wolfowitz (US Deputy Secretary), 136
Jahangir, 21, 54
Jammu & Kashmir, 143, 148, 248-50
  Pak-*mujahideen* in, 239-40
Janapadas, 64
Jangojin, R., 217
Japanese excavation, 73
Jatakas, 19, 80
Jiang Zemin (Chinese President), 140
Jihad, 174, 222
  against communist, 219
Jihangir Hassini, 116
Joint Working Group (JWG), 150
Jones, Elizabeth (Assistance Secretary of State), 132, 136
Joshi, Nirmala, 143
Judaism, 112
Juma Namangani, 234-35

Kablukov, Evgein, 78
Kabul, Hindu shahis of, 73-74
Kalidasa, 6, 39
K'ang Chu, 23
Kalhana, 71-72
Kalhan's *Rajatarangini,* 14
Kāmadhenu Cow, 37
Kamol Kharrazi (Iranian Foreign Minister), 169
Kamandalu, 37
Kambojas, 4, 12
Kamadhātu, 39
Kanishka, 5, 67
Kara-tepe inscriptions, 46
Kargil War, 1999, 148
Karimov, I., (President of Uzebekistan), 134, 145, 198-200, 220
Karma, 9
Kashika Sutra, 16
Kashmir, 9, 64-70, 74-75, 80-88, 96, 183, 228
  Brihad Buddhas of, 71-72
  Buddhism spread and development in, 75
  cultural activity in, 76-77
Kashmir-Gandhara region, 65-68
Kashmir University, 88
Kashmiris, 63
Kashmiri Plastic Art, 69-70
Kaushik, Devendra, 134,187
Kavya Mimansa, 13, 14
Kazakhstan, 3, 5, 15, 45-50, 78, 123-25, 125-30, 144-46, 150-54, 157-64, 174-80, 182-84, 187-88, 211-215, 236, 251-52, 260-64, 266-68, 273-80
  Indian relations with, 50-52
  Oil pipeline projects in, 278
Khalifatchilar (Caliphate supporters), 230
Khan, Sultan M., (Foreign Secretry of Pakistan), 92
Kharoshthi Script, 5, 25-26, 75, 79
Khrushchev, 84, 193
Khrustalev, M., 218
Khuda Bakhsh Library, 81
Khurshid, Salman (Indian Commerce Minister), 182
Kizil cave paintings, 6
Kshatriyas, 13-14
Kshemenda's *Brihat-Katha Manjari,* 14
Kumar, B.B., 3

Kumarajivas, 75
Kushana coins, 58
Kutb ud-din, 49
Kuwait, 158
Kuzmunaigas, 194
Kyrgyz diplomatic services, 78
Kyrghizstan, 3, 5, 15, 78-80, 123-25, 128-30, 140, 144-145, 148, 150-54, 157-62, 164-70, 174-80, 182-84, 187-88, 212-215, 226, 238-39, 251-52, 261, 264-66, 275-80

Lamas, 106
Lamaist terminology, 80
Lang Darma's assassination, 99-100
Languages, 24-25, 305-06
Language links between Central Asian and Indian culture, 117-18
Le-Cog, 35
League against Anti-imperialism, 84
Lekhaprakasha, 76
Lemmlein, G.G., 44
Lenin, 193
Linguistic relation with Indo-Uzbek, 111-120
Little Rajagriha,7
Lokakshema, 23
Lokeshwaras, 71
Lord Shiva, 92
Lynn Pascol (Deputy Assistant Secratary of State), 129

Mahabharata, 4, 8, 12, 13, 14, 15, 296
Mahajanapadas, 64
Mahallas, 21
Mahatma Gandhi, 83
Mahmood Gaznevi, 80
Mahmud Ibni, 302
Mahavamsha, 65, 66
Mahavihara, 67
Mahayana Buddhism, 24, 68, 75
Manu Smriti, 4, 14
Marco Polo, 7
Markandaya Purana, 11
Market economy, 183, 193
Masud, A.S., 218
Matrika chakra, 71
Matsya Purana, 11, 13
Maulana Abul Kalam Institute of Asian Studies,·39
Mazar-i-Sarif, 9, 155
Medieval literature, 15-16
*Meghdoota,*14
Merchants trading, 21
Metropolitan Museum of Art, New York, 34
Migration, 14, 213
Military aristocrecy, 50
Military action against Talibans, 154
Military operation against Afghanistan, 135
Mirkasymov, Surat, 247
Mir Kureish, 52
Mirza Ghalib, 16
Mongols, 113-15
Mongolian miniatures, 54
Mongolian war method, 50
Moscow, 20, 85, 86, 205-06
Mount Meru, 11
Mughal Court, 17
Muhammad-bin-Tughlaq, 17
Muhammad Gouri, 49
Muhammad Murad, 19
Mujahideen, 172, 176
Mukherji, B.N., 75
Mullah Omar, 134
Multiple Pipe line Policy (MPP), 163, 167
Mukhminova, R.G., 89
Muslim Lexion, 112
Musharraf, Parvez (President of Pakistan), 134

Nagan-She-Kao, 23
Najibullah (President of Afghanistan), 147

Najma Heptulla, 301
Nalanda, 39
Nalanda University, 100
Narasimha Rao, P.V., 186
National Ahmed Muslim Group, 218
Nazarbaev, Nursultan (President of Kazakh), 133, 178, 194
Nazis, 83
Near Abroad Policy, 167
Nehru, Jawaharlal, 83
Nehru Jawaharlal University, 88
Neolithic culture, 4, 43
Nestorian Christianity, 58
New Indo-Aryan language, 117
Nicolo Seals, 29
Nilakantha, Avaloketeśvara, 6, 22, 35-36
Niyazov, S. (Turkmanian President), 140,166, 200-02
North Atlantic Treaty Organization (NATO), 145, 151-54
  Conference of, 133
Nyatri Tsenpo, 93

October Revolution,123
Odessa-Brody Pipeline, 168
Oil exports, 160-62
Oil and Natural gas, politics of, 156-170
Oil Politics between CAS and Russia, 162-163
Oily Majlis, 232
Old Stone Age, 4
Operation Counter Terrorism, 132
Opinion production, 231-32
Opposition Nomenclature, 196-97
Oriental desposition, 127
Organization of Islamic Conference (OIC), 265
Osama Bin Laden, 149
Oxus valley, 9,24
ONGC, 181, 270
OPEC, 142, 144

Pahlavas, 4
Pakistan, 172, 176-79, 216-219, 227, 234-35, 240, 268, 283
  activities in Afghanistan, 147
Panchatantra, 49
Panchsheel Agreement, 107
Panini, 64
Patanjali, 13
Patrice Lumumba University, Moscow, 86
Peoples'Democratic Party, Uzbekistan, 197-99
Persianization, 174
Political organization, 79
Political system, 123-132
Pollution, 291
Poverty, 126, 226
Power vacuum, 172-73
Prayer-wheel cave, 38
Primokov, Y. (Prime Minister), 154
Proto Indian Seal, discovery of, 44
Puranas, 4, 10, 13, 19
Pushkalawati, 15
Pushkardvipa, 11
Putin, Vladimir (Russian President), 140, 165-67, 195, 205-208
Pyotr Pashino, 20

Qalmaq, 19
Qanungo, Kalika Ranjan, 118
Qarshi Khanabad, 153
Queen Didde, 74
Queen Mumtaj Mahal, 119
Queen Sugandha, 74

Rabbani, Burhanuddin, 138, 149, 173
Rais, Qamor, 86
Raj Kapur, 87
Raja Ranjit Singh, 21
Rajatarangini, 65

Rajiv Gandhi, 186
Ramayana, 4, 12-13, 296
Ranov,V., 4
Rashdi, H., 116
Ratu Boko inscription, 39
Refugees, 218
Regional Cooperative initiatives, 264-66
Relationship with China and Russia, 185-88
Religious extremism, 226-40
Religious organization, 218
Rigveda, 43, 64, 92
Rinchen Zongpo,101
Rivival in Tibet, 101
Rizwi, S.A.A., 116, 117
Roy, M.N., 21
Royal Geographic Society, 55
Ruski Zhurnal, 138
Russia, 180-88
Russian federation, 252
Russian languages, 27, 86-87
Russian monopoly, 175
Russian pipeline, 175-77
Russo-Indian Trade relation, 20

SAARC Summit, 248
Sachdeva, Gulshan, 251
Sagara King, 13-14
Sakya Lamas, 105
Samudramanthana, 6
Samye Debate, 98-99
Sanskrit Buddhism, 75-76
Sankrityayan, Rahul, 26
Sariputra Prakrana, 75
Sarkar, D.C., 22
Sarvastivada, 67, 76
Saundarananda, 75
Schimmel, A.M., 116
Second Domed Cave, 37
Second World War, 83
Secularism, 105
Shah Jahan, 53
Shamatov, Azad N., 111
Shanghai Cooperation Organization (SCO), 140-41, 153, 169, 170, 238-39, 299
Shangshung Script, 91-94
Sharda Script, 72-73
Shariat Law, 222
Sharma, Ram Villash, 27, 28
Sharma, R.R., 123
Shastri, Lal Bahadur (former Indian Prime Minister), 86
Shatpanchshatika, 76
Shih-kao, 23
Shunyavada, 68
Siddhiqi, Iqitidar, 22
Silk Route Extension, 79, 180
Smith, Dianne L., 182
Somdeva's *Katha Saritsagar*, 14
Songtsen Gampo, 96
Soviet Union, 126
Sponsoring Organization, 266
Stein, Sir Aurel, 26
Strategic Cooperation, 185-86
Sufism, 229
Sulemanov, R.H., 8
Sythian language, 26

Tajikistan, 25, 57, 78-80, 86-87, 123-25, 128-30, 140-45, 150-54, 157-62, 164-70, 174-80, 182-84, 187-88, 211-26, 236-39, 251-52, 261, 264-66, 273-80
  annual budget of, 204
  cooperation development of, 297-98
  democracy of, 202-04
  pre-election opposition alliance of, 204
Taj Mahal, 53, 297
Takshashila, 9, 44, 48
Takht-e-Suleiman, 81

Taliban, 145, 148, 176, 219, 221, 234-36, 239
activities of, 223
military action against, 134
policies of, 224
Taliban fundamentalists, 63
Talbot, Strobe (Deputy Secretry of State), 132, 152
Tantras, 100-101
Tantriks, 98
Tarapur Nuclear Power Plant, 186
Tarik-I-Rashidi, 52
Tashkent, 4, 8, 9, 15-16, 20, 55, 83-85, 146-48, 182-85, 216-18, 228-30, 235-36
Tashkent Declaration, 86
Tashkent University, 85, 199
Terrorism, 32, 176
Tibet, 91-93
cultural relations, 109-10
Tibet turns North and East, 106
Tibetan Buddhist system, 94
Tibetan culture, 93-95
Tibetan iconography, 39
Tibetan medicine, 102-04
Tibetan Monks, 99
Tibetan Script, 96-97
Tibetan University, Sarnath, 109
Tiered Stupa, 39-40
Timur Begs Mosque, 53
Tiwari, Bhola Nath, 86
Tōdaiji monostry, 39
Tohir Yuldasev, Abdulhalilovich, 231, 132, 134-35
Tokharian language, 25
Toshkhani, S.S., 63
Transoil pipeline system, 283
Tukhara Melody, 38-39
Tulips Revolution, 191, 206, 233
Tun-Huang, 7, 80
Turkic languages, 25-28
Turkistan, Islamic movement of, 226
Turkish literature, 115
Turkic-Muslim dynasty, 51
Turkman, Russian communique, 139
Turkistan, 5, 9, 12
Turkmenistan, 3, 5, 75, 78-80, 86-87, 125, 125-30, 144-46, 150, 157-60, 163-70, 174-75, 170-80, 182-84, 186-88, 200-01, 212-15, 226, 258-59, 251-52, 262, 264-65, 273-80
political opposition in, 201-202
political situation, 130
Turkmenistan National Museum, 82
Tusharas, 23
Tyrannical democracies, 125-26

U-Chen Script, 97
UNESCO, 195, 298
Unemployment, 306
Unipolor World Order, 185
United Tajik Opposition (UTO), 131, 218-20, 232
Unity of Central Asian-Trans-Caucasia, 188
Upadhyay, Bhagvat Sharan, 64, 74
Upanavarga, 76
Upanishads, 92
Urdu language, 24
Utpala dynastics, 70
US-led coalition against Iraq, 172
US-Senate Sub-committee, 154
USA, political and economic interests of, 167-68
Uttar Kura, 11-14
Uzbek-Tajik Conflicts, 203
Uzbekistan, 20, 25, 78, 86-88, 90, 123-25, 140-45, 147-150, 152-54, 157-64, 168, 174-75, 180-84, 187-89, 197-99, 211-15, 226, 236-39, 251-52, 261, 264-66, 273-80
economic development in, 247-50
Islamic movement of, 227-28
relegious extremism, 229-30, 239-40

group associations and educate people in urban ways of life (see Desai and Pillai 1970).

It should be noted that the slum exhibits mixed features of the presence of illegal or underground activities and of community organization involving residents engaged in both underground and overground activities. Slums differ in respect of the degree of cohesiveness of their social organization. The organized nature of a slum depends on the socio-economic and other characteristics of its population. Slums with a frequent floating population resulting in anonymity have the potential of turning into centres of prostitution, gambling, bootlegging, delinquency and crime. Slums, in some cases, are places of residence for the unemployed and destitutes with underground activities. Organized community living tends to be a feature of permanent settlements. In such a case new inmigrants feel emotionally secure, get socialized and gradually adjust themselves to the new environment notwithstanding the continuation of certain elements of rural or folk culture and styles of life to which they were accustomed. Thus any association of slums with the problems of law and order with civic problems of urbanization will be one sided. It is at best a subject of investigation. In this context, it is necessary to note that vices or illegal activities also exist in affluent neighbourhoods. They are not necessarily confined to slums.

Another important area of investigation in the study of slums is migration and settlement of migrants. Many studies show that inmigration to cities follows the networks of religion, caste, kinship, language and region (Gore 1970; Srinivas and Rao 1966). There is a tendency on the part of the people to sort themselves out and gather together on some of these lines. A fresh migrant lives in a familiar environment and gets more easily and smoothly initiated into the strange urban environment than the one who is forced to start his urban life in an altogether new social environment. When poor unskilled people migrate in a sizeable number, they tend to build their hutment colonies on any vacant land close to their workspot. Because of the advantages of prior contacts, fresh migrants prefer to live in the same colony irrespective of the poor physical conditions. While a few of them who might improve their life-chances considerably might move out of the area subsequently, others prefer to continue to stay in the same area. Needless to say that a group, over a period of time, develops its own social, economic and political structures, and these structures in turn keep the persons and families together. Hence, it would be necessary to investigate the nature of the community organization that the migrants build up in the place of destination.

Slum dwellers form part of the urban economy. Generally they are employed in the category of unskilled workers and in the informal sector of the economy as self-employed persons in petty trade, repairs and transport. They also participate in the urban political processes. Hence it would be necessary to study slums in relation to the wider economic and political organization in the city, in terms of informal sector, class formation and conditions of poverty.

In the light of the foregoing account of the various dimensions in the study of slums, we focus on the following areas in our study of Peta slum in the city of Vijayawada. First, we discuss the pattern of growth of the slum and the nature of its social organization in the general context of other slums in the city. Second, we analyse the process of migration and the adjustments of the migrants to the urban conditions of life. Third, we shall examine the occupational structure of the slum in relation to the city economy on the one hand, the occupational mobility patterns of the slum dwellers on the other. Fourth, we shall discuss the relations that the slum dwellers maintain with their places of origin. Finally, we shall consider the problem of slums in the context of clearance, development and control policies. Thus the main aim of the study is to understand the nature of the Bhaskara Rao Peta slum in the context of migration, urbanization and rural-urban interactions, and to reflect on the general problems of slums and urban development.

METHOD OF STUDY

In order to understand the general pattern and types of slums and their growth in the city, basic data available with the municipality were collected and analysed. The history of each slum in the city and the characteristics of its population were gathered through interviews with knowledgeable persons within and without the slum localities. To the extent possible the process and growth of each individual slum was linked up with the overall process of growth and development of the city itself. The ecological processes of succession, invasion and functional zones were taken into account.

It was felt that an appropriate strategy for analysing slum conditions was to study a slum intensively. An intensive study brings out more valuable insights than does a general survey. After making a general study of all the eleven designated slums in the city, Bhaskara Rao Peta, hence forth called Peta, was selected for intensive study, as it was more representative of slum situations in terms of physical features. Two procedures were adopted for collection of data. At one level information was gathered on social, economic, political, religious and cultural life in the slum through interviews, observations and participant observation. At another level schedules were made use of for eliciting information on some basic socio-economic factors from 362 households (25 per cent of the total households) distributed over thirteen caste-groups on a random sample basis. Details regarding migration were collected through a schedule from self-migrant heads of 292 households. Geneological data were obtained from 200 families spread over four important and populous caste groups—Vaddera, Madiga, Mala and Yadava. The data of the Socio-Economic Survey of Vijayawada City are used for comparative study of Peta with other localities of the city wherever possible.

2

VIJAYAWADA AND ITS SLUMS

VIJAYAWADA is located on the northern bank of the river Krishna, in the Krishna district of the state of Andhra Pradesh (Map 1). It is at the junction of the high roads from Madras to Calcutta and from Hyderabad to Machileepatnam. The Krishna canals connect Vijayawada with other cities like Madras, Eluru, Machileepatnam, Kakinada and Rajahmundry. The city is also one of the biggest railway junctions in the country. No other city in the state of Andhra Pradesh is so well connected as Vijayawada by a network of highways, roads, railways and canals (Government of Andhra Pradesh 1967).

Vijayawada is one of the ancient cities of the state of Andhra Pradesh. There is archeological and historical evidence to suggest that the existence of the city dates back to 10th century A.D. at least, though according to the folklore the city was in existence as early as the 5th century A.D. (Mckenzie 1883 217-18). The city was under the rule of the Kings of Vengi, Eastern Chalukyas, Kakatiyas and Muslims and subsequently under the British. Being located at the apex of the river Krishna it not only enjoyed favourable ecological advantage, which is one of the important factors for the city growth in pre-industrial times, but was also considered as a holy centre (Tataji and Satyamurthy 1975).

The city, of course, grew in size considerably only during British rule. The anicut constructed over the river Krishna at Vijayawada in 1855 changed the complexion not only of the town but also of the entire region surrounding the town which "was poverty-stricken, sparsely cultivated tract and subjected to recurring droughts prior to the construction of the anicut"

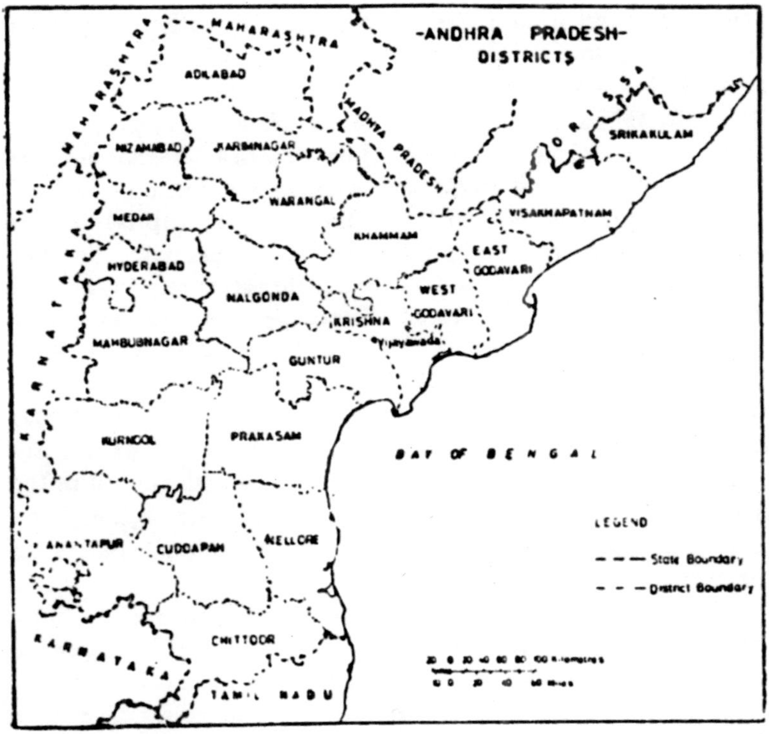

Map 1 : Andhra Pradesh—Districts

(Rajagopal 1969). Since then, after the transformation of the region into a rich agricultural delta, the city has acquired importance essentially as a centre of trade and commerce. It shares the common locational characteristics of Cuttack and Rajahmundry, which are also located at the apex of river deltas, such as dominance of commercial activities with a secondary emphasis on other services and administration and a weak industrial base (V.L.S.P. Rao and Ramachandran 1975). Within a radius of 50 miles from Vijayawada four cities, namely, Guntur, Tenali, Eluru and Machileepatnam and a cluster of small and medium size towns are located.

The city is widely regarded as the regional capital of the coastal Andhra Pradesh, by virtue of its commercial, economic, administrative, cultural and political importance. As already mentioned earlier, Vijayawada is mainly a commercial centre specializing in the export of agricultural produce. It caters to the commercial needs not only of the Krishna district but also of the other adjacent districts, namely, Guntur, West Godavari and East Godavari. Most of the Telugu daily newspapers are published from the city. There is a Broadcasting station in the city. Most of the film distribution companies are located here. Almost all the political parties have their regional offices in the city.

Though the city is not the headquarters of the Krishna district, several regional offices of the state and central governments are located in it because of its central location. Some of them are : The Divisional Headquarters of South-Central Railway, offices of the Income-tax Commissioner, Superintendent Engineers of the Electricity Board, Irrigation and Buildings Department, Public Works Department and the Revenue Divisional officers. Its importance in the state is next only to its capital city of Hyderabad.

Prior to 1905, the city constituted what is now called the old town. Gradually Kothapeta and Lalapeta areas were incorporated into the city limits. In 1905 the city expanded on the eastern side of the railway line and the new area came to be known as Governor Peta. Three canals run through the new city and the important roads run parallel to these canals. The new town expanded along Bandar road towards the east and to a lesser extent to the north.

Vijayawada Municipality is divided into 43 census localities (as in 1971). These census localities do not include Gunadala and Patamata panchayats which formed a part of the Vijayawada Urban Agglomeration in 1971. There is also a proposal to include the adjoining villages, namely, Bhavanipuram, Gollapudi, Enamalakuduru, Kanuru, Enikepadu, Prasadampadu and Ramavarappadu in the Vijayawada Municipality. Thus the city is growing not only due to its population growth within its municipal boundaries but also due to the inclusion of the surrounding villages into its fold.

Demographic features of the city in 1971

Vijayawada is one of the 13 class I cities of Andhra Pradesh, and 132 class I cities of India. It was the second largest urban agglomeration in the state for a long time that is, until 1971 when it moved to third place with a population of 3,44,607. Percentage variations of the city's population during the last one century are given in Table 2.1. It is clear from Table 2.1 that the growth rate of the city fluctuated during 1871 and 1901. But since 1901 the growth rate consistently and steadily increased until 1951, went down considerably in the following decade, and again slightly increased during the next decade. However, barring the decade ending in 1951 the growth rate has been steadily increasing. In terms of absolute numbers, the population growth has been very high since 1951 with more than 70 thousand persons being added to it in each of the decades.

The size, the density and the heterogeneity of social composition are considered as important variables differentiating cities from other forms of human settlements. Hence for a proper understanding of the nature of the city, information on these aspects is presented below.

The total population of the city municipality in 1971 is 3,17,258 and the total area is 7,504.35 acres. The density of the city is 10,791 persons per sq. km. as against 286 persons in the Krishna district, 2,665 persons in the other urban areas of the district, 4,706 in Machileepatnam, 8,997 in Guntur and 8,833 in Eluru.

TABLE 2.1 : The population of Vijayawada during 1871-1971

Year	Persons	Decade variation	Percentage variation
1871	8,206	—	—
1881	9,366	+ 1,160	+ 14.04
1891	20,224	+ 10,858	+115.93
1901	24,224	+ 4,000	+ 19.79
1911	32,867	+ 8,643	+ 35.68
1921	44,159	+ 11,292	+ 34.36
1931	60,427	+ 16,268	+ 36.84
1941	86,184	+ 25,757	+ 42.62
1951	161,198	+ 75,014	+ 87.04
1961	234,360	+ 73,162	+ 45.39
1971*	344,607	+110,247	+ 47.04

*The population of Vijayawada urban agglomeration. In 1981 the population of Vijayawada U.A. rose to 543,008 with the decade variation of + 198,401 and percentage variation of +57.57.

Religious composition

The population of the city is composed of 81.60 per cent of Hindus, 10.01 per cent of Muslims, 8.05 per cent of Christians and 0.32 per cent of other religions including Sikhs, Jains, etc. The proportion of Hindus in Vijayawada is slightly higher than the average for all the cities of the state (80.11%) and slightly less than the district percentage of 83.38. But in the case of Muslims, the proportion of the city is nearly two times higher then the proportion of the district of 5.71 per cent and less than the average proportion of Muslims of all the cities in the state which is at 14.17 per cent. The proportion of Christians in the city is 8.05 per cent as against 10.85 per cent in the district and 5.44 per cent for all the cities in the state.

Caste composition

The census reports do not provide information on all the caste groups. The proportion of Scheduled Castes in the city's population is 4.58 per cent as against 10.05 per cent for the district, 13.27 for the state and 3.65 for Machileepatnam, 3.75 for Guntur and 5.86 per cent for Eluru. The proportion of Scheduled Tribes in the city's population is 0.68 per cent as against 2.03 per cent of the district, 3.81 per cent of the state, 1.12 per cent for Machileepatnam, 2.14 per cent for Guntur and 0.54 per cent for Eluru. Thus the proportion of both the scheduled castes and tribes in the city's population is much lower when compared to the corresponding figures for the district and the state. But when compared to the other cities of the region there are variations.

The data on caste composition of the heads of the sample households in the *Socio-Economic Survey of Vijayawada City* are presented in Table 2.2. In all, 35 castes and 4 tribes with 859 households are represented in the total sample of 1,075 households. The remaining ones belong to religious groups other than Hindu. Out of the total, the three upper castes together account for 20.7 per cent, intermediate castes 32.9 per cent, lower castes for 9.6 per cent, scheduled castes for

TABLE 2.2 : Caste composition of the city

Castes	No. of sample households	Per cent
Upper Castes		
Brahmin	133	12.4
Kshatriya	30	2 8
Vysya	59	5.5
Sub-total	222	20.7
Intermediate Castes		
Viswa Brahmin	26	2.4
Kayastha	2	0.2
Reddi	24	2.2
Kamma	63	5.8
Telaga	160	14.9
Velama	15	1.4
Padmasali	25	2.3
Nagar	13	1.2
Bodili	1	0.1
Kummari	10	0.9
Yadava	6	0 5
Sisti Karanam	4	0.4
Mudaliar	4	0.4
Khatu	1	0.1
Vellala	1	0.1
Sub-total	355	32.9

TABLE 2.2—*Contd.*

Castes	No. of sample households	Per cent
Lower Castes		
Setti Balija	18	1.7
Nadar	4	0.4
Gavara	15	1.4
Rajaka	10	0.9
Palli	6	0.5
Vaddera	18	1.7
Kalavanthulu	6	0 5
Mangali	1	0.1
Enka	10	0.9
Relli	4	0.4
Anavadvavia	2	0.2
Nagavallu	3	0.3
Gomalla	3	0.3
Gonda	3	0.3
Sub-total	103	9.6
Scheduled Castes		
Mala	89	8.3
Madiga	65	6 0
Adi Andhra*	5	0 5
Sub-total	159	14.8
Scheduled Tribes		
Yenadi	2	0.2
Lambadi	7	0.7
Budabukkala	1	0.1
Yerukula	10	0.9
Sub-total	20	1.9
Total	859 out of a total of 1,075 sample households	

*Some Malas and Madigas call themselves Adi Andhras.
(Percentages are calculated for the total of 1,075 housholds)
Source : A Report on the Socio-Economic Survey of Vijayawada City, 1975.

14.8 per cent and scheduled tribes for 1.9 per cent. It is interesting to note that the representation of the scheduled castes and scheduled tribes in the sample is very high when compared to their proportions in the population of the city which are 4.58 per cent and 0.68 per cent respectively. The numerically important castes in the sample are Telaga, an agricultural caste, with 14.9 per cent, Brahmin with 12.4 per cent, and Mala, a scheduled caste with 8.3 per cent. Thus one each from upper, intermediate and scheduled caste groups emerge as numerically large groups in the sample. The proportion of not even one of the lower castes exceeds 2 per cent in the total sample. Among the intermediate caste groups the agricultural caste groups, namely, Reddi, Kamma, Telaga and Velama together constitute 24.3 per cent of the total sample. The artisan castes, namely, Viswa Brahmin (goldsmiths), Padmasali (weavers), and Kummari (potters) together constitute just 5.6 per cent of the sample. These data show that Vijayawada is a multi-caste city and predominantly populated by upper and intermediate caste groups as any other city (D'Souza 1976).

According to the 1971 census the number of females per 1,000 males is 948 in Vijayawada as against 957 in Machileepatnam, 975 in Guntur and 1,010 in Eluru. Thus the number of females in the city is less when compared to other cities in the region. However, according to the city sample the number of females is 979 per 1,000 males.

The information on the proportion of different age groups in the city's population for 1971 is not yet available. But, according to the 1961 census the proportions of the age groups of 0-14 years, 15-34 years, 35-59 years and 60 years and above are 38 per cent, 38 per cent, 20 per cent and 4 per cent respectively. Thus, those in the working age group account for 58 per cent of the total population.

According to the sample study, out of 5,557 persons belonging to 1,075 households, 42.0 per cent are in the age group of 0-15 years, 35.7 per cent in 16-35 years, 19.8 per cent in 36-60 years and 2.5 per cent in 61+ years. Thus the difference between 1961 figures and sample study figures is very little. It may also be noted that the classification of the age groups in the census is slightly different from that of the sample.

According to the 1971 census the literacy rate in the city is 54.39 per cent compared to 35.19 per cent in the district, 56.63 per cent in Machileepatnam, 47.93 per cent in Guntur and 51.32 per cent in Eluru. The literacy rate for males is 62.42 per cent and for females 45.93 per cent in the city.

The sample study shows that while 59 per cent of the total sample population received formal education, the remaining 41 per cent did not receive formal education. Those who completed 1-4 years of education accounted for 15.2 per cent; those who completed 5 years of education accounted for 7.3 per cent; those who completed 6-8 years accounted for 21.4 per cent; and those who completed 9-11 years accounted for 14.9 per cent. The proportion of matriculates, intermediates, graduates and post-graduates in the sample population is 4.8 per cent, 0.8 per cent, 1.5 per cent, and 0.5 per cent respectively.

Employment and occupational pattern

The data on occupational distribution of the workers in the city according to the 1971 census are presented in Table 2.3. It shows that the four important occupational categories which account for nearly 20 per cent or more are trade and commerce followed by transport, storage and communication, other services and manufacturing industries. The commercial importance of the city is evident from the fact that nearly 50 per cent of the workers are engaged in trade, commerce, transport, storage and communication categories.

TABLE 2.3 : **Proportion of workers in different occupational groups in 1971 census**

Sl. No.	Occupational category	Proportion of workers in each group
I	Cultivators	0.9
II	Agricultural labours	1.3
III	Livestock, Forestry, Fishing, Plantations, Orchards and Allied Activities	0.5
IV	Mining and quarrying	0.4
V	Household industry	1.3
VI	Manufacturing other than household industry	19.8
VII	Construction	6.4
VIII	Trade and Commerce	27.0
IX	Transport, storage and communication	22.8
X	Other Services	19.6
		100.0

Out of the total population of 5,557 persons covered under the sample study of the *Socio-Economic Survey of the City*, 3,080 persons (55.5%) are in the working age groups, and 1,529 persons (49.6%) out of 3,030 are gainfully employed. However, the remaining 50.4 per cent of the persons cannot be considered unemployed since only 6.4 per cent of the total population (197 persons) are seeking employment. In the sample study the occupations followed by the respondents are classified into five categories, namely, (I) very high status occupations (teachers, business executives, engineers); (II) high status occupations (class III employees of the government and railways, salesmen, shopkeepers and medical representatives); (III) medium status occupations (drivers and various skilled categories); (IV) low status occupations (class IV employees in the government, cultivators, tailors etc.); (V) very low status occupations (casual labourers, sweepers etc.). The percentages of the earners engaged in the above five categories of occupations are 5.73, 34.14, 14.01, 25.68 and 20.41 respectively.

As already noted, Vijayawada is mainly a centre of trade, commerce, transport and communications. As a commercial centre it specializes in the export of agricultural produces of the rich hinterland. Such commodities as grains, vegetables, fruits, fish, livestock, rubber and rubber products are supplied to distant places. Most of the industries in the city are of small-scale size, consisting largely of foundries and floor-mills, with the exception of a cement factory and the milk project with a combined employment of 1500 workers.

Slums of Vijayawada

The city is divided into 43 census localities, of which 11 are identified as slums. The area and population of eleven slums are given in Table 2.4. The city municipality has identified an area as a slum if it has a comparatively greater number of huts and has no proper civic amenities. Of 11 such slums, two are now classified as "Organised slums" for the reason that in the year 1962, 1784 households were allotted plots in these areas under a scheme of rehabilitation of the slum-dwellers. These two areas are on the eastern outskirts of the city. Being new and planned in terms of broad roads and independent house plots the two areas have not yet turned into slums with the attendant characteristics.

TABLE 2.4 : **Slums : area and population**

Name of the slum	Area in acres	Population	Density (people per acre)	Rank in Density
Chitti Nagar	111·58	4,376	39.0	8
Tailor Peta	157.06	12,215	77.0	5
Winch Peta	33.55	12,992	385.0	1
Bhaskara Rao Peta	166.31	7,887	47.5	6
Baptist Palem	92.66	10,114	108.0	3
Cement Factory Colony	132.83	2,580	19.3	9
Giripuram	5.92	1,190	200.7	2
Wood Peta	23.60	2,904	88.7	4
Badava Peta	32.95	1,316	39.0	7
Sub-total	756.46	54,764		
Mutyalampadu Housing Colony*	56.81	6,251	110.0	
Mutyalampadu*	1,098.24	2,337	2.1	
Grand total	1,911.51	63,352	31.2	

*Resettlement colonies.

The two 'organized slums' (Mutyalampadu and Mutyalampadu Housing Colony) together have a very extensive area of 1,155.05 acres with a population of 8,588 having a density of 7.4 persons per acre. For a realistic presentation of the situation of the slums the two so-called organized slums are kept out of the purview of the present analysis because the overall picture will then be distorted. Thus excluding the two resettled areas, the total population of the 9 slums in the city comes to 54,764, distributed over an area of 756.46 acres, whereas the population of the city is 3,08,670 in on area of 6,349.30 acres.

The nine slums (Chittinagar, Tailor Peta, Winch Peta, Bhaskara Rao Peta, Baptist Palem, Cement Factory Colony, Giripuram, Wood Peta and Badava Peta) constitute 17.4 per cent of the total population and 11.9 per cent of the total area of the city. Obviously the proportion of the slum population to the total population is far higher than the proportion of slum area to the total city area as reported to be the case in many other cities (Singh and deSouza 1980 : 17). While the overall density of the city works out at 49.10 persons per acre, the density of the slums is 72.4 persons per acre.

The foregoing comparison between the density of the city and that of slums does not, however, present a correct picture as the non-slum census tracts include large portions of vacant or agricultural lands. If we substract these vacant and agricultural lands, the overall density of the city, density of the non-slum area and that of the slums figure out to be 107.6, 106.0 and 118.8 persons per acre respectively. Thus there is no significant difference in the density of the slums and non-slums. In fact the non-slum areas still include a good proportion of land used for transportation and communication purposes and if this land is not taken into account, the density of these areas increases further.

If we take the individual census tract into consideration, we find that the non-slum areas have far higher density than the slums (Table 2.5). However, the slums which are encapsu-

TABLE 2.5 : **High density tracts in the city**

Name of the locality	Area in acres	Population	Density (persons per acre)
Sitanna Peta	3.59	2,977	829.0
Mahanthipuram	7.59	4,422	582.0
Winch Peta*	33.55	12,923	385.0
Kothapeta	82.39	29,923	363.0
Mallikharjuna Peta	32.63	9,730	298.0
Anjaneya Peta	41.34	11,282	273.0
Purnanandampeta	20.05	4,505	225.0
Giripuram*	5.92	1,190	201.7
Old Town	100.99	17,918	177.4
Satyanarayana Puram	131.46	15,346	116.7
Seetharamapuram	50.96	5,851	114.8
Labbi Peta	49.74	2,597	111.0

*Slum localities.

lated in the city register a higher density than the others. Thus one could reasonably say that slums are not more highly populous than the non-slums, nor does the higher density mark a slum from the non-slum area.

Besides the nine demarcated slum areas, hutments have sprung up in large numbers all along the canal banks and road-sides. No clear account is available about these slums. In the year 1962, efforts were made to rehabilitate the residents of slums on the canal banks in Mutyalampadu Housing Colony by way of giving house sites on a nominal rent. But this experiment seemed to have proved a failure in that reportedly many of them only sold away their plots in Mutyalampadu Housing Colony (popularly known as Ajith Singh Nagar named after Sri Ajith Singh, the then special officer of the Municipality) and returned to the original places.

Growth of the slums

The city of Vijayawada can be broadly divided into the old town (Census tracts, 4, 5, 6, 7, 8, 9, 10, 11, 12, 15, 16, 17, 18, 19 and 42) and the extended area (1 to 3, 13, 14, 20 to 43). In the old town we come across four slums : Chitti Nagar, Tailor Peta, Winch Peta and Baptist Palem (census tracts 5, 6, 8 and 17 respectively). The first three are adjacent to one another. Baptist Palem is separated from the other three slums by the railway station. As the city expanded, Peta slum (Census tract 13) in the south and Cement Factory Colony slum (Census tract 21) in the East sprang up. Subsequently three more slums, namely, Wood Peta, Badava Peta, Giripuram (Census tracts 35, 36, 37) came up in the far south (see Map 2).

We may now describe the features of these eight slums (excluding the Peta slum) one by one.

Chitti Nagar (Census tract No. 5)

This is encircled by Anjaneya Peta (Census tract No. 4) to its west, Rajarajeswari Peta (Census tract No. 19) to its east, and Tailor Peta slum area (Census tract No. 6) to its south. Anjaneya Peta and the adjacent area of Rajarajeswari Peta are mainly residential areas. This area is said to have become a slum around the 1930s. It covers an area of 111.58

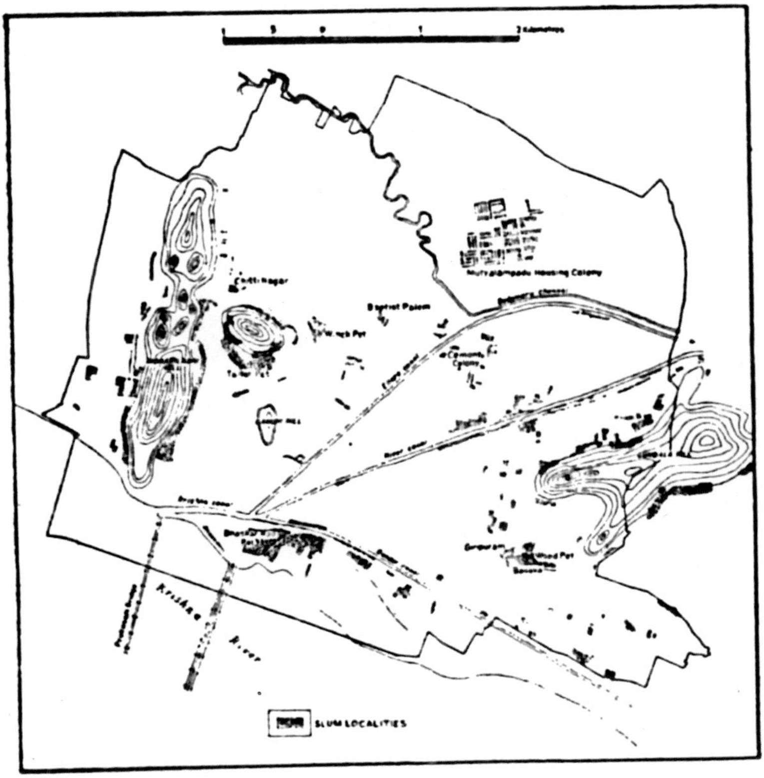

Map 2 : Vijayawada city: location of slums.

acres with a total population of 4,376. Density works out to 39 persons per acre, which is a little less than the average density of the city. It has nearly 460 thatched huts and 400 *kutcha* and *pucca* houses. Sullage is found in different parts. There are no drainage facilities and no metalled roads. In the rainy season the area becomes slushy with sullage water.

The social composition of the slum shows that out of a population of 4,376, as many as 450 persons belong to the Mala caste, 320 to the Madiga caste and around 100 to the Yerukula tribe. The rest belong to different intermediate castes, such as Nagara, Gauda and Telaga. This slum is named after a noted Congress leader Marupilla Chitti who belonged to the Nagara caste.

The people belonging to intermediate castes work as lathe and shed technicians, and fruit and vegetable sellers. The scheduled caste people are engaged as rickshaw pullers and unskilled labourers work on daily wages. Most of the residents of this slum are inmigrants from Visakhapatnam, Prakasam and Guntur districts.

Tailor Peta (Census tract No. 6)

This slum is surrounded by Chitti Nagar slum area (Census tract No. 5) to its north, Kotha Peta (Census tract No. 9) residential-cum-commercial area, to its west and south, Mahanti Puram (Census tract No. 7) a residential area, to its south, Winch Peta (Census tract No. 8) another slum to its south-east, and Rajarajeswari Peta (Census tract No. 19), a residential area to its north-east. Recently quite a number of huts have come up on the adjacent hill slopes. The total area is 157.06 acres with a population of 12,923. Density works out to 82.2 persons per acre. It has about 1,000 thatched huts and 800 *kutcha* and *pucca* houses. The hilly slope looks neat and clean because there is no stagnation of water. The lower plains area is dirty as there is no drainage. Except for three lanes, the roads are not metalled.

Out of the total population of 12,215, Malas number 1,350, Madigas 1,660, Pakees (scavengers) 500 and Rellis 150. Among these caste-groups, a good number are Christians. The rest belong to intermediate castes such as Nagara and Telaga.

The main occupations of the residents of this area are rickshaw pulling, casual labour, butchering (*kamela*) and sweeping (as employees of the municipality). The people belonging to intermediate castes are engaged in shopkeeping and contract labour.

Most of the residents of this slum are inmigrants from Krishna, Guntur, Prakasam and Visakhapatnam districts. The slum is said to have come up around 1910 and was named after a District Collector by name Tailor who allowed the inmigrants to settle down there.

Winch Peta (Census tract No. 8)

This is one of the oldest localities in the city being about 100 years old. But most of the huts came up in the 1930s. It is very near the main commercial centre as well as the railway station. It is surrounded by Tailor Peta (Census tract No. 6), Mahanti Puram (Census tract No. 7), Kotha Peta (Census tract No. 9), Lalapeta (Census tract No. 12) residential-cum-commercial area, Railway Land (Census tract No. 42) to its north, west, south-west. south and east respectively. It is spread over an area of 33.55 acres with a population of 12,992. Density works out at 385 persons per acre. It is the most dense slum, and it ranks third among high density areas in the city.

It has about 1,200 thatched huts and 740 *kutcha* and *pucca* houses. The huts are built in haphazard manner without any plan. There are no proper drainage facilities. Two roads are metalled. In the rainy season the area gets waterlogged.

Muslims constitute nearly 25 per cent of the total population and they are the single largest group in this slum with a population of 3,900. Scheduled castes and tribes constitute nearly 17 per cent of the total population. The relative strengths of these castes are as follows : Mala 850, Madiga 430, Yerukula 500 and Relli 310.

The residents are inmigrants from the adjacent areas of Krishna and Guntur districts. A sizeable number of the inhabitants are working as coolies and labourers in the railways. Muslims are small shopkeepers and butchers. The scheduled castes are employed as casual labour and as rickshaw pullers.

Baptist Palem (*Census tract No. 17*)
This is situated near the railway station. It is surrounded by railway land (Census tract No. 42) to its north, Kedareswara Peta (Census tract No. 18) residential-cum-commercial area to its north-east, Satyanarayana Puram (Census tract No. 23) residential area to its east, Seethanna Peta residential area to its south-east, and Purnanadam Peta (Census tract No. 16) residential area to its south. The slum came up around 1920.

The slum has a population of 10,114 spread over an area of 92.66 acres. Thus it records a density of 108 persons per acre. It has about 1,000 thatched huts and about 800 *kutcha* and *pucca* houses. The huts are built in clusters. The water gets stagnated in low-lying areas as there is no drainage. Only two roads are metalled.

Out of the total population of 10,114, Christians (many of them are Baptists) constitute nearly 50 per cent. There is a Baptist Church in the slum area and hence it is named as Baptist Palem. The scheduled castes constitute 10 per cent of the total population and many of the Christians are scheduled caste converts.

Many residents are employed as coolies in the railways. Others are engaged in lime work, rickshaw pulling and lorry driving. There are also about 50 Christian teachers.

The inhabitants of this slum are inmigrants from Krishna, Guntur and Prakasam districts.

Cement Factory Colony (*Census tract No. 20*)
This slum is of very recent origin. It came up in the 1950s. It is spread around the Cement Factory and the Timber Depots. It is situated in between Rajarajeswari Peta (Census tract No. 19), Mutyalampadu and Mutyalampadu Housing Colony (Census tracts No. 43 and No. 21), Satyanarayana Puram (Census tract No. 23) and Kedareswara Peta (Census tract No. 18) to its north, north-east, east, south-east and west respectively.

It covers an area of 132.43 acres with a population of 2,380. Its density accounts for 17.9 persons per acre, thus having the lowest density among all the slums. Out of the total population of 2,380, about 400 are Harijans, 100 are Yerukulas and 500 are Christians. The rest belong to different castes such as Telaga, Kamma, Reddi and Nagara.

The slum has 336 thatched huts and 147 *kutcha* houses. There are no proper roads nor drainage facilities in the locality. This is the only industrial slum in the city and many of the inhabitants work in the nearby cement factory. The rest of them are *mutha* (contract) labourers in timber depots.

Many of the inhabitants of this slum are migrants from Krishna, Guntur and Prakasam districts.

Giripuram (Census tract No. 35)

The slum came up around 1935. It is in continuation of and adjacent to Badava Peta (Census tract No. 36) and Wood Peta (Census tract No. 37) slum localities to the south-east of the city. It occupies an area of 5.92 acres, with a population of 1,190. Thus, the density of the slum works out to 201.0 persons per acre. From the point of view of density, it is the second among the slums, and occupies the eighth place among all the localities of the city. Out of the total population, 50 persons belong to the Mala caste and 350 to the Madiga caste. The rest are schedulded caste Christians.

It has in it 16 *kutcha* and *pucca* houses and 132 thatched huts. Because it is a low-lying area, the sullage water gets stagnated around the huts and in the streets. In the rainy season the condition becomes much worse. The roads are narrow, haphazard and not metalled. There is no drainage system in this slum.

The main occupations of the residents are leather work, rickshaw pulling and casual labour. There are a few taxi and lorry drivers.

The inhabitants are inmigrants from different districts such as Nalgonda, Khammam, Prakasam and Guntur.

Wood Peta (Census tract No. 36)

As already pointed out this slum is adjacent to Giri Puram and Badava Peta slums. This also came up around 1935 and was named after a District Collector by name Mr. Wood who allotted the land to the growing inmigrant population.

It is spread over an area of 23.60 acres and has a population of 2,094. The density works out at 88.7 persons per acre. Christians constitute roughly 25 per cent of the total population. Others belong to scheduled castes and scheduled tribes. There is one residential hostel for the scheduled tribes. It has in it 52 *kutcha* and *pucca* houses and 256 thatched huts. But the area looks clean and neat enough. Except for the huts it is in no way worse than many of the areas in the city which are not recognized as slums. There is no drainage system but the locality being situated on a mound, there is no problem of water stagnation. The main street is quite wide and black-topped and looks quite clean with *pucca* houses on either side. Only rear areas are somewhat congested. The residents are engaged in occupations like rickshaw pulling, low cadre services and casual labour. There are a good number of taxi and lorry drivers and school teachers, who own fairly decent houses. About half a dozen of them are college teachers.

The inhabitants are inmigrants from Guntur, Prakasam and Krishna districts.

Badava Peta (Census tract No. 37)

This slum came up around 1940. It is also situated adjacent to Giri Puram and Wood Peta slum localities.

It occupies an area of 32.96 acres. Its total population is 1,316. The density works out at 39 persons per acre, which is a little less than the average density of the city. Mala caste is the single largest caste-group with 600 persons. Next comes the Mala converted Christians. People belonging to the intermediate castes such as Telaga, Kamma and Reddi are also staying here. It has 30 *kutcha* and *pucca* houses and 245 huts. Roads are not metalled and there is no drainage system. Being a low lying area water gets stagnated in the streets. Most of the people are mechanics and fitters in Andhra Pradesh State Road Transport Corporation and Railways. There are about 40 school teachers. Some persons work as casual labourers and rickshaw-pullers. Many of the inhabitants are inmigrants from Krishna, Guntur, Prakasam and Khamman districts.

It is evident that the city of Vijayawada has been attracting population from not only the adjacent districts such as Guntur and Khammam but also from districts like Prakasam, Nalgonda and Visakhapatnam. Majority of the population in the eight slums belong to scheduled castes such as Mala and Madiga many of whom are converted Christians. There are also scheduled tribes such as Yerukula, Relli and Pakee.

The concentration of the scheduled castes and tribes is found in the slums of other cities also. More than 70 per cent of scheduled caste population of Madras live in slums and 37 per cent of the slum dwellers are the scheduled castes (Nambiar 1966). In the cities of Punjab most of the slum dwellers belonged to the scheduled caste (D'Souza 1976). In Vijayawada concentration of Muslims is to be found only in two slums. A sizeable number of the slum dwellers also belong to the intermediate castes such as Nagara, Telaga, Kamma and Reddi. Among other low castes Vadderas are in larger numbers.

The occupations followed by the residents of the slums reflect the dominant economic activities of the areas around. For example, a slum adjacent to the railway station has a sizeable population employed with the railways, and the residents of a slum adjacent to a commercial locality are engaged in contract and casual labour. In each slum, people belonging to a particular caste or religious group cluster together to a great extent, thus establishing identity within a slum. Such a formation promotes smooth intra-group interactions and ethnic cohesiveness.

The foregoing account shows that the hutment colonies and the localities consisting of a sizeable number of huts without civic amenities exhibit slum conditions. But the case of Woodpeta is slightly different from the others. Since it is situated on a mound and has broad roads it looks clean despite the lack of a drainage system. All the slums are predominantly inhabited by rural poor and unskilled migrants. The localities which are classified as slums by the municipality fall into the first category of our classificatory scheme mentioned earlier, namely, hutment colonies of migrants. However, there are some localities which consist of both *kutcha* and *pucca* houses, inhabited by the middle classes which may be considered as slums due to deteriorated conditions and the absence of satisfactory civic amenities. Though the third category of slums, namely, capsulated villages of fishermen or herdsmen and the like colonies are presently absent in the city, they are likely to emerge since the surrounding villages like Bhavanipuram, Gollapudi, Enamalakuduru, Ramavarappadu are going to be merged in the City Municipality. It may be mentioned that slums of this kind have already emerged in the city of Visakhapatnam in Andhra Pradesh (K. Ranga Rao and Raju 1971).

3

BHASKARA RAO PETA SLUM

PETA is one of the nine slums in Vijayawada City. It is situated very near Kaleswararao Market which is the main commercial centre in the city. It is surrounded by Bandaru Canal to its north, Krishna Lanka to its west, National Highway road to its south-west, Krishna river to its west and Vijayawada-Madras rail road to its east (see Map 3). Obviously there is no possibility for further expansion of the settlement on any side. As it is, about half of the houses are constructed on the railway land and the other half on the land belonging to the Department of the Roads and Buildings. The Railway Department has been constantly trying to evict the settlers with no success.

Peta has come up in the last quarter of the nineteenth century. It is said that around the year 1900 some people, belonging to Mala, Madiga and Vaddera castes from Guntur and Prakasam districts came to Vijayawada in search of livelihood. As this site was vacant they occupied the area and constructed their huts on it. Later some more scheduled caste families moved into this place from other parts of the city such as Kotha Peta and Mallikharjuna Peta, as they were forced to vacate these areas by the upper caste people. Since their caste people were already staying at Peta the scheduled castes migrants found it easier to settle down. The rate of inmigration has increased in course of time and people from Prakasam, Guntur and Krishna districts poured in. Some also came from Khammam and Nalgonda districts. Especially for the last thirty years (1940-70) there has been a heavy flow of inmigrants into Peta. The initial settlers helped their kin and

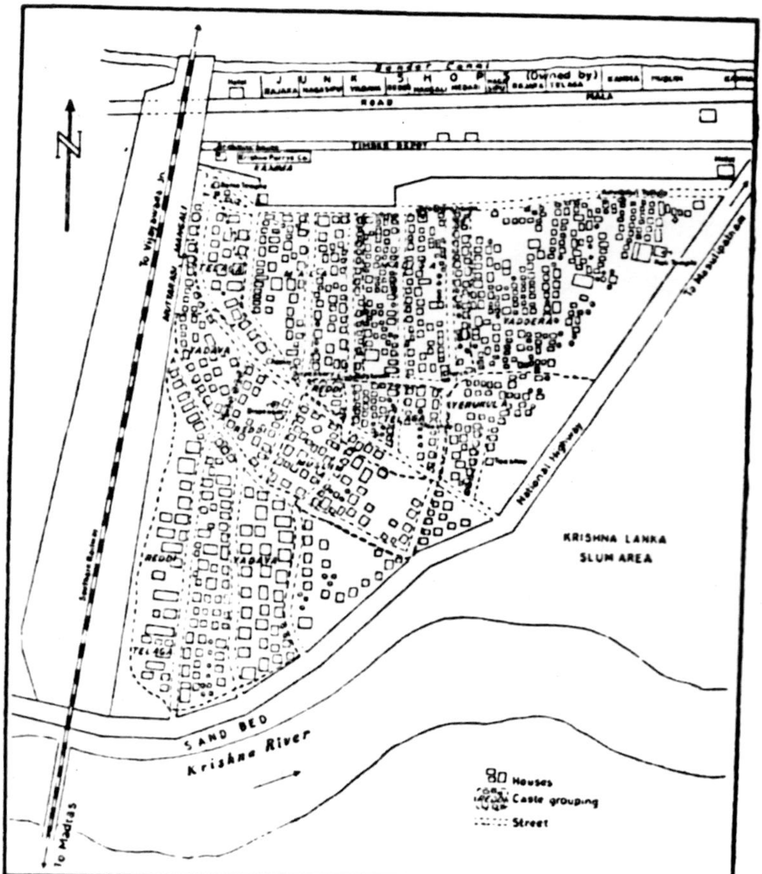

Map 3 : Bhaskar Rao Peta (not to scale)

castemen to move in. Besides, intermediate caste people such as Kammas, Reddis, Telagas and Yadavas also came into Peta. Muslims from rural areas also joined this stream of inmigrants. Thus in 1971 Peta had a population of 7,887 occupying an area of 166.31 acres with a density of 47.5 persons per acre.

There are 20 different Hindu castes, and one group of tribe and Muslims staying in Peta. The single largest caste is Vaddera with 263 households. Madiga caste occupies second place with 200 households. The relative strength of all the castes based on field census is given in Table 3.1.

Caste hierarchy

Taking the locally accepted norms of caste hierarchy Brahmin, Kshatriya and Vysya castes are shown as upper castes; Kamsali, Reddi, Kamma, Telaga, Kummari, Yadava, Nagasipu, Gauda, Nagara and Muttarasi as intermediate castes; Medari, Palli, Rajaka, Mangali and Vaddera as lower castes; Mala and Madiga as scheduled castes; and Yerukula as scheduled tribe.

Among the intermediate castes Reddi, Kamma, Telaga, Nagasipu are agricultural castes. Reddis are a numerically preponderant caste in Rayalaseema and Telangana regions of the state. It is one of the two important dominant castes along with Kamma in the state. Kammas are numerically strong in Krishna and Guntur districts. Telagas, another important cultivator caste, are preponderant in Krishna, East Godavari and West Godavari districts. Nagasipus are found only in Visakhapatnam district.

Kamsalis are goldsmiths by traditional occupation. Yadavas are largely cowherds and shepherds and some of them are also cultivators. The main occupation of Gaudas is toddy tapping. Vadderas are largely concentrated in Guntur and Prakasam districts. The Vaddera (earth workers) migrants are found even in metropolitan cities like Bombay and Bangalore.

Caste composition of Peta

While thirty-nine castes are represented in the sample of the socio-economic survey of the city, twenty castes are represented in Peta. The caste and tribal groups which are

TABLE 3.1 : Number of households according to castes in peta based on field census

Castes	Traditional occupation	Number of households	Per cent
Upper Castes			
Brahmin	Priesthood	3	0.2
Kshatriya	Agriculture	4	0.3
Vysya	Business	2	0.1
Intermediate Castes			
Kamsali	Goldsmithy	4	0.3
Reddi	Agriculture	152	10.5
Kamma	-do-	26	1.8
Telaga	-do-	144	9.9
Kummari	Pot-making	2	0.1
Nagasipu	Agriculture	38	2.6
Yadava	Agriculture, cowherd and shepherd	163	11.3
Gauda	Toddy-tapping	4	0.3
Nagara	Agriculture	3	0.2
Muttarasi	Fruit-selling	12	0 8
Lower Castes			
Medari	Basket-making	42	2.9
Palli	Fishing	3	0.2
Rajaka	Washerman	22	1.5
Mangali	Barber	12	0.8
Vaddera	Earth work	260	18.2
Scheduled Castes			
Mala	Agricultural labour and weaving	170	11.7
Madiga	Leather work	200	13.9
Scheduled Tribes			
Yerukula	Sooth-saying and Piggery	61	4.2
Others			
Muslims		118	8.2
Total		1,448	100.0

represented in the city sample but are absent in Peta are : Kayastha, Velama, Padmasali, Bodilis, Sisti Karanam, Mudaliar, Khatu, Vellala, Settibalija, Nadar, Kalavanthulu, Enka, Relli, Nagavallu, Gomalla, Gonda and scheduled tribes of Yenadi, Lambadi, and Buda Bukkala. The proportions of these caste groups in the city sample range between 0.1 per cent to 2.8 per cent. Thus these castes and tribes are numerically small in the city and no wonder that they are not represented in Peta. Some of these castes are also urban and well off.

There are some striking dissimilarities between the caste composition of the city and Peta. While the households of the three upper castes namely Brahmin, Kshatriya and Vysya together account for 20.7 per cent of the city sample, in Peta they account for just 0.6 per cent of the total households. The proportion of households belonging to intermediate castes, lower castes, scheduled castes and scheduled tribes to the total households of the sample in the city are 32.9 per cent, 9.6 per cent and 16.7 per cent as against 37.8 per cent, 23.6 per cent and 29.8 per cent respectively. Thus, while the representation of upper castes in Peta slum is almost negligible the proportion of lower castes and scheduled castes and scheduled tribes is higher by nearly two and a half times and twice respectively in Peta when compared to the city as a whole. Though the data on caste composition of individual census localities are not available, on the basis of the available data on caste composition of the slum localities, it can be surmised that the proportion of lower castes, scheduled castes and tribes would be much lower and the proportion of upper castes would be higher in the non-slum localities in the city.

The households of intermediate castes in the city sample from 32.9 per cent as against 37.8 per cent in Peta and thus the difference is very thin. However, certain intermediate castes appear to be numerically stronger in the city than those in Peta and *vice versa*. For example, Telagas are the single largest caste in the city with 14.9 per cent of the total households. But in Peta it is the sixth largest caste group with 9.9 per cent. The proportion of Kammas in the city sample and Peta are 5.8 per cent and 1.8 per cent respectively. Whereas Reddis and Yadavas are numerically large groups in Peta with 10.5 per cent and 11.3 per cent, they are numerically small groups in the city with 2.2 per cent and 0.5 per cent respectively. The relative preponderance of Reddis and Yadavas in the Peta slum compared to the city, could be due to the migration of the poor among these caste groups from agriculturally underdeveloped areas of Prakasam and Guntur districts into Peta.

The data on caste composition of the slums also suggest some significant differences between Peta and other slums. For example, three slums, namely, Giripuram, Woodpeta and Badava Peta are mostly, if not entirely, inhabited by the scheduled castes and scheduled tribes and the Christian converts of these groups. Out of the remaining five slums, only in Winch Peta Muslims constitute about 25 per cent of the total population, as against 8.2 per cent in Peta. In other slums, Muslims are either absent or form a very minor group.

The scheduled castes and the scheduled tribes and the Christian converts from these categories account for 30 per cent of the total population in Tailor Peta, 40 per cent in Cement Colony Area, 50 per cent in Winch Peta and 60 per cent in Baptist Palem. The other castes in these five slums are Reddi, Telaga, Nagara and Gauda. Thus the slums are by and large inhabited by scheduled castes and scheduled tribes, lower castes, and the poor belonging to intermediate castes, and Muslims. However, intermediate, lower and scheduled castes and tribes are substantially represented in Peta and hence it can be considered more heterogeneous than the other slums in the city.

Ecological distribution

There is a spatial segregation between clean castes and the untouchable castes in Peta. Normally the area of residence of the latter is separated from the former by lanes running in between. Thus the Malas, Madigas, Vadderas and Yerukulas are found residing in clearly demarcated areas. Along the railway tract are found the intermediate castes such as Reddis, Telagas and Yadavas, and Muslims. Even a stranger can easily notice the spatial separation between the scheduled castes and the intermediate castes. However, one intermediate caste is not spatially segregated from another. Depending upon the time of settlement, members of each caste constructed their own cluster of houses. The general tendency of each caste group, therefore, is to build their houses as closely as possible. Yadavas, Reddis and Telagas generally build houses in a single row. The Yadavas occupy a larger portion of the area and their settlements are found along the national highway. Other castes except Medaris are found in between and spread all over the locality.

In the comparatively new settlements along the canal, there are houses of Malas and Madigas in the midst of the intermediate castes such as Reddis, Telagas and Nagasipus. Here, the Scheduled Castes have built their houses first and subsequently others came in to settle down out of necessity. Even then, a fair measure of distance is maintained between Scheduled Castes and the others. This is in contrast with the absence of residential segregation by caste in a Madras slum (Wiebe 1975). But D'Souza (1976) reports segregation on caste lines in the slums of Chandigarh.

Housing pattern and other facilities

Almost the entire Peta consists of thatched mud huts. They number 1,170. As many as 1,448 households reside in them. There is a difference in the pattern of construction of the houses built by Reddis, Yadavas and Telagas on the one hand and those of other castes on the other. In the case of the former castes three to five households together construct a long structure and partition the same among themselves with one portion for each household. In the case of others each household builds its own separate hut. The huts of some of the Yerukulas, however, look different being conical in shape while the others are more or less rectangular, as the Yerukulas prefer to maintain their tribal identity.

The houses are constructed without any plan. With the result there is no straight passage or road anywhere except at the north-west side. No straight road is laid as such. The entire area gets slushy during the rainy season. For want of drainage facilities even in other seasons sullage water-logging takes place at various places. The entire locality is a low-lying area with high level roads on two sides and a railway tract on the third. During the rainy season water is supposed to flow towards the Krishna river but because of some obstruction at the bank, the water does not easily flow into the river. There is not even an open drainage for the discharge of sullage.

The municipality takes no interest in removing the waste or rubbish thrown on the streets. Normally each household tries to clean the street in front of its own hense. There are no street dust bins. Except for half-a-dozen *pucca* houses, others have no lavatories. Both men and women use the river and canal banks and the railway tracks for toilet purposes. A majority of the houses do not have any bathrooms. Only a few of them enclose small areas behind or by the side of or in front of the houses with palm leaves or bamboo curtains and use the same as bathrooms. However, only females use such enclosures. Males take their bath on the streets in the open. In such of those houses which do not have any enclosures women take their bath mostly at night erecting a temporary enclosure with the help of a cot or with a cloth curtain supported by poles.

Main social demographic features of Peta inhabitants

In this section we shall describe the household composition and type, marital status, age, literacy and education of the people of Peta on the basis of 362 sample households distributed over 13 Hindu castes, and Muslims, and forming 25 per cent of the total households.

For the sample households covered under the study, the average size of the household works out at 4.3 ranging between 3.6 (Nagasipu) and 5.7 (Mangali). The size of the intermediate caste households is comparatively smaller than that of the lower caste ones. In the intermediate castes the size varies from 3.6 (Nagasipu) to 4.6 (Kamma). But in the case of lower and scheduled castes with the exception of the Madigas where the size is 3.6, the household size ranges from 4.7 (Mala) to 5.7 (Mangali). The relative size of the sample households in different caste groups is given in Table 3.2.

The nuclear households account for 75 per cent (Table 3.3.) This shows that the urban slum household is largely nuclear (Woodruff 1960; Wiebe 1975). The percentage of the extended and compound households works out at 17.0 per cent and 8.0 per cent respectively. The extended households include joint families with the ego plus (a) married sons, (b) married brothers,

TABLE 3.2 : **Caste and size of the sample households in Peta**

Caste	No. of households	No. of persons	Size of the households
Kamsali	2	8	4.0
Reddi	50	201	4.0
Kamma	10	46	4.6
Telaga	30	114	3.8
Kummari	2	8	4.0
Yadava	55	233	4.0
Nagasipu	15	54	3.6
Medari	10	47	4.7
Rajaka	5	26	5.2
Mangali	3	17	5.7
Vaddera	50	251	5.0
Mala	60	286	4.7
Madiga	50	186	3.6
Muslim	20	87	4.4
Total	362	1,564	4.3

TABLE 3.3 : **Types of sample households**

Name of the caste	Nuclear household		Extended household		Compound household		Total
	No.	%age	No.	%age	No.	%age	
Kamsali	2	100.0	—	—	—	—	2
Reddi	34	63.0	6	12.0	10	20.0	50
Kamma	6	60.0	1	10.0	3	30.0	10
Telaga	26	83.3	3	10.0	2	6.7	30
Kammari	2	100.0	—	—	—	—	2
Yadava	42	76.4	5	9.1	8	14.5	55
Nagasipu	13	86.7	2	13.3	—	—	15
Medari	5	50.0	5	50.0	—	—	10
Rajaka	5	100.0	—	—	—	—	5
Mangali	2	66.7	1	33.3	—	—	3
Vaddera	31	62.0	16	32.0	3	3.0	50
Mala	40	66.7	17	28.3	3	5.0	60
Madiga	45	90.0	5	10.0	—	—	50
Muslim	19	90.0	1	10.0	—	—	20
Total	271	75.0	62	17.0	29	8.0	362

and (c) married and unmarried brothers. There are only eight (2.1 per cent of the total) extended households which include parents and married daughters. In the compound households we come across all sorts of relatives near and far, affinal and non-affinal. But among the 13 castes and Muslims under study eight (Kamsali, Kummari, Nagasipu, Medari, Rajaka, Mangali, Madiga and Muslim) have no compound households at all. The extended household is completely absent among the Kamsali, Kummari and Rajaka castes. The strength of these three castes is quite small (2.5 per cent of the total households studied). The percentage of nuclear households among different caste groups varies from 50 per cent (Medari) to 95 per cent (Muslim). Among the Kamsali, Kummari and Rajaka, it is 100 per cent.

The intermediate castes show a higher percentage of nuclear households, and the percentage ranges from 60 per cent to 100 per cent. The lower and scheduled castes, on the contrary, show a lesser percentage which varies from 50 to 66.5 with the single exception of the Madigas where it is as high as 90.0. This also means that the number of nuclear households is less in the case of comparatively old settlers such as Vadderas (62%), Malas (66.6%) and Medaris (50%) and is higher in the case of new settlers such as Yadavas (76.4%), Telagas (83.3%) and Nagasipus (86.7%). But for certain minor variations, it appears that the intermediate castes tend to migrate in nuclear households and still have a large number of relatives back at home.

The ratio of females to males in Peta is close to that of slums in Madras where it is 959 : 1000 (Aranganannal 1976 : 14) but varies from the large cities such as Delhi, Calcutta and Bombay. For example, in Delhi the ratio is 768 : 1000 and in Calcutta it is 721 : 1000 (Singh and deSouza 1980).

Males constitute 50.1 per cent of our total sample population whereas females constitute 49.9 per cent. It is not quite different from the overall sex-ratio in Peta which is at 51.4 : 48.6. If we take the number of females in different castes, it varies from 41.0 per cent (Mangali) to 54.5 per cent (Yadavas). The number of males is the lowest among the Yadavas (45.5%) and highest among the Mangali (59.0%). But generally there are no significant differences, the range being between 48 and 52 per cent, in most of the castes.

About 16 per cent of the total sample population (252 out of 1,564) are under five years of age and 22.4 per cent (348/1,564) are between the ages of six and fourteen years. Children thus account for 38.4 per cent (600/1,564) of the total persons. The persons who are in between 15 years and 25 years of age account for 24.3 per cent (379 out of 1,564) and another 31 per cent (484/1,564) are between 26 years and 50 years. Thus the population in the active working age-group of 15 to 50 years account for about 55 per cent (863/1,564). The persons who are above 50 years constitute only 6.3 per cent (99/1,564) of the total population. There are, however, only 2.3 per cent (16/664) people above 50 years of age in the intermediate castes whereas in the lower and scheduled castes they constitute 8.3 per cent (69/751). Thus among the intermediate castes the percentage of working population is larger than that among the lower and scheduled caste groups.

In the age-group of 6 to 14 years, only 10 persons are married out of 340 and account for 2.9 per cent. All these married persons are females. Out of these ten, nine belong to lower and scheduled castes such as Medari, Rajaka, Vaddera, Mala, and Madiga. Thus the incidence of child marriage is limited to the lower castes. The remaining one case belongs to the Reddi caste. No cases of widowhood and divorce are reported in this age-group.

In the age-group of 15 and 25 years, 72.5 per cent (275/379) are married and 24.5 per cent (93/379) are unmarried and only 3 per cent (11/379) are either widowed or divorced. Among the males of the intermediate castes in the age-group of 15 and 25 years, while 43 per cent (31/72) are married, 57 per cent (41/72) are unmarried. But among the males of lower and scheduled castes nearly 60 per cent (54/91) are ever-married and 57.2 per cent (52/91) are married, 2.3 per cent (2/91) are widowed and only a little more than 40 per cent (37/91) are unmarried. It shows that the age of marriage is higher in the intermediate castes than in the lower and scheduled castes. For the same reason among the lower and scheduled castes, the percentage of married is higher than that in the intermediate castes. Among the nine persons belonging to the Muslim group, four each are unmarried and married, and one is a widower.

The number of persons who are above 26 years is 583, and among them 99.7 per cent (581/583) are ever-married and only 0.3 per cent (2/583) are unmarried. Out of the total ever-married, 88.5 per cent (514/581) are married and 11.5 per cent (67) are either divorced or widowed.

On the whole among the persons who are above 14 years of age (964) 90.2 per cent are ever-married and 9.8 per cent are unmarried. Further, married persons account for 81.9 per cent, and 8.3 per cent are either widowed or divorced. But there is only a slight variation in the percentage of married, unmarried and widowed or divorced between the intermediate castes and lower and scheduled castes. Among the intermediate castes, the married constitute 83.2 per cent (347/417), unmarried are 10.8 per cent (45/417) and widowed/divorced are only 6 per cent (25/417). In lower and scheduled castes the percentage of unmarried is less and widowed/divorced is slightly higher than that among the intermediate castes. In this group the married account for 81 per cent (404/499), unmarried for 8.7 per cent (44/499) and widowed/divorced for 10.3 per cent (51/499).

A consideration of the marital status by sex shows that among males a little less than 80 per cent (399/502) are married and 16.7 per cent (84/502) are unmarried and only 3.8 per cent (19/502) are either widowed/divorced. But the number of married females is a little higher than that of the males (84.7 per cent—391/462). Similarly the number of widowed/divorced is about four times higher than that of males. There are about 13.2 per cent (61/462) widowed or divorced females whereas in males it is only 3.8 per cent (19/502). The unmarried females are only 10 (a little more than 2%) out of 462, whereas there are 84 unmarried (16.7%—502) males. Within the intermediate castes, there is only one case of a widower (out of 215). In the males of lower and scheduled castes there are 16 persons widowed and only two divorced. Among the females of the intermediate castes there are 24 widows and no divorced (out of 202 women), whereas there are 32 widows and 2 divorcees (out of 238) among the lower and scheduled castes. It is difficult to come to any basic conclusion, as divorce, remarriage and widow remarriage are permitted among all these castes. The greater number of widows among the lower and scheduled castes will have to be seen in relation to the age and most of them are above the productive age.

As pointed earlier 1,564 persons were covered under the sample study. Of these 252 were in the age-group of five years and below and the remaining 1,312 were above five years of age. So in order to find out the rate of literacy, 1,312 persons of above five years of age only were taken into consideration.

Out of 1,312 people nearly 75 per cent (982/1,312) were illiterate while 18.6 per cent (244/1,312) received primary education that is up to fifth standard, 5.2 per cent (68/1,312) received middle school level education that is sixth standard to eighth standard, and only 1.4 per cent (18/1,312) had education up to secondary level—ninth standard to S.S.L.C.

The proportion of literates among males is far higher than that of the females. While 39 per cent (262/672) of the males are literate, only 10.6 per cent (68/640) of females are literate. Of the total male population, those who received primary, middle and secondary education were 27.9, 8.4 and 2.7 per cent respectively. It is important to note that nearly 60 per cent (74/124) of the males of the Mala caste are literates. Of the total literates, 42.7 per cent (53/124) received primary education, 11.3 per cent (14/124) received middle education and 5.7 per cent (7/124) received secondary level education. Of the 18 persons who received secondary education, seven are from Mala caste and six from Madiga caste. The high rate of educated males of the Mala caste accounts for more number of people in salaried jobs. As many as 24.67 per cent (19/77) earning males of the Mala caste are in salaried jobs. For the above reason it is interesting to note that about 60.6 per cent (166/274) of the males among the intermediate castes had no education. Among males of the lower and scheduled castes, 58.6 per cent (214/365) are illiterate. Within the intermediate castes, there is a greater proportion of educated males in the Telaga caste (53.5%), and lowest in the Nagasipu caste (20.8%). Among the lower castes, the males of Rajaka and Vaddera castes show a very poor level of education that is 7.1 per cent and 14.0 per cent respectively.

Out of the total number of females above the age of 5 in the sample, only 10.6 per cent (63/640) are literate. Further, among them 8.7 per cent (56/640) and 1.9 per cent (12/640) received primary and middle education respectively. No case of any female receiving secondary education is reported. Among the females of the intermediate castes, literates are 12.4 per cent (34), whereas among the lower caste females they account for 9.1 per cent (31). But out of the total 31 literates from the lower and scheduled castes, 23 are from the Mala caste and six are from Madiga caste. Among the Medari and Vaddera castes not even a single woman is literate. Again, out of 12 women who received middle education, six and two are from Mala and Madiga castes respectively. Among all the intermediate castes there are only four women (out of 12) who received middle level education. The higher literacy rate among the Malas is due to their contact with and conversion to Christianity.

Out of a total number of persons who are in the age group of six to fourteen years, 30 per cent (105/350) are receiving primary education and 4.6 per cent are receiving middle level education. Those who are not receiving any sort of education account for 65.4 per cent. So the number of persons receiving education in this age group is 34.6 per cent as against the percentage of 24.4 in the age-group between 15 and 25 years, 20.0 per cent in the age-group between 26 and 50 years and 12.0 per cent in the age-group above 50 years. It clearly reveals the fact that the percentage of the educated is on the increase. The proportion of the educated in the age-group of 6 to 14 years is multiplied by nearly three times when compared to the age-group of above 50 years of age where it is only 12 per cent.

The educational status of persons has a close relationship with employment. While 38.4 per cent (600/1,564) of the total sample population are in the age-group of 14 years and below, the rest are in the age-group of 15 years and above. Thus 61.4 per cent (964) of the sample population are in the working age-group. The total number of earners in the working age group is 65.8 per cent (634/964). While as many as 98.4 per cent (494/502) of the males in the working age-group are earners, the female earners account for only 30.3 per cent (140/462). Caste-wise, while the percentage of the male earners varies from 84.3 (Malas) to 100.0 (Vadderas and Medaris), that of females ranges between a mere 2.8 (Telagas) and 100.0 (Vadderas and Medaris). None of the females of Kamsali, Reddi, Kummari, Yadava, Nagasipu, Mangali castes is an earner. Thus among the lower castes and particularly among Medari and Vaddera castes, a majority of the women in the working age-group are engaged in gainful employment. In these caste-groups, child labour is also prevalent both among the males and females. Child labour is almost non-existent among the Malas and Madigas since good many of their children go to school. Women labour among these scheduled caste groups is limited to about 30 per cent. Among the intermediate castes only three out of 202 women in the working age-group are earners. Thus lower caste women show a higher participation in work than the intermediate and scheduled caste women. Before we discuss the occupational pattern let us analyse the migration patterns of Peta slum dwellers in terms of process and purpose of migration.

4

MIGRATION PATTERNS AND PETA SETTLEMENT

MIGRATION is the key process by which people belonging to certain socio-economic backgrounds move to cities and find their way into slums. With a view to obtaining a general picture of the process of migration into Peta a brief historical account of the inmigrants and the areas from which the slum-dwellers arrived is given. Detailed analysis of the migratory process is based on the data collected through a special schedule from a sub-sample of 292 heads of first generation migrant households spread over 13 Hindu castes and one group of Muslims.

Generation-wise details of migration for each caste and for Muslims are shown in Table 4.1. The total number of households in Peta is 1,448. Among them, heads of 801 households (53.3%) are first generation migrants, 556 (38.4%) are second generation migrants, and 91 (6.3%) are third generation migrants. Vaddera, Madiga and Mala are the oldest inmigrants to Peta. Other castes followed them slowly. Continuous inflow is found mostly among the Mala, Madiga, Reddi, Yadava, Telaga, Medari, Nagasipu, Kamma, Rajaka and Mangali castes, and Muslims.

Places of origin of different castes

The members of all the castes have migrated from different districts within the state of Andhra Pradesh. There are only two heads of households who have migrated from outside the state—a Brahmin from Orissa and a Mangali, who originally

TABLE 4.1 : Caste and migration patterns of all castes

Caste	First generation migrants	Second generation migrants	Third generation migrants	Total
Brahmin	3	—	—	3
Kshatriya	3	1	—	4
Vysya	2	—	—	2
Kamsali	2	2	—	4
Reddi	130	22	—	152
Kamma	26	—	—	26
Telaga	96	48	—	144
Kummari	2	—	—	2
Yadava	139	24	—	163
Muttarasi	—	12	—	12
Nagara	3	—	—	3
Nagasipu	38	—	—	38
Gauda	5	—	—	4
Medari	27	15	—	42
Rajaka	12	10	—	22
Mangali	6	6	—	12
Vaddera	58	154	51	263
Palli	3	—	—	3
Yerukula	—	61	—	61
Mala	110	44	16	170
Madiga	82	98	20	200
Muslim	55	59	4	118
Total	801	556	91	1448

belonged to Andhra Pradesh, from Rangoon. We discern three patterns of movements of people within the state :

(i) all or a majority of those who have migrated from different Taluks within the Krishna district;

(ii) all or a majority of those who have migrated from particular Taluks within one district; and

(iii) those who have migrated from several different districts within the State.

The first category includes such castes as Kshatriya, Vysya, Gauda and Palli, and Muslims. The second category includes Yadavas, and Reddis coming from Prakasam district;

Nagaras, Nagasipus, Kamsalis, Kummaris and Medaris coming from Visakhapatnam district; Vadderas, Muttarasi and Yerukulas coming from Guntur district; and Rajaka coming from Prakasam district. The third category includes six castes—Brahmins, Telaga, Kamma, Mangali, Mala and Madiga. Members of these castes have migrated from several districts far and near—Krishna, Guntur, Prakasam, Khammam, Nalgonda, Karimnagar, West Godavari, East Godavari, Visakhapatnam and Srikakulam.

Thus while certain caste groups exhibit features of homogeneity in terms of their members coming from the same taluk or district, others show the features of heterogeneity as their members come from different districts, some of whom belong to other sub-castes. However, in the place of destination the inmigrants establish their identity on the basis of their caste.

Purpose of migration

For analysing the motivations behind migration we shall depend on our sample data from 292 first generation migrants who constitute a large majority (80%) of the inmigrants. According to the answers given by the respondents the information is classified into four categories: for livelihood, for higher income, for specific employment and others.

Those who had no work to do and no employment opportunities to earn their livelihood in their native villages came to Vijayawada in search of livelihood. About 77 per cent (225/292) of the self-migrants belong to this category. A majority of the persons belonging to the intermediate castes such as Reddi, Kamma, Telaga, Nagasipu and some from Yadava and Muslims were either agricultural labourers or small farmers at their native places. The people belonging to lower and scheduled castes such as Medari, Vaddera, Mala and Madiga were mainly engaged in their traditional occupations and agricultural labour.

Those who were already employed back at their homes, came to the city to earn higher incomes. This category works out at 8.3 per cent (24 out of 292). Among the Mala and Madiga castes the percentage of this category comes to 14 per cent (6 out of 43) and 13.9 per cent (4 out of 29) respectively.

Those who came to the city in search of some specific employment account for 7.5 per cent. These are the people who had some kind of education or some training and skills. Out of the 21 persons in this category, nine belong to Mala caste. Of the remaining twelve, five are Reddis, three Telagas, two Yadavas, and one each is a Madiga and a Muslim.

The other reasons include transfers, and nearness to work-place. This category accounts for 7.2 per cent of the self-migrants.

The first two categories, namely, those who came for livelihood and for higher income (85.3%) are almost of the same type with a minor difference. Those who are said to have come in search of livelihood were finding it difficult to make a living and thus were almost unemployed in the previous places of habitation. Some of them owned some landed property but their economic conditions were very bad because of drought conditions. Those who said that they came for higher incomes were very much underemployed at their respective places and wanted to have full employment and more income.

Associational migration

Out of 292 self-migrants, 30.8 per cent (90) came alone when they migrated. This tendency is predominant among the Reddis, Kammas and Madigas. Those who are reported to have come with relatives included persons of various castes who were either married or unmarried. Thus 66.6 per cent of Vadderas and 25 per cent of Madigas migrated along with relatives.

Out of the 292 self-migrants, 72.2 per cent (211 out of 292) said that they had some acquaintances in the city before they migrated. Among the intermediate castes about 68 per cent (121 out of 164) had acquaintances, whereas among the lower and scheduled castes around 79 per cent (85 out of 108) had prior acquaintances.

The major caste groups with higher percentages of migrants having prior acquaintances are : Nagasipu (93%), Mala (86%), Telaga (76%), Vaddera (72%), Muslims (70%), Reddis (68%), Madiga (67%), and Yadava (63%). As noted earlier, among the Vadderas and Madigas second and third generation migrants are more in number than among others. Moreover, migration process among these two castes started long ago around 1900. Nowadays we find that Malas, Telagas, Reddis and Yadavas are inmigrating more and in numbers. All the Kammas and Nagasipus are first generation migrants. Thus, while among Vadderas and Madigas and also to some extent among the Malas the acquaintances were largely of second and third generation people of their own caste and kinsmen, among the other castes many of the acquaintances belonged to first generation itself, mostly limited to one's own caste or village.

Taking the overall view, it appears that relatively lower castes depend more upon prior acquaintances for migration than the relatively upper castes. Our data show that, as against 90 per cent of the lower and scheduled caste heads of households, only 68 per cent heads of the intermediate castes had acquiantances in the city prior to inmigration. This would mean that while caste and kinship loyalties are strong among all categories of the population, they are much stronger among the lower castes.

The occupational distribution of 211 heads who had prior acquiantances in the city is like this : *mutha* labourers 58 per cent, salaried jobs 9.4 per cent, hereditary occupations 9.0 per cent, casual labourers 7.6 per cent and miscellaneous category 16.0 per cent. In a majority of the cases, the occupation of the acquaintances in the city has a direct bearing on the occupation of the migrants. For instance, among the Reddis, Telagas, Yadavas and Nagasipus the occupation of the majority of the acquaintances was contract labour and for the same reason the occupation of the majority of the migrants in these castes is also contract labour. The same trend is generally observed in other castes also. Thus our previous conclusion that the acquaintances living in the town, help absorb the migrants into their own occupational categories is valid. This is the strong reason why the same caste people prefer to live in the same area notwithstanding the congestion and unhygienic conditions.

Our data also reveal that among the total acquaintances, as high as 94.3 per cent were the residents of Peta and only 5.7 per cent were the residents of other areas among which Chitti Nagar is prominent. This again shows why the migrants continue to pour into this slum. It is also found that persons who have some hereditary skills such as leather work, basket-making, washing and hair-cutting engage themselves in occupations requiring these skills. Where individuals have multiple skills, they explore the one which is more profitable. For instance, although the Madigas have the skill in leather work, only a few of them take to leather work for the reason that the training they have had is not modern enough so as to enable them to compete in the urban market and earn enough money. However, some of them take to drumming (*dappu*) on various functions and this fetches them a fairly good amount of money.

The foregoing account reveals that most of the migrants selected Peta as the area of their residence because their caste people and near relatives were already residing there. This is how slums continuously absorb the people on caste, kinship, occupational and regional lines.

Choice of Peta for residence

With a view to probing further into the reasons for choosing Peta for their residence, the inmigrants were asked to specifically state the purpose of their stay in this slum. Many gave more reasons than one. We have pointed out earlier that a majority of the Reddis, Telagas, Yadavas, Nagasipus and about 50 per cent of the Vadderas are recruited as *mutha* labourers and sand labourers. Those who are *mutha* labourers work in the nearby market and in the case of the sand labourers the work spot is the river bed which is close by. The Rajakas also depend upon the nearby river or canal for washing clothes. As such, we find that more than 80 per cent of the residents prefer continuous residence in Peta. Availability of free plot for putting up the huts was also an important factor. About 30 per cent of the Vadderas and a majority of the Malas and Madigas who are either earth-workers, casual labourers or junk collectors prefer this place mainly because of the presence of their relatives. Many of the intermediate castes are relatively new migrants and they do not mention availability of free space as one of the factors. But, for them cheaper rent was an important factor. Hence, for all practical purposes, nearness of work-spot, presence of the river Krishna, and availability of free plot to put up a hut are the major factors in the choice of Peta as the place of residence. Vadderas, more than others, expressed more sentimental attachment to this area since they were the first settlers of Peta and claim to be the rightful owners of the area.

The migration process in Peta gives a different picture from that of slums in large cities like Bombay (Desai and Pillai 1972), Delhi (Bharat Sevak Samaj, 1958), Madras (Nambiar 1966) and Chandigarh (D'Souza 1968). Slums in these cities attracted migrants from various states near and far (see Singh and de Souza 1980 : 26-30). In Peta, on the contrary, with two exceptions all the migrants are from within the state. This difference may be attributed to the distinct nature of Vijayawada which is neither a metropolis nor a state capital.

With a view to providing a comparative picture on various aspects of migration like the factors causing migration, acquaintances of the migrants in the city, and the mode of migration, the data on the migrants in Peta and the migrants in the city are compared. The data on the migrants are taken from the sample study of the *Socio-Economic Survey of Vijayawada City*.

In the Peta sample those who migrated to the city in search of livelihood or for higher income, account for 85.3 per cent and those who migrated for specific employment account for only 7.2 per cent. In the city sample, 64.0 per cent of the migrants came to the city for employment, 14.1 per cent on account of transfer, 6.5 per cent for business, 6.5 per cent along with parents, 3.7 per cent because of marriage and 2.6 per cent for education. It is important to note that in Peta the reasons related to employment account for 92.5 per cent of the migrants as against 64.0 per cent in the city sample. Secondly, as the government employees constitute a small proportion among the migrants in Peta, transfer as a reason for moving into the city is negligible whereas the same reason accounts for 14 per cent of the migrants in the city sample. Education and business as factors causing migration are absent among the reasons stated by the migrants in the Peta sample.

Among the migrants in the city sample, only 33.6 per cent had acquaintances in the city prior to migration. The corresponding figure for Peta is 72.2 per cent. These figures further support our observation made earlier regarding the importance of acquaintances, caste and kinship ties in the process of migration among lower castes and poorer sections.

Out of 292 migrants in the Peta sample those who came alone, those who came with spouses and children, those who came with relatives, those who came with friends, and co-villagers account for 30.8 per cent, 45.5 per cent, 22.3 per cent and 1.4 per cent respectively. The corresponding figures for the city sample are 20.6 per cent, 55.1 per cent, 26.3 per cent and 0.1 per cent. These figures show that a larges number of the migrants in Peta migrated alone and a lesser number with spouses and children and parents when compared to migrants in the city sample.

In the second visit to the field in 1977, by the investigator it was found that the process of inmigration into Peta had been continuing. The flow of inmigration is found among Reddi, Telaga, Yadava, Nagasipu, Vaddera, Mala, and Madiga castes and also among Muslims. The number of heads of households who migrated into Peta during 1972-77 ranged between 10 among Muslims and 30 belonging to Nagasipu caste. Most of the migrants had prior acquaintances in the city and moved with their families into Peta.

Contacts with the places of origin

The degree to which the residents maintain contacts with their native villages depends upon three factors : (1) the duration of their stay in the city, (2) their economic interests in the villages and (3) the presence of close relatives in the places of origin. Depending upon these factors various caste groups exhibit different degrees of attachment and contacts with their natal villages. Among Vaddera, Madiga and Muslims who have a greater number of second and third generation migrants, and among Yerukula and Mutharasi who have no first generation migrants there is a tendency of having most of their close relatives like parents, children and brothers and sisters living in Peta. For them, Peta is as good as their native place. Besides, these groups do not have any property in the villages and consequently their contacts with the places of origin are not strong. The relatively old settlers such as these, normally do not go in for matrimonial alliances for their children outside the city.

The households belonging to the caste groups such as Reddi, Kamma, Yadava, Telaga and Nagasipu which have more of first generation migrants, have their close relatives in their places of origin and have economic interests in their villages also. Some of them have houses and lands and thus they tend to have stronger economic and social bonds with their places of origin. During 1972-77 twenty households each from Reddi, Kamma and Yadava caste groups returned to their villages for cultivating their lands, after having saved money from their earnings from urban occupations. The persons belonging to these intermediate caste groups still prefer matrimonial alliances from their places of origin. For example, Reddis and Yadavas get their daughters married in their villages and bring their sons-in-law to the city and help them get jobs.

Out of the total 362 heads covered under the major sample, 27 per cent have their parents and 41.7 per cent have their brothers and sisters staying at their native places. Only two heads, one each from Telaga and Muslim groups, have their children at their native places. Those who have relatives other than the above-mentioned categories back at home, account for 20.7 per cent.

All the intermediate castes, which have more recent migrants, have close relatives in their respective native places. And they visit their native place more frequently than the lower caste people do. Among the Reddis 54 per cent visit their native places twice a year and 32 per cent once a year. Those who never visit account for only 12 per cent. Among the Khammas 50 per cent visit twice a year and 30 per cent once a year. Those who make visits once a year account for 68 per cent among the Yadavas and 87 per cent among Nagasipus. While 30 per cent of Telagas make one visit a year, 27 per cent of them make it twice a year.

Thus, on the whole, good many people belonging to intermediate castes visit their native places comparatively more frequently than the lower caste people. It reveals the fact that they have still both social and economic interests in their native places. Among the lower castes Malas have more contacts with their native places and families. In a way their job facilitates frequent visits. When they visit different villages for purchase of scrap iron, on their way they visit their relatives in the villages. Among the other castes only about 30 per cent visit their native places once a year. Thus among the lower castes the relationships with the families in the villages are slender. Earlier we found that among the lower castes both close agnatic and affinal relations have settled down in good numbers in Peta and as such they do not seem to feel it necessary to visit their native villages.

Only about 5 per cent of the total number of heads (19/362) have obligations to their families at their native places. Out of nineteen heads, eleven heads send an amount to the tune of Rs. 300 per annum and seven heads send an amount between Rs. 301 and Rs. 600 and two heads send more than Rs. 600 to their parents in their native places. Thus, by and large, the inhabitants of Peta have no economic obligations to the members of their families residing in their native villages. A majority of them are in low income groups at the marginal subsistence level, and also they do not have close relatives staying at their places of origin.

Return migration

It is erroneous to think that once a migrant is always a migrant and those who migrate to the city will settle down in the city or migrate to other bigger cities. For various reasons, some of the migrants go back to their villages either permanently or temporarily.

From the data collected in 1977 that is, after a gap of five years from the first phase of the field work, it was found that 20 households from the intermediate castes such as Reddi, Kamma and Yadava went back to their villages with their savings in the city and invested it in agriculture, as most of these return migrants owned lands in their villages. Such cases come under the category of development migration (M.S.A. Rao 1976). There were also instances of return migration among the lower castes. The reasons for return migration in these cases were insufficient income and termination of employment or lack of work in the city. Connell *et al.* found that in India many return to villages "when they fail to get jobs or find life in the city unattractive" (Connell *et al.* 1976 : 161).

DISCUSSION

The foregoing analysis of the data on migration reveals that many of the inmigrants finding their way into slums are the people who have little or no technical skill or educational and other qualifications. A majority of the inmigrants especially among the lower castes moved into the city along with their kith and kin in search of regular employment. However, the cultivators who have some means of livelihood back at home, move alone into the city initially, and only after making sure that the means of livelihood are regular and better in the town, bring their families. Many of them still maintain contacts with their native places and occasionally visit them.

The process of migration in Peta shows that different sections of people moved because of diverse reasons. The major factor in moving from rural areas is no doubt economic. But it is not simply wage differential or expected higher wages as Harris and Todaro (1970) would posit. But what looms large in the minds of the rural working class is the prospect of getting regular employment and food for subsistence. The prospect of getting better income from urban jobs operates as a factor only among those who have some land to cultivate. In such cases the urban income should be considered supplementary to the rural. One basic limitation of the economic explanation is that it does not explain why among people who are placed in similar economic positions at the place of origin, some move and others do not.

Migration, however, does not actualize mainly because of perceived economic advantages but with the support network of caste, kin and regional contacts. A big majority of the inmigrants in Peta had such acquaintances. More often than not the acquaintances were their relatives. The choice of the occupation of the inmigrant is also conditioned by the occupation of the acquaintance. Thus a close group of relatives tend to follow the same occupation and reside in the same locality. The importance of the kin network in the recruitment of inmigrants to jobs and the choice of locality for residence is also evident. Availability of vacant land for constructing huts or availability of cheap housing near the work spot further strengthens the desire of the residents to continue to stay in the same place irrespective of the congestion and unhygienic conditions.

We have noted that some of the migrants returned to their villages, many settled down permanently in Peta, and still others had interest both in Peta and in the villages of origin. Whether or not a migrant settles down in the slum is a function of factors such as the skills he has at the time of migration, the skills he acquires after migration, the opportunities open to him in the town and his interests back home in the native village. At the beginning of the migration process one's own perceptions about the opportunities at the place of destination and an evaluation of one's perceptions of the life there in relation to the existential conditions at the place of origin form a stimulus for movement. In the case of lower classes relatives and friends are the important reference points and sources of their perceptions regarding the chances available at the place of destination. As regards the educated, their very knowledge and skill and their experiences of urban life act as the stimuli for movement to towns and cities. As such the dependence of the upper class and educated on their kith and kin in the places of destination may be insignificant when compared with that of the lower class uneducated migrants. Some of the migrants who have interests in land back at home may, after making sufficient earnings in the town, either go back to the village permanently or continue to live in the town and have an interest in the village as well. Urban areas with a variety of jobs available throughout the year allow migrants from rural areas to work in any capacity and earn a livelihood. Since these and possibly many other factors need to be taken into account in the analysis of the migration process, a simple push-pull dichotomous explanation of the process does not yield fruitful results.

5

OCCUPATIONAL PATTERNS, WORK ORGANISATION AND MOBILITY

WE SHALL discuss in this chapter the occupational patterns of Peta inhabitants, in terms of caste occupations, income and occupational mobility.

As the city is mainly a centre of trade, commerce and transport, the occupations followed by the inhabitants of Peta are by and large related to these activities. Both road and rail transport activity require a large number of manual labourers to load and unload goods and this demand is largely met by the rural unskilled migrants. The road transport activity also throws open opportunities to skilled persons in driving and ancillary services. White-collar clerical and broker jobs are also created by the lorry transport activity. The distribution of goods to various localities in the city requires the services of cart pullers. The city, as mentioned earlier, is one of the biggest railway and bus junctions in the country. The railways and the Andhra Pradesh Road Transport Corporation employs hundreds of skilled and educated persons. Some inhabitants of Peta are employees of these organisations. The floating population in the city creates a demand for cheap transport vehicles like man-driven three wheeler cycle rickshaws. Most of the rickshaw pullers in the city are slum dwellers. The construction activity which is a consequence of rapid growth of the city, coupled with the availability of cheap and good sand in the bed of the Krishna river provides employment largely to the Vadderas who work as sand labourers (loading and unloading the lorries) and as earth workers in construction. Another important occupation of the residents of Peta is junk collection. There are quite a number of merchants who buy junk iron and in turn sell it to the local iron foundries or export it to Visakhapatnam. The local iron foundries and small-scale industries employ some skilled and semi-skilled persons belonging to Peta. Thus the employment structure of Peta is closely integrated with the economy of the city. A significant number of the Peta dwellers is employed in the informal sector.

Caste, occupation and organisation of work

The twenty-one castes and Muslims are engaged in different occupations. While some follow the hereditary occupations others have taken up new ones. Table 5.1 gives a summary of the traditional and present occupations of all the castes in Peta, and Table 5.2 presents the occupational distribution of the earners in the sample households. We present below the occupations followed by the members of each caste in order to understand the variations from their caste occupations. We follow the order of the castes in terms of their numerical strength.

Vaddera is by far the largest caste-group having 263 households with an approximate population of thirteen hundred. The traditional occupation of the Vadderas is 'earth-work' such as digging of wells, trenches for foundations and construction of buildings. About 95 per cent of them are found engaged in the work of loading and unloading lorries with sand and other sorts of earth materials. The nearby Krishna river bed provides the perennial source of sand and earth. About 10 to 15 people form a gang and each gang enters into a contract with a contractor for loading and unloading the lorries. On an average each male, female and child (between 12-16 years) earns about Rs. 3, Rs. 2.50 and Rs. 1.50 respectively per day. Sand labour offers employment only for about nine months. During the rainy season they get employment as earth-workers in the city either on contract or daily wages. Children and women also work and earn. Children are rarely seen going to the local school which is run by the Catholic Church. Only a minority of the Vadderas are seen working as rickshaw pullers and daily wage earners.

TABLE 5.1 : **Caste and major occupation of all the castes in Peta**

Caste	Traditional occupations	Major occupations now followed	Minor occupations now followed
1	2	3	4
1. Vaddera	Earth-work	Earth-work and sand labour	Casual labour
2. Madiga	Leather work	Sand labour and Rickshaw pulling	Junk collection, casual labour
3. Mala	Agricultural labour and weaving	Junk collection and salaried jobs	Skilled work
4. Yadava	Shepherds and cowherds	Mutha gang labour	Casual labour
5. Reddi	Agriculture (cultivation)	-do-	Casual labour
6. Telaga	-do-	-do-	Skilled workers
7. Yerukula	Piggery	Piggery	Manure collection
8. Madari	Basket making	Basket making	—
9. Nagasipu	Agriculture (cultivation)	Mutha labour	Cart-pulling
10. Kamma	-do-	-do-	Business
11. Rajaka	Washermen	Washing clothes	Mutha labour
12. Mangali	Barber	Hair-cutting	Mutha labour
13. Muttarasi	Agriculture (cultivation)	Mutha labour	Casual labour

1	2	3	4
14. Kshatriya	Agriculture (cultivation)	Mutha labour	Casual labour
15. Kamsali	Jewel making	Miscellaneous	—
16. Gauda	Toddy tapping	-do-	—
17. Brahmin	Priest	Miscellaneous	—
18. Nagara	Agriculture (cultivation)	-do-	—
19. Palli	Fishing	-do-	—
20. Vysya	Commerce and business	Business	—
21. Kummari	Potter	Miscellaneous	—
Muslim	Agriculture	Skilled work	Kerosene selling

According to Peta sample, about 37 per cent of the Vaddera earners in the sample households are in their traditional occupation that is earth-work, including digging foundation for building construction. As many as 57.8 per cent are engaged in sand labour. The other 5 per cent of the earners are distributed over other categories such as rickshaw pulling and casual labour.

Madiga is the second largest caste group in Peta. There are 200 households. The traditional occupation of Madigas is leather-work, but only a small number of Madigas are now engaged in this job. Majority of the Madigas are engaged in occupations like sand-labour and rickshaw pulling. Some people are the salaried employees in the Municipality and others are engaged in buying and selling junk iron. A small number of women are sand labourers and graders in tobacco firms. But tobacco grading work offers employment only for six months in a year and for the rest of the year they work as casual labourers. There is not much child labour in this caste. Children either go to school or roam about.

About 27.5 per cent of the earners in the Madiga sample households are sand labourers and about 18.0 per cent rickshaw pullers. Out of the 18 rickshaw pullers in the sample, 13 are from this caste alone. Thus Madigas unlike others, are attracted to rickshaw pulling. About 29 per cent are in unclassified categories, mainly in junk collection. Those who are engaged in their traditional occupation, namely leather-work, account for less than 7 per cent. This clearly shows that there is a definite deviation in their occupational pattern from the traditional one.

Mala consists of 170 households. Most of the males are engaged in buying and selling junk iron. Out of a total of 180 junk sellers and buyers in this area, as many as 150 belong to this caste. A group of about 10 to 15 persons form a batch and go out into villages and towns for buying scrap iron and junk. On return they sell the material to the local merchants. The local merchants are Malas and Kammas. Among the Malas there are three merchants and among Kammas there are two. The general practice is that each local merchant would advance money to the group attached to him and the group would collect and sell the scrap iron to that merchant only. The local merchants in turn sell the junk to big wholesale merchants in the city. One of the three local Mala merchants and one of the two Kamma merchants also do wholesale business.

A good number of Malas are also in salaried jobs in the municipality, railways and electricity department. Some others are skilled blacksmiths. A few women of this caste earn as tobacco graders and casual labourers.

In the sample households nearly 19 per cent of the earners are in salaried jobs which is in tune with their level of literacy of 33.5 per cent. About 37 per cent of the earners are engaged in junk collection which is in a way monopolised by this caste. The number of skilled workers is also considerable, making a percentage of 19.0. Out of the 36 salaried people in the total sample, 19 come from this caste and similarly out of the total 98 skilled workers in the total sample, 38 are from this caste. Of the remaining earners, about 13.5 per cent are casual labourers and about 9.5 per cent are mutha labourers. Among the women earners of this caste, 54.0 per cent are tobacco graders and nearly 27.0 per cent are in the miscellaneous category.

Among the Yadavas as many as 90 per cent of the working population are *mutha* labourers. The term *mutha* labour here requires an explanation. The nature of work of a *mutha* labourer is loading and unloading of goods in and out of lorries and goods-wagons. Generally 15 to 20 people form a *mutha* (gang). Each mutha has a leader. He is called a *maistry*. Each *mutha* is attached to a particular type of commercial shop (vegetable shops, grain shops, etc.), and would undertake the work of loading and unloading of goods on a contract basis. The rate of payment for each operation is periodically fixed jointly by the muthas and the merchants. The daily income is shared by the members of the mutha. Mutha workers have formed a union, and according to its norms any one seeking admission into a particular mutha has to pay some fixed amount which is like an admission fee, and this amount is distributed among the existing members. Any member can nominate a new person in his place if he chooses to leave the mutha, provided the others do not have any specific objection, or else he can sell away his right. The membership can also be inherited by one's son.

The number of mutha labourers in the sample is as high as 88.6 per cent. Of all the castes, a large percentage of Yadavas are in this occupational category. The rest (11.4%) are engaged in salaried jobs, casual labour and other categories. Those who are engaged in casual labour and cart pulling (goods carriages) account for roughly six to seven per cent of the working population. Only a small number of people are in salaried jobs (e.g., clerks in commercial shops). The Yadava's hereditary occupation is rearing of sheep and cowherding, and the present occupational pattern is very different from their traditional occupation.

Nearly 90 per cent of the Reddi males are engaged in mutha labour. Of the remaining 10 per cent, some pull carts, and others work as clerks and peons. Some Reddis still own lands in their native villages. In the sample households there are 70 earners in this caste group forming 46.5 per cent (70/124) of the working age-group. No single female is an earner. The percentage of earners among the males works out at 98.7 per cent (70 out of 71). In the sample as high as 83 per cent are engaged in mutha labour, 7 per cent in salaried jobs, and 4.3 per cent in casual labour. Reddis are traditionally agriculturists and the present employment pattern shows a definite deviation in their occupational pattern.

Though a majority of the Telagas are mutha labourers, there are many skilled workers like automobile drivers and mechanics. A few of them earn their livelihood as casual labourers and cart pullers. There are three fuel depot owners. Some of them still have an interest in the land at their native villages. In this caste more than 37 per cent of the earners of the sample households are mutha labourers. It is the single largest occupational category in this caste. Next in importance is the category of skilled workers accounting for 17 per cent. It includes mechanics, fitters, lorry drivers and so on. About 36 per cent are in the miscellaneous category and 8.7 per cent are casual labourers. Only one is a clerk.

Most of the Muslims are engaged in skilled jobs like automobile driving, machine work, and so on. Further, some of the Muslims earn their livelihood by going round selling kerosene. Roughly only 10 per cent of them are engaged in mutha labour and casual labour. About 52 per cent of the working-age group in the sample households are earners. About 92 per cent of the males are earners and only one of the 22 women of the working agegroup is an earner. Among the males nearly half of the earners (12 out of 25) are employed in skilled jobs. The casual labourers and mutha labourers account for six per cent each. About thirty-two per cent are. in unclassified group and most of them are kerosene vendors.

As many as 95 per cent of Yerukulas, who are a tribe follow their traditional occupations such as piggery and collection of night soil and selling the same as manure.

Medaris are also engaged in their traditional occupation of basket-making. Both males and females actively work. All the children who are above 12 years of age help their elders. Just like the Vaddera children, Medari children are also gainfully employed in large numbers. It is important to note that cent per cent of the Medaris stick to their hereditary occupation of basket-making. Males, females, old and young, all are engaged in it.

About 70 per cent of the Nagasipus are in mutha labour. Salaried jobs, casual labour and skilled category claim 5 per cent each. The remaining 15 per cent are in the miscellaneous category. These people are traditionally agriculturists and there is a clear change in their occupational pattern.

Among the Kammas also mutha labour is the predominant occupation. Two Kammas are scrap iron merchants. About half a dozen people own fuel depots. Kammas are also traditionally agriculturists. But here the single largest occupation taken by them is mutha labour which claims 71.5 per cent of the total earning members in the sample. Rest of them are distributed over different occupations.

While a majority of the Rajakas (about 60%) are engaged in their caste occupation that is, washing clothes, others earn their livelihood through mutha labour.

Among the Mangali caste, most of the males are engaged in their caste occupation (hair-cutting). A few people are in skilled jobs and mutha labour. One Mangali is a medical doctor with an L.M.P. certificate.

While half of the male Muttarasis are engaged in sand labour, the other half are earning their livelihood through casual labour.

There are four households of Kshatriyas in Peta. Among them two household heads are lorry drivers and the other two are mutha labourers.

Out of four heads of Kamsali households, two are mutha labourers and the other two are casual labourers.

Gauda consists of four households. While two heads are engaged in mutha labour, the other two have taken to liquor selling, which is their traditional occupation.

Out of the three Brahmin households, one head is working in the State Electricity Board as a skilled worker. The second who migrated from Orissa is a sweet meat vendor and the third is a private teacher.

Nagara consists of three households. Two heads are mutha labourers and the third is engaged in business.

The heads of the three households belonging to Palli caste are engaged in mutha labour.

Out of the two Kummari heads, one is a mutha labourer and the other is a buttermilk vendor. No one follows the hereditary occupation of pottery.

There are two Vysya households in Peta. Both the heads are running grocery shops.

Occupational distribution

Table 5.2 gives the occupational distribution of the earners in the sample households. The occupations are classified into six main divisions, each of them includes one or more allied occupations : (1) The mutha labour connected with wholesale merchants and railways occupies first place. Nearly half of the working people are mutha labourers (45.7%—290/634). This category also includes sand labour, which requires no special skill. (2) Those who are engaged in hereditary occupations account for 17.6 per cent (112/634) of the total employed. This category includes basket-making (Medari caste), laundry (Rajakas), hair-cutting (Mangalis), footwear making (Madigas) and earth-work (Vadderas). (3) A little more than seven per cent (40/634) of the earners are in skilled jobs such as mechanics, fitters, drivers and tobacco graders. (4) Salaried

TABLE 5.2 : Occupational distribution of earners in the sample households

		Kamsali	Reddi	Kamma	Telaga	Kummari	Yadava	Nagasipu	Medari	Rajaka	Mangali	Vaddera	Mala	Madiga	Muslim	Total
		1	2	3	4	5	6	7	8	9	10	11	12	13	14	15
No. of households		2	50	10	30	2	55	15	10	5	3	50	60	50	20	362
Total population		8	201	46	114	8	233	54	47	26	17	251	286	186	87	1564
Total males population		4	108	24	55	4	106	26	26	14	9	131	147	90	40	784
Earners		2	70	14	35	2	70	20	20	12	6	86	77	56	24	494
Total female population		4	93	22	59	4	127	28	21	12	8	120	139	96	47	780
Earners		—	—	2	1	—	—	—	16	4	—	73	26	17	1	140
Salaried jobs	Total	—	5	—	1	—	3	1	—	—	—	—	19	6	1	36
	%	—	7.1	—	2.8	—	4.3	5.0	—	—	—	—	18.5	8.2	4.0	5.7
Casual labour	Total	—	3	—	3	—	2	1	—	—	—	4	14	5	2	34
	%	—	4.3	—	8.2	—	2.8	5.0	—	—	—	2.5	13.6	6.8	8.0	5.4
Caste occupations	Total	—	—	—	—	—	—	—	36	8	4	59	—	75	—	112
	%	—	—	—	—	—	—	—	100	50.0	66.7	37.1	—	6.8	—	17.6
Contract labour	Total	—	58	10	13	1	62	14	—	8	—	92	10	20	2	290
	%	—	83.0	62.5	26.0	50.0	88.6	70.0	—	50.0	—	57.8	9.7	27.5	8.0	45.7

TABLE 5.2—*contd.*

		1	2	3	4	5	6	7	8	9	10	11	12	13	14	15
Rickshaw	Total	1	—	—	—	—	—	—	—	—	—	2	2	13	—	18
pulling	%	50	—	—	—	—	—	—	—	—	—	1.3	1.9	17.8	—	2.9
Skilled	Total	—	1	—	6	—	—	1	—	—	2	1	20	3	12	46
jobs	%	—	1.46	—	17.0	—	—	5.0	—	—	33.3	0.65	19.4	4.1	48.0	7.2
Others	Total	1	43	26	13	1	3	3	—	—	—	1	38	21	8	98
	%	50.0	4.3	27.5	30.0	50.0	4.3	15.0	—	—	—	0.65	36.9	28.8	32.0	15.5
Total Earners		2	70	16	36	2	70	20	36	16	6	159	103	73	25	634

jobs which include government, municipal and private services and school teachers account for 5.7 per cent (36/634). (5) Casual labourers account for 5.4 per cent (34/634). This includes workers who carry goods on heads, maidservants and the like. Rickshaw pullers constitute only 2.9 per cent (18/634) of the total earners. Among the Madigas 17.8 per cent (13/73) are rickshaw pullers. In respect of the other castes this occupation is either absent or insignificant. The remaining miscellaneous occupations claim 15.5 per cent of the earners. This category includes scrap iron selling and purchasing, cart pulling, collecting old clothes and paper and petty business activities.

Income

Out of the total households in the sample as many as 58 per cent are in the income-groups of Rs. 1,001 to Rs. 2,000 per annum. Those who are in the income-groups below Rs. 1,000, between Rs. 2,001 and Rs. 3,000, and above Rs. 3,000 account for 17.4 per cent, 18.5 per cent and 6.1 per cent respectively.

Table 5.3 gives the distribution of households by income-group and caste. It is seen that while a majority of the Madigas fall in the income-group of below Rs. 1,000 per annum, a significant majority of the Malas are in the income group of above Rs. 1,000. There are in all 22 households in the income group of above Rs. 3,000, and nearly one-third of them are Malas. The following castes are found in some significant proportion in the upper income brackets : Reddi, Kamma, Telaga, Yadava, Vaddera and Mala.

OCCUPATIONAL PATTERNS OF EARNERS OF THE PETA SAMPLE AND THE CITY SAMPLE

With a view to examining the number of earners and the occupational pattern in the two sample studies from a comparative angle, the relevant data are presented below.

Among 5,557 persons belonging to 1,075 households of the city sample, 42.0 per cent are in the age-group of 15 years

Table 5.3 : Distribution of households by caste and income groups

Caste	Number of households	Annual income of the household			
		Below Rs. 1,000	Between Rs. 1,001 & Rs. 2,000	Between Rs. 2,001 & Rs. 3,000	Above Rs. 3,000
Kamsali	2	1	1	—	—
Reddi	50	1	34	12	3
Kamma	10	1	7	1	2
Telaga	30	1	18	10	1
Kummari	2	1	1	—	—
Yadava	55	—	42	10	3
Nagasipu	15	—	13	1	1
Medari	10	5	5	—	—
Rajaka	5	—	4	—	—
Mangali	3	2	—	1	—
Vaddera	50	7	25	15	3
Mala	60	10	24	18	8
Madiga	50	28	22	—	—
Muslims	20	6	14	—	—
Total	362	63	210	67	22

and below.* Thus the proportion of persons in the working age-group in the city sample is 58.0 per cent as against 61.4 per cent in Peta sample. It may be noted that the figures on employment rates for different sex, age and caste groups are not available as far as the city sample study is concerned. In the total city sample population only 27.5 per cent are gainfully employed. But in Peta 61.4 per cent of the total persons are in the working age-group and 65.8 per cent of the persons in working age-group are earners. This means 40.5 per cent (634/1,564) of Peta sample are earners. The incidence of child labour in the city sample should be negligible since the city study covers largely non-slum areas. Even in Peta child labour is largely confined to two caste groups namely, Vaddera

*The classificatory scheme of the age-groups in the two samples are slightly different. In the city sample those who are 15 years and below are considered as children, and in the Peta sample those who are 14 years and below are considered as children.

and Medari. Hence it is not improper to consider that by and large the earners in the city sample belong to the working age-group. Even if child labour is excluded, the proportion of earners in the slum sample would be much higher when compared to the earners in the city sample. This difference may be explained by two factors :

(1) The females in the non-slum areas, which largely constitute the city sample, do not take to employment. In the slum sample, around 30 per cent of the females in the working age-group are earners. This must have contributed to the high proportion of earners in the Peta sample and low proportion of earners in the city sample to some extent.

(2) In the Peta sample as much as 98.4 per cent of the males in the working age-group are earners. In other words, there is a tendency among the poorer sections to engage themselves in some kind of occupation or the other. There is no unemployed male in the working age group in Peta. Whereas in non-slum areas the persons with higher education level and skills tend to be more choosy of the nature of the occupation and work and remain unemployed until they get jobs of their choice. This is illustrated by the fact that approximately 12 per cent of the labour force is unemployed in the city sample and most of them seek jobs in government service or jobs that earn a regular income.

In the city sample study the occupations followed by the earners are classified into five categories. They are :

I. Very high status occupations : professionals (doctors, engineers, teachers, government officers, advocates, business executives, journalists).

II. High status occupations : (salesmen, government employees, class III clerks, shop-keepers and businessmen, and class III railway employees).

III. Medium status occupations : blue collar workers (drivers, mechanics and factory workers).

IV. Low status occupations : (traditional occupations and government and railway class IV employees, watchmen, carpenters, tailors, barbers, street vendors and caste occupations of service castes etc.).

V. Very low status occupations : casual labourers, rickshaw pullers, sweepers, cart pullers etc.

It should be pointed out that the classificatory schemes of the occupations in the city sample study and Peta sample study are different. Hence, for comparative purposes the occupational distribution of the earners in the Peta sample were re-classified more or less on the lines of the city sample study. However, the proportions for the Peta sample given below are only approximate ones which help us understand the broad patterns for comparative analysis.

Table 5.4 shows that there is a wide difference between the city sample and the Peta sample in terms of the proportions of various occupational-status categories. It can be seen that around 40 per cent of the earners in the city sample are in high and very high status occupations whereas in the Peta sample the corresponding figure is negligible. More or less an

TABLE 5.4 : **Occupational distribution of the earners in the city sample and the Peta sample**

Category of occupation	City sample	Peta sample
I Very high status	5.73	Negligible
II High status	34.14	Negligible
III Medium status	14.01	5.0
IV Low status	25.68	25.0
V Very low status	20.41	70 0

equal proportion of both the samples account for lower level employees in the organised sector and traditional caste occupations. The proportion of those in very low status occupationas in the Peta sample is nearly three and a half times higher than that of the same category in the city sample. Thus these figures suggest that there is a wide gulf between the slum and the city as a whole at least in terms of occupational status.

Occupational mobility

One of the important consequences of rural-urban migration is occupational mobility. Many of the migrants pursued their traditional occupations relating to agriculture or the caste occupations in their villages prior to coming to Peta. When they migrated into the city, in a majority of the cases changes occurred not only in the income levels but also in the nature of work the migrants pursued in the city. Of course, these changes may not be very significant in the case of migrants with little education and skills who are largely engaged in occupations which require only manual labour.

Any discussion on occupational mobility should focus on two aspects: (1) inter-generational mobility, and (2) intra-generational mobility. For probing into the first aspect, data on the occupations of the fathers of the heads of all the 362 households, and the present occupations of all the heads of the households and their own brothers living in Peta were collected. Their combined number was 387. For understanding the second aspects of the problem, information regarding occupational changes among the heads of all the 362 households in terms of total number of changes and the reasons for change from one occupation to another was collected.

Table 5.5 presents data on inter-generational occupational mobility. The occupations of the fathers can be seen in the horizontal rows and those of the sons in the vertical columms. The number of cases with no mobility are shown in brackets. It can be seen that in 82 out of 387 (21.2%) cases there is no mobility. In other words, 82 persons are engaged in occupations which were pursued by their fathers. This means that as many as 304 out of 387 cases, the heads of the households and their brothers moved away from their fathers' occupations.

When the changes are examined on the basis of the occupational groups of the fathers it is found that the mobility is high among the sons of the fathers whose occupation was farming. Out of 139 such sons as many as 90 are engaged in contract labour, 11 in salaried jobs, 8 in skilled occupations and 30 in 'others' category. High mobility is not strange because of the simple fact that farming is not possible in the city.

The sons of those who were either agricultural labourers or casual labourers are engaged largely in contract labour (42/103) followed by 'others' category (37/103), salaried jobs (9/103), rickshaw pulling (6/103), and so on. Though there is continuity in terms of manual labour, the nature and conditions of employment are different. In the urban context the labourers work on the basis of contractual relations governed by certain

TABLE 5.5 : **Inter-generational occupational mobility**

Occupation of Father / Occupation of Son	Salaried job	Casual and agricultural labour	Caste occupations	Contract labour	Rickshaw pulling	Skilled jobs	Farmers	Others	Total
Salaried jobs	(2)	—	1	3	1	1	–	6	14
Casual and agricultural labour	9	(5)	1	42	6	3	—	37	103
Caste occupations	—	1	(18)	19	2	1	—	6	47
Contract labour	—	—	2	(39)	1	2	—	2	46
Rickshaw pulling	—	—	—	—	(3)	—	—	—	3
Skilled jobs	—	5	—	1	1	(6)	—	1	14
Farmers	11	—	—	90	—	8	(—)	30	139
Others	1	1	—	7	—	3	—	(9)	21
Total	23	12	22	201	14	24	—	91	387

Note : Figures in brackets show the number of cases with no mobility.

norms. The occupational category where the inter-generational mobility is strikingly low is the contract labour. Out of 46 sons as many as 39 are in their fathers' occupation in this category. Many of the sons are second generation inmigrants entering the same occupations as their fathers. This shows that mutha labour is highly organised and to some extent, entry into it is based on succession. The significance of this type of work-group organisation to the controversial concept of the informal sector is discussed in the concluding chapter.

Intra-generational mobility

In order to analyse intra-generational mobility, those who changed their occupations at least once are taken into account. For example, in the case of Medaris, Rajakas, Mangalis, and some of the Madigas, the place of work and levels of income only changed. Even after migration into the city they are engaged in their respective caste occupations. These cases have been left out since there is no change in the nature of work in spite of the other changes.

Out of à total of 634 earners in the 362 sample households, 347 (54.7%) have been in the same occupation since they became earners. The remaining 287 persons (45.3%) changed their occupations once or more. Out of these 287 persons, 263 changed their occupations once, 20 persons twice and 4 persons thrice or more.

The pattern of changes in the occupations of these 287 persons can be seen in Table 5.6. It is seen that out of 25 persons who started their career in salaried jobs, only four remained in salaried jobs category and the remaining 21 persons took to casual labour, rickshaw pulling and so on. The main reasons for leaving the salaried jobs were retrenchment and retirement. Among 62 persons, who were either agricultural labourers or casual labourers in their villages or casual labourers in the city, 36 joined muthas as contract labourers and the remaining 28 persons took to junk collection, kerosene selling, rickshaw pulling etc. Out of 20 persons who gave up their caste occupations, 16 eke out their living on contract labour, while four are engaged in other occupations. Among these 20 persons many belong to Rajaka caste.

Out of a total of 18 persons who started as skilled workers,

TABLE 5.6 : **Intra generational occupational mobility**

Occupation / Present occupation	Salaried jobs	Agricultural labour	Caste occupations	Contract labour	Rickshaw pulling	Skilled jobs	Farming	Others	Total
Salaried jobs	(4)	4	—	5	3	1	—	8	25
Agricultural and Casual labour	1	(—)	1	36	4	2	—	18	62
Caste occupations	—	—	(—)	16	—	—	—	4	20
Contract labour	1	—	—	(7)	3	—	—	2	13
Rickshaw pulling	—	—	1	1	(—)	—	—	2	4
Skilled jobs	1	2	2	3	—	(4)	—	6	18
Farming	3	—	—	93	—	1	(—)	15	112
Other	1	1	—	3	1	7	—	(20)	33
Total	11	7	4	164	11	15	—	75	287

Note : Figures in brackets show the number of cases with no mobility.

14 changed to various unskilled occupations and the remaining four remained in the skilled category but moved to jobs different from the previous ones.

Among 112 persons whose first occupation was farming, as many as 93 are in contract labour and 3 are in salaried jobs and 15 are in the 'others' category.

It is also seen that the number of persons in salaried jobs fell from 25 to 11, casual labour from 62 to 7, caste occupations from 20 to 7 and, of course, farming from 112 to 0. The increase in the number of persons in contract labour is from 13 to 164, rickshaw pulling from 4 to 15 and 'others' category from 23 to 75. By and large the occupations which attract the slum dwellers in general and recent migrants in particular is contract labour. The other important occupations which readily provide employment are rickshaw pulling and scrap iron collection. The importance of contract labour is much greater when compared to other occupations since it provides regular work and higher incomes.

Reasons for changing the occupations

Among the important reasons for changing the occupations are low income from the previous occupation, expiry of contract or lack of work. Out of 287 persons, as many as 204 mentioned 'low income', and 45 mentioned 'lack of work' as the reasons for their leaving the previous occupations. The other reasons include retrenchment, retirement and ill health which together account for 31 cases of change. It may be said that the reasons which largely account for migration are also the important reasons for occupational changes.

Occupational mobility results not only in changes in the nature of work but also in changes in the prestige of the occupation and the income levels. It is difficult to determine whether there is an increase or decrease in the prestige of the occupation. Even increase in income levels may be sometimes misleading due to the changing value and purchasing power of the money from time to time. In some cases deterioration of economic position after migration into the city is also reported (K. Ranga Rao *et al.* 1977).

The changes in the income levels can be seen in Table 5.7. It is seen that there was considerable increase in income levels

TABLE 5.7 : Changes in the income-levels between the first and present occupation

Occupation	Income levels per annum				Total
	Rs. 1,000 and below	Rs. 1,001-2,000	Rs. 2,001-3,000	Rs. 3,001 & above	
First occupation	269	16	2	—	287
Present occupation	75	203	8	1	287

of the persons at least in absolute figures. While in the first occupation as many as 269 out of 287 persons are in the bracket of Rs. 1,000 and below per annum, the number in the same bracket decreased to 75 after changing to the present occupation. This also means that around 25 per cent of the persons are in the same bracket in spite of the change in the occupations. The number of persons in the bracket of Rs. 1,001 to Rs. 2,000 p.a. increased from 16 to 203, and in the bracket of Rs. 2,001 to Rs. 3,000 p.a. from 2 to 8 as a result of the change in the occupation. In only one case the income has gone above the level of Rs. 3,001 p.a. Thus, incomes increased with the changes in occupations.

The foregoing account of the occupational pattern and mobility among the Peta residents shows that, by and large, they are employed in the category of manual jobs and in the informal sector of the city economy. There is no unemployment and a majority of them are in the income group of Rs. 1,000-2,000 per annum. There has been both inter-generational and intra-generational mobility although the former is more significant. Thus obviously the general level of living of the migrants in the slum has registered a slight improvement when compared to the living standards in their places of origin. Continuous inflow of people into the slum, therefore, should be understood from this comparative background of the migrants (also see Mangin 1970 : XXVIII).

6

COMMUNITY ORGANISATION OF PETA

WE SHALL discuss in this chapter the community organisation of Peta in terms of kin relations, caste panchayats, political parties, voluntary associations, religious activities, community services and anti-social activities.

KIN NETWORKS

The importance of kin network is borne out by the fact that, out of a total 362 households covered under the major sample, 90.3 per cent of them have relatives in the city. While 83.3 per cent of the households have relatives within Peta, seven per cent have relatives in different parts of the city.

In order to find out the nature of kin links between the households of the same caste groups, genealogical information was collected from households distributed over the four major caste groups : Yadava (40), Vaddera (50), Mala (60) and Madiga (50). It was found that the kin network of the 200 households covered as many as 416 households of which 52 were single households. The remaining 364 households are divided into 108 kin-groups. The 108 kin-groups can be further divided into 46 agnatic groups, 32 affinal groups, and 30 with both agnatic and affinal relations. Thus agnatic relationships seem to be slightly more important than the affinal relationships in the matter of migration. The 30 kin-groups with both agnatic and affinal relationships are those which have been in Peta for a longer period. This means that, they prefer to maintain their marital relations within the city besides bringing their agnatic and affinal relations gradually to the city.

In terms of the number of households in each kin-group we find that the number of kin-groups with 2, 3, 4, 5, 6, 7, 8 and 9 households each, are 43, 27, 19, 7, 7, 5, 0 and 1 respectively. Thus a majority of the kin-groups consist of 2 to 4 households and the kin-group with two households is the largest of all (see Table 6.1).

In terms of variation between castes, we find that many Malas and Yadavas do not have close relatives in the town. On the contrary Vadderas and Madigas have a wide network of relatives. Among the Madigas there is one kin-group with nine households. Taking the agnatic and affinal relationships separately, we find that while Yadavas have a greater percentage of affines (55 %), the other castes have more agnates. Thus besides caste, kin relations also provide the basis of cohesiveness and security for the residents of Peta.

Caste panchayat

It is found that only the Yerukulas maintain the traditional caste panchayat headed by a single headman. The Malas and Madigas have caste panchayats but the members are elected. No other caste has a caste panchayat as such, but some have associations. Table 6.2 summarizes the information on the presence or otherwise of caste panchayats and the political affiliations of the major caste groups in Peta.

Malas belong to two religious groups, Hindus and Christians. But so far as caste matters are concerned, religion seems to make no difference. Until the year 1965 each kin-group or a group of people coming from nearby villages used to have its own informal head who would work as a mediator in various matters of disputes and conflict or would act as an elderly person in functions and ceremonies. But as the situation became complex, it was felt that they should have a formal kind of organisation to look after ritual, social and political matters. Hence, in 1965 the Malas decided to elect every year a set of six leaders. The present set of six leaders were elected in January 1972. These leaders are mostly concerned with settlement of disputes and other social-ritual matters.

TABLE 6.1: **Kin network by caste**

	Caste				Total
	Yadava	Vaddera	Mala	Madiga	
Number of sample households	40	50	60	50	200
Number of total kin-groups	32	40	54	34	160
Number of total kin-groups having relations in the city	20 (62.5%)	32 (80.0%)	32 (61.5%)	24 (70.6%)	108
Number of total kin-groups having no relations in the city	12 (37.5%)	8 (20.0%)	22 (40.7%)	10 (29.4%)	52
Number of kin-groups having agnatic relations in the city	6 (30.0%)	14 (43.7%)	14 (43.7%)	12 (50.0%)	46
Number of kin-groups having affinal relations in the city	11 (55.5%)	8 (25.0%)	8 (25.0%)	5 (20.8%)	32
Number of kin-groups having both the relations in the city	3 (15.0%)	10 (31.3%)	10 (31.3%)	7 (29.2%)	30
Kin-groups consisting one household	12	8	22	10	52
Kin-groups having two households	11	10	13	9	43
Kin-groups having three households	8	7	6	6	27
Kin-groups having four households	1	6	6	6	19
Kin-groups having five households	—	5	1	1	7
Kin-groups having six households	—	1	3	3	7
Kin-groups having seven households	—	3	1	1	5
Kin-groups having eight households	—	—	—	—	—
Kin-groups having nine households	—	—	—	1	1
Total heads among all kin-groups (8-16 rows)	62	125	123	89	399

TABLE 6.2 : **Political affiliations of the major caste-groups**

Caste	Whether has a caste panchayat	No. of leaders	Membership of leaders in political parties			General sympathy of the people towards political parties		
			Congress	CPI	CPI(M)	Congress	CPI	CPI(M)
Vaddera	No	2	—	—	—	—	Minority	Majority
Madiga	Yes	4+5+2	—	—	—	—	-do-	-do-
Mala	Yes	6	1	2	—	Minority	Majority	Minority
Yadava	No	1	1	1	—	—	-do-	—
Reddi	No	2	—	2	—	—	-do-	—
Telaga	No	1	—	—	—	Minority	-do-	—
Muslim	No	2	—	2	—	—	-do-	Minority
Yerukula	Yes	1	—	—	—	—	-do-	-do-
Medari	No	—	—	—	—	—	-do-	—
Nagasipu	No	1	—	1	—	—	-do-	—
Kamma	No	2	—	2	—	—	-do-	—

Malas are politically quite conscious. Out of the six leaders three have strong political affiliations. One is a member of a Ward Congress Committee and the other two are members of a Ward Committee of the Communist Party of India (CPI). The most influential of the six is a Christian who is the secretary of the Old Iron Collectors Union (OICU). Since many of the Malas are engaged in the work of buying and selling of junk the Secretary of the Old Iron Collectors Union normally has more influence on the caste as a whole. The present Secretary, however, does not have any formal membership in any political party, although he is said to be a supporter of the Communists. For the same reason many of the Malas are sympathizers of Communists whether CPI or CPI(M).

Madigas are divided into three groups and each is headed by a different set of caste leaders. It is said that until 1963 there was only one caste panchayat and later (in 1964) it was divided into three groups on the lines of kinship affiliations. Now each group has its own separate caste panchayat. The first group consists of Hindu Madigas, the second group of converted Christians and the third of both Hindus and Christians.

The first group is headed by four leaders who are elected by consensus. It is the single largest group among Madigas with about 120 households under its control. Though the leaders of this group do not have any membership in any political party, it is politically conscious. While a majority of the members are sympathizers of the CPI(M) the rest have affiliation with the CPI. The panchayat of the second group is headed by a set of five leaders. Nearly 80 households are under the control of this group. Members of this group are sympathizers of CPI. The third group is comparatively smaller than the other two. It consists of roughly 60 households and is headed by a two-member caste panchayat. It comprises both Hindus as well as converted Christians. The elder men of this group do not have any political affiliations, so also the members.

Yerukulas have a traditional caste panchayat headed by a headman whose office is hereditary. As most of the Yerukulas migrated from more or less the same region the leader is accepted by one and all. Those who migrated from other regions also accept his headship. The present head is a P.W.D. employee and is economically better off than the other members of the caste. He himself does not have any political affiliation. But half of the caste members are sympathizers of CPI while the others are sympathizers of CPI(M).

In the caste groups where the caste panchayats are active, almost all the cases of divorce, desertion, marriage settlement are taken care of by the caste panchayats. The caste leaders thus perform both the traditional and modern functions relating to socio-economic amelioration of the people. Therefore, the leadership among the three castes Mala, Madiga and Yerukula may be said to be of neotraditional category. Among the Medaris, however, their headman in the city also serves as the caste-head in Peta. In other castes, matters such as divorce and desertion are settled by the elderly persons and political matters of the modern type (elections and party organisation) are separated from the purely social and semi-religious matters. Because of a lack of distinction between the traditional and modern activities among the Malas, Madigas and Yerukulas any minor interpersonal problem becomes a large group problem, whereas such minor problems ordinarily do not become major group problems in the case of other castes.

Community leadership and political parties

At the level of Peta as a whole, the overall leadership can be said to be in the hands of the two Communist parties. The political leadership can be expressed in terms of ecological pattern as well. The area surrounding 'Sundarayya Chowk' (named after P. Sundarayya, the CPI(M) leader) is largely under the leadership of CPI(M). The rest of the slum with a few exceptions is under the leadership of CPI.

The above mentioned ecological pattern of political leadership emerges because of the fact that a majority of the Vadderas and Madigas live side by side around the Sundarayya Chowk and many of them, being either sand labourers or rickshaw pullers, are members of the labour unions dominated by CPI(M). Although kin links play their part in party affiliations, ecological solidarity is an important factor in keeping the people around Sundarayya Chowk under the leadership of CPI(M). The leader of the CPI(M) belongs to the Nagara caste and he himself lives near the Chowk.

It is to be noted here that all the political leaders as well as caste leaders in Peta are in better occupations and are comparatively economically better off than other members of their respective caste men. This is true in all the cases. A majority of the leaders also live in better houses.

Marriage, divorce and dispute settlements

With the Mala and Madiga castes the norms governing marriage and divorce are well defined. The caste heads play an important part in the settlement of marriage. The parents of the bride or bridegroom belonging to Peta should take one or more caste heads along with them to the other party to advise them in choosing the bride or bridegroom. In fact, it is the caste head who represents the parents of the bride or bridegroom and negotiates the terms regarding dowry and other conditions with the other party. The caste heads collect a fee of Rs. 3 from the bride's side and Rs. 5 from the bridegroom's side, which is called *Kalagalupu*, on the day of engagement. The money is spent on liquor on the same day.

The boy or girl belonging to Peta wears new clothes and is recognized as a bridegroom or bride for the first time in the house of one of the caste heads and later in his or her own house. The attendance of the caste heads at the marriage ceremony is considered very important. In case they do not attend, the other castemen also do not attend. When a male member belonging to Peta is married to a girl outside Peta, the caste heads go to the bride's house with *Pasupu-Kumkuma* (turmeric and vermilion). The caste heads charge the local party Rs. 11.50 as *Pandiri Katnam* (pandal payment). This money goes to the caste fund. The accumulated money is spent on purchase of large cooking vessels which are lent free of cost to the castemen to be used in various ceremonies.

Divorce is granted by the caste heads under two conditions: (1) when the husband is incapable of or unwilling to support his wife and children, (2) when the husband or wife is found to be involved in extra-marital relations. But the willingness of both the partners is necessary for granting divorce. If either of the partners is suspicious of the moral behaviour of the other he or she has to lodge a complaint with the caste head. The allegation can be proved only on the basis of an eye-witness. If he or she is caught sleeping with anybody other than his wife or her husband, the culprit is brought and is tied to a pole. After examining the case the divorce is granted. The guilty will be fined and the fine may range between Rs. 5 and Rs. 200. Usually the fine for the first crime will be around Rs. 5. But if the person repeats the mistake the fine may go up to Rs. 200. Of course, the amount of fine also depends on how the person behaves in the presence of the caste heads in the course of the trial of the case. If he fails to pay the fine he will be expelled from the caste, and he has to face social boycott. If he wants time to pay the fine, he has to produce a security. The money collected in the form of fines is largely spent on liquor. The norms governing marriage and divorce are the same in the Mala and Madiga castes.

Most of the disputes in Peta occur between neighbours over garbage disposal or children attending nature's calls near the neighboure's houses. Such disputes are usually settled by the involved people themselves. The persons involved shout abusive words at each other for about 15 to 20 minutes and then keep quiet. But if such disputes take a serious turn and become violent, they will be brought to the notice of the caste heads or the political leaders. The disputes of a social and economic nature and the disputes between parents and children arising out of the manner in which the property is shared at the time of partition will be settled either by the caste heads or by the political leaders.

When a dispute arises between the persons or households belonging to different caste groups, it is resolved by the heads of the castes involved jointly. In such a situation the intervention of political leaders is not uncommon. The intervention of political leaders tends to be more if the castes involved in the disputes do not have caste panchayats as such. In caste groups other than Mala, Madiga and Yerukula, the inter-caste disputes are resolved by the caste heads and committee members of the local units of the political parties. The intervention and participation in the dispute settlement process by the political leaders depends upon the political party to which the persons involved in the dispute owe their allegiance. For example, the disputes between Vadderas and other caste-groups are resolved sometimes by CPI Committee members, sometimes by CPI(M) Committee members and at other times by both since roughly half of the Vadderas are with the CPI and the other half with CPI(M). Intra-caste disputes of Vadderas are settled either by the CPI or CPI(M) Committee members or by both depending on the political allegiance of the persons involved in the disputes. In some cases the caste heads also participate in the process of dispute settlement. One incident of dispute settlement is described below.

A Vaddera girl threw water in the living premises of her neighbour, who was an ordinary but influential member of the CPI, a youth leader, a liquor seller by profession and Yerukula by caste. (He will be referred to as Mr. Yerukula). The wife of Mr. Yerukula and the Vaddera girl exchanged heated words over this. Meanwhile Mr. Yerukula came out of the house and joined his wife in abusing the Vaddera girl. Then a passer by who was also Vaddera by caste, observed the incident for five minutes and warned Mr. Yerukula not to scold the Vaddera girl. They too exchanged heated words while Mr. Yerukula's friends gathered around. When the tension heightened, Mr. Yerukula and his friends beat the Vaddera man. He left quietly and told his castemen about the incident and within a few minutes about 50 Vaddera men were on the spot of the trouble. When asked by the Vaddera men about the incident, Mr. Yerukula told them everything except that he and his friends had beaten the Vaddera man. When the Vaddera man angrily said that he was beaten by them, Mr. Yerukula lied saying he had never beaten him. Then the Vadderas (they are sympathizers of CPI) and Mr. Yerukula and his friends started shouting at each other and the situation became tense. At this moment Mr. Yadava, who was one of the Committee members of CPI, came and asked them about the dispute. He listened to the versions of both the parties and said,

> Mr. Yerukula says they didn't beat him. This boy says he was beaten. Whose words should we believe ? Anyway,

it is not good on your part to quarrel like this. All of you should disperse from here.

Without saying a word the Vadderas went away. Their unhappiness over the judgement was, however, evident on their faces. After Mr. Yadava left, Mr. Yerukula laughed triumphantly. But, had the Vadderas chosen to make a complaint to their caste head or to the CPI Committee, its meeting would have become a necessity. However, even if the committee were to meet, its judgement would not have been different in view of Mr. Yerukula's personal influence and his position in the Party. Thus the political leaders assume the role of village panchayat leaders in the settlement of disputes in Peta. The leaders combine both traditional and modern functions.

Trade unions

Almost all the numerically large and important occupational groups like the sand labourers, contract labourers, old iron workers, and rickhaw pullers have their own trade unions. While the unions of sand and contract labourers and rickhaw pullers are affiliated to various political parties, that is CPI, CPI(M), and Congress, the Union of Old Iron Collectors is not affiliated to any political party. The contract labourers working with private goods transport corporations, wholesale shop owners, railways, the Andhra Pradesh State Transport Corporation are members of unions of their respective organisations and the sand labourers working with different contractors have different unions. But all the workers engaged in collecting and selling of old iron are members of a single union and the leadership is in the hands of the local persons only. In the case of rickshaw pullers and contract labourers most of the union leaders are from outside Peta.

Voluntary associations

Besides political parties and trade unions there are different voluntary associations in Peta. Ambedkar Youngmen's Association and Sanghika Seva Dalam are two such voluntary associations. These associations which were active for a few years were started by some educated youth belonging to

Madiga and Mala castes respectively. Interestingly the other caste groups did not seem to have made any effort to form such voluntary associations. The reasons for the formation of the voluntary associations among the Mala and Madiga castes are : (a) higher rate of literacy, (b) intra-caste solidarity, (c) higher percentage of salaried employees, and (d) higher rate of participation of members in union activities.

The Ambedkar Youngmen's Association was formed by some educated Madiga boys around 1965, and it was active for about four years in organising the youth for conducting socio-cultural activities. However, the association became inactive from 1969 onwards. Though there is an office for the association in the Madiga locality, it is now used for gossip. Activities or meetings of the association no longer take place.

The Sanghika Seva Dalam (Social Service league) was established by the educated Mala youth in 1969 with an initial membership of 20. The objectives of the association were (a) starting a library, and (b) developing friendliness and cultivating good habits among the youth. The members decided not to allow drunkards and gamblers into the association. The association functioned only for a year. When one of the political parties conducted *hartal* against the rising prices, the president of the association asked its members to participate in the hartal if they were willing. This gave raise to a doubt in the minds of the members who were averse to that political party. They thought that the association was going to be tagged on to that political party. As a result they left the association. Thus the association became defunct. After a lapse of one year, efforts were made by the ex-office bearers to revive the association but the response from the youth was poor.

In 1971 Yadavas formed a caste association under the presidentship of a local member of the CPI. But soon it was dissolved on the advice of the CPI leaders. There are no organised neighbourhood clubs of any kind in Peta.

Religious-cultural activities

There are three temples and one church. Of the three temples, one is devoted to the worship of the goddess Kali, the second to

Amma Varu and the third to Rama. The Kali temple was built by the Vadderas out of donations. The priest is a Vaddera. In 1961 a statue of a late priest was erected in the temple premises. It is believed that the late priest had some occult powers and was a great devotee of Kali, and of Sri Pothuluri Veera Brahman, the saint. Not only the inhabitants of Peta but also people from surrounding areas visit the temple. Malas and Madigas are not allowed to enter the temple. During the nine-day Dassera period, services are conducted on a very large scale. The Amma Varu temple is built to commemorate the memory of a Vaddera lady who committed suicide and was believed to be a pious lady with supernatural powers. But now-a-days no regular worship is offered in this temple.

The Rama temple is situated in the Mala area and was built by the Malas. Although there is no regular priest attached to the temple, celebrations are conducted during the Sri Rama Navami period (March-April). Only the scheduled castes i.e. Malas and Madigas, worship the deity. Converted Christians also join the celebrations. The temple does not get have an idol in it. During the celebrations a picture of Lord Rama is placed and worshipped.

The church was built about twenty years ago by a Roman Catholic missionary and the converted Malas and Madigas visit this place of worship. A missionary primary school is also run in this church building. A Catholic priest residing in the city visits this church every Sunday to conduct services. Christmas is celebrated on a big scale.

During the festivals of Sankranti, Sri Rama Navami and Dasera, *Harikathas* and *Burrakathas* are performed. Disco dance (dance by professional girls and boys to the tune of recorded music and songs) has become a very popular variety entertainment. During Sankranti days, cock-fights are a regular feature.

Recreation and leisure-time activities

Since most of the adult male members in the slum are earners, they are busily engaged in their work on all days except Sundays and other holidays. Those who are engaged in contract labour, salaried jobs, skilled jobs, cart pulling and so on are free on Sundays. The persons who are engaged in rickshaw pulling, and old iron collection and so on are not free even on Sundays and hence do not enjoy leisure except on festival days. The non-earning women are busy with house-keeping and looking after children. When the male members are free, they spend their leisure time mostly with their friends and relatives residing in Peta. Some of them also visit their relatives living in other parts of the city. When asked about their way of spending holidays more than 90 per cent of the heads replied that they visited their relatives and friends. It is quite interesting to note that in the city sample, nearly 80 per cent did not visit their relatives residing in the city even on holidays. This brings out a striking difference in the behaviour pattern of the predominantly poor population of the slum and predominantly middle-class population of the city. Among the heads of the slum households those who go to the movies on holidays account for 28 per cent. Nearly 50 per cent or more among Reddi, Telaga and Rajaka heads of households go to the movies on most of the holidays. But most of them visit their relatives and friends and/or prefer to stay at home, spend their time with the members of the family and relax rather than spending money and time on movies. Another thing which marks out a holiday is a special menu which invariably includes some kind of non-vegetarian preparations. Some of the male members also heavily drink on holidays and festival days.

However, it should be noted that the pattern of recreation and leisure-time activities of the youth is different from that of relatively elder members of Peta. The youth, especially in the age-group of 15-25 years, gather at the *pan*-shops and tea shops after their night meal and on Sundays and other holidays. Movie-going and gossiping are the important sources of entertainment for them. Some of them stay around the *pan*-shops until 11.00 P.M. The main topics which frequently find place in their conversations are movies, charms of the female stars, fighting capabilities and historionics of male stars of the Telugu screen, local girls, sex, dress and fashions. Debates over the talents of the Telugu matinee idols are not uncommon. The cinema-hero-worship is prevalent in south India with various fans' associations, though heroine-worship is not much less significant. During the times of elections and other important political events they discuss the state, national and international politics with some seriousness. During the Indo-Pakistan war of 1971 most of the youngsters used to listen to the radio news bulletins and read newspapers and discuss the events. In March, 1977 the main topic of the discussion was the *Janatha gali* (Janata wave).

Some enthusiasts gather daily in one of their houses to conduct rehearsals of mythological dramas and practise lengthy *Padyalu* (a kind of sonnet) between 9.00 and 12.00 in the night. On festival days they stage plays.

Community services

As mentioned above the only primary school in the slum is run by a Christian missionary. One Brahmin offers tuitions for students of the intermediate castes. There is no government or municipal hospital. Three private doctors run their private dispensaries. All the three are L.M.P. Certificate holders. Two of them, one Reddi and one Mangali, are local residents and the third, a Brahmin doctor, resides in the city.

There are small and medium-sized grocery and provision stores. The medium-sized shops are four in number and they are managed by two Vysyas, one Telaga and one Nagasipu. The six relatively big fire-wood depots are run by Kammas, Reddis, Muslims and Yadavas.

Small tea shops (*buddies*) are found at various places. But near the Sundarayya Chowk, Railway Gate and by the side of the railway track there are comparatively big tea stalls. These big ones are run by Kerala Muslims.

Housing and civic amenities

Among the 362 heads of households in Peta 267 (73.3%) own their homes. The rest live in rented houses. As high as 78.7 per cent (285/362) of the houses occupy a plinth area of below 30 sq. yards whereas 14.6 per cent (53/362) are between 31 and 50 sq. yards. Only 6.7 per cent (24/362) of the houses have an area between 50 and 100 sq. yards. This makes it clear that the housing standards are very poor.

Out of the total sample houses, 71.6 per cent (259/362) are single room houses; 26.5 per cent (96/362) are two room ones and only 1.9 per cent (7/362) are with three or more rooms. A majority of the houses are thatched huts (99.2%), and *kutcha* and *pucca* houses account only for less than one per cent.

Among the households covered under the sample, no house has a lavatory of its own. There are no public latrines either. Only a little more than 30 per cent of the total sample houses are provided with bathrooms with bamboo or palm leaf enclosures. Around 11 per cent (40 houses) of the total sample houses have boring-pumps and all these but one belong to the intermediate castes. Almost all the people of the lower castes are dependent either on public wells or the canal for water. No house has a proper drain around it, and in the absence of drainage dirty water stagnates in front of and around the houses.

The quality of food consumed by the residents of Peta is very low. Consumption of milk is either too little or nil. Usually the menu includes rice, a *chutney*, chillie powder, a vegetable curry or *dal*. Except on Sundays and festival days the residents do not go in for non-vegetarian food. Some of them eat *idli* or *dosa* or *vada* in the tea stalls in Peta. Women usually do not eat in hotels. The residents spend more money on buying tea from stalls rather on vegetables, milk and curds.

In Peta the common diseases among the children are diarrhoea and fever, and among the elders venereal diseases and tuberculosis. Desai's study of a Bombay slum also shows that intestinal disorders, fevers and tuberculosis are the common diseases among the slum-dwellers (Desai and Pillai 1970). However, epidemics like small-pox and cholera are conspicuous by their absence. It is reported that among the Peta residents venereal diseases are more common among those who live without their wives and among the bachelors. Most of such people visit prostitutes.

Crimes and social evils

Once Peta was very notorious for different types of social evils like prostitution, pick-pocketing, wagon robbery and gambling. Whenever a stranger stepped into the area along the railway line, he used to be robbed of his possessions. Therefore, every one in the city was frightened to enter the locality alone during night time. The investigator was also warned by many not to stay in Peta. But fortunately no untoward incident took place in his case. In fact, no case of robbery was reported during his eight month stay in Peta. However, there was a wagon robbery case during one of the nights and it was said that wagon theft was a usual occurrence. Peta has an ecological advantage for goods wagon robbery. The railway track is on a bridge and there is the sand bed of the river Krishna beneath it. During nights when the goods trains cross the bridge at a low speed, the wagons are unlocked and emptied on the sand bed. The members of the gang remove the goods and sell them to the merchants. The Railway Police are said to be in collusion with the robbers. Apart from the organised wagon robbery, other kinds of crime are not significant in Peta. It is said that around 1967 the local leaders drove the gamblers, prostitutes and pick-pocketers away from the locality. However, illicit sale of liquor continues to exist. Some persons also engage in black-marketing of cinema tickets, and in gambling relating to New York cotton market locally known as *bracket*.

Occasionally some prostitutes and new recruits are brought to Peta by one or two agents. They are placed in the huts in between the national highway and the Krishna river. It is said that periodically a batch of three to four girls are brought in and kept for a few months and are later sent to Gandhinagar area which is the red-light area in the city. Thus Peta acts as the marginal area for traffic in women. It may be noted in this connection that prostitutes are recruited and moved from one area to another in a city and from one city to another, on an organised basis. Many 'lodges' in different localities act as brothel houses. Vijayawada, with a large floating population, provides a fertile ground for prostitution.

SUMMARY

The foregoing analysis of the community organisation of Peta shows that, contrary to the general expectation of slums, it is well organised. In its essential characteristics the area is somewhat like a large village with its own socio-economic and political set-up and at the same time closely interlinked with the wider social organisation and culture of the city. In this Peta resembles the slums in many other cities in India (Singh and de Souza 1980). The area is roughly divided into different caste settlements and each caste-group works as a social unit by itself. Individuals and households are thus connected through their primordial relations and no one exhibits the feeling of leading a life of isolation. The social structure maintains the traditional hierarchical nature of caste even though the gradation is not as rigid as it is in rural areas. Some of the lower caste-groups still maintain their traditional caste panchayats with some modifications. As against the traditional system of hereditary caste-headman, they have now come to adopt the method of electing panchayat members. This pattern is in contrast to the replacement of caste panchayats by voluntary associations in a Madras slum (Wiebe 1975).

Keeping in line with the urban occupational structure, the slum population is divided into different occupational groups, and it is important to stress that a caste group is not co-terminous with the occupational group although generally the intermediate castes tend to follow better paid occupations than the lower castes. Nevertheless each occupational group maintains its own occupational association and the members, irrespective of their caste affiliations, show work solidarity, guided by the norms of the work associations. This phenomenon of occupational solidarity is clearly the result of urban economic organisation, and trade union organisation of labourers.

The occupational structure of the slum is closely interlinked with the economic opportunities that the city provides. Vijayawada is largely a commercial city with wholesale trade in several agricultural commodities, including fruits. It has a cement factory and inexhaustible source of sand supply from the river bed. Inmigrants get employment in these occupations which are largely manual in nature. Vadderas with the advantage of their traditional occupation of earth work get easily employed as sand workers. Inmigrants of intermediate castes enter mutha labour attached to merchants and railways. Some lower caste men also join muthas attached to railways. The demand for baskets to export mangoes and other fruits and vegetables keeps the Medaris busy weaving baskets.

Generally a city provides opportunities in transport

(rickshaw driving), junk collection, casual labour and petty trade, and those employed in these occupations settle down in slums because of kin and village links and because of the cheaper cost of living.

The slum dwellers are in no way indolent or weak (Desai and Pillai 1972). They show a fair degree of political conciousness. In this respect Peta dwellers show similarity with the slum dwellers of others cities like Bomaby (Lynch 1974) and Madras (Wiebe 1975). Many of them are radically oriented and are affiliated to the Communist parties. This is the result of their economic backwardness, and their work situations which are amenable for unionization. The political parties cut across the occupational and caste categories. Many of the residents take active interest in political matters like elections, meetings, processions, etc. What happens in the community is not completely independent of the external political system of the city even though the local socio-economic structure and leadership has its own political implications. As is usual with any community, the leadership is by and large controlled by leaders having higher socio-economic status (Wiebe 1975).

Slum life is generally associated with a number of social evils like gambling, prostitution, organized robbery, juvenile delinquency, etc. We have noted the occurrence of some such cases in Peta. However, it is important to note two facts in this connection. One is, that at one time the area was reputed for its vices and crimes. The situation has changed now. With the increase of inmigrants having jobs and closer kin networks it has become difficult for stray individuals to carry on these anti-social activities any more. Secondly, the incidence and magnitude of undesirable activities is not higher in this area when compared to some other areas in the city which are not slums. The so-called 'red-light' area in the city is situated right by the side of a decent residential-cum-commercial locality. This indicates that evils such as prostitution and alcoholism thrive in areas where there is a high floating population and where the settled community life is minimal. It is because of a more organised social life that in Peta regular prostitutes and professional bootleggers do not thrive. Similar finding is noted by Woodruff (1960) regarding a

Bangalore slum. However, one cannot help but note the existence of traffic in women, gambling connected with the cotton market, occasional sale of illicit liquor and the like. Leaders of all political parties seem to accept this as normal to modern urban life and therefore turn a blind eye at them.

The slum dwellers are as eager as non-slum dwellers to celebrate or conduct religious and other festivals. Thus obviously what makes the slum distinct from the other areas in the city are the appalling conditions of housing, congestion, insanitation, and conditions of poverty, which we shall discuss as a part of the general features of slums in the concluding chapter.

7

CITIES, SLUMS AND URBAN DEVELOPMENT

In the light of our study of Peta Squatter Settlement we shall discuss in the concluding chapter three general problems : (i) the occupational structure and work organisation of Peta in relation to the concept of urban 'informal sector'; (ii) the conditions of life of the Peta slum dwellers in the context of the notion of the 'culture of poverty'; and (iii) the Peta squatter slum in the wider framework of urban development including measures of slum clearance, improvement and control.

Informal sector

The occupational structure and work organisation throw new light on the question of the informal sector of the urban economy. Since the first systematic formulation of the concept of informal sector by the ILO (1972) Employment Mission to Kenya in terms of its features—easy entry for the new enterprises, reliance on indigenous resources, family ownership, small scale operations, unregulated and competitive markets, labour intensive technology and informally acquired skills of workers – it has been subjected to refinements and criticisms of various kinds. Papola (1980 : 22) points out the continuity in each of the features of informal sector rather than the dichotomy between the formal and the informal and pleads for considering inter sectoral linkages into a growth pattern. Breman (1976) argues for looking at the nature of the entire labour market rather than divide the urban system into two sectors; distinguishing different articulated production relations which can be found within the economic system of third world countries. In his study of South Gujarat, he found the fragmented labour market more useful than formal/informal dichotomy. Sinclairs' (1978 : 96) criticisms of the concept of informal sector are more substantial. He considers that the use of the concept impedes analysis. It implies a greater degree of homogeneity regarding those within the sector than is actually justified in the light of empirical studies. The term observes and does not allow examination of the linkages between different parts of the informal sector and other parts of the city economy. The concept does not facilitate analysis of the dynamic forces in changing the informal sector's parts through time.

While we agree with the criticisms of the concept of the informal sector that are mentioned above, we want to highlight the part played by caste, kinship and political party in the recruitment and organisation of workers and the employer-employee relationships. In Peta we have seen the degree of heterogeneity in the occupational structure of the slum dwellers, falling within the informal sector. Each of the major occupations is organised into unions such as the mutha workers' union, sand workers' union, junk-collectors' union and so on. Each is dominated by one or more caste groups and is affiliated either to the CPI, CPI(M) or the Congress parties. While the mutha workers' union is dominated by Reddis and Yadavas, the sand workers' union is dominated by Vadderas. We also found that the migration was both caste and job specific. Vaddera migrants got into sand work and migrant Reddis, Yadavas and other intermediate castes got into mutha work through prior kin contacts. This provided the continuum between the rural and the urban.

There are four means of entry into the occupations in the urban informal sector. First, the caste specific skills which are in demand in particular occupations. For instance, the Vadderas traditionally known for their skills in earth and stone work are recruited as sand workers on a preferential basis by the agents of the contractors. Secondly, the kin and caste contacts in certain jobs attract migrants belonging to these. For instance mutha work as loaders and unloaders with big merchants is well paid and here the caste and kin links are significant in gaining an entry into mutha work. Thirdly, others can enter the specialized work groups through bribing or by buying the work token from a person who is leaving. Lastly, others can enter the jobs on the basis of certain skills and initiative, which is largely true of self-employed persons in Peta such as junk collectors and rickshaw pullers but not without the support of the kin-caste infrastructure.

The different work-groups and categories which organised into unions are politically articulated. This type of organisation serves three purposes : it restricts the entry into these jobs; it establishes certain norms governing the employer-employee relations; and links the specific work-group to others with similar interests in the framework of trade union and political party. Hence in Peta different work-groups within the informal sector have a potential to get integrated with the trade unions in the formal sector controlled by state level and national political parties thereby facilitating class formation. In the context of Peta, however, we find both class and ethnic relations assuming significance in different contexts.

Such a view of the informal sector emphasizing the specific nature of the work-groups and categories in terms of their social composition and organisation provides insights into the pattern of employment and recruitment to understand both intra sectoral differences and linkages between the informal and formal sectors in the wider framework of economic and political processes. The informal sector as a blanket term does not permit the analysis of exploitative relationships, hence the unit of analysis should be work-groups and categories either of the self-employed or of the employer-employee relations, rather than the enterprises. The advantage of having the work-group or category as the unit of analysis is that it will bring out the different forms of labour use and conflicting relations in production processes. It also focuses on the problem of the living conditions of the urban poor.

Culture of poverty

It is argued that wherever there are cities there will be slums and they are associated with poverty and a specific culture. Oscar Lewis (1966) who developed the notion of culture of poverty maintained that this was not just a matter of deprivation or disorganisation, but a design of living with a readymade set of solutions for human problems. Hence it serves a significant adaptive function. He developed this in the context of his investigations of urban Latin America and New York. He showed how the culture of poverty was manifest in urban slums as a subculture. In the words of Lewis (1966 : xiv):

> The lack of effective participation and integration in the major institutions of the larger society is one of the crucial characteristics of the culture of poverty.

This is characterized by many factors such as uprootedness and isolation, cash economy and wage-labour, high rate of unemployment, low wages, lack of social, economic and political organisation and personal inadequacy and inferiority complex arising out of the dominant value on accumulation of wealth and property. Stokes (1962) also attributed poverty to incapability. Distinguishing slums of hope and despair, he held the view that the slums of despair are the homes of the poor not only in income terms but in terms of poor ability to be employable.

Valentine (1968) and others have rightly criticized the concept of the culture of poverty on logical-conceptual and empirical grounds and it is hardly necessary for us to go into its details. Lewis himself agreed that under a revolutionary government in the slums of Cuba there was no evidence of the culture of poverty. We may, however quote the apt statement made by Mangin even in the context of the U.S.A. and Latin America. Mangin (1970 : XXXI-XXXII) writes:

> My own interpretation of the Latin American and United States situations is that the traits mentioned by Lewis, and the phenomenon of apathy and cyclical poverty, are much more tenuous and temporary in both areas than he says.

He agrees with Saul Alinsky that there is no such thing as an apathetic group, culture or class. The political factors that lead to the disparities in wealth and power are much more important than personality and cultural characteristics.

As we have indicated in the Introduction, a social group with stable relations and societal networks could hardly exhibit the characteristics of total disorganisation or no organisation. Peta dwellers not only have a community organisation but have a sense of belonging to a caste and kin group. They also maintain close links with their native villages. Hence they do not feel isolated nor harbour a feeling of despair. Further, there is little unemployment and only a few are below the poverty line. A majority of the slum dwellers belong to one or the other work-group of labour organization. Although it is not a formal trade union, it protects their interests and regulates the entry of others into it. They also belong to political parties. Thus they are economically and politically more integrated with the urban political economy.

Hence, our analysis of the social, economic and political aspects of Peta clearly refute the applicability of the notion of 'culture of poverty' as characterised by Oscar Lewis. Paul Wiebe (1975 : 160) also came to this conclusion with regard to the slum life in Chennanagar, a slum in Madras city. It is simplistic to associate a specific style of life of a people with poverty, and locate it only in the slums. This is a much more complicated issue which calls for a systematic investigation. Poverty is not necessarily associated with uncleanness (slum conditions). No is tidiness the characteristic feature of the well-to-do. Many middle class squatter settlements in cities like Delhi exhibit slum conditions. Squatting is not the monopoly of the poor. People belonging to the middle-income group often buy plots in an unauthorised area at a low cost and built *pucca* houses there (M.S.A. Rao 1974). Since these colonies are illegal the Corporation does not give any water, electricity, drainage and sewerage facilities. The houses also get overcrowded and due to non-civic habits of the residents slum conditions prevail. On the contrary some hut-ment colonies maintain grerter cleanliness than colonies with *pucca* houses. Although people live in huts, the walls and floors are plastered with cowdung which is a free disinfectant. They keep the surroundings and roads clean. With less over-crowding the sanitary conditions do not deteriorate. Thus by following a civic culture, slum conditions can be avoided. Under conditions of urban living a minimum of infrastructure, (even given the proper attitude and concern) namely, water, drainage, sewerage and toilets, and clearance of garbage and other municipal services, is necessary. Given these facilities, even hutment settlements can be kept clean. Hence it is a question of poverty of civic culture that characterizes slum conditions rather than a culture of poverty.

Often even middle class residents in the congested parts of the city are seen throwing rubbish into the street, and near-slum conditions prevail both inside and outside their houses. They allow their children to defecate on the streets, even though they have toilets inside the house. One of the distinguishing features of slum conditions in Indian cities is the practice of people to defacate in the open. If only this is eliminated half of the slum conditions will be under control. When such styles of life prevail among some sections of the middle class, it would be biased to associate them only with the poor.

It is necessary to note that civic culture does not necessarily mean a westernized civic culture. Mahatma Gandhi has shown how people can lead a simple and hygienically clean life in the *ashram* type settlement that he built. Houses there were neither expensive nor westernized, but cheap with environmental cleanliness. Thus we need an indigenous low cost technology and appropriate civic culture, to avoid slum conditions. However, this in itself does not solve the problem of slums beyond pointing out that the slum conditions are not necessarily associated with poverty. Slums are hard facts of our cities and the question is what do we do with them or how we prevent them from growing and emerging.

The basic ideology behind the problem of slums needs a careful examination. It needs to be recognized that the problem of slum is associated with the exploitative system of the capitalist society (see D.G. Epstein 1972; Desai and Pillai 1972). The city is for the rich and the middle classes who can pay for the infrastructure and other urban facilities and luxuries. The city administration safeguards the rights of the propertied class and the corporation or municipality renders services to those who reside in authorized areas and who pay taxes for these services.

The authorities take the view that those who illegally occupy public land should not be provided with any service or infrastructure. In fact, some corporations and city administrations work like business houses making huge profits by charging more and spending less (Bose 1973). Often they buy agricultural land at a nominal price and sell the plots at a very high price, far beyond the means of people in the middle income groups. The city administration only has a marginal policy for the housing of the low income groups and none for the poor who cannot afford to pay for rent, water and other facilities.

The industrialists, traders and others who recruit a large number of unskilled workers do not care for welfare. The former get cheap labour supply from the slums without their having to provide them with house or other facilities. Thus both the administration and the employers exploit the slum dwellers. Under such circumstances slums are to be looked upon as solutions that the poor migrants have sought for themselves rather than as problems.

It is essential therefore to bring about a basic change in the exploitative system in the direction of socialistic ideology. It is the responsibility of the state to care more for the poor urban dwellers who live in huts or on pavements by recognizing them as full citizens. At present they have the right to vote but not the right to claim civic amenities. They should not be considered as criminals (as squatters) in the first instance. There should be a whole programme of meeting the minimum needs of the poor, starting with employment as part of the urban renewal policy.

It is also necessary to note that welfare should not turn into a charity system in which the poor slum dwellers expect everything free of cost. There is always a tendency to avoid paying taxes and rent, in the name of poverty, but to spend on alcohol and other vices. Hence it is necessary to build up an expectation that they have to pay for the facilities although at a subsidized rate and to fix the premium on proper maintenance and use of facilities. Having provided the minimum facilities, municipal laws should be implemented strictly. Hence neither charity nor laxity in the enforcement of civic norms should be the approach to the problem of slum dwellers.

Urban development : slum clearance, development and control

The common measure that is in vogue to deal with the problem of slums is clearance with two main variations. One is to clear the slums and resettle the slum dwellers on the periphery of the city far away from their places of work as there will be no land available within the city, and the other is to resettle the slum dwellers nearer their places of work. While the latter was adopted by the Madras Corporation in resettling the fishermen near the Marina beach, the former measure is the most common one adopted by many city development authorities. Let us now consider this measure in the context of Vijayawada and its slums.

We have already noted that in the 1960s as many as 1784 families of slum dwellers living on the banks of three canals were allotted housing plots in Mutyalampadu Colony situated on the eastern outskirts of the city and were compelled to move there. Each family was allotted a plot of 1,200 square feet on a nominal rent. According to the reports gathered from the local residents and some of the municipal employees, a sizeable number of families returned to the slums having either sold away or rented out their plots. Many such plots are now occupied by middle class families. The main reason for this was the non-availability of any jobs in that area and the long distances from the places of work or from the main commercial areas, where only the uneducated slum dwellers could seek employment. Transfer of such right of ownership of plots is not recognized by the municipality and hence no such transfer could be officially registered. All the transfers were purely unofficial without any sale or transfer deeds. Thus this experience of rehabilitating the slum dwellers in Mutyalampadu Colony far away from the centre of the city was a failure and the only lesson that one can draw from this is that such of those slum dwellers who are not in secure salaried jobs always like to reside at places which are closer to their work spots.

We now present the attitudes of the Peta residents in respect of slum clearance.

Out of all the groups in Peta the Vadderas and Yerukulas are highly reluctant to move out of Peta. The Vadderas earn their livelihood by engaging themselves in work connected with loading and unloading lorries with sand available in the adjacent Krishna river bed. Moving out of the area in any direction far from the river bed is considered detrimental to their occupation. Peta being closer to the important business-cum-residential localities in the city the Vadderas feel assured of easy access to the contractors and of regular work. Many of their women work as sand labourers. At regular intervals, the mothers visit their homes to breast feed the children. This is possible because the work spot is very close by. Further, the Vadderas have a kind of sentimental attachment to the area and being one of the oldest and largest group of inmigrants in the area, they feel that they are its rightful residents. The temple constructed by them adds to their feeling of belonging to this area. The Yerukulas feel it almost impossible to find any place elsewhere in the town where their domesticated pigs would have enough place to move around and have enough of water supply as they have in and around Peta. Here the pigs move freely around along the river bed and the Yerukulas need not bother about them except to provide some kind of a shelter at night.

Some of the Vaddera youths, however, expressed their willingness to move out of this area and settle down anywhere else in the city provided better employment and housing facilities were made available. This is because they exhibit a tendency to deviate from the traditional kind of work which demands hard manual labour and the work which they consider "mean" (for example pig raising and carrying night soil). However, they have neither skills nor training to take up other jobs. Hence they are involved in activities such as blackmarketing of cinema tickets and gambling connected with the cotton market. Among the scheduled castes (Malas and Madigas) a sizeable number is engaged in purchasing and selling junk iron. Some are in salaried jobs. Such people are willing to move out of Peta to any nearby site where they could be provided with good housing facilities. But they strongly expressed a view to move together to one area without dispersal. The work of purchasing and selling scrap iron is done in groups and hence the need to be together. The rickshaw pullers, sand labourers, and casual labourers and others belonging to different castes and religious groups prefer to continue to stay here, for they feel that residing far from the business-cum-commercial localities would deprive them of the easy availability of work throughout the year. Those who are in salaried jobs are quite willing to move into quarters if their employers are willing to provide the same.

Yadavas, Reddis and Telagas are also numerically significant caste-groups in Peta. A majority of the earners in all the three caste-groups are in mutha labour connected with business and commercial activities. Many of them are well disposed towards moving to other areas but closer to the commercial centres. They are comparatively recent inhabitants of this locality and therefore have built their huts on the land belonging to the railways. Many a time the railway authorities have tried in vain to make them vacate the land. But these groups fear that some day they will be forced to vacate and hence are prepared to move out to any nearby place where free or cheap housing is made available. They expect the government or the municipality to provide land and build houses for them free of cost. Some upper caste individuals also seem to entertain the idea of getting out of this place and settling down somewhere else in order to be able to be away from the lower and scheduled castes. They seem to be only awaiting government's offer of a suitable alternative site and/or free housing. The talk of slum-clearance and the like makes these people strongly hope for such favours.

With regard to the other castes it was found that all those individuals who are employed in skilled jobs, who are somewhat better off and whose places of work are not nearby, are willing to move out provided some assistance is extended by the government. Those who are engaged in small business such as hotel-running, firewood selling and soon would like to continue in the same area because they are directly dependent upon the locality and do not have financial means either to build houses outside, or to rent shop accommodation elsewhere.

The problem of slum-clearance and rehabilitation of the slum dwellers is not merely a social and economic problem, but has assumed some political significance as well. As we have noted earlier while some individuals and groups personally are for moving out of the area provided necessary facilities are extended, collectively and publicly they express opinions in favour of continued residence in the same area. This kind of discrepancy in their opinions is due to some political pressures.

At the time of this survey there was a rumour afloat that the Congress government and the municipality controlled by the Congress Party were in favour of slum clearance because they wanted to disperse these groups in order to weaken the stronghold of the Communist parties on the local residents. Hence the suspicion of the motives of the government makes even those who are otherwise willing to move out hesitate to do so. Local leaders thrive politically on such rumours. The immediate beneficiaries of all this confusion are, however, the relatively economically powerful individuals who also wield political power. In either case it is the vested interests of some individuals and groups that work against the possible programmes of slum clearance. One of the vested interest groups is the slum lords who have built rows of huts and have rented them out.

Where only the migrants get a job in a locality they would naturally not like to leave it. Living together in the midst of known people or relatives is not only socially and emotionally satisfying, but also economically desirable in that even at the risk of underemployment or unemployment the group members feel obliged to support the new entrants and the latter get socialized to the new urban situation. In this sense the slums may be said to be performing a social function but this argument should not be stretched beyond a limit.

Since the fresh migrants stay in the same houses or locality, it results in further congestion and overcrowding. While on the one hand many of the inhabitants do not have means to improve their housing conditions, even a few of those who can afford, find it impossible to do so for want of free vacant land. The municipalities do not assume any responsibility to spend on an unauthorized area wherefrom there is no possibility of any revenue in return. Municipalities are prone to neglect such areas. Very often it so happens that the land does not belong to the municipality and therefore the slum area does not come under its purview at all and therefore the municipality feels hesitant to make any improvements in such areas. Besides the negligence of municipalities, most newly established industries also leave their lower class employees to their fate without making any provision for their housing.

These two problems thus arise due to unplanned urban and industrial growth.

On the basis of our data on Peta we may suggest the following measures of slum improvement, clearance and control.

There is a minority section of people living in slums who are willing to move out and reside or build houses if suitable places are made available. These are the people who are in salaried jobs. They may be provided with cheap plots or housing on a reasonable rent or hire-purchase basis near their work spots. The municipality and the employing agencies together should take the lead in this direction.

Secondly some of the casual or mutha labourers would like to move to nearby suitable areas provided they are allowed to move out in groups. These groups could be caste-based or occupation-based or both. The municipality should be able to earmark and allot suitable areas. Financial assistance in building improvised huts would be an additional attraction to such people. In Peta those who are located on the railway land are more prone to such movement than others. Incidentally they also belong to upper caste groups and are somewhat economically better off.

Thirdly when the above mentioned two sections of the residents move out, the remaining ones would be Vadderas, Yerukulas, Rajakas and some of the Malas and Madigas, and others. They could be allowed to stay on and the housing, drainage, sewerage and the sanitary conditions could be provided. A carefully worked out programme of slum development needs to be planned and implemented.

It is obvious that in the case of the second and third measures both the municipality and the government have to plan and invest necessary amounts of money, and the plots and houses are to be given to the inhabitants on nominal rent or hire-purchase system. As a social welfare measure the government should come forward with a sizeable subsidy. Unni (1977) also suggests such a programme of action.

Growth of new slums and deterioration of the conditions of the existing slums need to be controlled through coordinated planning. One way out is to indirectly restrict and direct the inflow of inmigrants into the city. This means long term plans of urban redevelopment, location of industries and business districts, proper allotment of sites for inmigrant workers to build houses, and providing drainage and sewerage facilities in each area. Secondly, if the landless agricultural labourers and small farmers are provided with employment in the rural areas as in the case of Food for Work and employment guarantee scheme, the magnitude of urbanward migration can be reduced. All these measures need a change in the ideology of municipal development in favour of the urban poor. As Desai and Pillai (1972 : 246) argue the logic of priorities of resource disbursement underlying economic planning needs to be changed in favour of the slum dwellers.

SELECT BIBLIOGRAPHY

Abrams, Charles (1964) : *Man's Struggle for Shelter in an Urbanizing World*, Cambridge, M.I.T. Press.

Anderson, Nels (1960) : *Urban Community*, London : Routledge and Kegan Paul.

Aranganannal (1975) : *Socio-Economic Survey of Madras Slums*, (1971 Survey) Madras : Tamil Nadu Slum Clearance Board.

Bharat Sevak Samaj (1958) : *Slums of Old Delhi*, Delhi : Atma Ram and Sons.

Bhat, Chandra Sekhar (1978) : "Politics in a Slum", A paper presented at 10th International Conference of Anthropological and Ethnological Sciences held at Delhi 1978.

Bose, Ashish (1973) : *Studies in India's Urbanization : 1901-71*, Bombay : Tata McGraw Hill.

Breman, Jan C. (1976) : "A Dualistic Labour System : A Critique of the 'Informal Sector' Concept", *Economic and Political Weekly*, 11(48) 1870-1876; 11(49) 1905-8 and 11(50) 1939-44.

Calcutta Metropolitan Development Authority (N.D.) : *Some Facts and Figures*, Calcutta : Directorate of Planning : CMDA.

Clindard, Marshal B. (1966) : *Slums and Community Development*, New York : Macmillan.

Connel, John *et al.* (1976) : *Migration from Rural Areas*, Delhi : Oxford University Press.

Desai, A.R. and Pillai, S.D. (ed.) (1970) : *Slums and Urbanization*, Bombay : Popular Prakasan.

Desai, A.R. and Pillai, S.D. (ed.) (1972) : *A Profile of An Indian Slum*, Bombay : University of Bombay.

D'Souza, Victor S. (1968) : *Social Structure of a Planned City*, Bombay : Orient Longmans.

D'Souza, Victor S. (1976) : "Urban Development in India :

Demographic, Functional and Socio-Cultural Perspectives" in Muttangi, P.K. (ed.), *Urban Development—A Perspective*, Bombay : Tata Institute of Social Sciences.

Dwyer, D.J. (1975) : *People and Housing in Third World Cities*, London : Longman.

Epstein, D.G. (1972) : "The Genesis and Functions of a Squatter Settlement in Brasilia", in Weaver, T. and White, D. (ed.), *The Anthropology of Urban Environments*.

Gore, M.S. (1970) : *Immigrants and Neighbourhoods*, Bombay : Tata Institute of Social Sciences.

Government of Andhra Pradesh (1967) : *Vijayawada, Outline Development Plan*, Hyderabad : Government Central Press.

Harris, J.R. and Todaro, M.P. (1970) : "Migration Unemployment and Development : A Two-Section Analysis", *American Economic Review*, 60(1) March, pp. 126-142.

I.L.O. (1972) : *Employment, Incomes and Equality : A Strategy for Increasing Productive Employment in Kenya*, Geneva.

Jagannadham, V. and Palvia, C.M. (1977) : *Slums and Squatter Settlements in an Indian Million (+) City*, New Delhi : The Indian Institute of Public Administration (Mimeographed).

Lewis, Oscar (1966) : *La Vida*, New York : Random House.

Lynch, Owen M. (1974) : "Political Mobilization and Ethnicity among Adi-Dravidas in a Bombay Slum" in *Economic and Political Weekly*, IX(39) : Sept. 28.

Majumdar, Tapan K. (1978) : "The Urban Poor and Social Change : A Study of Squatter Settlements in Delhi", in Alfred de Souza (ed.), *The Indian City* : New Delhi : Manohar.

Mangin, William (1970) : *Peasants in Cities*, Boston : Houghton Mifflin Co.

Mayur, Rashmi (1981) : "Mumbai Today and Tomorrow" in *The Illustrated Weekly of India*, Vol. CII : 23, July 5-11, 1981.

Meckenzie, Gordon (1883) : *A Manual of Krishna District*, Madras : The Presidency of Madras.

Naidu, Ratna (1978) : "A Study of Slums in Hyderabad-Secunderabad", *The Indian Journal of Social Work*, 39(3), October, 297-312.

Nambiar, P.K. (1966) : *Slums in Madras City*, Census of India 1961, vol. IX, Madras, Part XI-C.

Papola, T.S. (1980) : *Urban Informal Sector in a Developing Economy*, Delhi : Vikas.

Rajagopal, M.N. (1960) : *Krishna District, Draft Gazetteer* (Mimeographed).

Ramachandran, P. (1972) : *Pavement Dwellers in Bombay City*, Bombay : Tata Institute of Social Sciences.

Rao, K. Ranga and Raju, B.R.K. (1972) : "Slums of Visakhapatnam : A Perspective" in *Seminar on Town Planning in Visakhapatnam*, Waltair : Andhra University Press.

Rao, K. Ranga (1971) : "City and Social Life : A Review of Sociological Theory" in Rajeswar Prasad, G.C., Hallen and Kusum Pathak (eds.), *Conspectus of Indian Society*, Agra : Satish Book Enterprise.

Rao, K. Ranga *et al*. (1977) : "Migration Experience of Urban Slum-Dwellers" in *The Indian Journal of Social Work*, vol. 38, No. 1, April.

Rao, M.S.A. (1974) : "Migrant in the City" in *Yojana*, 18(20), November, 7-13.

Rao, M.S.A. (1976) : "Migration and Urban Area Development" in *Social Change*, 6(3 and 4), September-December, 3-7.

Rao, V.L.S.P. and Ramachandran, R. (1974) : *A Report on the Socio-Economic Survey of Vijayawada City*, Department of Human Geography, Delhi School of Economics (Mimeographed).

Sen, S.N. (1962) : *The City of Calcutta, A Socio-Economic Survey*.

Sinclair, Stuart W. (1978) : *Urbanization and Labour Markets in Developing Countries*, London : Croomhelm.

Singh, Andrea Menefee and Alfred de Souza (1980) : *The Urban Poor*, Delhi : Manohar.

Srinivas, M.N. and Rao M.S.A. (1966) : "Sociological Study of Okhla Industrial Estate" in *Small Industries and Social Change*, Delhi : UNESCO.

Stokes, Charles J. (1962) : "A Theory of Slums", *Land Economics*, vol. 38(3), August, pp. 187-197.

Sunday Standard (1973) : Madras.

Tataji, U. and Satyamurty, B. (1975) : "Urbanization and Urban Growth in Andhra Pradesh" in *Indian Journal of Comparative Sociology*, vol. 3, February 1975, No. 2.

Unni, K. Raman (1977) : "Slum Relocation and Urban Planning" in *Social Action*, vol. 27, No. 4, October-December, 1977.

Valentine C.A. (1968) : *Culture and Poverty*, Chicago : University of chicago Press.

Venkatarayappa, K. (1972) : *Slums*, Delhi : Sterling.

Whyte, W.F. (1943) : *Street Corner Society*, Chicago and London : University of Chicago Press.

Wiebe, Paul, D. (1975) : *Social Life in an Indian Slum*, Delhi : Vikas Publishing House.

Woodruff, Gertrude, M. (1960) : "Family Migration into Bangalore" in *The Economic Weekly*, (Annual Number), vol. XII, January 1960, No. 1.

Index

Abrams, Charles, 2
Affinal groups, 77
Age groups, 15
Agnatic group, 77
Agricultural labour, 46, 71
Alcoholism, 94
Alinsky, Saul, 99
Ambedkar Youngmen's Association, 86, 87
Anderson, Nels, 2
Anonymity, 15
Anti-social activities, 77; problems, 4
Aranganannal, 2, 38
Ashram type settlement, 101

Bangalore, 1, 2, 31, 95
Bhat, Chandrasekhar, 2
Bombay, 1, 2, 31, 38, 50, 94
Boot leggers, 94
Bose, Ashish, 102
Brahmin caste, 64, 90
Breman, Jan C., 96

Calcutta, 1, 2, 8, 38
Capitalist society, 101
Castes, artisan, 15, 31, 44, 67, 68; association, 87; categories, 94; composition, 12, 13t, 31, 34; groups, 7, 33, 93, 105; headman, 93;hierarchy, 31, 93; occupations, 56, 57, 60, 62, 63, 70, 73, 78; panchayat, 77, 81, 82, 93; places of origin of, 44; settlements, 93
Casual labours, 24, 26, 62, 64, 67, 71, 73, 75, 104
Chandigarh, 2, 35, 50
Child labour, 60, 69
Christians, 12, 22, 24, 26, 27, 28, 88; missionary, 90
Church, 57, 87, 88
Cinema-hero-worship, 89
City, administration, 101, 102; development, 103; growth, 8; municipality, 11; sample, 33, 67, 68, 70
Civic, amenities, 102; culture, 100, 101; norms, 102
Class formation, 6, 98
Clindard, Marshal B., 2
Communist Party of India (M), 81, 82, 85, 94, 97
Community organization, 6; services, 77, 90
Commercial centre, 10
Congestion, 106
Congress Political Parties, 97, 106; committee, 81
Connel, John, 54
Contract labour, 23, 71, 73, 75, 86, 88
Crimes and social evils, 91

Delhi, 1, 2, 38, 50, 100
Demographic features, 11
Desai, A.R., 1, 2, 5, 50, 91, 94, 101, 108
D'Souza Victor S., 2, 4, 15, 19, 27, 35, 50, 93
Disparities, 99, 100
Disputes, inter-caste, 84, 85; participation of political parties, 84; settlements, 83

Divorc (ed), 40, 82, 83
Dowry, 83
Drainage, 100, 107, 108
Droughts, 8; conditions, 47
Dwyer, D.J., 1

Earners, occupational distribution of, 57, 65t
East Godavari, 10, 46
Ecological distribution, 34
Educational status, 42
Election, time of, 89
Eluru, 8, 11, 15
Employment, 42; guarantee scheme, 108
Environmental cleanliness, 101
Epstein, D.G., 101
Ethnic relations, 98

Festivals, 88, 89
Floating population, 56
Food consumed, 91
Formal sector, 98

Gambling, 91, 94, 104
Garg, J.S., 160
Gauda caste, 64
Gore, M.S., 2, 5
Gossiping, 89
Guntur, 10, 11, 13, 15, 22, 23, 24, 25, 26, 27, 31, 34, 46

Harris, J.R., 54
High density tracts, 19, 20
Hindus, 12, 43, 81
Housing facilities, 35, 105, 106, 107; and civic amenities, 90
Households, distribution of, 67
Hutment colonies, 27
Hyderabad, 1, 8, 10

Income, 67; groups, 67, 68; levels, changing in, 75
Informal sector, 6, 96, 97
Inmigrants, 23, 24, 25, 93, 104, 107, 108; majority of, 54; streams of, 31, 49; third generation, 47, 51; workers, 108
Intergenerational mobility, 71, 72
Intermediate castes, 13, 15, 22, 23, 27, 31, 33, 38, 40, 48, 90, 93
International Labour Office (ILO), 96

Janatha gali (Janata wave), 90
Juvenile delinquency, 94

Kakinada, 8
Kamma caste, 25, 27, 31, 33, 36, 44, 46, 48, 51, 52, 53, 60, 63, 67, 90
Kamsali, 31, 38, 64
Kanpur, 1
Karimnagar, 46
Khammam, 25, 26, 27, 29
Kin-caste infrastructure, 98; group, 78; links, 82; network, 54, 77, 79t; relations, 48, 77
Kinship, 49, 51, 97; affiliations, 81
Krishna river, 8, 23, 24, 25, 26, 29, 31, 35, 45, 56, 103
Kshatriyas, 64
Kummari caste, 31, 38, 43, 64

Labour force, 69; market, 97; organization, 100; supply, 102
Leadership, 94, 95
Lewis, Oscar, 98, 99, 100
Literacy rate, 15
Living conditions, 94
Lower castes, 14, 15, 32, 39, 48, 52, 55, 91, 93; class, 106
Lynch, Owen M., 94

Machileepatnam, 8, 11, 13, 15
Madigas casete, 22, 25, 29, 34, 39, 41, 44, 49, 51, 60, 67, 73, 77, 82, 84, 88, 104, 107
Madras, 1, 2, 8, 27, 29, 35, 38, 50, 93, 100, 103
Mahatma Gandhi, 101
Major caste-groups, political affiliations of, 80t

Majumdar, Tapan K., 2
Malas caste, 7, 22, 25, 29, 31, 34, 36, 39, 44, 47 49, 52, 60, 67, 77, 81, 82, 84, 88, 104, 107
Mangali caste, 31, 36, 38, 43, 44, 63, 64, 73, 90
Mangin, William, 76, 99
Marital relations, 77; status, 40
Marriage, 39, 50, 83; norms, 84; settlement, 82
Matrimonial alliances, 51, 52
Mayur, Rashmi, 1
Meckenzie, Gordon, 8
Medari caste, 31, 38, 39, 42, 44, 46, 63, 73, 93
Middle castes, 27, 101, 103; class, squatter settlements, 100
Middle income groups, 102
Migrant(s). 5, 6, 25, 31, 47, 48, 50, 51, 55, 70, 71, 106
Migration, 5, 43, 46, 47, 48, 50, 51, 53, 55; analysis of, 54; associational, 47; caste kinship in process of, 51, 97, 100; development, 53; economic advantages, 54; factors causing, 50; prior acquaintances for, 48, 51; purpose of, 46; push-pull, 55; reason for, 75
Movies, 89
Municipal, development, 108; laws, 102; services, 101
Municipality, 6, 27, 36, 60, 61, 101, 105, 107
Muslims, 12, 23, 27, 31, 34, 36, 38, 43, 44, 47, 52, 62, 90
Mutha, 49; labour, 61, 63, 64, 73, 105, 107; workers, 97
Muttarasi caste, 31, 51, 64

Nagara caste. 25, 27, 31, 64, 83
Nagasipu, 31, 36, 38, 41, 43, 46, 48, 49, 52, 63, 90
Naidu, Ratna, 1
Nalgonda, 29, 46
Nambiar, P.K., 27, 50
Native places, 52, 53
Neighbourhood clubs, 47
Non-civic habits, 100
Non-slums areas, 19, 20, 68, 69, 95

Occupations, classified, 69, 70; hereditory, 64; prestige of, 75; reasons for changing, 75
Occupational association, 93; categories, 48; distribution, 48, 57, 70; groups, 86, 93; intergenerational, 76; mobility, 56, 70, 71, 72, 75, 76; pattern, 16, 60, 67
Old Iron Collectors Union (OICU), 81
Organized robbery, 94; slums, 17, 57
Orissa, 44, 64

Palvia, C.M., 1
Panchayat, 93
Papola, T.S., 96
Peta, 4, 6, 10, 29, 33 34, 48, 55, 58, 65, 67, 70, 76, 88, 94, 96, 98, 103, 105, 107; castes absent in, 33; caste leader in, 83; choice of residence of, 49; caste composition of, 33; cummunity organization of, 77; education, 16, 41, 42, 50; groups in, 78; households according to caste in, 32; immigrants into, 29, 51, 54; literates, 41; occupational distribution, 64; sample, 68, 69, 70; slum, 2, 3; social demographic features of, 36
Pick-pocketing, 91
Pillai, S.D., 1, 2, 5, 50, 91, 94, 101, 108
Political affiliations, 81, 82; economy, 100; leaders, 82, 84; parties, 77, 81, 94, 95, 97, 98, 100; processes, 6
Poor immigrants, 5
Poverty, 8, 95, 100, 102; culture of, 96, 98, 101; insanitation and, 95; line, 100
Prakasam, 22, 23, 24ff, 34, 45, 96
Production processes, 98

Prostitution, 91, 94

Rajagopal, M N., 10
Rajahmundry, 8, 10
Rajaka caste, 31, 38, 41, 44, 63, 73, 99, 107
Raju, B.R.K., 2, 28
Ramachandran, P., 2
Ramachandran, R., 111
Rangoon, 45
Rao, K. Ranga, 2, 28, 75
Rao, M.S.A., 5, 53, 100, 111
Rao, V.L.S.P., 10, 111
Red-light area, 94
Reddi caste, 25, 27, 31, 33, 35, 40, 43, 45, 48, 52, 62, 67, 89, 97, 105
Recreation and leisure time activities, 88
Rehabilitation, 17, 105
Religious composition, 12; cultural activities, 77, 87
Regional lines, 49
Return migration, reason for, 53
Rickshaw pullers, 67, 71, 86, 88, 104
Robbery, 91
Roman catholic missionary, 88
Rural poor, 27, 34, 99, 101, 102
Rural urban continnum, 97; migration, 70

Salaried jobs, 62, 71, 88
Sample households, types of, 37
Sand labour, 60, 64, 80, 104
Sanghika Seva Dalam, 86, 87
Scheduled castes (see also Madigas and Malas), 12, 14, 15, 23, 25, 27, 32, 34, 38, 40, 47, 88, 105; Tribes, 14, 23, 26, 27, 32, 34
Sewarage, 107, 108
Sinclair, Stuart W., 97
Singh, Andrea Menefee, 2, 4, 18, 38
Slum, 1, 2, 3, 5, 6, 17, 20, 24, 27, 35, 43, 48, 50, 88, 94, 96, 101, 107; area attributes of, 2, 3; categories, 28; cities, 50; clearance, 96, 102ff, 105; conditions, 27, 100, 101; cultural life, 7; definition of, 2; density of, 19; dwellers, 27, 56, 103, 105, 108; function, 4; growth of, 3, 20, 107; localities, 33; measures of, 107; planning, 107; organization, 5, 78; population, 11, 19; problem of, 6, 102; social composition of, 11, 22; social function of, 106

Societal networks, 99
Spatial segregation, 34
Srikakulan, 46
Srinivas, M.N., 5, 111
Stokes, Charles J., 98
Sundarayya, P., 82, 83

Tataji, U., 8
Telega castes, 25, 26, 27, 31, 33, 35, 41, 46, 47, 49, 52, 62, 67, 89, 105
Tea *buddies*, 90
Temples, 87
Thatched huts, 90
Todaro, M.P., 54
Trade Union, 86, 93, 98, 100
Tribal identity, 35
Tribe (*see* Yerukulas)

Underground activities, 5
Unhygienic conditions, 48, 55
Unni, K. Raman, 107
Upper caste groups, 107
Urban Agglomeration, 11; development, 6, 96, 102; economy, 6; poor, 98, 104; renewal policy, 102; slums, 99; unplanned, 107

Vaddera, 7, 27, 29, 31, 34, 38, 41, 42, 43, 46, 48, 51, 56, 60, 63, 64, 67, 77, 78, 82, 84, 85, 93, 97, 103, 107
Valentine, 99, 112
Venerial diseases, 91
Venkatarayappa, K., 2, 3, 112
Vijayawada, 2, 6, 8, 10, 12, 13, 15, 17, 20, 26, 29, 46, 93, 103; centre of trade, 17; city limits, 10; municipality, 11; population of,